THE NEW GROVE

Italian Baroque Masters

MONTEVERDI
FRESCOBALDI CAVALLI
CORELLI
A. SCARLATTI VIVALDI
D. SCARLATTI

Denis Arnold
Anthony Newcomb
Thomas Walker
Michael Talbot
Donald J. Grout
Joel Sheveloff

W. W. NORTON & COMPANY
NEW YORK LONDON

First published in
The New Grove Dictionary of Music and Musicians,
edited by Stanley Sadie, 1980

First published in UK in paperback with additions 1984 by
PAPERMAC
a division of Macmillan Publishers Limited
London and Basingstoke

First published in UK in hardback with additions 1984 by
MACMILLAN LONDON LIMITED
4 Little Essex Street London WC2R 3LF
and Basingstoke

British Library Cataloguing in Publication Data
The New Grove Italian baroque masters.—
(The New Grove composer biography series)
1. Composers—Italy—Biography
I. Arnold, Denis II. Series
780'.92'2 ML390
ISBN 0–333–38235–8 (hardback)
ISBN 0–333–38236–6 (paperback)

First American edition in book form with additions 1984 by
W. W. NORTON & COMPANY
New York and London

ISBN 0-393-30094-3 (paperback)
ISBN 0-393-01690-0 (hardback)

Printed in Great Britain

Contents

List of illustrations

Illustration acknowledgments

We are grateful to the following for permission to reproduce illustrative material: Tiroler Landesmuseum Ferdinandeum, Innsbruck (fig.1); Music Division, Library of Congress, Washington, DC (fig.2); British Library, London (figs.3, 7, 11, 15, 23); Archivio di Stato, Mantua (fig.4); Ecole Nationale Supérieure des Beaux-Arts, Paris (fig.5); Royal College of Music, London (fig.6); Biblioteca Nazionale Marciana, Venice (fig.8); Institut für Theaterwissenschaft (Niessen Collection), University of Cologne (fig.9); Richard Macnutt, Tunbridge Wells (figs.10, 18); Biblioteca del Conservatorio di Musica S Pietro a Majella, Naples (fig.13); Staatliche Kunstsammlungen, Kupferstichkabinett, Dresden (fig.14); Civico Museo Bibliografico Musicale, Bologna (fig.16); Biblioteca Apostolica Vaticana, Rome (fig.17); Biblioteca Nazionale Universitaria, Turin (fig.19); Calcografía Nacional, Real Academia de Bellas Artes de San Fernando, Madrid (fig.20); Instituição José Relvas, Alpiarça (fig.21); Rowe Music Library, King's College, Cambridge (fig.22).

General abbreviations

A	alto, contralto
addl	additional
addn	addition
Ag	Agnus Dei
Anh.	Anhang [appendix]
ant	antiphon
aut.	autumn
B	bass [voice]
b	bass [instrument]
b	born
bc	basso continuo
bn	bassoon
BWV	Bach-Werke-Verzeichnis [Schmieder, catalogue of J. S. Bach's works]
c	circa [about]
carn.	Carnival
chit	chitarrone
cl	clarinet
collab.	in collaboration with
conc.	concerto
Cr	Credo
d	died
db	double bass
edn.	edition
ens	ensemble
facs.	facsimile
fl	flute
frag.	fragment
Gl	Gloria
hn	horn
hpd	harpsichord
inc.	incomplete
inst(s)	instrument(s), instrumental
K	Kirkpatrick catalogue [D. Scarlatti]
kbd	keyboard
Ky	Kyrie
lib	libretto
mand	mandolin
Mez	mezzo-soprano
movt	movement
n.d.	no date of publication
n.	note
ob	oboe
obbl	obbligato
off	offertory
opt.	optional
orch	orchestra, orchestral
org	organ
ov.	overture
p.	pars (lp. = *prima pars*, etc)
perf.	performance, performed (by)
pic	piccolo
prol	prologue
pubd	published
R	photographic reprint
r	recto
RAI	Radio Audizioni Italiane
rec	recorder
repr.	reprinted
rev.	revision, revised (by/for)
RV	Ryom catalogue [Vivaldi]
S	San, Santa, Santo [Saint]; soprano voice

San	Sanctus	U.	University
spr.	spring		
SS	Saints	v, vv	voice, voices
Ss	Santissima, Santissimo	*v*	verso
str	string(s)	va	viola
		vc	cello
T	tenor	vle	violone
timp	timpani	vn	violin
transcr.	transcription, transcribed by/for		
trbn	trombone		

Symbols for the library sources of works, printed in *italic*, correspond to those used in *RISM*, Ser. A.

Bibliographical abbreviations

AcM	*Acta musicologica*
AMw	*Archiv für Musikwissenschaft*
AnMc	*Analecta musicologica*
AnnM	*Annales musicologiques*
BJb	*Bach-Jahrbuch*
BMB	Biblioteca musica bononiensis
BMw	*Beiträge zur Musikwissenschaft*
BSIM	*Bulletin français de la S[ociété] I[nternationale de] M[usique]*
BurneyH	C. Burney: *A General History of Music from the Earliest Ages to the Present* (London, 1776–89)
CEKM	Corpus of Early Keyboard Music
CHM	*Collectanea historiae musicae* (in series Biblioteca historiae musicae cultores) (Florence, 1953–)
CMc	*Current Musicology*
DAM	*Dansk aarbog for musikforskning*
DBI	*Dizionario biografico degli italiani*
DJbM	*Deutsches Jahrbuch der Musikwissenschaft*
EitnerQ	R. Eitner: *Biographisch-bibliographisches Quellen-Lexikon*
EMDC	*Encyclopédie de la musique et dictionnaire du Conservatoire*
ES	*Enciclopedia dello spettacolo*
FétisB	F.-J. Fétis: *Biographie universelle des musiciens* (2/1860–65) (and suppl.)
GerberL	R. Gerber: *Historisch-biographisches Lexikon der Tonkünstler*
GerberNL	R. Gerber: *Neues historisch-biographisches Lexikon der Tonkünstler*
GfMKB	*Gesellschaft für Musikforschung Kongressbericht*
Grove 5	*Grove's Dictionary of Music and Musicians* [5th edn.]
GSJ	*The Galpin Society Journal*
HawkinsH	J. Hawkins: *A General History of the Science and Practice of Music* (London, 1776)
HMw	Handbuch der Musikwissenschaft, ed. E. Bücken (Potsdam, 1927–)
HPM	Harvard Publications in Music
IMSCR	*International Musicological Society Congress Report*
IMusSCR	*International Musical Society Congress Report*
JAMS	*Journal of the American Musicological Society*
JbMP	*Jahrbuch der Musikbibliothek Peters*

KJb	*Kirchenmusikalisches Jahrbuch*
LaMusicaE	*La musica: enciclopedia storica*
MA	*The Musical Antiquary*
MD	*Musica disciplina*
Mf	*Die Musikforschung*
MGG	*Die Musik in Geschichte und Gegenwart*
ML	*Music and Letters*
MMA	*Miscellanea musicologica* [Australia]
MMg	*Monatshefte für Musikgeschichte*
MMI	Monumenti di musica italiana
MMR	*The Monthly Musical Record*
MQ	*The Musical Quarterly*
MR	*The Music Review*
MSD	Musicological Studies and Documents, ed. A. Carapetyan (Rome, 1951–)
MT	*The Musical Times*
NA	*Note d'archivio per la storia musicale*
NOHM	*The New Oxford History of Music*, ed. E. Wellesz, J. A. Westrup and G. Abraham (London, 1954–)
NRMI	*Nuova rivista musicale italiana*
NZM	*Neue Zeitschrift für Musik*
ÖMz	*Österreichische Musikzeitschrift*
PÄMw	Publikationen älterer praktischer und theoretischer Musikwerke
PMA	*Proceedings of the Musical Association*
PRMA	*Proceedings of the Royal Musical Association*
RaM	*La rassegna musicale*
RdM	*Revue de musicologie*
ReM	*La revue musicale*
RicordiE	*Enciclopedia della musica* (Milan: Ricordi, 1963–4)
RIM	*Rivista italiana di musicologia*
RISM	*Répertoire international des sources musicales*
RMI	*Rivista musicale italiana*
SartoriB	C. Sartori: *Bibliografia della musica strumentale italiana stampata in Italia fino al 1700* (Florence, 1952–68)
SIMG	*Sammelbände der Internationalen Musik-Gesellschaft*
SMA	*Studies in Music* [Australia]
SMN	*Studia musicologica norvegica*
SMw	*Studien zur Musikwissenschaft*
VMw	*Vierteljahrsschrift für Musikwissenschaft*

VogelB — E. Vogel: *Bibliothek der gedruckten weltlichen Vocalmusik Italiens, aus den Jahren 1500 bis 1700* (Berlin, 1892); rev., enlarged, by A. Einstein (Hildesheim, 1962); further addns in *AnMc*, nos.4, 5, 9 and 12; further rev. by F. Lesure and C. Sartori as *Bibliografia della musica italiana vocale profana pubblicata dal 1500 al 1700* (Geneva, 1977)

ZMw — *Zeitschrift für Musikwissenschaft*

Preface

This volume is one of a series of collections of biographical essays derived from *The New Grove Dictionary of Music and Musicians* (London, 1980). In its original form, the text was written in the mid-1970s, and finalized at the end of that decade. For this reprint, the texts have been re-read and modified, mostly by their original authors. For the material on Alessandro Scarlatti, Donald Grout has been assisted by Hermine Williams, and Malcolm Boyd (work-list) by Hermine Williams and Lowell Lindgren (operas, oratorios) and Thomas Griffin (serenatas); for Domenico Scarlatti the material has been modified by Malcolm Boyd. The bibliographies have been brought up to date and the work-lists in particular incorporate the findings of recent research.

The fact that the texts of the books in this series originated as dictionary articles inevitably gives them a character somewhat different from that of books conceived as such. They are designed, first of all, to accommodate a very great deal of information in a manner that makes reference quick and easy. Their first concern is with fact rather than opinion, and this leads to a larger than usual proportion of the texts being devoted to biography than to critical discussion. The nature of a reference work gives it a particular obligation to convey received knowledge and to treat of composers' lives and works in an encyclopedic fashion, with proper acknowledgment of sources and due care to reflect different standpoints, rather than to embody imaginative or speculative writing about a composer's character or his music.

It is hoped that the comprehensive work-lists and extended bibliographies, indicative of the origins of the books in a reference work, will be valuable to the reader who is eager for full and accurate reference information and who may not have ready access to *The New Grove Dictionary* or who may prefer to have it in this more compact form.

S.S.

CLAUDIO MONTEVERDI

Denis Arnold

CHAPTER ONE

Life

Although Claudio Monteverdi has often been called a revolutionary composer, he was in fact less an inventor of forms and techniques than one who refined them and made them viable for lesser men. He did so throughout a long life, in which he showed an astonishing capacity for keeping abreast of the latest ideas. His major achievement lay in his penetrating expression of human psychology. The early madrigals can be considered as studies of emotions more varied and powerful than those of any other composer. His first opera, *L'Orfeo*, was the earliest to reveal the potential of this then novel genre, while his second, *L'Arianna*, may well have been responsible for its survival; the refinement of psychological attitudes in his late operas meant that the form became capable, like all great drama, of creating a new and satisfying world. In his sacred works, notably the famous Vespers, he brought a secular, up-to-date manner into church music. He can, in sum, be justly appraised as one of the most powerful figures in the history of music.

I Early years at Cremona

Monteverdi was born in Cremona on 15 May 1567 and was baptized Claudio Giovanni Antonio Monteverdi. In his letters he commonly used the spelling 'Monteverdi', but the variant 'Monteverde' frequently appeared on title-pages whose production he may well have supervised. He was born in the parish of SS Nazaro e Celso, where his father was living at the time and was eventually to be buried. His father, Baldassare Monteverdi (*b c*1542), was a chemist, who practised medicine in the way of barber surgeons, even though this was not strictly legal. Claudio's mother, Maddalena (née Zignani), gave birth to a daughter and two boys. She died probably before 1576. His father remarried and had three more children, the eldest of whom was born in 1579; but his second wife, Giovanna Gadio, also died young, in 1583, and in the following year he married for a third time. His circumstances during Claudio's formative years seem to have been modest. Until 1566 he carried on his business in a small shop or stall rented from the chapter of Cremona Cathedral in the square in front of the cathedral; he then transferred it to his own parish. As late as 1582 he needed time to find a comparatively small sum that he owed the cathedral authorities. Nevertheless the two sons of his first marriage were given a good musical education under Marc'Antonio Ingegneri, *maestro di cappella* of the cathedral; the lessons seem to have been private, since there is no evidence that either brother sang in the choir.

Claudio was clearly a precocious boy, for as early as 1582 he published a volume of three-part motets with the famous Venetian printing house of Gardane and in 1583 a book of sacred madrigals, a more local enterprise with a publisher in nearby Brescia. Within a year a further volume, of canzonettas, appeared under the imprint of another leading Venetian publisher, the house of Amadino and Vincenti, who were to publish much of his later music. The cost of printing these volumes must have been borne to some extent by the Cremonese patrons to whom they were dedicated, and Baldassare may have been gaining some useful social acquaintances, since in 1583 he was involved in negotiations with the health authorities in Milan to legalize the practice of medicine by the chemists of Cremona, on the grounds that there was no college of surgeons there. These negotiations took some three years to complete, and from 1587 he was allowed to call himself 'dottore'. In the same year Claudio produced a book of madrigals, on whose title-page he still acknowledged Ingegneri as his teacher, but it is clear that now he was looking for work outside Cremona. In 1589 he visited Milan, and it seems likely that about then he was obtaining engagements, probably as a player of string instruments, at the court of the Gonzaga family at Mantua. He published a second book of madrigals in 1590, and before a third appeared two years later he was in full-time employment at Mantua.

II Mantua

Duke Vincenzo I Gonzaga maintained a comparatively small but virtuoso establishment of musicians at his court at Mantua, augmenting it for special occasions. Monteverdi held a post as 'suonatore di vivuola', which could mean a player of either a viol (viola da gamba) or a violin (viola da braccio) or both. His duties included taking part in weekly concerts given in the ducal palace, and it was probably for these that he produced a new set of madrigals soon after his appointment. These pieces show such a strong influence of Giaches de Wert, the *maestro di cappella* to the court, that he must be assumed to have replaced Ingegneri as Monteverdi's spiritual master, though nothing is known of their formal relationship. This third madrigal book was popular enough to be reprinted in 1594. Although he did not assemble another collection for publication until 1603, it is clear that Monteverdi quickly became one of the leading musicians at Mantua, since he was included in the train of courtiers accompanying the duke on his expedition to Austria and Hungary against the Turks in 1595. Wert died in 1596, and though Monteverdi expected to succeed him (as is apparent from a letter he wrote in 1601), the post went to a senior colleague, Benedetto Pallavicino. Monteverdi's reputation was spreading, however, and he was known at the court of Ferrara, for he was about to dedicate a book of madrigals to Duke Alfonso d'Este when the duke died in 1597. On 20 May 1599 he married Claudia de Cattaneis, one of the court singers, but almost immediately he again had to accompany his employer abroad, this time to Flanders, where the duke went for a cure at Spa. Claudia bore him three children, Francesco (Baldassare) (baptized 27 August 1601), Leonora (Caiulla) (baptized 20 February 1603) and Massimiliano (Giacomo) (baptized 10 May 1604). The daughter died shortly after she was born (for the sons see below, p.9).

Monteverdi's reputation as a composer was firmly established by 1600. In that year the first attacks by G. M. Artusi on his supposed harmonic innovations appeared, though the works Artusi discussed had not yet been published; henceforward Monteverdi was considered a leading exponent of the modern approach to text expression. In 1601 he was appointed *maestro di cappella* at Mantua on the death of Pallavicino. In 1603 he published his fourth book of madrigals, which was followed in 1605 by the fifth, the two together forming a retrospective collection of his work over more than ten years and including pieces already known to Artusi. In the fifth book he included the outline of a reply to Artusi, which was amplified by his younger brother Giulio Cesare (*b* 1573, *d* probably 1630 or 1631, also a composer) in the famous *Dichiaratione* in the *Scherzi musicali* (1607). Such public discussion did even more to promote Monteverdi's music, and both the latest and earlier madrigal books quickly went into new editions.

In February 1607 his first opera, *L'Orfeo*, was produced before the Accademia degli Invaghiti of Mantua. Little is known about this production, but some at least of the singers and players were brought from Florence and elsewhere, and it may be assumed that it was given on a substantial scale. During August of the same year Monteverdi was made a member of the Accademia degli Animosi, Cremona, and some of his music, possibly part of *L'Orfeo*, was performed at one of its meetings. But his main reason for being in his home town at this time was probably the illness of his wife, who had been unwell since the previous year and who was being cared for by his father. She died on 10 September and was buried at SS Nazaro e Celso (her grave does not survive).

After Claudia's death Monteverdi refused at first to return to his duties at Mantua, but by October it became expedient for him to do so since another opera by him, *L'Arianna*, was planned for production. It proved impossible, however, to adhere to the original date during Carnival, and Marco da Gagliano's *La Dafne* was substituted. It was decided to stage it instead as part of the celebrations marking the homecoming of the Gonzaga heir-apparent, Francesco, with his bride, Margaret of Savoy, after their marriage at Turin in May 1608. There was thus plenty of time for rehearsal, though the preparations were complicated by the death from smallpox of the singer engaged for the title role, Caterina Martinelli; this was another great sadness for Monteverdi, for she had been living in his house for several years, possibly as a pupil of his wife. Her part was taken at short notice by Virginia Andreini, a member of the Comici Fedeli, a troupe then in Mantua. *L'Arianna* was given on 28 May and was enthusiastically received. Andreini scored a big success in the famous and influential lament, on which the opera's reputation largely rested. Monteverdi contributed to two further events in the nuptial celebrations: the music for the prologue to the pastoral play *L'Idropica*, performed by the Comici Fedeli, and a full-length French-style ballet, *Il ballo delle ingrate*.

After this period of intensive work Monteverdi returned to Cremona in a state of virtual collapse and depression that lasted for over a year. His father was alarmed enough in the autumn of 1608 to ask for his son's release from the service of the Gonzaga family, and when this was denied, Monteverdi himself wrote a bitter letter that showed his complete disenchantment with Mantua. He accused the authorities of the duke's household of meanness and insulting behaviour towards him, and although he was granted a pension in return for his recent labours he continued to feel unhappy and by 1610 was looking for a new post. This was probably the main reason for his visiting Rome during that year, though a subsidiary reason was to try to obtain a place in the papal seminary for his elder son. He seems also to have gone to Venice to supervise the printing of a large volume of his church music, dedicated to Pope Paul V and significantly containing a type of music that might prove attractive to the authorities of St Mark's, Venice. At this time he was planning another madrigal book, to include three extended laments, but before it was completed his employer, Duke Vincenzo, died, and his successor, Francesco, dismissed him, together with a number of other artists, in July 1612, apparently without warning. He went back to Cremona and seems to have done little for about a year, although he gave a concert in Milan. Then, on the death of the *maestro di cappella* of St Mark's, G. C. Martinengo, he was invited to Venice, where on 19 August he performed some of his church music as a test in front of the procurators. He was appointed to the post at an annual salary of 300 ducats and given an immediate present of 50 ducats to cover his expenses. He returned to Cremona to make arrangements for moving. On his way back to Venice he was robbed by highwaymen.

III Venice

Since the *cappella* of St Mark's in Venice was at a low ebb, Monteverdi's first few years there were largely concerned with its reorganization. He seems to have been an efficient and energetic administrator: he brought the choir up to strength, found new virtuoso singers, transferred the instrumental ensemble from a per diem basis to the full-time payroll, bought new music and brought a new repertory to the custom of singing masses on ferial days as well as festivals, using works by 16th-century composers like Lassus and Palestrina. He must also have written large-scale works for use at St Mark's but none of them was published at this time; the works that did appear were either motets for small forces, which were included in several anthologies from 1615 onwards, or, like the pieces in the sixth book of madrigals (1614), had been written at Mantua. During his early years at St Mark's little music was published by his colleagues, but gradually he appointed younger men, among them Cavalli, Alessandro Grandi (*d* 1630) and Giovanni Rovetta, who took some of the burden off him.

Monteverdi was thus able to accept commissions from elsewhere, notably from Mantua, where he was again persona grata, Duke Francesco having died and been succeeded by his brother Ferdinando, whom Monteverdi had known well. He composed a ballet, *Tirsi e Clori*, which was produced at Mantua in 1616. In the same year he began work on a *favola marittima* called *Le nozze di Tetide*, though he was unhappy with the libretto and never completed the music, even when it transpired that the work was intended simply as a set of *intermedi*, not as a continuous, unified whole. In 1618 he began composing another dramatic work, *Andromeda*, which he also left unfinished, after two years of intermittent work. In letters to Mantua his main excuses for his slow progress on these commissions refer to his duties in St Mark's, for which the procurators raised his salary in 1616 to the unique height of 400 ducats.

There can be no doubt, however, that Monteverdi was also composing music for secular academies, since his ample seventh book of madrigals (1619) is full of concertato music in an up-to-date style. In 1620 there was some discussion of a revival of *L'Arianna* at Mantua. It was also in 1620 that he received an offer to return to

Mantuan service; in his indignant refusal of it he catalogued all his old grievances, which clearly were still alive in his mind. In doing so he revealed that his income in Venice was much augmented by commissions from the religious confraternities, a fact confirmed by the accounts of the Scuola Grande di S Rocco, for which he wrote music for the day of its patron saint in 1623 and 1628. Other works from the 1620s include the dramatic dialogue *Combattimento di Tancredi e Clorinda*, which was staged in the home of a Venetian nobleman, Girolamo Mocenigo, in 1624. But the most important is a full-length opera, *La finta pazza Licori*, about which his long correspondence with the Gonzagas' chancellor, the younger Alessandro Striggio, survives. It was intended for performance at Mantua in 1627 (with a well-known opera singer, Margherita Basile, in the title role), probably to celebrate the succession of Vincenzo II on the death of Duke Ferdinando; but Vincenzo was constantly ill, and the work was never performed. Immediately after completing it, Monteverdi was asked to write music for *intermedi* and a torneo to be given at the Farnese court at Parma, and the procurators gave him leave of absence to go there.

During this period of activity there was worrying news of his younger son, Massimiliano, who was studying medicine at Bologna. In 1627 he was arrested on the orders of the Inquisition for reading forbidden books. He was acquitted in 1628 but only after a short period in prison, during which his father had to raise bail for his release. He eventually became a fully qualified doctor and practised at Cremona, where he died in 1661. Monteverdi's elder son, Francesco, after briefly studying, probably law, at the universities of Padua and

Bologna, entered the Carmelite order shortly after 1620. In 1623 he became a singer at St Mark's, Venice. He was still included in a list of singers drawn up in 1677, but he probably died shortly after this, since in 1678 several new appointments were made to fill unspecified places in the choir. He sang at Padua in 1636 in *Ermiona*, an 'introduction to a torneo' by Pio Enea degli Obizzi, with music by G. F. Sances. There are two typically Venetian ariettas by him in Carlo Milanuzzi's *Quarto scherzo delle ariose vaghezze* (Venice, 2/1624).

After about 1629 Monteverdi seems to have become less active as a composer. This was probably because of external circumstances. In 1628, on the death of Vincenzo II, Mantua was left without a male heir and promptly became the cause of a major war, during which it was sacked by imperial troops. He thus received no further commissions from there. Venice itself suffered from a disastrous attack of plague in the winter of 1630–31, which caused a complete cessation of activity for several months and a noticeable diminution of music publishing for several years. In 1630, before the arrival of the plague, Monteverdi set Giulio Strozzi's drama *Proserpina rapita* for a wedding of nobility (Mocenigo–Giustiniani). He composed the mass of thanksgiving for deliverance from the plague in November 1631. In 1632 he published a slim volume of pieces for one and two voices under the title *Scherzi musicali* and was away from Venice for a while, probably at Cremona seeing to family affairs; at about this time he took holy orders. Little is heard of him during the next few years, although it is known that he was considering the completion of a book explaining his basic principles of composition that he had promised some 30 years earlier. He published a grand retrospective collection of his secular music in 1638 and a similar volume of church music in 1641. Yet his life's work was by no means over. Following the opening of public opera houses in Venice from 1637, he was much sought after as a composer of operas. In 1640 *L'Arianna* was revived, and in the following two years three new works, *Il ritorno d'Ulisse in patria*, *Le nozze d'Enea con Lavinia* and *L'incoronazione di Poppea*, were given first performances. The first of these was also performed in Bologna with certain Venetian singers, and he wrote a ballet, *La vittoria d'Amore*, on a commission from Piacenza. In 1643 he was given leave to visit Cremona. He died shortly after returning to Venice, on 29 November 1643. He was buried in the church of the Frari, where a commemorative plaque was erected; a copy still exists in the chapel to the north of the high altar.

CHAPTER TWO

Theoretical basis of works

Throughout most of his mature working life Monteverdi consciously strove to achieve certain intellectual concepts common in the High Renaissance, and it is impossible to understand his stylistic development without taking them into account. Although it is unlikely that he read Greek, at least with any fluency, he held, like many musicians and theorists of his time, that the highest achievement of the artist was the Platonic goal of moving the affections, which can be translated less literally but more cogently as 'affecting the whole man'. His lack of Greek, and probably his lack of mathematical training too, inclined him against the interest, current in his youth, in acoustical experiments that attempted to revive the temperament of ancient music. He therefore turned to Plato's general artistic ideas, the most important of which seemed to him to be one discussed by Zarlino that Ficino had rendered from the Greek as 'melodia ex tribus constare, oratione, harmonia, rhythmus'.

Monteverdi's interpretation of this influential concept insisted on the order in which Plato mentioned the three elements of music – the text ('oratio'), the combination of notes ('harmonia') and rhythm. In his view, therefore, the music should be second in importance to the words. Not all commentators of the time considered that this order was of supreme significance. Caccini was one who did, but unlike him and other members of the Florentine school, Monteverdi, thoroughly grounded in traditional techniques, believed that Plato's ideal could be realized within the framework of polyphony. Certainly some elements in the generally accepted procedure of polyphonic composition would have to be modified, notably those relating to harmony, and he was convinced too that the modal structure as explained and defended by Artusi was completely outdated. He also saw the necessity for a wider use of dissonance. Although he found analogies in current methods of improvised ornamentation to explain his own free use of dissonance, there can be no doubt that he sought to make it a much more significant means of expression.

Later in his life Monteverdi turned his attention to the interpretation of Plato's idea of rhythm. Whereas in his earlier attempts at recreating ancient concepts by modern means he had left the technical terms distinctly vague, he here accepted the direct correlation between certain rhythmic patterns and certain emotional states. Influenced, perhaps, by his family's medical background, he believed that the emotions could be divided in the manner of the humours of the body and that music might follow these divisions. He worked out this idea in some detail in certain pieces in the *stile concitato*, but in general he remained a pragmatist and never allowed his natural musicality to be overruled by academic ideas, even when these were at their most influential in his work. This pragmatism is shown at its best in his avowed acceptance of a completely different style of music that was absolutely traditional and needed no explanation by reference to the Greek philosophers. While his views on dissonance and modality can be found in other writers of the time, the crystallization of his idea of two 'practices' – the one based on the purity of the style developed from the Netherlands school, the other a modern one based, paradoxically, on ancient principles – was unique. Though not directly responsible for the way in which later Baroque composers were to use this division, Monteverdi himself clearly derived great benefit as a composer from his theoretical thinking, even if much of it was imprecise.

CHAPTER THREE

Madrigals, Books 1–6

Monteverdi wrote music in most of the madrigalian genres current from about 1580 to 1640. Those he ignored were largely of no emotional weight, like the mascherata or villanella, though they offered opportunities for caricature, in which he showed some interest in his last operas. It is difficult to date many of his pieces because of the long gaps between some of the publications in which they appeared, but evidence from his letters and occasionally from the texts he set enables the continuity of his stylistic development from 1584 until the late 1630s to be charted with some certainty. It is thus possible to assert that he worked almost continuously throughout his life in this medium.

His first published pieces were *madrigali spirituali*, which appeared in 1583, his 17th year, and obviously followed a fashion for such pieces that was also exploited by Marenzio, the Gabrielis and several other composers in the mid-1580s. Only the bass part of Monteverdi's volume survives, but it is enough to show that the music was rather old-fashioned, as might be expected from a pupil of Ingegneri, whose own madrigal style was typical of the early 1570s. Monteverdi's canzonettas for three voices (1584) equally show Ingegneri's influence, for instead of the very simple homophonic textures of most examples of the genre there is a certain amount of genuine polyphony that is

1. Claudio Monteverdi: portrait by Bernardo Strozzi (1581–1644)

not always suitable for the small-scale proportions of the bipartite form. Also unusual for canzonettas is Monteverdi's marked interest in word-painting, another feature that seems to stretch beyond the confines of a strophic genre. At the same time, the need for compactness in working on a small scale made him appreciate two main ideals of such music: crisp rhythmic motifs based on the natural accentuation of the words, and short singable phrases rather than the extended vocal lines of the larger contrapuntal forms.

This mixture of old and new informs Monteverdi's first secular madrigal book (1587), which appeared after the vogue of the Marenzian madrigal style had become well established. He seems at times a shade unsure in the handling of five voices, some parts being not well integrated into the texture, but on the whole he again shows the soundness of Ingegneri's tuition in counterpoint, many of the madrigals being written in a manner not far from that of his teacher. Yet several contain hints of the newer style, setting the fashionable pastoral verse in a more obviously melodious way and underlining the text with the musical images of the Marenzian school. The texture in these pieces is not strictly contrapuntal but rather a quasi-polyphonic interweaving of motifs giving a lighter feeling and a brighter sound. Two further traits that assume importance in later works are a distinct interest in the deriving of formal patterns from musical motifs with similar rhythms, as in the cycle *Ardo, sì, ma non t'amo*, where the opening lines of the two succeeding madrigals, *Ardi o gela a tua voglia* and *Arsi e alsi a mia voglia*, provide obvious material for such integration; and the use of dissonance, treated with perfect circumspection according to Zarlino's practice but nonetheless extended in places to some length.

The second book of madrigals (1590) is much more assured in technique, with no signs of weakness in the counterpoint and a better sense of proportion in setting the words, so that important phrases are given ample development. There are still a few pieces in the manner of Ingegneri, but most are now in the Marenzian style. The chosen verse is in the courtly pastoral tradition of Tasso (and Guarini), and the musical setting is based on the detailed expression of rich imagery. Monteverdi had not only mastered conventional devices, such as a broken melody for 'sospiri' (sighs) and scales for the ideas of ascending and descending, but was full of original imaginative ideas, such as that at the beginning of *Non si levav'ancor*, where the idea of the sun having not yet risen is expressed by simultaneous motifs, one rising, the other falling, and in the 'mirror' image to convey the reflection of the dawn on the sea in *Ecco mormorar l'onde*. To the crispness of rhythm suggested by a syllabic word-setting is added a more brilliant sound than formerly, largely based on the upper voices of the ensemble. A few madrigals show a knowledge of the school of composers at Ferrara; they wrote for an ensemble of virtuoso women singers, and Monteverdi imitated the florid style of their soprano parts. This volume represents the zenith of his work at Cremona, forward-looking but never going beyond the technical limits of the amateur circle of a provincial town academy.

Though a few numbers in the third madrigal book (1592) are also in this style and may therefore be assumed to have been written for Cremona, the volume as a whole represents a major change in direction. For now, after cultivating the popular manner of Marenzio, Monteverdi adopted a distinctly modern approach. Although this new style was to become fashionable in the 1590s, it is significant that Monteverdi was among the first to adopt it. The effect of Platonic thinking is evident in several ways. In contrast to the essentially hedonist attitude of the Marenzian style, the progressive traits are revealed in a greater seriousness, obviously with the intention of moving the affections. To this end the Tasso-like verse of the second book, with its tendency towards concrete images allowing obvious equivalents in the music, was supplanted by the more introverted poems of Guarini, which needed a new kind of interpretation. This interpretation was obviously based on that of Wert, who had been attempting something of the kind for several years. Since the words were of the greatest importance in this new approach, Wert tried both to make them audible and to express their emotional meaning, rather than just their external images. In ensuring audibility Wert created melodies that approached rhythms of spoken declamation both in their frequent eliding of syllables and in the use of very short notes, often repeated on a monotone, giving the effect of quasi-recitative. While the logic of this was to be followed by the monodists, Wert attempted to work within a conventional framework by simplifying the textures of the madrigal ensemble to produce virtual homophony, thus effectively abolishing counterpoint, though since he did not pursue his principles to their logical extreme there are still conventional sections even in his most unusual works. For the purposes of expression Wert abandoned the usual confines of singable melody, writing angular lines sometimes of great difficulty, with wide or awkward leaps to underline the astringencies of the verse. Noticeably he did not go beyond the normal handling of dissonance, and his basic sonorities were those derived from his experience with the Ferrarese ensemble.

Monteverdi followed Wert's principles very closely in certain respects and took up his general attitude in several works included in his third book. Much of the volume consists of settings of Guarini, though there are two Tasso cycles. He came nearest to Wert's style in one of these, *Vattene pur, crudel*, which contains a great deal of choral recitative, whose monotoned melody is broken by expressive intervals pointing emotional words. Using predominantly homophonic textures he sought variety by using different combinations of voices, which resulted in a series of trio sections clearly related to those of the Ferrara school. As with Wert, his music assumes virtuosity on the part of the performers, and, as adumbrated in certain pieces in the second book, the upper voices especially are treated in a florid manner. Monteverdi was, however, less consistent than Wert in this respect, for he periodically broke into his former style to express the concrete images of the verse. He also made much greater use of dissonance than Wert. In its details it still obeys the criteria of the conservatives, but in a piece such as *Stracciami pur il core* (which Martini and Burney were to use in the 18th century to prove Monteverdi's revolutionary nature) it is extended to such a degree as to make it the most noticeable feature of the madrigal, especially since the discords are made harsher by double suspensions and by including the note of resolution simultaneously with the actual dissonant note. There are signs that Monteverdi had not completely assimilated this new idiom, largely in the imbalance between sections and in the extreme nature of the difficult passages. These signs may well have been the result of his quick production of these more modern madrigals, which he must have composed soon after arriving at Mantua.

The fact that his next madrigal book did not appear until 11 years later, in 1603, suggests that it took Monteverdi some time to integrate the various new elements in his style. There seems to have been no practical reason for the long wait, since the third book achieved a second edition within two years, indicating a certain popularity, as does the inclusion of a number of canzonettas in an anthology assembled by Antonio Morsolino in 1594. These latter works are much more up-to-date than the similar essays of ten years earlier. In them Monteverdi put aside counterpoint in favour of the trio textures current in his colleague Gastoldi's three-part ballettos of the same period, which are the main influence on these canzonettas.

The madrigals in the fourth and fifth books (best considered together since between them they represent the work of the 13 years from 1592) are more mature in every way than anything that had gone before and must be considered the peak of the music that Monteverdi produced in the first half of his life. The verse that he set is nearly all by Guarini (more than half of the poems in the fifth book come from *Il pastor fido*) and often has a strongly erotic flavour more intense than that of the usual pastoral verse. The musical style is an extension of that of the third book, with a deep concern for the audibility and expression of the words. Again it is the madrigal cycles, *Ecco Silvio* in five sections and *Ch'io t'ami* in three, that use the Wertian chordal recitative most extensively; indeed in *Ecco Silvio* there is little relief from it. There are many passages of it in the single madrigals, but they are integrated into a more normal texture to form a smaller part of the whole than is usual in the third book. The manner can be seen at its most imaginative in *Sfogava con le stelle*, where the recitative is actually notated in the manner of psalmodic chanting so that the declamation can be exactly as in speech. These passages occur several times and on each occasion give rise to extensive free counterpoint, using expressive harmony and melody which are thrown into strong relief by their recitative context. More often still, the recitative in these madrigals is felt to be part of a normal motif, as in *A un giro sol*, where there is extensive use of the monotone; yet the phrases are completed with figuration completely in a 16th-century idiom, so the parlando writing becomes no more than incidental. Expressiveness is achieved without the extreme awkwardness of melody of the third book. The wide leaps of Wert are rare, though diminished and augmented intervals are common, as is the downward minor 6th, which from now on was a hallmark of Monteverdi's melodic style. Such difficulties as do exist for the singers come largely from the way in which major and minor are juxtaposed, for they are presented with an unpredictable freedom that is untypical of the formal chromatic writing of the late 16th century. This results in an unusually rich harmony, which, without seeming extravagant in Gesualdo's later manner, completely breaks with the rules laid down by Zarlino.

As Artusi found, Monteverdi's use of dissonance is highly original, although in several respects it is based on the common practice of the period. First, he wrote down ornaments that would previously have been improvised. These are much less revolutionary than those suggested by Caccini, for they were culled from such treatises on embellishment as those by Bassano, Bovicelli and Conforti. But Monteverdi's application of them seems at times deliberately to flout the methods of those writers by making the discords appear in their harshest form. Secondly, he extended the idea of passing notes by missing out the consonances from and to which the dissonance should proceed, thus making the discord more prominent, even though in itself it could well have been found in works by very conservative composers. Thirdly, suspensions are irregularly resolved, so that instead of proceeding by step they leap on to a consonant note of the succeeding chord. This procedure is not strictly original, since Vincenzo Galilei had advocated it about 1590, but it too is used in a such a way as to intensify the dissonant feeling. Finally, there is a frequent holding of bass notes to give the effect of a pedal, which appears to increase the actual number of passing notes and chords, even if all the details lie within the conventions codified by 16th-century theorists. By such extensions of previous practice, Monteverdi appeared to have invented a completely revolutionary idiom, in which chords of the 7th and 9th could be treated freely; it was this that gave him the reputation of being a progressive composer. The remarkable feature of this novelty is less its supposed originality than the purposes to which it is put. There is a vast range of emotion within these madrigals: some are tragic in the sustained use of dissonance, others are playful by virtue of the lightly touched discords, while the richness of the integrated chromaticism conveys the eroticism of Guarini's verse with uncanny exactness. Achieving a nice balance between the painting of the concrete image and the introverted intensity that is the basic feature of the poetry, Monteverdi's middle-period madrigals are never merely clever or shocking in the mannerist way, for they show acute psychological penetration allied to a sense of proportion whereby the musical material never seems under-developed and is thus wholly appropriate to the terseness of the verse.

The fifth book was published with the addition of a basso continuo part. For all except the last six numbers this is virtually a *basso seguente* and is unnecessary in performance. A harmony instrument is an essential ingredient in the other six madrigals, where it is largely used instead of a third voice as the bass in the trio sections derived from the earlier madrigal style. It therefore provides a new freedom in the handling of sonorities, since a solo voice could now be used to contrast with the tutti without complete disruption of the harmony. The immediate effect of the innovation on Monteverdi's style was that it made for greater contrasts. The vocal lines of the solo sections (including duets) have more elaborate embellishments, while the instrumental bass tends to move quite slowly, to allow a feeling of improvisation suggested by the rhythmically more irregular ornaments he now used. The tutti sections usually have very plain melodies, with a simple homophonic texture. To give a sense of shape, Monteverdi replaced the contrapuntal devices of previous madrigals by rondo patterns in which the tutti sing the recurrent refrain and the soloists provide the episodes. Emotionally these works are less sophisticated than the others in the volume, though they have a new charm resulting from their concentration on melody rather than on rich harmony and textures.

The same can be said of the *Scherzi musicali* (1607). His brother's *Dichiaratione* in explanation of Monteverdi's principle of two 'practices' mentions that Monteverdi had imported a 'canto alla francese' into Italy, and this has been taken by some scholars to mean that in this volume he was experimenting with *musique mesurée*. There are certain points of resemblance: the metrical novelties of Chiabrera's strophic verse reflect a knowledge of Ronsard and the French classicizing lyric (see Pirrotta, *NRMI*, 1968), and the regularity of the contents of the *Scherzi musicali* derives from its patterns. Nonetheless they are really hemiola songs – a genre that was to become extremely fashionable in the first two decades of the 17th century – which are given a texture very similar to that of Gastoldi's three-part ballettos already mentioned in connection with Monteverdi's canzonettas of 1584. In such respects these pieces are forward-looking, for regular rhythmic patterns and simple textures are the main features of the monodic arias that were now replacing polyphonic madrigals in public esteem.

Monteverdi's sixth book of madrigals (1614) seems retrogressive since in it he reverted to the mannerist style, which he now took to a new extreme point. It consists chiefly of two extended cycles, both laments dating from the period 1608–10 (a third was planned but was apparently not completed). The first of these is an arrangement of the climactic scene of the opera *L'Arianna*. The scene does not survive in its original form, but the extant versions and the libretto show that it was an extended arioso with choral interjections. Monteverdi clearly reworked it extensively in his madrigalian version for five voices, which highlights the close relationship between his monodic style and that of his Wertian recitative ensemble madrigals, both in the nature of the melody and in the expressive dissonance that is amply used throughout. Unity between the sections is achieved by a subtle repetition of thematic fragments, and the first part is virtually a rondo, with the episodes providing an imaginative concept of surprise in their novel development of material. Although there are few signs that the *Lamento d'Arianna* is an arrangement, a comparison with the other cycle, the threnody for Caterina Martinelli, *Incenerite spoglie*, shows that the textures and sonorities of a work originally designed for ensemble can be more varied. This is the finest work of Monteverdi's mannerist period, with the recitative style thoroughly integrated into the madrigal idiom. The verse, by a Mantuan poetaster, is bad, offering few concrete images but a plethora of emotional words, which Monteverdi set in an austere melodic style. The harmony is highly expressive, extreme dissonance being saved for the climaxes in a restrained manner, which makes the cry of despair in the final section seem, in its astringency, even more moving. The sixth book includes two other, shorter works in this vein, and the remainder of the volume consists of madrigals of the newer, continuo type, among them the joyous *Qui rise, O Tirsi*, in which the duet texture possible in this idiom is used to the utmost advantage.

CHAPTER FOUR

Madrigals, Book 7 onwards

The sixth book was the last of Monteverdi's madrigal books in which he persisted with forms directly related to those of the 16th century, for the seventh book (published in 1619), entitled *Concerto* (perhaps in deference to a Venetian tradition dating back to Andrea Gabrieli's similarly-named volume of 1587), is entirely devoted to genres developed since 1600. It is an unusual collection in displaying a great variety of works; it is virtually a retrospective view of his secular oeuvre over several years. It may owe this pattern to Marco da Gagliano's *Musiche* (1615), but it contains an even greater diversity of means and idiom than that widely ranging volume.

Surprisingly little of the seventh book is given over to purely monodic genres. The two pieces that can be described unequivocally as monodies both seem to be essays in the Florentine manner of recitative. They are *lettere amorose* and consist of syllabic declamation over a narrow range, obviously in imitation of speech inflection. Expressiveness is achieved by the use of ornaments and occasionally by raising the voice above this narrow range. By contrast Monteverdi's usual harmonic style is totally lacking, the basso continuo being given simple consonances in slow motion. While they are not ineffective in the hands of a dramatic singer, these pieces are so unlike Monteverdi's operatic recitative that they seem to have been experiments in an academic manner that he quickly abandoned. A third work for solo voice, *Tempro la cetra*, is more characteristic. It is a sonnet, divided into a set of strophic variations for tenor, preceded by a short overture whose last phrase is used as a ritornello and followed by a dance for instrumental ensemble. This seems to be part of a dramatic entertainment of some kind, possibly a prologue to a play or an *intermedio*, as it closely resembles the prologue to *L'Orfeo* in the expressiveness of both melody and harmony and in its realization of the potentialities offered by the variation form. The fourth work for a single voice, *Con che soavità*, is completely *sui generis*. Related less to monody than to the Venetian concertato motet, it is written for three groups of musicians, two of string and keyboard instruments, the third a soprano with continuo instruments. The interest lies less in the vocal line than in the kaleidoscope of sonorities, which are conceived as a variety of pastel shades rather than in terms of strong contrasts. The other work written for a large concerted ensemble is *A quest'olmo*, for six voices with violins and recorders, which in spite of the presence of instruments is essentially in the idiom of previous madrigal books.

The bulk of the seventh book consists of duets, which now succeeded the five-part madrigal in Monteverdi's work as the medium for the sophisticated psychological expression of a wide range of emotions. The duets divide into three main types, one derived from the solo madrigal with continuo, another from the aria (in the early 17th-century meaning of the word), while the third is a set of variations over a stock bass such as the romanesca. The relationships between the older madrigal and the first type is seen in the seventh book in *O come sei gentile*, a setting of Guarini including a great

CLAVDIO MONTE VERDE
FIORI POETICI
Raccolti nel Funerale
DEL MOLTO ILLVSTRE;
E Molto Reuerendo
SIGNOR CLAVDIO
Monte verde
Maestro di Cappella della Du-
cale di S. Marco.
Consecrati
DA D. GIO: BATTISTA
Marinoni, detto Gioue:
Maestro di Cappella del Do-
mo di Padoua
ALL' ILLVSTRSSIMI
& Ecceilentissimi
SIG. PROCVRATORI
Di Chicsa di S. Marco.
In VENETIA, Presso Francesco Miloco.
Con Lic. de Sup. MDCXLIV.

2. Title-page, with portrait of Monteverdi, from G. B. Marinoni's 'Fiori poetici' (1644)

deal of detailed word-painting and displaying the virtuosity of the singers very much in the manner of the Ferrarese madrigals of the previous century. There are also echoes of Wertian melody in the awkward melodic leaps of *Ah, che non si conviene*; but it is the word-setting in these duets that gives the feeling of continuity from Monteverdi's earlier work. The intensity of *Interrotte speranze*, created largely by harmonic means, resembles that of several madrigals from the fourth book, and the close way in which the varying emotions of the verse are reflected achieves the same degree of subtlety. The aria-type duets are essentially projections of the canzonetta, although the simple strophic patterns of that genre are modified by the introduction of ritornellos and by making the succeeding verses different in detail. Although not as popular a melodist as some of his younger contemporaries, Monteverdi shows an appreciation of current tastes in the regular phrasing and harmonic changes and the strongly diatonic melody of a piece such as the well-known *Chiome d'oro*. The type of duet in which variations unfold over a bass reveals his craftsmanship in the new medium, which is seen at its best in *Ohimè, dov'è il mio ben?*, where the recurring bass suggests an ample variety of harmony and does not impede his imagination in allowing the melody to express the words in considerable detail. In all the duets he achieved a relationship between the voices like those in the former madrigalian idiom, not despising homophonic euphony but often suggesting contrapuntal interplay, with motifs passed freely between the voices. The fact that the bass rarely takes its part in such quasi-polyphony emphasizes the fact that the modern idiom dominates these works.

Madrigals

The few pieces that appeared in the 1620s in anthologies persist in the same vein. Two duets (in *RISM* 1624[11]) are excellent examples of their kind; one of them, *O come vaghi*, is a re-creation for the smaller ensemble of the spirit of a madrigal in the fourth book, *A un giro sol*. Three ariettas for solo voice also published in 1624 were Monteverdi's first pieces in this popular genre to be printed. Interestingly he differed from his younger contemporaries in his liking for word-painting even within the very restricted scope of the light strophic genre, though the songs are not less attractive melodically on that account. His liking for the greater possibilities in this direction offered by variation form is plain in the *Scherzi musicali* of 1632, where the most ambitious works use a repeated bass pattern rather than a simple melodic repetition. The three sections of *Quel sguardo sdegnosetto* are specially masterly because of Monteverdi's capacity for finding seemingly new harmonic progressions from the same bass notes, while the almost madrigalian imagery through which he ennobled trivial verse is even more remarkable. The masterpiece of the volume is again a duet, *Zefiro torna*, set as a chaconne. A two-bar pattern is repeated exactly many times, while the voices are manipulated to form differing phrase lengths; there is thus not a hint of monotony. Monteverdi's penchant for word-painting again results in a highly imaginative setting of the detail of the poem, a sonnet by Rinuccini similar in its use of concrete imagery to the poems by Tasso that he had set earlier. *Zefiro torna* is the first great vocal chaconne, and it heralded a tradition that was to last until the middle of the 18th century.

The final book of madrigals produced under

Monteverdi's supervision is unusual not only for its large size and because it seems to have been designed as a grand retrospective collection of music that he had composed over some 30 years, but mainly because it appears to be a manifesto for his theories of the three styles of humours. It is divided into two parts, 'Canti guerrieri' and 'Canti amorosi'. The volume includes *Il ballo delle ingrate*, first performed at Mantua in 1608 but here revised with adaptations probably made for a later performance in Vienna; *Combattimento di Tancredi e Clorinda* (1624); and a ballet probably written for the festivities celebrating the coronation of Ferdinand III as Holy Roman Emperor in 1636. The dating of these works (which are discussed on pp.43–7 below) suggests equally wide dating for the other pieces, which show an equal diversity of manner. The earliest of these are probably two pieces 'in the French style', *Dolcissimo uscignolo* and *Vago augelletto*. These have little, if any, relationship with the *Scherzi musicali* of 1607 previously mentioned in this connection except that they too adopt a metrical rhythmic pattern rather than one based on Italian speech rhythms; but their connection with the writers of *musique mesurée* is strengthened by the alternation of solo sections and tuttis that are full harmonizations of them, a feature known in France about 1600. The cycles of concerted madrigals for a few voices and continuo seem to belong to the period 1620–35, the duets in particular developing the techniques of those in the seventh book. Of these, *Ardo e scoprir* has the sexual passion associated with Monteverdi's Mantuan works, though the continuo technique belongs to the 1620s; while the equally fine *O sia tranquill'il mare* is a study in loneliness that seems to anticipate Penelope's mood in *Il ritorno d'Ulisse*.

The greatest of the pieces requiring small forces, the *Lamento della ninfa*, develops this same mood. It is a triptych whose main central section, a soprano lament over a four-note ground bass, is framed by an introduction and conclusion that set the scene. The harmonic resource in this section is astonishing, the dissonances normal in Monteverdi's tragic music made more prominent by the use of three male voices as a background to the soprano's melody. Another remarkable feature is the instruction that the soprano must use tempo rubato while the remainder of the ensemble keep in strict time, thus accentuating the dissonance while underlining the emotional separation of the lovelorn nymph from the rest of the world. In its use of the ostinato this extraordinary work acts as a link between the earlier monodic laments following the vogue set by that in *L'Arianna* and those in later operas, by Cavalli, Cesti, Purcell and others, which usually employ some repeated bass formula.

If few of these works show much sign of Monteverdi's theorizing, the large-scale pieces show more obvious connection with it. His invention of the *stile concitato* was ostensibly the outcome of his reflections on Plato's concept of arousing the warlike or agitated state in Man. Monteverdi interpreted this to mean that a semibreve should be divided into 16 semiquavers repeated on a single note. This clearly could not be done to any great extent in voice parts whose words are sung, so it is mainly given to string instruments, where the effect can be achieved by bowing. This isolating of a rhythm tends to make the harmony static, since the repetition of the single note allows for little variety, and much of

Monteverdi's *stile concitato* music is from this point of view rather dull. His natural pragmatism, however, tends to cause an integration of other elements into the style, notably those associated with the realism of the earlier madrigals. He had several times set texts including references to battle and in doing so had used quasi-fanfare motifs probably borrowed from the battaglia and deriving ultimately from Janequin's *La bataille de Marignan*. He now adapted these to this new context. The avowed new style thus has a number of older traits within it. The realistic word-painting of *Altri canti d'amor*, probably written for the Emperor Ferdinand III, is thus in many ways nearer to the madrigal style of the 1580s, in spite of external features that point to an appreciation of the newer sonorities available with modern string playing. More interesting emotionally are the works in which the *stile concitato* is an incidental ingredient rather than the raison d'être. Such a work is the excellent setting of Petrarch's sonnet *Hor ch'el ciel e la terra*, in which the three humours, 'molle', 'temperato' and 'concitato', are contrasted in music that succeeds not only in painting the words but in expressing their inner meaning with the sophistication of the great psychological madrigals of the fourth book.

A third of the contents of the posthumous ninth book consists of previously published music, the remaining pieces being largely trios of a lighter kind, attractively written in the regular triple rhythms fashionable in the 1620s though not attempting the intensity of Monteverdi's grand manner. One of these, *Come dolce hoggi l'auretta*, is from the opera *Proserpina rapita*. From this it may be deduced that all the music that

Monteverdi wished to preserve had already been printed under his own auspices and that we thus possess the entire corpus of his music in madrigalian genres.

Some scholars have viewed the later works not as truly madrigalian pieces but as incipient cantatas. The sectional structure of such a work as *Ninfa che scalza il piede* in the eighth book, in which each *parte* is written for a different combination of voices, may lead to this conclusion. Yet in spite of its formal variety Monteverdi's secular chamber music all belongs to the tradition he inherited in the 16th century. It is significant that at a time when solo music was predominating he preferred to write for an ensemble, if only of two or three voices. This allowed him a greater variety of texture, enhanced by the possibilities of the loose counterpoint that after the 1580s was all that conventional madrigals contained. It is also significant that even when he did write solo pieces the principles of word-painting, learnt from the Marenzian madrigal, still informed his approach to the madrigalian genre. The roots of the real developments in 17th-century music must therefore be sought elsewhere. Monteverdi's madrigals, however, form the finest corpus of work by any composer working in this sphere. He was as technically accomplished as Marenzio but had a much greater emotional range. He was as speculative as Gesualdo, but his much greater compositional skill means that his experimental writing is better integrated into his works and is of greater value in expressing emotion. If he lacked the lightness of touch of Vecchi, this is essentially because, as an 'academic' composer, his main preoccupation was with realizing the Greek concept of 'affecting the whole man'. He was also writing, after his Cremona years, for professional performers of great skill. Thus virtually all his 250 works in this genre are of some interest, a high proportion are masterly and some are masterpieces.

CHAPTER FIVE

Early dramatic works

Monteverdi was probably engaged in the production of various kinds of theatrical entertainment from his earliest years at Mantua. It is unlikely that he had a chance to gain such experience at Cremona. His models for dramatic works were thus those of his colleagues serving the Gonzagas. Their activities undoubtedly included providing music for ballets, a favourite amusement of Vincenzo I, who had probably acquired some knowledge of it from the court at Ferrara. Monteverdi's participation in dance music is made the more probable by virtue of his employment as a string player, as it was the five-part ensemble of viols and violins that was used in such entertainments. He must also have performed in *intermedi* and music for plays, notably Guarini's celebrated pastoral comedy *Il pastor fido*, originally planned for 1591 but finally produced early in 1598. The music for 1591 was probably by Wert and Gastoldi, but the production of 1598 may well have included some by Monteverdi. Cavicchi (*Congresso internazionale . . .1968*) has pointed out that in the preface to a volume of contrafacta including some taken from the Guarini settings in the fifth book of madrigals the editor, Aquilino Coppini, referred to 'La Musica rappresentata del Quinto libro de' Madrigali del Signor Claudio Monteverdi' and that this, taken literally, would imply that they were originally monodic theatre music, for which five-part versions had been made later in the manner of the *Lamento d'Arianna*. Whether or not this is true, it is certain that Monteverdi's experience of stage music began well before he could have become acquainted with the Florentine operatic experiments and that it is an important factor in the consideration of his stylistic development.

The first knowledge of Monteverdi's working in this area comes in a letter dating from 1604, while he was awaiting details of choreography from the Mantuan dancing-master before writing the music for a ballet. This shows a concern for practical matters that was to prove typical of his approach to later projects for theatre music. It may be assumed that he was involved in similar works for Mantua during the next two years, since one of the reasons given by Giulio Cesare Monteverdi for writing his *Dichiaratione* to the *Scherzi musicali* of 1607 was that his brother was too busy 'ora in Tornei, ora in Balletti, ora in Commedie'. The first score to survive, however, is that for an opera, *L'Orfeo*, called a 'favola in musica' and produced at Mantua in 1607. Where exactly the production took place is unknown, since the Accademia degli Invaghiti, before whom it was given, had no permanent premises at this time, and speculation that it was in the Galleria dei Fiumi in the Palazzo Ducale is so far unproven. It seems likely that the ambience was a relatively small hall, where the grand effects customary in productions of pastorals had to be reduced to modest proportions. Although both Monteverdi and his librettist, Alessandro Striggio, almost certainly knew Peri's *Euridice*, there are notable differences between the two. In both works the classical story is treated as a pastoral, with the usual semi-happy conclusion, but the printed libretto of *L'Orfeo* shows that either composer or poet intended an ending closer to the myth, with Orpheus menaced by the Bacchantes. Why this was put aside is unknown, but it indicates an altogether grander conception than that of *L'Euridice*, and helps to explain the greater length of *L'Orfeo*, with its five acts demanding different scenes, whereby the classical concept of unity of place is abandoned. In addition to pastoral there are strong elements of the *intermedio*, notably in the scene depicting Orpheus's descent to Hades, for which precedents can be found in several 16th-century entertainments. Opportunities for dancing are also included, both in the first act and at the conclusion of the opera. Thus elements from the genres in which Monteverdi had been working for at least a decade were present to allow him to move away from recitative-dominated drama in the Florentine pattern.

The music of *L'Orfeo* is therefore a mixture of monody, madrigal, and instrumental music of various kinds. Since it derived from *intermedi* and ballet music, Monteverdi demanded an instrumental ensemble of a similar kind to those used in such entertainments. It is accordingly larger and more varied than that of *L'Euridice* and includes the trombones traditionally used in infernal scenes, and recorders and strings for pastoral scenes. It is somewhat smaller than the largest ensemble used in 16th-century *intermedi*, and a new feature is the great variety of harmony instruments accompanying the voices. It is exceptional in deliberately demanding virtuosity from several players, especially those of cornettos, small violins (dancing-masters' kits) and harp, the player of the last-named at the first performance probably being a famous harpist from Naples. On the other hand, its deployment to gain dramatic atmosphere was not very unusual, except perhaps in the simultaneous use of various continuo instruments, which is sometimes highly imaginative in its exploration of sonorities.

The individual items from which the opera is built are also largely traditional. The pastoral first act includes a choral canzonetta which in style derives from Gastoldi's ballettos and the large-scale chorus lamenting the death of Eurydice in Act 2 is a homophonic madrigal whose rich harmony is typically Monteverdian. The instrumental pieces in the body of the opera are mostly short and in five parts, and they are often based on dance rhythms such as that of the pavan. They resemble similarly short pieces by Monteverdi's colleague Salamone Rossi, another string player, which apparently were written for dramatic entertainments of some kind. The toccata for the total ensemble, including trumpets, that begins the opera is a military fanfare, which could well have been played *al fresco* by the town musicians; again this was not an unusual prelude to a play or *intermedio*.

The greatest stylistic variety is to be found in the monodic music, in which Monteverdi shows a flair beyond the reach of the Florentines. Comparatively little of it is recitative, but the narration of the messenger describing Eurydice's death clearly owes much to Peri, whose expressive power and interesting harmonies in a similar style furnished an inviting model. Monteverdi preferred more organized patterns of solo music such as strophic variation, which he used most effectively for the Prologue; the duet, used less as dialogue than as the expression of two shepherds or of Apollo and Orpheus, who voice the same emotions simultaneously; and the continuo madrigal after the manner of the last six numbers of his fifth book, duet sections alternating with tuttis which often repeat the same material to give an elementary rondo form. Thus much of the music is based on the madrigalian style, the melody having a shape similar to that in the fourth and fifth books. The harmony is equally expressive, with a great deal of dissonance brought about by a melodic anticipation of a succeeding chord or by the irregular resolution of passing notes. The desire for organization informs the structure both of the individual acts and of the work as a whole. Ritornellos occur frequently to provide small-scale patterns, but Act 1 is conceived virtually as an arch, an example of large-scale planning unprecedented at this epoch. Even more remarkable is the fact that the opera has a grand, carefully placed climax, Orpheus's great aria in Act 3, 'Possente spirto', which, with its display of vocal and instrumental virtuosity, has something of the role of a grand scena in later operas (see fig.3).

From the point of view of drama *L'Orfeo* belongs to the tradition of the late Renaissance and thus does not pretend to depict rounded human characters. The only role aspiring to such a condition is that of Orpheus himself, but even he is seen more as an allegorical figure representing the power of music. On the other hand, there are many touches of excellent theatrical effect in the music: the unexpected breaking off of the Prologue to allow the drama to begin; the simple style of the last verse of 'Possente spirto' after the previously embellished melody, to show that Orpheus's increasing desperation results in a human rather than a virtuoso plea to be allowed to cross the Styx; the use of sinfonias to

3. Opening of Act 3 of Monteverdi's 'Orfeo' from the 1615 edition, published by Amadino

change the mood between scenes. It is such things, not to mention the excellence of the music itself, that made *L'Orfeo* the first viable opera in the repertory.

Only the libretto and several versions of the lament survive from *L'Arianna*. These, together with the sketchy description of its first performance by the Mantuan court chronicler Follino, suggest a somewhat more ample scale of production than in *L'Orfeo*, as would be expected for such a formal occasion. Monteverdi maintained, however, the general approach of the earlier opera. The monodic versions of the lament reveal the same expressive, malleable melodic style, based on his madrigalian experience, while the libretto shows that this scena had interpolations from a chorus of fishermen, suggesting the same concern for musical shape, as opposed to simple declamation.

The score of *Il ballo delle ingrate* of the same year was published only in 1638, though the surviving libretto of the 1608 performance suggests there were some changes in the published version. Whether all the instrumental sections were published is more doubtful, since as it stands the ballet is both short and somewhat lacking in proportion. Follino's description mentions the participation of all kinds of instruments, so it may well be that a large continuo section was deployed after the manner of *L'Orfeo*. The dance music may well have been expanded by repetition of the various short sections in different orders (the instructions for the dances by Cavalieri in the sixth *intermedio* for the 1589 Florentine production of *La Pellegrina* may offer a useful model). The monodic opening section, a dialogue between Venus and Cupid, is written in a stricter recitative style than is usual in *L'Orfeo*, though the harmony is effective, and at one point there is a hint of a triple-time aria, looking forward to the style of the 1620s. The short duet which ends this dialogue is in Monteverdi's best vein, and the strophic-variation aria for Pluto surrounding the dances shows a melodiousness combined with a care for expressing the detail of the words worthy of his best madrigals. The concluding aria for the last remaining *ingrata* is the finest part of the work, a miniature masterpiece written in the same emotional spirit as the *Lamento d'Arianna.* The dances display the methods of rhythmic transformation common in pavan–galliard pairs, and their five-part texture emphasizes the three upper lines, which are allotted to violins. The production was probably quite elaborate, with machines or *carri* for Venus and Cupid and an *intermedio*-like representation of the jaws of Hades. The lack of virtuosity in the women's parts, as in the surviving scena from *L'Arianna*, almost certainly stems from the employment of the actress Virginia Andreini after the death of Caterina Martinelli, but if this caused practical difficulties at the time the exploitation of a limited vocal range and a simpler melodic style in the *ingrata*'s aria showed the way forward to a genuine dramatic manner in solo music.

CHAPTER SIX

Later dramatic works

Monteverdi's next surviving theatre piece, *Tirsi e Clori* (1616), was also a ballet for Mantua, but smaller-scale and lacking the *intermedi* ingredients of *Il ballo*. The musical forces show the trend towards the monochrome string ensemble and away from the variety of the Renaissance orchestra: Monteverdi asked for nine players of the viola da braccio family and eight singers, two of whom take the parts of Thyrsis and Chloris. The continuo team is equally modest, with a chitarrone and harpsichord (or a harp for Chloris) to accompany the two protagonists and a spinet and two lutes to support the general ensemble. The work is in the form of a dialogue madrigal, a type popular by 1616, with flowing triple-time melody after the manner of the monodic aria, followed by the ballet, an extended madrigal for five voices (notwithstanding the eight suggested by Monteverdi) with more complicated rhythms than in the dance music of either *L'Orfeo* or *Il ballo delle ingrate*. Noticeably there are no allegorical elements in the brief story of pastoral courtship. That this is symptomatic of Monteverdi's thinking about the nature of music drama is revealed by a series of letters to Striggio concerning the music for *Le nozze di Tetide*, a *favola marittima*, which he started to compose later the same year. He thought at the outset that the libretto was to be set completely to music in the manner of *L'Arianna*. For this purpose, however, it seemed, because of the lack of human interest, very inadequate:

> I see that the characters are winds, *amoretti*, *zeffiretti* and sirens, so that many sopranos will be needed; and also that the winds – west winds and north winds – have to sing. How, dear sir, since winds do not speak, shall I be able to imitate their speech? And how, by such means, shall I be able to move the passions? Ariadne moved the audience because she was a woman, and Orpheus did the same because he was a man and not a wind . . . I find that this tale does not move me at all and is even difficult to understand; nor do I feel that it can naturally inspire me to a moving climax. Ariadne inspired in me a true lament, and Orpheus a true prayer, but I do not know what this will inspire in me.

This letter, one of the first contributions to an aesthetic of opera written by a composer who had experience of the genre, was in fact based on a misunderstanding, since the verse was intended for a set of *intermedi*; it is interesting that when this was explained to him Monteverdi did not challenge its suitability. He wrote madrigals for the nereids and solo music for Venus, the latter with fashionable echo effects, and he suggested dancing at certain points. Thus he was clearly differentiating by this time between operas, serious works that must move the affections, and less organic forms of entertainment. The correspondence about the abortive *Andromeda* of 1618–20 reveals nothing of aesthetic importance except that Monteverdi was still interested in madrigalian choruses and dances. The conception of the lost *Apollo* emerges even more vaguely from the letters, but it seems to have been some kind of dramatic cantata, the centrepiece of which was a lament, presumably monodic.

As a piece of music-theatre *Apollo* may thus have resembled Monteverdi's next such work to survive, *Combattimento di Tancredi e Clorinda* (1624), a setting of stanzas from Tasso's epic poem *Gerusalemme liberata.* This in itself denotes that it was not to be a conventional operatic work, since, whereas he usually insisted on all kinds of changes and additions to librettos to make them more effective for his purposes, he here set a text that afforded no opportunity for this kind of adaptation. The scene is that of a fight in single combat between a Crusader, Tancred, and the Muslim girl Clorinda, of whose sex he could not be aware since she was dressed in armour; Monteverdi used a narrator to sing the words not given to these two protagonists. The form of the cantata (for want of a better word) is therefore based on the dialogue madrigal. The central action, however, is largely created by the orchestra of strings, the writing for which demonstrates the potentialities of the *stile concitato,* with its division of long notes into short, measured repeated notes – not, as has sometimes been stated, with the modern string tremolando. Though in outline the work is not all that different from *Tirsi e Clori,* the writing for both instruments and voices is completely different. The vocal parts are set as expressive arioso, at times highly ornamented, and lack the pure lyricism of the earlier piece. The absence of theatrical realism implied by the use of a narrator is more than made up for by the realistic effects of the orchestra, which imitates the trotting of horses in triple time, the clashing of swords by pizzicato and the shortness of breath in the dying Clorinda by sustained bowing changing suddenly from *forte* to *piano* and by both instruments and the voice as Clorinda actually dies. What could so easily have been simply a demonstration of an academic idea is in fact a vivid drama of human feeling.

It is evident from the important series of letters to Striggio in 1627 (see fig.4) about the lost opera *La finta pazza Licori* that human psychology was now Monteverdi's principal concern in dramatic music. This opera was planned as a comedy, which was certainly unusual at this time and suggests that Giulio Strozzi's drama had been written as a play rather than for musical setting. There is no mention of any allegorical figures, but the heroine, Licoris, intended for the singer Margherita Basile, was to simulate madness in order to make Amyntas desire to marry her. The complicated psychology of the heroine was one of the greatest attractions of this idea for Monteverdi, who instructs the singer to act 'from the single word rather than the sense of the phrase'. Realism was again to be sought: offstage music and noises, arias (one a lullaby) and the necessity for as much variety as possible are mentioned in the descriptions of how Strozzi was adapting the play to Monteverdi's needs. The fact that three virtuoso singers were available made them reorganize the plot to give each a more equal role than in the first conception, where the burden was very strongly on Licoris. While it is impossible to surmise exactly what form Monteverdi's music took, the correspondence indicates a radical departure from the earlier operas in aim and approach in spite of the fact that the royal occasion for which it was designed was not basically different from the one for which *L'Arianna* had been composed. The letters concerning the *intermedi* at Parma in 1628 show a more conventional attitude, indicating that Monteverdi still subscribed to the idea of a difference in seriousness between an opera and other theatre music.

The ballet for Ferdinand III published in the eighth

4. Final page of autograph letter (10 September 1627) from Monteverdi to the Mantuan court chancellor, Alessandro Striggio, giving his reasons for refusing to return to the service of the Gonzagas (trans. in Stevens, 1980, p.355) book of madrigals is not strikingly original in plan. It consists of strophic variations for tenor, with instrumental ritornellos, followed by two choral madrigals using the *stile concitato*; the latter were originally separated by dances, but these were not printed. The ritornellos are scored for two violins and continuo, but the five-part texture of the choruses and the style of the tenor solo are both developed from *Tempro la cetra* and *Tirsi e Clori* of some 20 years earlier.

Little is known about the conception of the three operas of Monteverdi's final years or even about the conditions under which they were performed. One, *Le nozze d'Enea con Lavinia*, is lost, but the synopsis and scenario, which do survive, indicate that it was 'a tragedy with a happy ending'. There were dances and choruses, first in *intermedi* between the acts and later integrated into the drama. The authenticity of one of the two surviving works, *Il ritorno d'Ulisse in patria*, has sometimes been challenged, since its only surviving score is in Vienna and is different in many details from the manuscript librettos presumably used in Venice. The style of the music is so like that of Monteverdi's other late works that there can be few doubts that the Vienna score is by him, but it may well have been altered by another hand while some scenic effects with chorus seem to have been fashioned with the tastes of the Viennese court in mind. The opera was first performed in Venice early in 1640, given in Bologna later that year, and repeated in Venice the following Carnival. It is known that some of the singers at St Mark's were given leave of absence to go to Bologna, presumably to take part in the performances there; this may explain the preponderance of male roles of quite modest proportions, whereas in other Venetian operas of the 1640s both women and castratos were used more lavishly. The demands on the designer and machinist were little different from those in the early operas, and, with the frequent participation of gods, the libretto still shows elements from *intermedi*. But the Homeric basis of the story allows for much of the interest in human emotion on which the correspondence concerning *La finta pazza Licori* insisted, and Badoaro provided a great variety of characters, from the comic, represented by Iro, the parasite accompanying Penelope's suitors, to the intensely serious, Ariadne-like figure of Penelope herself. There is also a genuine attempt at dialogue between the participants, and a grand climax, allowing for the equivalent of Orpheus's 'Possente spirto' at the moment when Ulysses defeats the suitors through being the only one to have the strength to draw his bow.

Musically, the score is remarkable for its lack of academicism compared with what might have been expected from Monteverdi's letters and eighth book of madrigals. The climactic scene uses the *stile concitato* most effectively. Elsewhere he displayed complete mastery of the genres in which he had been working for over 30 years. Much of Penelope's music consists of expressive recitative. It is somewhat less dissonant than his earliest music in this manner, but it shows a notable command of phrase structure, sometimes involving the repetition of words, which, while never obscuring their meaning, gives the recitative a hitherto unrivalled sense of shape. The variety of closed forms is equally noteworthy. The duets are specially fine and never obstruct the movement of the drama. Both strophic variation and the ostinato bass are freely used in the closed forms, where the melodic writing varies from smoothly flowing triple-time arias to catchy ariettas. It is clear that the orchestral and choral music is incomplete in the Vienna manuscript, but five-part textures are again common, and the strings are occasionally used to accompany the voice. Monteverdi's intentions are sometimes obscure – for example, when only a single chord, meant to be repeated but with no other instructions, is given to accompany the departure of the Thracian boat escorting the sleeping Ulysses – but this very fact shows that the orchestra was exploited for such effects; and as was customary, ritornellos are used to shape the vocal music.

Monteverdi's final opera, *L'incoronazione di Poppea*, is on an even more ample scale and involves a still greater number of characters. The principal parts – Poppaea, Nero (written for a high castrato) and Octavia (taken by Anna Renzi, one of the most celebrated singers of the mid-17th century) – require first-class singers, and a number of minor roles demand considerable skill.

G. F. Busenello's libretto still contains allegorical elements, and the dénouement, whereby the sleeping Poppaea is protected from murder by Love, relies literally on a *deus ex machina*. Yet in part because the story is an adaptation of Tacitus and no longer a matter of mythology, supernatural characters play a proportionally lesser role in the opera, which has a strongly human basis. The characters represent a cross-section of society ranging (apart from deities) from the emperor and his consort and their courtiers and associates to servants and common soldiers. In spite of this immense range the libretto is skilfully constructed, so the lack of continuity sometimes apparent in *Il ritorno d'Ulisse* is rarely found, and cause and effect follow each other cogently, only a few disparate scenes providing obvious relief from the progress of the drama. The only thing lacking is the grand dramatic climax for which Monteverdi's letters about other projects indicate his liking.

Monteverdi set the libretto with considerable freedom, repeating and rearranging passages to heighten the dramatic effect, as in the confrontation between Nero and Seneca in the first act. He consistently underscored variety of emotion within a single character, and Nero is drawn in a way reminiscent of Monteverdi's instructions concerning Licoris, in that a single phrase can suddenly change his mood, giving a lively, realistic picture of a neurotic ruler. The music has greater variety than any other opera by Monteverdi, and the purely solo music is intrinsically more interesting than that of *Il ritorno d'Ulisse*. There are specially fine laments, written in the customary arioso, for the deposed empress, Octavia, and Poppaea's husband, Otho. Nero's music is still more remarkable; in it the detailed imagery of the verse is set with the utmost imagination, such devices as the *stile concitato* having lost their academic flavour and become an essential expression of mood. The duets are frequent, and in them Monteverdi displayed an astonishing capacity for expressing widely differing kinds of love-making.

Discussion of the detail of the opera is made difficult because the two surviving scores were probably used by travelling companies which took the piece outside Venice (one score was made for performance in Naples). Comparison of these scores, and also of librettos, shows that alterations were made to suit changing circumstances, and that some of the extant music is probably not by Monteverdi at all; even the authenticity of the final duet is in doubt (it may be by Benedetto Ferrari). The nature of the instrumental ensemble is not known, the ritornellos in the Venice score being given to a 'trio' combination – probably two violins and bass – while the Neapolitan version indicates a four-part ensemble. Nevertheless, such evidence as exists of Venetian theatres makes it probable that a very small ensemble had now replaced the massive panoply of the Renaissance band that accompanied *L'Orfeo*; certainly the role of the instruments is reduced, and there is no necessity at all for a chorus, though 'extras' were possibly used for visual effects in the penultimate scene.

Nevertheless, despite uncertainties such as these, it is generally possible to follow the workings of Monteverdi's dramatic imagination. The scene of the death of Seneca, a chromatic madrigal in a style whose origins go back to Monteverdi's Mantuan years, shows a tragic power rarely seen in 17th-century opera. From the point of view of construction the most impressive flair is shown in the way that closed forms never seem to be the object of the music but convey necessary elements of the drama; with few exceptions it is thus impossible to extract the arias and duets from the fabric of the opera. The realism of the world picture given by *L'incoronazione di Poppea* has a strange by-product in that Nero and Poppaea are anti-hero and anti-heroine, and virtue is defeated in their victory. The idea of the opera yet remains a typically 17th-century allegory of the triumph of love in which the fate of individual human beings is less important. For all that, it is difficult not to see Monteverdi's experience of princes and their courts in this work, his greatest masterpiece and arguably the finest opera of the century.

CHAPTER SEVEN

Sacred music

The great multiplicity of styles that can be found in Monteverdi's sacred music owes much to the fact that although he spent the greater part of his working life in the service of the church he was not so employed during the vital years of his early maturity. His music therefore does not fit naturally into a continuing tradition, and it shows many signs of individuality, not only in details of style but also in his general approach to its peculiar problems.

Just as there is no real evidence to suggest that he was ever a choirboy at Cremona Cathedral, equally there is none to show that he was seriously concerned in the composition of church music in his pre-Mantuan years. The *Sacrae cantiunculae* (1582) consists not of liturgical pieces but of motets probably written to acquire contrapuntal technique. As such they reveal an efficiency surprising for a boy of 15, though both in the handling of words and in a lack of interesting sonorities they also show some inexperience. At Mantua, Monteverdi seems to have had no responsibility whatever for church music until his promotion to *maestro di cappella* in 1601; and for the rest of his career there his duties in this sphere were nominal, especially up to 1609, while Gastoldi was in charge of the music at the ducal church of S Barbara. It may have been because there was no church musician of any eminence in Mantua from that year that Monteverdi was

e composition of the music included in
:ction published in 1610, though its
ıe pope indicates an outward-looking
than a desire to please his employer.
...ever, so strongly reflects the resources and attitudes common at Mantua that it is unique in the history of church music and belongs to neither of the established Roman and Venetian traditions so influential at this period.

The full title of this famous volume is *Sanctissimae virgini missa senis vocibus ad ecclesiarum choros ac Vespere pluribus decantandae – cum nonnullis sacris concentibus ad sacella sive principum cubicula accommodata*. It is clear from this that there are three elements in the collection: a mass; the vesper psalms and *Magnificat* settings appropriate to festivals of the Virgin Mary; and motets of a not strictly liturgical nature. It has sometimes been interpreted to mean that these three elements were intended to be kept separate in performance, but the motets are placed unusually in between the settings of the vesper psalms, thus encouraging the belief that they were considered part of the Vespers music and acted as antiphon substitutes in a well authenticated manner of the time. There still remains the problem of why Monteverdi provided two settings of the *Magnificat*, which are so similar in technique and material that they must be considered alternatives rather than complementary. It has been suggested that one was meant for First Vespers, the other for Second, but there is no evidence that the music was so intended. A more plausible explanation may lie in the fact that the essentials of the liturgy of Vespers may be obeyed without using instruments (other than the organ) if the second

Magnificat is used; and it would therefore be possib. to use this music in cathedrals where a skilled instrumental ensemble was not available.

Although it can be seen that Monteverdi's liturgical intentions are open to varying interpretations, his general intention, to show himself a capable composer in differing styles of church music and to make plain his belief in the *prima* and *seconda prattica*, is hardly in doubt. The mass is a monument of the *prima prattica.* Written on themes from Gombert's motet *In illo tempore* (published in 1554), its academic intent is clear from the printing of ten *fughe* or contrapuntal tags from the motet at the head of the mass in the partbooks. It thus differs considerably from the masses using motets as parody material common in the later decades of the 16th century. Not only is there a more thorough polyphonic working-out of these tags but there is much close canonic writing and few places where imitative counterpoint gives way to the sonorous homophony of the Roman composers. Austerity rules too in the treatment of the words, for the conventional painting of the text is almost completely lacking. The mass is therefore most unusual for its period, its main resemblances to other settings lying in the diatonic harmony, with its many academic progressions, and in the wide range between upper and lower parts, which results in great splendour of sound.

The vesper psalms, on the other hand, are in the modern style, though they are not entirely *seconda prattica* works, since formal design, not the words, was the primary consideration. The mixture of elements is unique. Much of the melodic material is derived from plainsong, which is sometimes used as cantus firmi in netimes woven into the fabric of counter- the use of strong rhythms and imitative cit *Dominus* it is the basis of a strophic- and in the hymn for Vespers, *Ave maris stella*, it is given the accentuation of a strophic hemiola song. Chordal chanting in the manner of *falsobordone* is freely used in several places. Alongside these seemingly backward-looking elements are traits derived from the most recent madrigal style, notably trios with decorated melody, 'walking' bass patterns given to the continuo instruments, and ritornellos (sometimes optional) for a five-part instrumental ensemble. The larger-scale works show a knowledge of the Venetian style, though the use of *cori spezzati* rarely resembles that of the Gabrielis since the use of plainsong material does not allow for closely argued dialogue. The psalm settings are, however, conceived sectionally, verse by verse, the sections ending with full cadences, and the diversity between them is emphasized by complete changes of sonority, a trio of upper voices, for example, being replaced by one of lower voices or some similar effect. This is the antithesis of 16th-century practice and is one of the earliest appearances of a method that became the norm in later Baroque music. Where counterpoint is still extensively employed, as in *Lauda, Jerusalem*, the close imitations and dense textures of the mass on *In illo tempore* are also found.

The motets in the collection are the most thoroughgoing exhibitions of the modern style and the *seconda prattica*. They were written with Mantuan virtuoso singers in mind, and few church works of the time equal them in their exploitation of ornamental melody, in which figuration developed in secular monody is freely used in ensemble. Harmonically they are akin to the arioso sections in the operas, dissonance arising from the conflict between the slower movement of the bass and the anticipations or delays in the melody, which itself uses such expressive devices as the descending 6th and augmented and diminished intervals to express the words. One motet is an echo piece, less in the manner of Venetian echo motets than of theatre music such as Peri's 'Dunque fra torbid'onde' in the Florentine *intermedi* of 1589. Instruments are prominent in two items.

The opening versicle, *Domine ad adiuvandum*, is remarkable for being the toccata from *L'Orfeo* with added choral parts chanting the words rhythmically. The other, the *Sonata sopra 'Sancta Maria'*, is in effect a large-scale 'quilt' canzona, with a soprano repeating a plainsong prayer to the Virgin Mary 11 times. Though there were precedents for it, the virtuosity of the instrumental writing and the expansiveness of its form make this unique too. The *Magnificat* settings bring all the afore-mentioned devices into play. The smaller one is for six voices and organ and is thus one of the first concertato settings. It is composed in separate sections, each using a different combination of voices, but unity is achieved by the constant repetition of a plainsong cantus firmus. The ornamental melody suggests that it was intended for solo voices though it is possible that some verses were sung chorally. The larger setting is designed in the same way except that the inclusion of instruments makes possible even greater variety between the sections. Operatic influences are here very strong, one section being virtually an echo scene, another using cornett and violin duets in the manner of Orpheus's great aria in *L'Orfeo*. In one verse, treated in the manner of the *Sonata sopra 'Sancta Maria'*, the plainsong cantus firmus is accompanied by instruments playing lively rhythms.

Whether Monteverdi composed further church music in his years at Mantua is unknown, and dating his Venetian works is difficult since they appeared in two collections, both huge, one published under his supervision in 1640, the other issued posthumously in 1650. Some developments in style can be traced by means of various works by him that appeared in anthologies between 1615 and 1629, but they are mainly pieces for modest forces, and thus do not give a rounded picture. It seems certain that much of his church music for Venice is lost, for, since he was expected to compose fresh music for the important festivals each year, even the two ample collections can hardly represent 30 years' work.

The surviving works suggest that he continued to develop the three major trends revealed in the 1610 volume, adapting them to the changing tastes of three decades. He largely abandoned the older Venetian style, using *cori spezzati*, in favour of various types of concertato music, in which the expansive manner of the late Renaissance was reduced to the more restricted but elegant style of the early Baroque period. He continued to make use of the *prima prattica*, in which he composed at least two masses and several psalms. The extreme scholarliness of the 1610 mass is, however, modified in the two later mass settings. Both are for four voices with organ bass and use the old *misura da breve* and white note values. Dissonance is restricted to prepared suspensions and passing notes that move by step, while the melody and verbal underlay follow the principles of

Zarlino. The main difference between this style and that of the 16th century lies in its diatonicism, the increasing regularity of rhythm and the predictability of its imitative counterpoint, whose texture is rarely varied by homophony. There is little word-painting, though suspensions express the word 'passus' in one of the masses, and Monteverdi was obviously determined to remain strictly within the tenets of the *prima prattica* and to essay a pure musical idiom. The resulting music is thus somewhat lacking in emotional power, though it is of profound historical importance in the development of the *stile antico*, which was practised successfully in Venice by several composers even in the 18th century.

The works written in the concertato manner are mainly psalm settings for Vespers and were probably meant for ceremonial occasions at St Mark's. In keeping with the general trend of the time, they are for comparatively small instrumental forces; two violin parts are normal, with trombones to support the voices (though the parts are often optional), and occasionally a bassoon is given an independent part. The brilliance of the Gabrielian orchestra is thus substantially reduced to monochrome. The writing for voices also tends to be of a less obviously virtuoso nature, though it is often both effective and imaginative. The earliest of Monteverdi's published Venetian choral works are four motets (in *RISM* 1620[3]); they are in a style akin to that of the Cremona madrigals, with the concrete images painted in an almost Marenzian way, and the continuo is little more than a *basso seguente*. There are some similar works in the retrospective collections, but the bulk of the concertato music uses the continuo as an essential feature, and it often acts as an important structural device.

Monteverdi did not repeat the experiment of the Vespers music in using plainsong cantus firmi as unifying agents, probably because the harmonic implications of modal material were difficult to reconcile with the increasing diatonicism of 17th-century music. Instead he sought formal designs either in rondo structures or in repeated bass figuration. There are a number of rondo motets, in which a solo group of two or three singers usually alternates with a tutti repeating a refrain. Unlike earlier Venetian rondo motets, in which the refrains are settings of the word 'Alleluja', Monteverdi repeated words from the psalm, even though this destroyed their continuity; he thus shows his concern for musical design at the expense of the text. He did likewise in works where there is no rondo form but merely short repetitions of motifs and phrases. Ostinato basses allowed for textual continuity, and Monteverdi showed a mastery of the genre to an even greater extent than in his secular music, since his psalm settings are often much longer than the *Lamento della ninfa* and the 1632 *Zefiro torna*. His tour de force occurs in a setting of *Laetatus sum*, where a single-bar figure is repeated over 100 times while variety is achieved through a succession of duets for differing combinations of voices, violins, trombones and bassoon. The melodies in such works are often close to those in contemporary secular songs, and Monteverdi used his own popular canzonetta *Chiome d'oro* in a setting of *Beatus vir*, which mixes ostinato and rondo techniques. As a result he forged an attractive, modern style unusual in church music at this time.

Monteverdi's Venetian motets for a few voices are

more closely related to those in the 1610 collection, though with necessary modifications to suit Venetian conditions. His first published solos and duets appeared in anthologies from 1615 onwards and show that, lacking the virtuosos of Mantua, he largely renounced decorative melody in favour of a pleasant tunefulness. Some of the motets of the 1620s especially owe much to the secular arias of the songbooks and achieve a lightness that makes them seem secular in spirit. Other pieces look back to the intensity of the 1610 motets, especially four Marian motets (published in *RISM* 1625^2), which seem to derive from the version of the *Lamento d'Arianna* as a prayer to the Blessed Virgin. These works use virtuoso *fioriture*, dissonance and expressive melody to give extraordinarily passionate meaning to the words in the *seconda prattica* manner. There is also a small group of works which are constructed sectionally; with their passages of quasi-recitative and aria they look forward to the later Baroque solo cantata.

The fact that in much of Monteverdi's sacred music secular material and techniques are to be found is of great significance in the history of church music, since many 17th-century church composers were not experienced in opera or other modern genres. By his application of methods first explored in secular music he helped to prevent the ossification of style that otherwise might well have occurred.

CHAPTER EIGHT

Historical position

Monteverdi's reputation, both in his lifetime and after, has been that of a revolutionary, responsible to a considerable degree for drastic changes in musical style around 1600. This picture, encouraged by the polemic with Artusi, was confirmed in essentials by the two leading historians of the 18th century, Martini and Burney, probably because Artusi was more accessible than scores of Monteverdi's madrigals (the original sources being partbooks); and it persisted during most of the 19th century. Increased knowledge of the background of the period has modified this point of view in recent years. Monteverdi can now be seen as a principal figure in a progressive movement that included a number of composers and theorists. His greatest gifts lay in finding how traditional means could be applied to novel ends. Thus he persisted with the ensemble madrigal when the logical step for a composer interested in the declamation of the words was to adopt monody after the Florentine manner. His early operas were full of devices developed in *intermedi* and ballets. His church music is, in the *prima prattica* works, very traditional; elsewhere it is a mixture of traditional and new techniques, as in the Vespers of 1610, where cantus firmus technique and operatic scena mingle to produce a unique effect. His one real invention was the *stile concitato*, which has no exact precedent, though with its vivid realism the practical result is reminiscent of the battle pieces of the 16th century. As a theorist he was unable, even after a lifetime's thought, to arrive at a complete system or aesthetic of composition. His originality here lay in his realization that there was not one method of approach, but two, to the problems involved and that it was possible to use traditional as well as new techniques in attaining the desired goal of moving the passions.

It was because of his moderate views that Monteverdi's influence was less than might have been assumed for so famous and long-lived a composer. Few Italian composers followed his madrigal style, since the younger ones in particular were absorbed in the writing of monodic works. In this sphere his invention of the lament was particularly influential, for the genre became fashionable at the hands of such composers as d'India, Saracini and, later, Cavalli. Neither did his operas give rise to direct imitations. The style of the early works remains unique, while that of the later works was taken up less by his Venetian successors than has often been imagined. The profound humanity based on a historical theme which is the essence of *L'incoronazione di Poppea* has no exact equivalent in the works of Cavalli, though comic personages do infiltrate the operas of the period around 1650. The *stile concitato* certainly inspired: in Italy it was used by Grandi and Merula, while in Germany, Schütz made it an integral part of his style. It was in northern countries too that the theoretical basis of the *stile concitato* took root in the attempt by Schütz's pupil Christoph Bernhard and others to categorize musical figuration to correspond with human emotions, a process that contributed to the emergence of the doctrine of the Affections. It was in the practical application of this expression of human emotions in music that Monteverdi rightly held himself to be a master; and his position in music history rests on the fact that he showed how this could be done.

WORKS

Editions: *C. Monteverdi: Tutte le opere*, ed. G. F. Malipiero (Asolo, 1926–42, rev. 2/1954; with added vol.xvii [suppl.], 1966) [M]
C. Monteverdi: Opera Omnia, ed. Fondazione Claudio Monteverdi, IMa, *Monumenta*, v (1970–)
C. Monteverdi: Composizioni vocali profane e sacre (inedite), ed. W. Osthoff (Milan, 1958) [O]

Numbers in right-hand margins denote references in the text.

DRAMATIC — 37–54

Endimion, dance music, Mantua, 1604–5, music lost

L'Orfeo, favola in musica (A. Striggio (?1573–1630)), Mantua, Feb 1607 (Venice, 1609 and 1615); M xi, 1 — 1, 5, 28, 38–43, 45, 54, 59

L'Arianna, opera (O. Rinuccini), Mantua, 28 May 1608, music lost except for lament (see 'Secular vocal') — 1, 5–6, 8, 11, 25, 33, 43, 44, 45, 48, 160

Il ballo delle ingrate, ballet (Rinuccini), Mantua, 1608, pubd in Madrigali guerrieri et amorosi, 1638; M viii, 314 — 6, 32, 43–4, 45

Prologue to L'Idropica, comedy with music (G. B. Guarini), Mantua, 2 June 1608, music lost — 6

Tirsi e Clori, ballet (Striggio), Mantua, 1616, pubd in Concerto: settimo libro, 1619; M vii, 191 — 8, 45, 47, 50

Le nozze di Tetide, favola marittima, begun 1616 but never completed, lost — 8, 45–6

Andromeda, opera (E. Marigliani), begun 1618–20 but never completed, lost — 8, 46

Apollo, dramatic cantata, never completed, lost — 46

Intermezzi for Le tre costanti (Marigliani), 1622, music lost

Combattimento di Tancredi e Clorinda (Tasso), Venice, 1624, pubd in Madrigali guerrieri et amorosi, 1638; M viii, 132 — 9, 32, 46–7

Armida, dramatic scena, 1624–7, music lost

La finta pazza Licori (G. Strozzi), intended for Mantua, 1627, but never perf., music lost — 9, 48, *49*, 51

Gli amori di Diana e di Endimione (A. Pio), Parma, 1628, music lost

Mercurio e Marte, torneo (C. Achillini), Parma, 1628, music lost

Proserpina rapita, opera (Strozzi), Venice, 1630, music lost except for 1 trio (see 'Secular vocal': Come dolce hoggi) — 10, 34

Volgendo il ciel, ballet, Vienna, ?1636, pubd in Madrigali guerrieri et amorosi, 1638; M viii, 157 — 32, 48, 50

Adone, 1639, music lost

Il ritorno d'Ulisse in patria (G. Badoaro), Venice, 1640; M xii — 11, 33, 50–52, 53

Le nozze d'Enea con Lavinia, opera, Venice, 1641, music lost — 11, 50

La vittoria d'Amore, ballet, Piacenza, 1641, music lost — 11

L'incoronazione di Poppea (G. F. Busenello), Venice, 1642; M xiii — 11, 52–4, 65, 138, 144

Prologue to La Maddalena, sacra rappresentazione (G. B. Andreini), 1617 (see 'Sacred vocal': Su le penne de' venti)

SECULAR VOCAL — 15–36, 64

Canzonette, 3vv (Venice, 1584) [1584] — 2, 15–17, 25

Il primo libro de madrigali, 5vv (Venice, 1587) [1587] — 3, 17

Il secondo libro de madrigali, 5vv (Venice, 1590) [1590] — 3, 17–18, 20

Il terzo libro de madrigali, 5vv (Venice, 1592) [1592] — 3, 4, 18–21, 22

Il quarto libro de madrigali, 5vv (Venice, 1603) [1603] — 4, 5, 21–4, 31, 34, 41

Il quinto libro de madrigali, 5vv, bc (Venice, 1605) [1605] — 5, 21, 24, 37, 41

Musica tolta da i madrigali di Claudio Monteverde e d'altri autori, e fatta spirituale da Aquilino Coppini, 5, 6vv (Milan, 1607[20]) [incl. 11 sacred contrafacta of madrigals by Monteverdi] [1607[20]]

Scherzi musicali di Claudio Monteverde, raccolti da Giulio Cesare Monteverde suo fratello, 3vv (Venice, 1607[21]) [1607[21]] — 5, 25, 32, 38

Il secondo libro della musica di Claudio Monteverde e d'altri autori, fatta spirituale da Aquilino Coppini, 5vv (Milan, 1608) [incl. 8 sacred contrafacta of madrigals by Monteverdi] [1608]

Il terzo libro della musica di Claudio Monteverde e d'altri autori, fatta spirituale da Aquilino Coppini, 5vv (Milan, 1609) [incl. 19 sacred contrafacta of madrigals by Monteverdi] [1609]

Il sesto libro de madrigali, 5vv, con uno dialogo, 7vv, bc (Venice, 1614) [1614] — 8, 25–6

Concerto: settimo libro de madrigali, con altri generi de canti, 1–4, 6vv, bc (Venice, 1619) [1619] — 8, 27–30, 32

Scherzi musicali cioè arie, et madrigali in stil recitativo, con una ciaccona . . . raccolti da Bartholomeo Magni, 1, 2vv, bc (Venice, 1632) [1632] — 10, 31

Madrigali guerrieri et amorosi con alcuni opuscoli in genere rappresentativo, che saranno per brevi episodii frà i canti senza gesto: libro ottavo, 1–8vv, insts, bc (Venice, 1638) [1638] 11, 32–4, 35, 48–9, 51

Madrigali e canzonette . . . libro nono, 2, 3vv, bc (Venice, 1651) [1651] 34

Works in 1594[15], 1605[12], 1624[11], C. Milanuzzi: Quarto scherzo delle ariose vaghezze . . . con una cantata et altre arie del Signor Monteverde, e del Sig. Francesco suo figliolo, 1v (Venice, 1624 [lost], 2/1624), 1634[7] 10, 21, 31

A che tormi il ben mio, 5vv, 1587; M i, 8

A Dio, Florida bella (G. B. Marini [Marino]), 5vv, insts, 1614; M vi, 38

Ah, che non si conviene romper la fede?, 2vv, 1619; M vii, 62 30

Ah dolente partita (Guarini: *Il pastor fido*) (= O infelix recessus), 5vv, 1603; M iv, 1

Ahi, che si parti il mio bel sol adorno, 3vv, *I-MOe*; M xvii, 38

Ahi, com'a un vago sol (Guarini) (= Vives in corde), 5vv, 1605; M v, 62

Alcun non mi consigli, 3vv, 1651; M ix, 42

Alle danze, alle gioie, 3vv, 1651; M ix, 68

Al lume delle stelle (Tasso) (= O rex supreme), 4vv, 1619; M vii, 129

Altri canti d'amor (Marini), 6vv, 2 vn, 4 va, 1638; M viii, 2 34

Altri canti di Marte (Marini) (= Pascha concelebranda) (2p. Due belli occhi fur l'armi [= Ergo gaude, laetare and Lauda, anima mea]), 6vv, 2 vn, 1638; M viii, 181

Amarilli onde m'assale (G. Chiabrera), 3vv, 1607[21]; M x, 31

Amor che deggio far?, canzonetta, 4vv, 2 vn, chit/hpd, 1619; M vii, 182

Amorosa pupilletta, 3vv, 1607[21]; M x, 44

Amor per tua mercè vatene a quella, 5vv, 1587; M i, 11

Amor, se giusto sei (?Guarini) (= Amemus te), 5vv, 1605; M v, 81

Amor, s'il tuo ferire, 5vv, 1587; M i, 54

Anima del cor mio, 5vv (= Anima quam dilexi), 5vv, 1603; M iv, 88

Anima dolorosa (= Anima miseranda), 5vv, 1603; M iv, 84

Anima mia, perdona (Guarini: *Il pastor fido*) (= Domine Deus) (2p. Che se tu se'il cor mio [= O gloriose martyr]), 5vv, 1603; M iv, 26

A quest'olmo, a quest'ombre (Marini), 6vv, 2 vn, 2 rec/fl, 1619; M vii, 14 28

Ardo, avvampo, mi struggo (= Alleluja, kommet, jauchzet and Frewde, kommet, lasset uns gehen), 8vv, 2 vn, 1638; M viii, 107

Ardo e scoprir, ahi lasso, io non ardisco, 2vv, 1638; M ix, 32 32

Ardo, sì, ma non t'amo (Guarini) (2p. Ardi o gela a tua voglia (Tasso), risposta; 3p. Arsi e alsi a mia voglia (Tasso), contrarisposta), 5vv, 1587; M i, 61 17

Armato il cor d'adamantina fede (= Heus, bone vir), 2vv, 1632; M ix, 27

Augellin, che la voce al canto spieghi, 3vv, 1619; M vii, 98

A un giro sol de' bell'occhi lucenti (Guarini) (= Cantemus), 5vv, 1603; M iv, 49 22, 31

Baci soavi e cari (Guarini), 5vv, 1587; M i, 14

Batto qui pianse Ergasto (Marini), 5vv, hpd, 1614; M vi, 101

Bel pastor dal cui bel guardo (Rinuccini), 2vv, 1651; M ix, 1

Bevea Fillide mia (G. Casoni), 5vv, 1590; M ii, 15

Cantai un tempo, e se fu dolc'il canto (P. Bembo), 5vv, 1590; M ii, 102

Canzonette d'amore, 3vv, 1584; M x, 3

Che dar più vi poss'io? (?Guarini) (= Qui regnas), 5vv, 1605; M v, 51

Ch'io ami la mia vita, 5vv, 1587; M i, 1

Chiome d'oro, bel thesoro, canzonetta, 2vv, 2 vn, chit/hpd, 1619; M vii, 176 30, 62

Ch'io non t'ami, cor mio (Guarini), 5vv, 1592; M iii, 76

Ch'io t'ami e t'ami più de la mia vita (Guarini: *Il pastor fido*) (= Te sequar) (2p. Deh, bella e cara [= Sancta Maria]; 3p. Ma tu più che mai dura [= Spernit Deus]), 5vv, 1605; M v, 39 21

Chi vol haver felice e lieto il core, 'cantato a voce piena, alla francese' (Guarini), 5vv, 1638; M viii, 280

Chi vuol veder d'inverno un dolce aprile, 3vv, 1584; M x, 17

Chi vuol veder un bosco, 3vv, 1584; M x, 23

Clori amorosa (Chiabrera), 5vv, 1607[21]; M x, 54

Come dolce hoggi l'auretta spira (Strozzi, from Proserpina rapita), 3vv, 1651; M ix, 60 34

Come farò, cuor mio?, 3vv, 1584; M x, 14

Con che soavità, labbra odorate (Guarini), 1v, str, lutes, hpds, org, 1619; M vii, 137 28

Cor mio, mentre vi miro (Guarini) (= Jesu, dum te), 5vv, 1603; M iv, 7

Cor mio, non mori? (= Jesu, tu obis), 5vv, 1603; M iv, 11

Corse a la morte il povero Narciso, 3vv, 1584; M x, 15
Cruda Amarilli (Guarini: *Il pastor fido*) (= Felle amaro), 5vv, 1605; M v, 1
Crudel, perchè mi fuggi? (Guarini), 5vv, 1590; M ii, 83
Damigella tutta bella (Chiabrera), 3vv, 1607[21]; M x, 40
De la bellezza le dovute lodi, 3vv, 1607 (doubtful)
Dice la mia bellissima Licori (Guarini), 2vv, 1619; M vii, 58
Di far sempre gioire amor speranza, 3vv, 1651; M ix, 50
Dolcemente dormiva la mia Clori (Tasso), 5vv, 1590; M ii, 78
Dolci miei sospiri (Chiabrera), 5vv, 1607[21]; M x, 52
Dolcissimi legami di parole amorose (Tasso), 5vv, 1590; M ii, 19
Dolcissimo uscignolo, 'cantato a voce piena, alla francese' (Guarini), 5vv, 1638; M viii, 271 32
Donna, nel mio ritorno (Tasso), 5vv, 1590; M ii, 44
Donna, s'io miro voi, giaccio divengo, 5vv, 1587; M i, 58
Ecco di dolci raggi (2p. Io che armato sin hor [= Spera in Domino]), 1v, 1632; M x, 81
Eccomi pronta ai baci (Marini), 3vv, 1619; M vii, 111
Ecco mormorar l'onde (Tasso), 5vv, 1590; M ii, 68 18
Ecco Silvio (Guarini: *Il pastor fido*) (= Qui pependit) (2p. Ma se con la pietà [= Qui pietate]; 3p. Dorinda, ah dirò mia [= Maria, quid ploras]; 4p. Ecco piegando le ginocchie a terra [= Te, Jesu Christe]; 5p. Ferir quel petto, Silvio [= Pulchrae sunt]), 5vv, 1605; M v, 14
Ecco vicine, o bella tigre (Achillini), 2vv, 1619; M vii, 71 21
E così a poc'a poco torno farfalla (Guarini), 6vv, 1605; M v, 96
Era l'anima mia già presso a l'ultim' hore (Guarini) (= Stabat virgo), 5vv, 1605; M v, 9
Eri già tutta mia, lv, 1632; M x, 80
Et è pur dunque vero, lv, insts, 1632; M x, 82
Filli cara e amata (A. Parma), 5vv, 1587; M i, 21
Fugge il verno dei dolori (Chiabrera), 3vv, 1607[21]; M x, 34
Fumia la pastorella (A. Allegretti), 5vv, 1587; M i, 27
Già mi credev'un sol esser in cielo, 3vv, 1584; M x, 18
Giovinetta ritrosetta, 5vv, 1607[21]; M x, 50
Gira il nemico insidioso, 3vv, 1638; M viii, 75
Giù lì a quel petto giace, 3vv, 1584; M x, 20
Godi pur del bel sen felice, 3vv, 1584; M x, 19

Hor, care canzonette, 3vv, 1584; M x, 24
Hor ch'el ciel e la terra (Petrarch) (= O du mächtiger Herr) (2p. Così sol d'una chiara fonte [= Dein allein ist ja]), 6vv, 2 vn, 1638; M viii, 39 34
I bei legami (Chiabrera), 3vv, 1607[21]; M x, 29
Il mio martir tengo, 3vv, 1584; M x, 9
Incenerite spoglie (see Sestina) 26
Interrotte speranze (Guarini), 2vv, 1619; M vii, 94 30
Intorno a due vermiglie, 5vv, 1590; M ii, 29
Io ardo, si ma'l fuoco di tal sorte, 3vv, 1594[15]; M xvii, 1; O, 2
Io mi son giovinetta (= Rutilante in nocte), 5vv, 1603; M iv, 59
Io mi vivea com'aquila, 3vv, 1584; M x, 11
Io son fenice e voi sete la fiamma, 3vv, 1584; M x, 22
Io son pur vezzosetta pastorella, 2vv, 1619; M vii, 41
La bocc'onde l'asprissime (E. Bentivoglio), 5vv, 1590; M ii, 75
La fiera vista, 3vv, 1584; M x, 4
La giovinetta pianta (= Florea serta), 5vv, 1592; M iii, 1
Lamento d'Arianna: Lasciatemi morire (Rinuccini), 5vv, 1614; M vi, 1 25–6, 38
Lamento d'Arianna: Lasciatemi morire (Rinuccini), lv (Venice, 1623); M xi, 161 43, 44, 63
Lamento della ninfa: Non havea Febo ancora (Rinuccini), 1–4vv, 1638; M viii, 286 33, 62
Lamento d'Olimpia: Voglio morir: van'è'l conforto tuo, lv, *GB-Lbm*; O, 10
La mia turca che d'amor, 1v, in C. Milanuzzi: Quarto scherzo delle ariose vaghezze (Venice, 2/1624); M ix, 117
La pastorella mia spietata (Sannazaro), 3vv, 1607[21]; M x, 41
La piaga c'ho nel core (= Plagas tuas), 5vv, 1603; M iv, 41
Lasciatemi morire (see Lamento d'Arianna)
La vaga pastorella sen va tra fiori, 5vv, 1587; M i, 50
La violetta (Chiabrera), 3vv, 1607[21]; M x, 48
Lidia, spina del mio core, 5vv, 1607[21]; M x, 56
Longe da te, cor mio (= Longe a te), 5vv, 1603; M iv, 92
Luci serene e chiare (R. Arlotti), 5vv, 1603; M iv, 35
Lumi miei, cari lumi (Guarini), 5vv, 1592; M iii, 99
Maledetto sia l'aspetto, 1v, 1632; M x, 76
Mentre io miravo fiso (Tasso), 5vv, 1590; M ii, 58

Mentre vaga Angioletta ogn'anima (Guarini), 2vv, 1638; **M** viii, 246
M'è più dolce il penar per Amarilli (Guarini: *Il pastor fido*) (= Animas eruit), 5vv, 1605; **M** v, 56
Misero Alceo (Marini), 5vv, insts, 1614; **M** vi, 91
Ninfa che scalza il piede, 1–3vv, 1638; **M** viii, 259 35
Non così tosto io miro (Chiabrera), 3vv, 1607[21]; **M** x, 38
Non è di gentil core (Guarini), 2vv, 1619; **M** vii, 8
Non giacinti o narcisi (Casoni), 5vv, 1590; **M** ii, 24
Non havea Febo (see Lamento della ninfa)
Non m'è grave'l morire, 5vv, 1590; **M** ii, 92
Non partir, ritrosetta, 3vv, 1638; **M** viii, 305
Non più guerra, pietate (Guarini), 5vv, 1603; **M** iv, 72
Non si levav'ancor (Tasso), 5vv, 1590; **M** ii, 1 18
Non sono in queste rive fiori (Tasso), 5vv, 1590; **M** ii, 35
Non vedrò mai le stelle, 2vv, 1619; **M** vii, 66
Non voglio amare per non penare, 3vv, 1651; **M** ix, 58
Occhi miei, se mirar, più non debb'io, 3vv, 1594[15]; **M** xvii, 2; O, 3
Occhi un tempo, mia vita, occhi di questo cor fido sostegno (Guarini), 5vv, 1592; **M** iii, 82
O come è gran martire (Guarini) (= O dies infelices), 5vv, 1592; **M** iii, 8
O come sei gentile, caro augellino (Guarini), 2vv, 1619; **M** vii, 41 28
O come vaghi, o come cari (**G. B. Anselmi**), 2vv, 1624[11]; **M** ix, 102 31
O dolce anima mia (Guarini), 5vv, 1592; **M** iii, 19
Ogni amante è guerrier (Rinuccini), 2–3vv, 1638; **M** viii, 88
Ohimè ch'io cado, ohimè ch'inciampo, 1v, in C. Milanuzzi: Quarto scherzo delle ariose vaghezze (Venice, 2/1624); **M** ix, 111
Ohimè, dov'è il mio ben?, 'romanesca' (B. Tasso), 2vv, 1619; **M** vii, 152 30
Ohimè, il bel viso (Petrarch), 5vv, 1614; **M** vi, 70
Ohimè, se tanto amate (Guarini), 5vv, 1603; **M** iv, 54
O mio bene, o mia vita, 3vv, 1651, **M** ix, 95
O Mirtillo, Mirtill'anima mia (Guarini: *Il pastor fido*) (= O mi Fili), 5vv, 1605; **M** v, 5
O primavera, gioventù de l'anno (Guarini: *Il pastor fido*) (= Praecipitantur), 5vv, 1592; **M** iii, 62
O rosetta, che rosetta (Chiabrera), 3vv, 1607[21]; **M** x, 43
O rossignuol ch'in queste verdi fronde (Bembo), 5vv, 1592; **M** iii, 33
O sia tranquill'il mare, 2vv, 1638; **M** ix, 36 32
O viva fiamma, o miei sospiri ardenti, 2vv, 1619; **M** vii, 47

Parlo, miser'o taccio? (Guarini) (= Longe, mi Jesu), 3vv, 1619; **M** vii, 116
Perchè fuggi tra salci, ritrosetta? (Marini), 2vv, 1619; **M** vii, 76
Perchè, se m'odiavi, 1v, 1634[7]; **M** xvii, 24
Perchè se m'odiavi, 3vv, 1651; **M** ix, 79
Perchè t'en fuggi, O Fillide?, 3vv, 1638; **M** viii, 295
Perfidissimo volto (Guarini), 5vv, 1592; **M** iii, 68
Piagne e sospira (Tasso) (= Plorat amare), 5vv, 1603; M iv, 96
Più lieto il guardo, 1v, 1634[7]; **M** xvii, 22
Poi che del mio dolore, 5vv, 1587; **M** i, 24
Presso un fiume tranquillo, dialogue (Marini), 7vv, insts, 1614; **M** vi, 113
Prima vedrò ch'in questi prati, 3vv, 1605[12]; **M** xvii, 5; O, 6
Qual si può dir maggiore, 3vv, 1584; **M** x, 2
Quando dentro al tuo seno, 3vv, 1651; **M** ix, 56
Quando l'alba in oriente (Chiabrera), 3vv, 1607[21]; **M** x, 36
Quando sperai del mio servir mercede, 3vv, 1584; **M** x, 13
Quante son stelle in ciel (G. B. da Cerreto), 3vv, 1594[15]; **M** xvii, 3; O, 4
Quel augellin che canta (Guarini) (= Qui laudes), 5vv, 1603; M iv, 66
Quell'ombra esser vorrei (Casoni), 5vv, 1590; **M** ii, 49
Quel sguardo sdegnosetto, 1v, 1632; **M** x, 77 31
Questa ordì il laccio (Strozzi), 5vv, 1587; **M** i, 46
Questi vaghi concenti (?Guarini), 9vv, 1605; M v, 104
Questo specchio ti dono, Rosa, 5vv, 1590; **M** ii, 87
Qui rise, O Tirsi (Marini), 5vv, insts, 1614; **M** vi, 77 26
Raggi, dov'è il mio bene?, 3vv, 1584; **M** x, 6
Rimanti in pace a la dolente e bella Fillida (L. Celiano), 5vv, 1592; **M** iii, 104
S'andasse amor a caccia (T. Tasso), 5vv, 1590; **M** ii, 53
Se i languidi miei sguardi, 'lettera amorosa', 1v, 1619; **M** vii, 160
S'el vostro cor, madonna (Guarini), 2vv, 1619; **M** vii, 90
Se nel partir da voi, vita mia, 5vv, 1587; M i, 36
Se non mi date aita, 3vv, 1594[15]; M xvii, 4
Se per estremo ardore morir potesse un core (Guarini), 5vv, 1592; M iii, 41
Se per havervi oimè, 5vv, 1587; M i, 5
Se pur destina e vole il cielo, 'partenza amorosa', 1v, 1619; M vii, 167

Se pur non mi consenti, 5vv, 1587; M i, 18
Sestina: Lagrime d'amante al sepolcro dell'amata [incipit: Incenerite spoglie] (S. Agnelli), 5vv, 1614; M vi, 46 — 26
Se tu mi lassi, perfida (Tasso), 5vv, 1590; M ii, 65
Se vittorie si belle, 2vv, 1638; M ix, 21
Sfogava con le stelle (Rinuccini) (= O stellae), 5vv, 1603; M iv, 15 — 22
Si ch'io vorrei morire (M. Moro) (= O Jesu, mea vita), 5vv, 1603; M iv, 78
Si come crescon alla terra i fiori, 3vv, 1584; M x, 21
Si dolce è'l tormento, 1v, in C. Milanuzzi: Quarto scherzo delle ariose vaghezze (Venice, 2/1624); M ix, 119
Si si ch'io v'amo, occhi vaghi, occhi belli, 3vv, 1651; M ix, 82
Soave libertate (Chiabrera), 2vv, 1619; M vii, 85
Son questi i crespi crini?, 3vv, 1584; M x, 10
Sovra tenere herbette, 5vv, 1592; M iii, 13
Stracciami pur il core (Guarini), 5vv, 1592; M iii, 26 — 20
Su su, su che'l giorno è fore, 3vv, 1584; M x, 12
Su su, su pastorelli vezzosi, 3vv, 1638; M viii, 310
Su su, su pastorelli vezzosi, 3vv, 1651; M ix, 89
Taci, Armelin, deh taci (Anselmi), 3vv, 1624^{11}; M ix, 106
T'amo, mia vita (Guarini) (= Gloria tua), 5vv, 1605; M v, 90
Tempro la cetra (Marini), 1v, str, 1619; M vii, 1 — 28, 50
Ti spontò l'ali amor, la donna mia (F. Alberti), 5vv, 1590; M ii, 97
Tornate, o cari baci (Marini), 2vv, 1619; M vii, 81
Tra mille fiamme e tra mille cathene, 5vv, 1587; M i, 39
Troppo ben può questo tiranno amore (Guarini) (= Ure me), 5vv, 1605; M v, 71
Tu dormi? Ah crudo core (= O Jesu, lindere meinen Schmertzen), 4vv, 1619; M vii, 123
Tu ridi sempre mai, 3vv, 1584; M x, 16
Tutte le bocche belle in questo nero volto (Alberti), 5vv, 1590; M ii, 39
Una donna fra l'altre honesta e bella vidi (= Una es), 5vv, hpd, 1614; M vi, 29
Usciam, ninfe, homai fuor di questi boschi, 5vv, 1587; M i, 42
Vaga su spina ascosa (Chiabrera) (= Ave regina mundi and Jesum viri senesque), 3vv, 1619; M vii, 104
Vaghi rai di cigli ardenti (Chiabrera), 3vv, 1607^{21}; M x, 46
Vago augelletto, che cantando vai (Petrarch) (= Resurrexit de sepulcro and Veni, veni, soror mea), 6–7vv, 2 vn, db, 1638; M viii, 222 — 32

Vattene pur, crudel, con quella pace (Tasso), 5vv, 1592; M iii, 48 — 20
Vita de l'alma mia, 3vv, 1584; M x, 8
Vivrò fra i miei tormenti (Tasso), 5vv, 1592; M iii, 87
Voglio di vita uscir, 1v, *I-Nf*; O, 18
Voi pur da me partite (Guarini) (= Tu vis a me), 5vv, 1603; M iv, 44
Volgea l'anima mia soavemente (Guarini) (= Ardebat igne), 5vv, 1603; M iv, 20
Vorrei baciarti, O Filli (Marini), 2vv, 1619; M vii, 52
Zefiro torna (Petrarch), 5vv, 1614; M vi, 22
Zefiro torna, 'ciacona' (Rinuccini), 2vv, 1632; M ix, 9 — 31, 62

SACRED VOCAL — 10, 55–63, 64

Sacrae cantiunculae . . . liber primus, 3vv (Venice, 1582) [1582] — 2, 55
Madrigali spirituali, 4vv (Brescia, 1583) [1583] — 2, 15
Musica tolta da i madrigali di Claudio Monteverde e d'altri autori, e fatta spirituale da Aquilino Coppini, 5, 6vv (Milan, 1607^{20}) [incl. 11 contrafacta of madrigals by Monteverdi] [1607^{20}]
Il secondo libro della musica di Claudio Monteverde e d'altri autori, fatta spirituale da Aquilino Coppini, 5vv (Milan, 1608) [incl. 8 contrafacta of madrigals by Monteverdi] [1608]
Il terzo libro della musica di Claudio Monteverdi e d'altri autori, fatta spirituale da Aquilino Coppini, 5vv (Milan, 1609) [incl. 19 contrafacta of madrigals by Monteverdi] [1609]
Sanctissimae virgini missa senis vocibus ad ecclesiarum choros ac Vespere pluribus decantandae – cum nonnullis sacris concentibus ad sacella sive principum cubicula accommodata, 1–3, 6–8, 10vv, insts, bc (Venice, 1610) [1610] — 56–60, 63
Selva morale e spirituale, 1–8vv, insts (Venice, 1640) [1640] — 11, 60
Messa, 4vv, et salmi, 1–8vv, concertati, e parte da cappella, et con le letanie della beata vergine, 6vv (Venice, 1650) [1650] — 60, 138
Works in 1615^{13}, 1617^{3}, 1620^{2}, 1620^{3}, 1622^{2}, P. P. Lappi: Concerti sacri . . . libro secondo (Venice, 1623), 1624^{2}, 1625^{1}, 1625^{2}, 1627^{1}, 1627^{4}, 1629^{5}, 1641^{2}, 1641^{3}, 1642^{4}, 1645^{3}, 1649^{6}, 1651^{2}

(*Latin*)

Missa de cappella, 6vv, 1710 (on Gombert's In illo tempore); M xiv, 57 — 57, 58
Messa da cappella, 4vv, org (with alternative settings of Crucifixus, 4vv, 4 trbn/va da braccio; Et resurrexit, 2vv, 2 vn; Et iterum venturus est, 3vv), 1640; M xv, 59 — 60–61
Messa da cappella, 4vv, org, 1650; M xvi, 1 — 60–61

Ab aeterno ordinata sum, 1v, 1640; **M** xv, 189
Adoramus te, Christe, 6vv, bc, 1620[3]; **M** xvi, 439 61
Amemus te (= Amor, se giusto sei), 5vv, 1609
Angelus ad pastores ait, 3vv, 1582; **M** xiv, 36
Animas eruit (= M'è più dolce il penar), 5vv, 1608
Anima miseranda (= Anima dolorosa), 5vv, 1609
Anima quam dilexi (= Anima del cor mio), 5vv, 1609
Ardebat igne (= Volgea l'anima mea), 5vv, 1609
Ave Maria, gratia plena, 3vv, 1582; **M** xiv, 15
Ave regina mundi (= Vaga su spina ascosa), 3vv, in P. P. Lappi: Concerti sacri . . . libro secondo (Venice, 1623)
Beatus vir, 6vv, 2 vn, 3 va da brazzo/trbn, 1640; **M** xv, 368 62
Beatus vir, 5vv, 1640; **M** xv, 418
Beatus vir, 7vv, 2 vn, 1650; **M** xvi, 167
Cantate Domino, 2vv, 1615[13]; **M** xvi, 409
Cantate Domino, 6vv, bc, 1620[3]; **M** xvi, 422 61
Cantemus (= A un giro sol), 5vv, 1609
Christe, adoramus te, 5vv, bc, 1620[3]; **M** xvi, 428 61
Confitebor tibi, Domine, 4vv, 1627[4]; O, 45
Confitebor tibi, Domine, 3vv, chorus 5vv, 1640; **M** xv, 297
Confitebor tibi, Domine, 3vv, 2 vn, 1640; **M** xv, 338
Confitebor tibi, Domine, 5vv or 1v and 4 str, 1640; **M** xv, 352
Confitebor tibi, Domine, 1v, 2 vn, 1650; **M** xvi, 129
Confitebor tibi, Domine, 2vv, 2 vn, 1650; **M** xvi, 144
Credidi propter quod locutus sum, 8vv, 1640; **M** xv, 544
Currite populi, T, 1625[2]; **M** xvi, 491 63
Deus tuorum militum, 1v, 2 vn, 1640 (= Sanctorum meritis (ii) and Iste confessor); **M** xv, 614
Deus tuorum militum, 3vv, 2 vn, 1640; **M** xv, 636
Dixit Dominus (i), 8vv, 2 vn, 4 va/trbn, 1640; **M** xv, 195
Dixit Dominus (ii), 8vv, 2 vn, 4 va/trbn, 1640; **M** xv, 246
Dixit Dominus (iii), 8vv, 1650; **M** xvi, 54
Dixit Dominus (iv), 8vv, 1650; **M** xvi, 94
Domine Deus (= Anima mia, perdona), 5vv, 1609
Domine, ne in furore, 6vv, bc, 1620[3]; **M** xvi, 432 61
Domine Pater et Deus vitae meae, 3vv, 1582; **M** xiv, 17
Ecce sacrum paratum, 1v, 1625[2]; **M** xvi, 497 63
Ego dormio et cor meum vigilat, 2vv, 1625[1]; **M** xvi, 481
Ego flos campi, 1v, 1624[2]; **M** xvi, 464

Ego sum pastor bonus, 3vv, 1582; **M** xiv, 6
En gratulemur hodie, 1v, 2 vn, 1651[2]; **M** xvi, 517
Ergo gaude, laetare (= Due belli occhi, 2p. of Altri canti di Marte), 6vv, 1641[3]
Exulta, filia Sion, 1v, 1629[5]; **M** xvii, 8; O, 32
Exultent caeli, 5vv, 1629[5]; **M** xvii, 15; O, 39
Felle amaro (= Cruda Amarilli), 5vv, 1607[20]
Florea serta (= La giovinetta pianta), 5vv, 1608
Fugge, anima mea, mundum, 2vv, vn, 1620[2]; **M** xvi, 444
Gloria in excelsis Deo, 7vv, 2 vn, 4 va da braccio/trbn, 1640; **M** xv, 117
Gloria in excelsis Deo, 8 vv, *I-Nf*; O, 65
Gloria tua (= T'amo, mia vita), 5vv, 1607[20]
Haec dicit Deus (= Voi ch'ascoltate in rime sparse), 5vv, 1642[4]
Heus, bone vir (= Armato il cor), 2vv, 1642[4]
Hodie Christus natus est, 3vv, 1582; **M** xiv, 26
Iam moriar, mi Fili, 'Pianto della Madonna sopra il Lamento d'Arianna', 1v, 1640; **M** xv, 757
In tua patientia, 3vv, 1582; **M** xiv, 34
Iste confessor (= Deus tuorum militum and Sanctorum meritis (ii)), 1v, 2 vn, 1640; **M** xv, 618
Iste confessor (= Ut queant laxis), 2vv, 2 vn, 1640; **M** xv, 622
Jesu, dum te (= Cor mio, mentre vi miro), 5vv, 1609
Jesum viri senesque (= Vaga su spina ascosa), 3vv, 1641[2]
Jesu, tu obis (= Cor mio, non mori?), 5vv, 1609
Jubilet tota civitas, 1v, 1640; **M** xv, 748
Justi tulerunt spolia impiorum, 3vv, 1582; **M** xiv, 50
Laetaniae della beata vergine, 6vv, 1650; **M** xvi, 382
Laetatus sum, 6vv, 2 vn, bn, 2 trbn, 1650; **M** xvi, 231 62
Laetatus sum, 5vv, 1650; **M** xvi, 276
Lapidabant Stephanum, 3vv, 1582; **M** xiv, 1
Lauda, anima mea (= Due belli occhi, 2p. of Altri canti di Marte), 6vv, 1641[3]
Lauda, Jerusalem, 3vv, 1650; **M** xvi, 344
Lauda, Jerusalem, 5vv, 1650; **M** xvi, 358
Lauda, Sion, salvatorem, 3vv, 1582; **M** xiv, 42
Laudate Dominum, 5vv, chorus 4vv, 2 vn, 4 va/trbn, 1640; **M** xv, 481
Laudate Dominum, 8vv, 2 vn, 1640; **M** xv, 503
Laudate Dominum, 8vv, 1640; **M** xv, 521

Laudate Dominum in sanctis eius, 1v, 1640; M xv, 753
Laudate Dominum, B, 1650; M xvi, 227
Laudate Dominum, B, 1651[2]; M xvi, 519
Laudate Dominum, 6vv, org, *D-Kl*
Laudate pueri, 5vv, 2 vn, 1640; M xv, 438
Laudate pueri, 5vv, 1640; M xv, 460
Laudate pueri, Dominum, 5vv, 1650; M xvi, 211
Longe a te (= Longe da te, cor mio), 5vv, 1609
Longe, mi Jesu (= Parlo, miser'o taccio?), 3vv, 1649[6]
Magnificat, 8vv, 2 vn, 4 va trbn, 1640; M xv, 639
Magnificat, 4vv, 1640; M xiv, 703
Maria, quid ploras? (= Dorinda, ah dirò mia, 3p. of Ecco Silvio), 5vv, 1607[20]
Memento [Domine, David] et omnis mansuetudinis, 8vv, 1640; M xv, 567
Nisi Dominus, 3vv, 2 vn, 1650; M xvi, 299
Nisi Dominus, 6vv, 1650; M xvi, 318
O beatae viae, O felices gressus, 2vv, 1620[2]; M xvi, 454
O bone Jesu, illumina oculos meos, 3vv, 1582; M xiv, 44
O bone Jesu, o piissime Jesu, 2vv, 1622[2]; M xvi, 506
O crux benedicta, 3vv, 1582; M xiv, 25
O dies infelices (= O come è gran martire), 5vv, 1608
O Domine Jesu Christe, 3vv, 1582; M xvi, 29
O gloriose martyr (= Che se tu se'il cor mio, 2p. of Anima mia, perdona), 5vv, 1609
O infelix recessus (= Ah dolente partita), 5vv, 1608
O Jesu, mea vita (= Sì ch'io vorrei morire), 5vv, 1609
O magnum pietatis opus, 3vv, 1582, M xiv, 22
O mi Fili (= O Mirtillo), 5vv, 1608
O quam pulchra es, 1v, 1625[2]; M xvi, 486 63
O rex supreme (= Al lume delle stelle), 4vv, 1649[6]
O stellae (= Sfogava con le stelle), 5vv, 1609
Pascha concelebranda (= Altri canti di Marte), 6vv, 1641[3]
Pater, venit hora, 3vv, 1582; M xiv, 33
Plagas tuas (= La piaga c'ho nel core), 5vv, 1609
Plorat amare (= Piagne e sospira), 5vv, 1609
Praecipitantur, Jesu Christe (= O primavera), 5vv, 1608
Pulchrae sunt (= Ferir quel petto, 5p. of Ecco Silvio), 5vv, 1607[20]

Quam pulchra es, 3vv, 1582; M xiv, 13
Qui laudes (= Quel augellin che canta), 5vv, 1609
Quia vidisti me, Thoma, credidisti, 3vv, 1582; M xiv, 40
Qui pependit (= Ecco Silvio), 5vv, 1607[20]
Qui pietate (= Ma se con la pietà, 2p. of Ecco Silvio), 5vv, 1609
Qui regnas (= Che dar più vi poss'io?), 5vv, 1608
Qui vult venire post me, 3vv, 1582; M xiv, 48
Resurrexit de sepulcro (= Vago augelletto), 6–7vv, 1649[6]
Rutilante in nocte (= Io mi son giovinetta), 5vv, 1609
Salve, crux pretiosa, 3vv, 1582; M xiv, 38
Salve, O regina, 1v, 1624[2]; M xvi, 475
Salve regina, 1v, 1625[2]; M xvi, 502 63
Salve regina, 2vv, 2 vn, 1640; M xv, 724
Salve regina, 2vv, 1640; M xv, 736
Salve regina, 3vv, 1640; M xv, 741
Sancta Maria (= Deh, bella e cara, 2p. of Ch'io t'ami e t'ami più), 5vv, 1607[20]
Sancta Maria, succurre miseris, 2vv, 1627[1]; M xvi, 511
Sanctorum meritis inclita gaudia (i), 1v, 2 vn, 1640; M xv, 606
Sanctorum meritis inclita gaudia (ii) (= Deus tuorum militum and Iste confessor), 1v, 2 vn, 1640; M xv, 610
Spera in Domino (= Io che armato sin hor), 1v, 1642[4]
Spernit Deus (= Ma tu più che mai dura, 3p. of Ch'io t'ami e t'ami più), 5vv, 1607[20]
Stabat virgo (= Era l'anima mia), 5vv, 1607[20]
Surgens Jesus, Dominus noster, 3vv, 1582; M xiv, 46
Surge propera, amica mea, 3vv, 1582; M xiv, 8
Te, Jesu Christe (= Ecco piegando, 4p. of Ecco Silvio), 5vv, 1607[20]
Te sequar (= Ch'io t'ami), 5vv, 1608
Tu es pastor ovium, 3vv, 1582; M xiv, 19
Tu vis a me (= Voi pur da me partite), 5vv, 1609
Ubi duo vel tres congregati fuerint, 3vv, 1582; M xiv, 11
Una es (= Una donna fra l'altre), 5vv, 1609
Ure me (= Troppo ben può questo tiranno amore), 5vv, 1607[20]
Ut queant laxis (= Iste confessor), 2vv, 2 vn, 1640; M xv, 629
Veni in hortum meum, 3vv, 1582; M xiv, 3
Venite siccientes ad aquas Domini, 2vv, 1624[2]; M xvi, 467
Venite, videte martyrem, 1v, 1645[3]; M xvii, 25

Veni, veni, soror mea (= Vago augelletto), 6–7vv, 1649[6]
Vespro della Beata Vergine, 'composto sopra canti fermi', 6vv, 6 insts, 1610: — 1, 56–60, 62, 64
Domine ad adiuvandum, 6vv, 3 trbn, 2 cornetts, 6 str; M xiv, 123 — 58
Dixit Dominus, 6vv, 6 insts; M xiv, 133 — 58
Nigra sum, 1v; M xiv, 150
Laudate pueri, 8vv, org; M xiv, 153
Pulchra es, amica mea, 2vv; M xiv, 170
Laetatus sum, 6vv; M xiv, 174
Duo Seraphim clamabant, 3vv; M xiv, 190
Nisi Dominus, 10vv; M xiv, 198
Audi coelum, 1v, chorus 6vv; M xiv, 227
Lauda, Jerusalem, 7vv; M xiv, 237 — 58
Sonata sopra 'Sancta Maria', 1v, 2 cornetts, 3 trbn, 2 vn, vc; M xiv, 250 — 59, 60, 115
Ave maris stella, 2vv, chorus 8vv (2 choirs), 5 insts; M xiv, 274 — 58
Magnificat, 7vv, 2 fl, 2 rec, 3 cornetts, 2 trbn, 2 vn, vc; M xiv, 285 — 56, 59
Magnificat, 6vv, org; M, xiv, 327 — 56, 57, 59
Vives in corde (= Ahi, com'a un vago sol), 5vv, 1607[20]

(*Italian*)

Afflitto e scalz'ove la sacra sponda, 4vv, 1583
Aventurosa notte, 4vv, 1583
Chi vol che m'innamori, 3vv, 3 str, 1640; M xv, 54
Dal sacro petto esce veloce dardo, 4vv, 1583
Dei miei giovenil anni, 4vv, 1583
D'empi martiri, 4vv, 1583
È questa vita un lampo, 5vv, 1640; M xv, 35
Laura del ciel sempre feconda, 4vv, 1583
L'empio vestia di porpora, 4vv, 1583
Le rose, gli amaranti e gigli, 4vv, 1583
L'human discorso, 4vv, 1583
Mentre la stell'appar, 4vv, 1583
O ciechi il tanto affaticar (Petrarch), 5vv, 2 vn, 1640; M xv, 1
Sacrosanta di Dio verace imago, 4vv, 1583
Spuntava il dì, 3vv, 1640; M xv, 42
Su le penne de' venti (prol to La Maddalena), 1v, 5 insts, 1617[3]; M xi, 170
Voi ch'ascoltate in rime sparse (Petrarch) (= Haec dicit Deus), 5vv, 2 vn, 1640; M xv, 15

(*German*)

Alleluja, kommet, jauchzet (= Ardo, avvampo), 8vv, 1649[6]
Dein allein ist ja (= Così sol d'una chiara fonte, 2p. of Hor ch'el ciel e la terra), 6vv, 1649[6]
Frewde, kommet lasset uns gehen (= Ardo, avvampo), 8vv, 1649[6]
O du mächtiger Herr (= Hor ch'el ciel e la terra), 6vv, 1649[6]
O Jesu, lindere meinen Schmertzen (= Tu dormi?), 4vv, 1649[6]

BIBLIOGRAPHY

SOURCE MATERIAL

G. Sommi Picenardi: 'D'alcuni documenti concernenti Claudio Monteverde', *Archivio storico lombardo*, 3rd ser., iv (1895)
G. F. Malipiero: *Claudio Monteverdi* (Milan, 1929)
Anon.: 'Preziose scoperte di autografi di Claudio Monteverdi', *La bibliofilia*, xxxviii (1937)
R. Lunelli: 'Iconografia monteverdiana', *RMI*, xlvii (1943), 38
C. Gallico: 'Newly Discovered Documents concerning Monteverdi', *MQ*, xlviii (1962), 68
A. Rosenthal: 'A Hitherto Unpublished Letter of Claudio Monteverdi', *Essays Presented to Egon Wellesz* (Oxford, 1966), 103
F. Lesure: 'Un nouveau portrait de Monteverdi', *RdM*, liii (1967), 60
G. de Logu: 'An Unknown Portrait of Monteverdi by Domenico Feti', *The Burlington Magazine*, cix (1967), 706
Monteverdi's letters: a selection in Eng. trans. with commentary, in D. Arnold and N. Fortune, eds.: *The Monteverdi Companion* (London, 1968), 19–87
W. Siegmund-Schultze: 'Beiträge zu einem neuen Monteverdi-Bild', *Wissenschaftliche Beiträge der Universität Halle*, ser. G, viii/1 (1968), 11
Monteverdi: lettere, dediche e prefazioni, ed. D. de' Paoli (Rome, 1973)
The Letters of Claudio Monteverdi, ed. and trans. D. Stevens (London, 1980)

BIOGRAPHY AND CRITICAL STUDIES

G. M. Artusi: *L'Artusi, ovvero Delle imperfettioni della moderna musica*, i (Venice, 1600); ii (Venice, 1603)
——: *Discorso secondo musicale di Antonio Braccino da Todi* (Venice, 1608, repr. 1924)
F. Caffi: *Storia della musica sacra nella già cappella ducale di San Marco in Venezia dal 1318 al 1797* (Venice, 1854–5, repr. 1931)
P. Canal: *Della musica in Mantova* (Venice, 1881)
S. Davari: *Notizie biografiche del distinto maestro di musica Claudio Monteverdi* (Mantua, 1884)
E. Vogel: 'Claudio Monteverdi', *VMw*, iii (1887), 315–450
A. Bertolotti: *Musici alla corte dei Gonzaga in Mantova dal secolo XV al XVIII* (Milan, 1890/*R*1969)
H. Goldschmidt: *Studien zur Geschichte der italienischen Oper* (Leipzig, 1901–4/*R*1967)
——: Monteverdis Ritorno d'Ulisse, *SIMG*, iv (1902–3), 671
——: 'Claudio Monteverdis Oper: Il ritorno d'Ulisse in patria', *SIMG*, ix (1907–8), 570
G. Cesari: 'Die Entwicklung der Monteverdischen Kammermusik', *IMusSCR*, iii *Vienna 1909*, 153

H. Leichtentritt: 'Claudio Monteverdi als Madrigalkomponist', *SIMG*, xi (1909–10), 255–91
R. Schwartz: 'Zu den Texten der ersten fünf Bücher der Madrigale Monteverdis', *Festschrift Hermann Kretzschmar* (Leipzig, 1918), 147
L. Schneider: *Un précurseur de la musique italienne aux XVIe et XVIIe siècles: Claudio Monteverdi: l'homme et son temps* (Paris, 1921)
R. Haas: 'Zur Neuausgabe von Claudio Monteverdis "Il ritorno d'Ulisse in patria" ', *SMw*, ix (1922), 3–42
A. Tessier: 'Les deux styles de Monteverde', *ReM*, iii/8 (1922), 223–54
H. Prunières: *La vie et l'oeuvre de C. Monteverdi* (Paris, 1926, 2/1931; Eng. trans., 1926/*R*1972)
——: 'Monteverdi's Venetian Operas', *MQ*, x (1924), 178
C. van den Borren: ' "Il ritorno d'Ulisse in patria" de Claudio Monteverdi', *Revue de l'Université de Bruxelles*, iii (1925)
J. A. Westrup: 'Monteverde's "Il ritorno d'Ulisse in patria" ', *MMR*, lviii (1928), 106
A. Tessier: 'Monteverdi e la filosofia dell'arte', *RaM*, ii (1929), 459
K. F. Müller: *Die Technik der Ausdrucksdarstellung in Monteverdis monodischen Frühwerken* (Berlin, 1931)
H. F. Redlich: *Claudio Monteverdi: ein formgeschichtlicher Versuch* (Berlin, 1932)
J. A. Westrup: 'The Originality of Monteverde', *PMA*, lx (1933–4), 1
W. Kreidler: *Heinrich Schütz und der Stile Concitato von Claudio Monteverdi* (Stuttgart, 1934)
G. Benvenuti: 'Il manoscritto veneziano della "Incoronazione di Poppea" ', *RMI*, xli (1937), 176
H. F. Redlich: 'Notationsprobleme in Cl. Monteverdis "Incoronazione di Poppea" ', *AcM*, x (1938), 129
J. A. Westrup: 'Monteverdi and the Orchestra', *ML*, xxi (1940), 230
——: 'Monteverdi's "Lamento d'Arianna" ', *MR*, i (1940), 144
P. Collaer: 'L'orchestra di Claudio Monteverdi', *Musica*, ii (Florence, 1943), 86
B. Lupo: 'Sacre monodie monteverdiane', *Musica*, ii (Florence, 1943), 51–85
F. Torrefranca: 'Il lamento di Erminia di Claudio Monteverdi', *Inedito*, ii (1944), 31; suppl., 1
O. Tiby: *Claudio Monteverdi* (Turin, 1944)
D. de' Paoli: *Claudio Monteverdi* (Milan, 1945)
L. Ronga: 'Tasso e Monteverdi', *Poesia*, i (1945)
H. F. Redlich: 'Monteverdi's Religious Music', *ML*, xxvii (1946), 208
A. Einstein: *The Italian Madrigal* (Princeton, 1949/*R*1971)
H. F. Redlich: *Claudio Monteverdi: Leben und Werk* (Olten, 1949; Eng. trans., rev., 1952)

J. A. Westrup: 'Monteverdi and the Madrigal', *The Score*, i (1949), 33
L. Schrade: *Monteverdi, Creator of Modern Music* (London, 1950/*R*1964)
W. Apel: 'Anent a Ritornello in Monteverdi's Orfeo', *MD*, v (1951), 213
M. le Roux: *Claudio Monteverdi* (Paris, 1951)
C. Sartori: *Monteverdi* (Brescia, 1953)
A. A. Abert: *Claudio Monteverdi und das musikalische Drama* (Lippstadt, 1954); review by L. Ronga, *RMI*, lvii (1955), 140
D. Arnold: 'Notes on Two Movements of the Monteverdi "Vespers" ', *MMR*, lxxxiv (1954), 59
W. Osthoff: 'Die venezianische und neapolitanische Fassung von Monteverdis "Incoronazione di Poppea" ', *AcM*, xxvi (1954), 88
H. F. Redlich: 'Claudio Monteverdi: Some Problems of Textual Interpretation', *MQ*, xli (1955), 66
W. Osthoff: 'Zu den Quellen von Monteverdis Ritorno d'Ulisse in Patria', *SMw*, xxiii (1956), 67
D. Arnold: ' "Seconda pratica": a Background to Monteverdi's Madrigals', *ML*, xxxviii (1957), 341
——: 'Monteverdi's Church Music: Some Venetian Traits', *MMR*, lxxxviii (1958), 83
W. Osthoff: 'Neue Beobachtungen zu Quellen und Geschichte von Monteverdis "Incoronazione di Poppea" ', *Mf*, xi (1958), 129
——: 'Zur Bologneser Aufführung von Monteverdis "Ritorno d'Ulisse" im Jahre 1640', *Anzeiger der phil.-hist. Klasse der Österreichischen Akademie der Wissenschaften*, xcv (1958), 155
D. Stevens: 'Ornamentation in Monteverdi's Shorter Dramatic Works', *IMSCR*, vii *Cologne 1958*, 284
J. A. Westrup: 'Two First Performances: Monteverdi's "Orfeo" and Mozart's "Clemenza di Tito" ', *ML*, xxxix (1958), 327
F. B. Zimmerman: 'Purcell and Monteverdi', *MT*, xcix (1958), 368
G. Pannain: 'Studi monteverdiani', *RaM*, xxviii (1958), 7, 97, 187, 281; xix (1959), 42, 95, 234, 310; xxx (1960), 24, 230, 312; xxxi (1961), 14; *Quaderni della RaM*, iii (1965), 13
D. D. Boyden: 'Monteverdi's *violini piccoli alla francese* and *viole da brazzo*', *AnnM*, vi (1958–63), 387
L. Passuth: *A mantuai herceg muzsikusa, Claudio Monteverdi korának regényes törtenete* (Budapest, 1959; Ger. trans., 1959 as *Monteverdi: der Roman eines grossen Musikers*)
W. Osthoff: *Das dramatische Spätwerk Claudio Monteverdis* (Tutzing, 1960)
D. Arnold: 'The Monteverdian Succession at St Mark's', *ML*, xlii (1961), 205
W. Osthoff: 'Monteverdis Combattimento in deutscher Sprache und Heinrich Schütz', *Festschrift Helmuth Osthoff* (Tutzing, 1961), 195

D. Stevens: 'Where are the Vespers of Yesteryear?', *MQ*, xlvii (1961), 315
F. Ghisi: 'L'orchestra in Monteverdi', *Karl Gustav Fellerer zum 60. Geburtstag* (Cologne, 1962), 187
D. Arnold: ' "L'incoronazione di Poppea" and its Orchestral Requirements', *MT*, civ (1963), 176
——: *Monteverdi* (London, 1963)
——: 'The Monteverdi Vespers – a Postscript', *MT*, civ (1963), 24
S. Reiner: 'Preparations in Parma – 1618, 1627–28', *MR*, xxv (1964), 273
R. Tellart: *Claudio Monteverdi: l'homme et son oeuvre* (Paris, 1964)
G. Biella: 'La Messa, il Vespro e i sacri concenti di Claudio Monteverdi nella stampa Amadino del 1610', *Musica sacra*, 2nd ser., ix (Milan, 1964)
D. Arnold: ' "Il ritorno d'Ulisse" and the chamber duet', *MT*, cvi (1965), 183
G. Biella: 'I "Vespri dei Santi" di Claudio Monteverdi', *Musica sacra*, 2nd ser., xi (Milan, 1966), 144
A. Damerini: 'Il senso religioso nelle musiche sacre di Claudio Monteverdi', *CHM*, iv (1966), 47
C. Gallico: 'Monteverdi e i dazi di Viadana', *RIM*, i (1966), 242
RIM, ii/2 (1967) [special Monteverdi no.]
D. Arnold: 'Monteverdi and the Art of War', *MT*, cviii (1967), 412
——: *Monteverdi Madrigals* (London, 1967)
——: 'Monteverdi the Instrumentalist', *Recorder and Music Magazine*, ii (1967), 130
G. Barblan and others: *Claudio Monteverdi nel quarto centenario della nascita* (Turin, 1967)
S. Bonta: 'Liturgical Problems in Monteverdi's Marian Vespers', *JAMS*, xx (1967), 87
N. Fortune: 'Duet and Trio in Monteverdi', *MT*, cviii (1967), 417
C. Gallico: 'La "lettera amorosa" di Monteverdi e lo stile rappresentativo', *NRMI*, i (1967), 287
E. Santoro: *La famiglia e la formazione di Claudio Monteverdi: note biografiche con documenti inediti* (Cremona, 1967)
D. Stevens: '*Madrigali guerrieri, et amorosi:* a Reappraisal for the Quatercentenary', *MQ*, liii (1967), 161; also pubd in D. Arnold and N. Fortune, eds.: *The Monteverdi Companion* (London, 1968)
——: 'Monteverdi's Venetian Church Music', *MT*, cviii (1967), 414
D. Arnold and N. Fortune, eds.: *The Monteverdi Companion* (London, 1968, rev. 2/1984)
N. Pirrotta: 'Early Opera and Aria', *New Looks at Italian Opera: Essays in Honor of Donald J. Grout* (Ithaca, 1968), 39–107
——: 'Scelte poetiche di Monteverdi', *NRMI*, ii (1968), 10–42, 226

Congresso internazionale sul tema Claudio Monteverdi e il suo tempo: Venezia, Mantova e Cremona 1968
N. Anfuso and A. Gianuario: *'Lamento d'Arianna': Studio e interpretazione sulla edizione a stampa del Gardano, Venezia 1623* (Florence, 1969)
A. Gianuario: 'Proemio all' "Oratione di Monteverdi" ', *RIM*, iv (1969), 32
N. Pirrotta: 'Early Venetian Libretti at Los Angeles', *Essays in Musicology: in Honor of Dragan Plamenac* (Pittsburgh, 1969), 233
D. Arnold: 'Monteverdi's Singers', *MT*, cxi (1970), 982
N. Anfuso and A. Gianuario: *Preparazione alla interpretazione della Poiēsis Monteverdiana* (Florence, 1971)
T. Antonicek: 'Claudio Monteverdi und Österreich', *ÖMz*, xxvi (1971), 266
W. Frobenius: 'Zur Notation eines Ritornells in Monteverdis "L'Orfeo" ', *AMw*, xxviii (1971), 201
K. R. Mays: *Harmonic Style in the Madrigals of Claudio Monteverdi* (diss., Indiana U., 1971)
D. Arnold: 'A Background Note on Monteverdi's Hymn Settings', *Scritti in onore di Luigi Ronga* (Milan and Naples, 1973), 33
D. Stevens: 'Monteverdi's Necklace', *MQ*, lix (1973), 370
A. Chiarelli: '*L'incoronazione di Poppea* o *Il Nerone:* problemi di filologia testuale', *RIM*, ix (1974), 117–51
S. Reiner: 'La vag'Angioletta (and others), Part I', *AnMc*, no.14 (1974), 26–88
C. Gallico: ' "contra Claudium Montiuiridum" ', *RIM*, x (1975), 346
H. Hell: 'Zu Rhythmus und Notierung des "Vi ricorda" in Claudio Monteverdis *Orfeo*', *AnMc*, no.15 (1975), 87–157
J. G. Kurtzman: 'Some Historical Perspectives on the Monteverdi Vespers', *AnMc*, no.15 (1975), 29–86
I. Fenlon: 'The Monteverdi Vespers: Suggested Answers to some Fundamental Questions', *Early Music*, v (1977), 380
D. Stevens: 'Monteverdi, Petratti, and the Duke of Bracciano', *MQ*, lxiv (1978), 275
——: *Monteverdi: Sacred, Secular and Occasional Music* (Rutherford, 1978)
D. de' Paoli: *Monteverdi* (Milan, 1979)
J. G. Kurtzman: *Essays on the Monteverdi Mass and Vespers of 1610* (Houston, 1979)
J. H. Moore: *Vespers at St Mark's, 1625–1675: Music of Alessandro Grandi, Giovanni Rovetta and Francesco Cavalli* (diss., U. of California, Los Angeles, 1979; Ann Arbor, 1980)
I. Fenlon: *Music and Patronage in Sixteenth-century Mantua* (Cambridge, 1981–2)

GIROLAMO FRESCOBALDI

Anthony Newcomb

CHAPTER ONE

Life

I Childhood and youth, 1583–1603

Girolamo Frescobaldi was born in the town of Ferrara, in northern Italy, in mid-September 1583. Although the record of his baptism still survives, there is no unanimity of opinion as to how to read it. 9 September (Haberl, 1887), 13 September (Bennati) and 15 September (Cametti, 1927, and Casimiri, 1937) have been proposed. The last date should probably be accepted. A photograph of a part of the page in question is published in Bennati (p.134), but the section photographed is too small to clarify the question completely. About Frescobaldi's ancestors not a great deal is known. Busi (see Haberl, 1887, p.67) claimed that his father, Filippo, was an organist. Certainly he seems to have been a fairly important citizen of Ferrara, since he is called 'illustrissimus' in a legal document connected with the purchase in 1584 of a sizable house, appropriate for a prosperous citizen. The house is still standing in what is now the Via Frescobaldi. That Luzzaschi was godfather to one of Filippo's children would seem to indicate that Filippo, whether or not he was a musician, at least had musical friends.

During Frescobaldi's childhood Ferrara was one of the most brilliant and progressive musical centres in Europe (see Newcomb, 1980). Duke Alfonso II d'Este was a melomaniac, who listened to music for between two and four hours a day. Frescobaldi's connections with, and knowledge of, the musical life of the court are likely to have been considerable, for he seems to have been something of a prodigy as an organist, and his teacher, Luzzaschi, was the court organist. Luzzaschi is consistently mentioned both by his contemporaries and by somewhat later writers (Diruta, Banchieri, Monteverdi, Giustiniani, Della Valle, Penna) as one of the four or five most important organists and keyboard composers of the second half of the 16th century; he remained famous well into the 17th century. By an unexplained and unfortunate anomaly, little of the organ music that he is known to have published (the inventory in Waldner, 1916, lists a second and third book of ricercares) seemed until recently to have survived. The two brief ricercares in Diruta's *Il transilvano* (reprinted and discussed in Newcomb, 1979) were virtually all that remained from which one could gain a summary idea of his mastery of the imitative instrumental forms. A recently identified group of ricercares in a late 16th-century manuscript and a recently uncovered manuscript copy of Luzzaschi's second book of ricercares now permit the formation of a better idea of the style of instrumental music with which Frescobaldi grew up (see Newcomb, Madison 1983, and pp.104–5 below).

One has, however, long been able to form a satisfactory idea of Luzzaschi's musical personality from his vocal music. His madrigals for one to three sopranos (1601) demonstrate his highly personal and expressive style of written-out diminution (see Cavicchi, 1965), one of the immediate ancestors of the distinctive ornamental style of Frescobaldi's A.3–4. As a composer of five-part madrigals Luzzaschi was exceptionally bold in his harmonies and especially in his use of texture, although his style remained essentially polyphonically rather than chordally based. All these features recall Gesualdo, who expressly pointed to Luzzaschi as his mentor (see Newcomb, 1968 and 1980). Frescobaldi too must have been greatly influenced by him, for he proudly proclaimed himself his disciple in two of his dedications (A.6 and B.4).

Two developments in the Ferrarese court musical establishment during the 1580s and 1590s seem clearly to have left an imprint on the young Frescobaldi. First, in the 1580s the duke assembled there an internationally famous and widely imitated group of singers, which included up to four ladies of astounding musicianship and virtuosity. Because of the possibilities offered by this new group, Ferrara became a centre for the development of written-out ornamentation (e.g. Luzzaschi's madrigals of 1601). Second, with Gesualdo's arrival at the court in 1594 Ferrara became the breeding-ground for a new style of polyphonic madrigal, whose harmonic, melodic and textural experiments led directly to the *seconda prattica* proclaimed by Monteverdi in 1605. It may be presumed that Frescobaldi was influenced not only by Gesualdo, who was almost exclusively a composer of vocal music, but also by the sizable group of musicians who accompanied him to Ferrara and who included Scipione Stella, Fabritio Filamarino and Rinaldo dall'Arpa; these composers are in turn represented in a manuscript of southern Italian keyboard music (see Silbiger, 1980, pp.86–92; published in CEKM, xxiv). The visit of Gesualdo and his retinue may have stimulated Frescobaldi's interest in Neapolitan keyboard music; Apel has long maintained (1938 and 1967) that the unusual style of the Neapolitans Macque, Mayone and Trabaci influenced him greatly. With a greater knowledge of the Ferrarese style of instrumental music in the last decades of the century, however – the style of Luzzaschi, of the 'Giaches' of the Bourdenay ricercares (Paris, Bibliothèque Nationale, Rés. Vma 851) and of Ercole Pasquini – one will perhaps conclude that the southern Italian and the Frescobaldi style represent two interdependent developments from this same 'Po valley' style. Jackson (1964), for example, has pointed out the substantial differences between the styles of Frescobaldi and of Trabaci.

It is not known exactly how long Frescobaldi remained in Ferrara. The Este court there was disbanded late in 1597, when Duke Alfonso died without an heir. The duchy reverted to the church, and the remainder of the Este family, together with part of the court, moved to Modena (which had been ceded to the Este family not by the church but by the Holy Roman Empire). Luzzaschi, however, remained in Ferrara, and so, it seems, did Frescobaldi. The first three names in a list of the organists of the important Accademia della Morte of Ferrara are Luzzaschi, Pasquini and Frescobaldi (see Cavicchi, 1962). Since Pasquini assumed his duties at St Peter's in 1597, it may be supposed that it was then – when he was only 14 – that Frescobaldi became organist of the academy. It is not certain how long he stayed in this post. In the 19th century a secretary of the Accademia di S Cecilia (the musicians' brotherhood in Rome) asserted that Frescobaldi became a member in 1604 (see Cametti, 1908), but there is no extant document to support that, and the reliability of the 19th-century research has been questioned (see Hammond, 1983, p.333, n.2). The members of this brotherhood seem to have been either fairly prominent musicians in Rome or established and famous ones elsewhere (e.g. Costanzo Porta, Lassus, Zacconi, Monteverdi). Although the documentary issue may never be settled, it seems likely that by 1604 Frescobaldi was working in Rome. He may well have gone there as early as 1601 (see p.88 below).

II Early manhood, 1604–15

In outlining Frescobaldi's career in Rome it is at no time at all appropriate to speak of his being employed by any single institution or person, in the sense that Luzzaschi, for example, had been employed by Duke Alfonso and the court of Ferrara. The situation in Rome was different from that in virtually every other Italian centre of patronage, for it boasted not one but several rich and powerful patrons and courts. The successful artist – musician and painter alike – was often active at the courts of several of these patrons, sometimes within a politically determined circle. Every young artist, however, needed one patron to launch him on his career. This position was usually assumed by a member of an important family from the artist's native province, who perhaps housed and fed him and paid him a little; above all he introduced him to other powerful friends and found him commissions, students and positions. For Frescobaldi, Enzo and Guido Bentivoglio seem to have filled this role. In this Frescobaldi was fortunate.

Guido, who is the first of the Bentivoglio family to loom large in Frescobaldi's biography, was the son of Cornelio Bentivoglio, the most important nobleman in the Este court next to the duke himself, and Isabella

Bendidio, a beautiful and cultivated lady, often praised as a singer at the Ferrarese court in the 1570s. Only six years older than Frescobaldi, he became one of the most cultivated and intelligent patrons in early 17th-century Rome (his portrait, painted by Van Dyck in 1623 and now in the Pitti Palace, Florence, is reproduced in Haskell, p.4*a*). He took his degree at Padua in 1600 and then went to Rome to pursue an ecclesiastical career. Since Luzzaschi can be traced in Rome early in 1601 (see Palisca, p.353), one might speculate that Frescobaldi went to Rome with him at that time and remained there under Bentivoglio's protection.

There is no record of Frescobaldi's having held a specific post before the beginning of 1607, when he may be the 'Girolamo organista' of S Maria in Trastevere (see Casimiri, 1937, and Cannon, 1969). In June 1607 Bentivoglio, recently made an archbishop and nuncio to Flanders, took Frescobaldi to Brussels, perhaps as an educational experience. (It should be noted here that the lutenist Girolamo mentioned by Alessandro Piccinini in his *Intavolatura di liuto* (1623) as having gone to Flanders in Bentivoglio's service was definitely not Frescobaldi but Piccinini's own brother. Confusion between the two Girolamos led Machabey (p.16) to think that there was a reliable witness to Frescobaldi's activity as a lutenist.) The potential effect on Frescobaldi of this journey was tremendous. Brussels was the city of Peter Philips and Pieter Cornet, and was not far from the Amsterdam of Sweelinck. It is unlikely that Frescobaldi ever met Sweelinck: Curtis wrote of the unlikelihood of Sweelinck's having come to Brussels during this period; had Frescobaldi gone to Amsterdam to meet him, he would probably have boasted of it in one of the dedications of 1608. As a young organ virtuoso and composer, however, he must certainly have met Philips and Cornet (see the dedication to B.2, where he stated that he had shown the pieces to the principal musicians in Brussels).

The actual effect of his stay in a northern centre of keyboard music seems to have been to call forth a collection of Italian madrigals. The explanation of this paradox may lie in the fame and popularity of the Italian madrigal in northern Europe: Phalèse, the printer of B.2, had brought out at least a dozen enormously successful anthologies of Italian madrigals in the quarter-century before 1608. The paradox goes a bit deeper, however. Frescobaldi was also in a flourishing centre of harpsichord and organ builders such as Ruckers of Antwerp, and it is known (Newcomb, 1964–77, p. 121) that Guido Bentivoglio sent back a Flemish harpsichord soon after his arrival in Brussels which was much admired in Rome. Yet, as Lunelli has remarked, the advanced northern instruments, markedly different from their Italian counterparts, left virtually no trace either on Frescobaldi's music or on the organs of St Peter's, which were rebuilt during his tenure there. It would seem that both the keyboard instruments and the keyboard music of north-west Europe left remarkably little imprint on him. He probably arrived in Brussels with Guido Bentivoglio in August 1607; he must have left even before the dating of the dedication of B.2 in June 1608, for a letter of 25 June 1608 shows that he was then in Milan. He stayed in Flanders about ten months (reports of a longer stay or of his employment there as a church organist have long been discredited). On his return to Italy he went to Milan to oversee the printing of his fantasias and then went on to Ferrara. Bentivoglio, who remained nuncio in Flanders until 1616, assigned him to the protection of his brother Enzo, who was in 1608 named Ferrarese ambassador in Rome and settled there that autumn.

Meanwhile, on 21 July 1608, Frescobaldi had been elected organist of St Peter's, Rome, mostly through the good offices of Enzo Bentivoglio (Fabbris, Ferrara 1983), since he was not in Rome to participate in the 'competition'. It is possible that, upon his arrival in Rome in October, he stayed with Bentivoglio in his residence in what is now the Palazzo Sacchetti, just across the Tiber from St Peter's. He took up his duties at St Peter's on 31 October 1608, though he was paid only from 1 November. When he took office, the choir of the Cappella Giulia was composed of six boy sopranos, four male contraltos, four tenors and four basses, all under the direction of Francesco Soriano, who held his post from 1603 to 1620. The two small organs of St Peter's are thoroughly discussed in Lunelli. The newer and the more frequently used one was built in the 1580s. Precise descriptions of both must remain speculative, since they are based on descriptions of the organs only as they were in the middle of the 18th century. Both were of one manual, with a very limited (probably *C* to *A*) pedalboard that was not independent. The newer organ probably had 50 keys and 14 ranks. Like the typical Italian 16th- and 17th-century organ, each was characterized by a full chorus (ripieno) of narrow principals (from 16′ to perhaps 1′), two flutes and a reed (which at St Peter's seems to have been rather poor and may never have functioned during Frescobaldi's tenure as organist). There is no sign in the descriptions of the 18th century of a stop rather characteristic of the early

Italian organ, the Vox humana, or acoustical tremulant, produced by two registers of pipes tuned to slightly different pitch levels. The two organs of St Peter's were located in the two deep lateral chapels in each side of the nave and compass east (i.e. in front) of the great dome. Each organ could be heard clearly only from nearby (Hammond, 1983, pp.33–5). A fine example of the Roman organ of Frescobaldi's time, built in 1598 by Luca Blasi, may still be seen and heard in the right transept of St John Lateran.

Libanori – the source of several tales about Frescobaldi, some of which can be proved to be either false or wildly exaggerated and all of which should be discounted – reported that Frescobaldi gave an inaugural recital to an audience of 30,000. A letter dating from 5 November 1608 (see Newcomb, 1964–77) reports rather more modestly that he arrived in Rome on 29 October 'safe, sound and happy' and 'on the eve of All Saints' Day took possession of the organ of St Peter's. He has also played for the two following feasts, to the great satisfaction and praise of the canons and of other fine musicians'. Thus even in St Peter's he played the organ in modest circumstances and to a restricted public. This was not his only activity as a musician. He was paid six scudi a month for his work at St Peter's; in 1615 this probably amounted to about 15% of his income (see Cametti, 1908; Hammond, 1983, pp.49, 60–62, gives further details of Frescobaldi's sources of outside income). For example, it is known from Maugars that he played in other religious institutions, and from various sources that he played the harpsichord in the apartments of several prominent cardinals. Thus he played on a wide variety of instruments, in both sacred and secular surroundings (Hammond, 1983, chap.8, offers a fine compendium of the instruments he may have encountered).

Frescobaldi's activity as harpsichordist in the apartments of cardinals was particularly important, and his fame and professional standing in this area seem to have grown rapidly. In mid-1609 Enzo Bentivoglio tried to attract one of Caccini's daughters to Rome as Frescobaldi's bride, perhaps also intending that she form part of the group of lady singers that Enzo had formed in imitation of the famous Ferrarese group of 25 years earlier. Caccini's response was a counter-offer of marriage with his daughter and employment for both at the Florentine court, with a high salary and few duties. The offer was not accepted. Individual studies by Newcomb (1964–77), Hill (Madison 1983) and Fabbris (Ferrara 1983) give further details of this thriving world of private Roman secular music in the 1610s – a world in which Frescobaldi immediately became active and which may have been the focus of his activity during his first years in Rome (the situation is summarized in Hammond, 1983, chap.3).

As his relationship with the Bentivoglio family declined, Frescobaldi found, apparently around 1612, a new patron in Cardinal Pietro Aldobrandini, who was the man who took possession of Ferrara for the church in 1598, the nephew of Pope Clement VIII and one of the richest and most important prelates of the period. Frescobaldi received from him a regular salary (probably between 100 and 150 scudi a year) as well as payments in goods. This position seems not, however, to have entailed his complete allegiance to Aldobrandini; in 1619, for example, he is recorded as playing in the musical academy in the palace of Cardinal Alessandro d'Este. Moreover, Annibaldi has shown (Madison 1983) that Frescobaldi was sufficiently independent and headstrong to sue Aldobrandini in a civil case regarding the enforced sale of Frescobaldi's house (on what is now the Piazza Colonna) for the enlargement of Aldobrandini's palace.

Although much information regarding Frescobaldi's first years in Rome has been uncovered only recently, the principal events in his life from around 1612 to 1627 have long been known from the magisterial study by Cametti (1908) and have been brought up to date by Hammond (1983). In May 1612 his first son, Francesco, was born out of wedlock. On 18 February 1613 he married the boy's mother, a certain Orsola del Pino, who came of a Milanese family and brought as dowry the house over which Frescobaldi was to struggle with Aldobrandini. Five months later a daughter, Maddalena, was born. The irregularity in the order and timing of these events cannot easily be explained. It seems most unlikely, given the information presented above, that Frescobaldi in 1612 lacked the funds to marry, as Reimann (1952) suggested. It should also be noted that the Girolamo Frescobaldi who may have stepped beyond the limits of propriety in his relations with a certain Angiolina in Rome in the summer of 1609 (see Newcomb, 1964–77, and Reiner, 1974) was indeed he and not another of that name, as Casimiri suggested (1942). This difficulty and the order of events around his marriage suggest that Frescobaldi was a rather hot-blooded young man. Another son, Domenico, who became a priest and poet and an art collector of some note, was born in November 1614; that his godfather was Cardinal Ginnasi is another indication of Frescobaldi's rising position in Roman society. Two more children were born to the couple: the baptismal record of the first, Stefano, born during 1616–17, has not been found; the second, Caterina, was born in September 1619 and held at the baptismal font by Evangelista Carbonesi, the Inquisitor of Malta.

Shortly after the birth of Domenico the two important prints were published by which may be judged the development of Frescobaldi's style during the crucial years 1609–14. One (A.5) is dedicated to Cardinal Aldobrandini, who had been Frescobaldi's patron for some three years. The other (A.3–4) looks to Cardinal (now also Duke) Ferdinando Gonzaga, with whom Frescobaldi was negotiating during the winter of 1614–15 concerning a possible position at the court of Mantua (Monteverdi had only recently left there for Venice). The documents surrounding these negotiations are presented and examined by Newcomb (1964–77) and Hammond (1983). Frescobaldi was offered 600 scudi a year by Ferdinando; in return he asked that the salary be in goods and willable property and be augmented by a house for himself and his family, plus 300 scudi to help with the large cost (500 scudi) of engraving A.3–4. These terms seem to have been accepted, for he went to Mantua (without his family) in the second half of February 1615. Once there, however, he seems to have found the reality far short of the promise: towards him, as towards Monteverdi, the Gonzaga family seem to have been exasperating masters, for he left Mantua after less than three months. In a letter of 16 May 1615, written from Rome, he cited as the reason for his return the lack of attention on the part of the authorities in Mantua both to his person and to his financial appeals. Prudently he seems not to have severed his Roman connections before going to Mantua; indeed he was paid by St Peter's throughout his absence, and there is no record of his being given permission to leave his post, though the period included the six weeks of Lent, when his duties would in any case have been light.

III Middle age, 1616–28

For over ten years Frescobaldi's life proceeded without extraordinary recorded incident. As has been noted above, two more children were born to him during this period. Cametti (1908) noted several changes of residence. It is known that in 1625 Frescobaldi had living in his house, in addition to his own family, two Polish students, an Italian lutenist and a German; it is not specified whether they were pupils or simply boarders. The little information regarding this period may be supplemented by the dedications of the publications of 1624–8 (A.6, A.7, B.1 and A.8). The dedication of A.6 to Alfonso d'Este (later Duke Alfonso III) poses a question. Frescobaldi had maintained his connections with the Este family by playing in the musical academy at the palace of Cardinal Alessandro d'Este in Rome. The dedication may show Frescobaldi looking hopefully once more to a princely court as a place of stable employment, as he had looked years before to Mantua and would look again shortly to Florence. Or it may be, as its prose implies, a simple homage to his native city and to the former employers of his teacher Luzzaschi. The two dedications of 1627 (A.7 and B.1, to Monsignor Luigi Gallo and Cardinal Scipione Borghese respectively) show that he was moving in the most powerful circles of Roman patronage (see Hammond, 1983, p.68, and Haskell, pp.27f). Finally the de-

5. Girolamo Frescobaldi: drawing by Claude Mellan

dication of A.8 to the young Grand Duke of Tuscany, Ferdinando II de' Medici, looks forward to his next experiment outside Rome. There occurred in this period the publication of the first print of his music by a large Venetian printer (a reprint of A.5 and A.6 by Alessandro

Vincenti in 1626), without a dedication and presumably without the financial aid that a dedication implied. This may be taken as an indication of the growing fame and commercial value of his music; Vincenti was to become his regular printer in the 1630s after his return from Florence.

The famous engraved portrait of Frescobaldi was published for the first time, as far as can be ascertained, in A.7 (1627). Yet one reads in the engraving that the portrait was made when Frescobaldi was 36, i.e. in 1619–20. According to Hammond (1983, pp.56 and 348) the drawing reproduced here as fig.5 was made around 1624, the first year of Mellan's stay in Rome, the engraving in A.7 derives from this, and either Mellan or the engraver was mistaken about Frescobaldi's age at the time of the drawing. All later portraits (except for the Bernini caricature possibly of Frescobaldi, reproduced in Hammond, 1983, p.59) are derived from this drawing or this engraving.

IV **Last years, 1629–43**

In early March 1628 Ferdinando II de' Medici was received by the Aldobrandini family both in Rome and in their magnificent villa at Frascati (see Cametti, 1908). Frescobaldi probably met him, and, as noted above, he dedicated to him in the same year a new collection of instrumental canzonas (the mention in *SartoriB* of an edition of 1623 is an error). In November 1628 Frescobaldi was given leave of absence from his post at St Peter's and went to the Florentine court, where some documents call him court organist, some *maestro di cappella.* He was paid 300 scudi a year, later raised to 348. It is not known whether his employment with the

Aldobrandini family lasted beyond this point, although it survived the death of Cardinal Pietro in 1621. Recently discovered information about music in Florence during Frescobaldi's years there is presented by Hammond (1978 and 1983, chap.6).

In 1634 Frescobaldi left Florence to return to Rome. Haberl (1887) proposed that he left because of the plague, although this had afflicted Florence since 1631. Hammond (1979) has since shown that he was lured back to Rome by an offer of service with the Barberini, the family of the reigning pope, Urban VIII, and perhaps the most munificent patrons of the arts that Rome had yet known. In May he reassumed his duties as organist of St Peter's. His new patron, Cardinal Francesco Barberini, was responsible for a supplement to his salary of 24 scudi a year, and for obtaining a benefice for his son Domenico. The cardinal also paid him 60 scudi a year towards the rent of a house near Trajan's Column, and a monthly salary of 3.6 scudi (Hammond). The dedications of the works sent to the printers during the next three years recognize the generosity of the Barberini family: A.11 (1635) is dedicated to Cardinal Antonio, Francesco's brother, and A.12 (1637) bears the arms of Francesco. Hammond supplies much recently uncovered information about this period of Frescobaldi's professional life – both in Francesco Barberini's private musical establishment, where Frescobaldi was joined by Virgilio Mazzocchi, J. H. Kapsberger and numerous other singers and instrumentalists, resident and non-resident, and at the Oratorio del Crocifisso, where the French viol player Maugars heard Frescobaldi play and described a performance of 1639.

Frescobaldi's fame was by now international. Mentions

of his music and his phenomenal playing began to appear with ever greater frequency. After repeated requests Froberger gained permission in 1637 to absent himself from his post at the Viennese court in order to study with him; he remained in Rome for over three years. Although many other German organists (e.g. Kerll and Tunder) have been called pupils of Frescobaldi, this may be evidence only of his great prestige in Germany after his death (in a German pamphlet of 1687 the claim to have studied with him was ridiculed as a typical boast). Given the extent of his influence at this period, it is particularly regrettable that nothing is known of his life or musical style during the last six years of his life. Pietro della Valle (1640) mentioned his new manner, 'with more *galanterie* in the modern style', but evidence of this is limited to scattered manuscript works (see pp.123–4 below), in which the reliability of the attributions has been widely questioned (see especially Silbiger, *Italian Manuscript Sources*, 1980).

Frescobaldi died in Rome on 1 March 1643, after ten days of fever, and was buried in the church of the SS Apostoli, near where he had lived for the last nine years. A contemporary chronicler (cited in Cametti, 1908) reported that his Requiem Mass was sung by the most famous musicians in Rome.

CHAPTER TWO

Personality and reputation

One is on uncertain ground in trying to assess Frescobaldi's personality, for there are few documents to help, and some of those that do exist are at present unavailable. Two things are suggested, however, by what is now known. First, the events of 1609–13 suggest that he was impetuous, at least in his relations with the opposite sex, and tended to be inconsistent, even abrasive, in his behaviour. Second, there are vague indications that he was not a man of broad general culture. Those of his letters that are at present available (one is reproduced as fig.6) are more than usually capricious in their spelling and syntax. Paolo Facconi, in a letter of 1615 (see Newcomb, 1964–77, and Hammond, 1983), described him as 'not very skilful beyond his own four walls' ('uomo poco esperto fuor di casa'), which may indicate either that he was not very experienced outside his own field or that he was not a skilled negotiator on his own behalf. Finally, two conservative 17th-century theorists described him as rather untutored. Doni, in a letter to Mersenne of July 1640, said that he was 'a very coarse man', that 'all his knowledge is at the ends of his fingertips' and that in his vocal music (he seems to have been thinking of B.3 and B.4) he failed to set the text properly and did not even know the meaning of words that are somewhat uncommon (see Pirro, 1925, p.47f). Liberati (pp.55f) placed him among those composers who are 'so ignorant in letters that they scarcely know how to write their name correctly'. Both Doni and Liberati had axes to grind, however, and it is difficult to know what weight to give to their remarks. Doni, in particular, was Francesco Barberini's private secretary and may have been influenced by Frescobaldi's abrasive personal style.

One is on firmer ground in assessing Frescobaldi's reputation. His fame was immense, both in Italy and north of the Alps and both at the end of his life and for well over a century afterwards. As early as the 1620s Giustiniani wrote that 'for Organ and Cembalo Geronimo Frescobaldi of Ferrara carries off all the honours, both in his skill and in the agility of his hands'. Bonini said that Frescobaldi 'has found a new style of playing, especially on the harpsichord' and that 'today whoever does not play in [his] style is not esteemed'. Such tributes are paralleled by those in Maugars, Della Valle, Penna, Liberati and Gasparini, as well as those of Alessandro Vincenti (in A.13) and those in Giovanni Scipione's op.3 (1652) and Luigi Battiferri's op.3 (1669). Battiferri seems to have been the first to call Frescobaldi a 'giant among organists', a phrase carried over into Penna's musical primer and thence to other books and manuscripts. It should be noted that both Penna and Gasparini in their very popular and much reprinted instruction books referred the student of the keyboard to the study of Frescobaldi in particular.

Although Silbiger ('The Roman Frescobaldi Tradition', 1980) and Hammond (1983, pp.75f) have uncovered a few details concerning Frescobaldi's direct activity as a teacher in Florence and Rome, our view of this important part of his career remains incomplete. The use of his published music as a model in the educa-

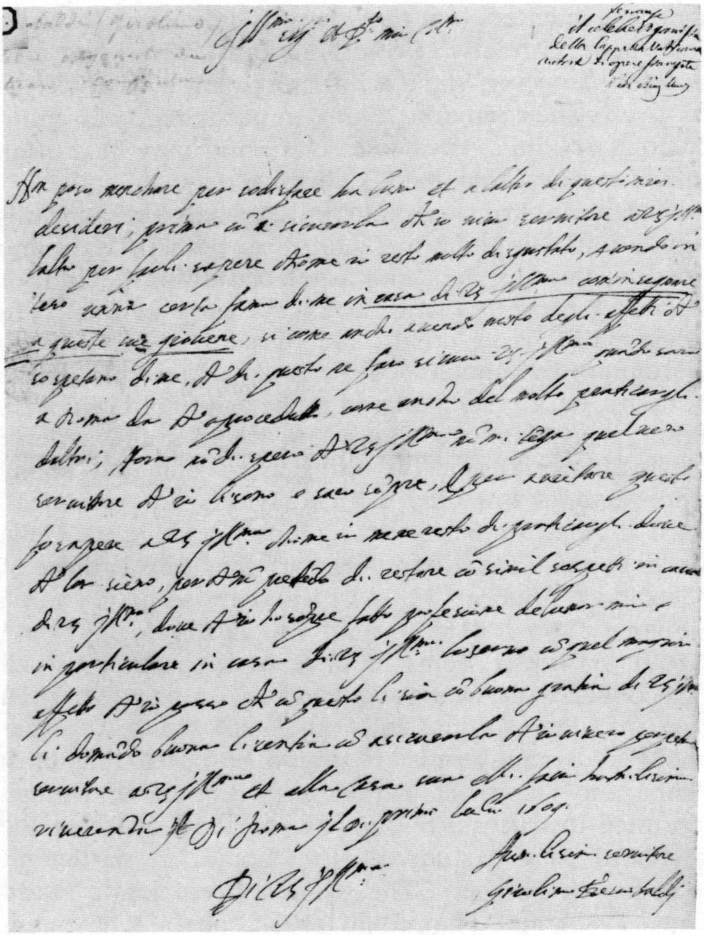

6. *Autograph letter (1 July 1609) from Frescobaldi in Rome, complaining of some calumnious reports regarding his conduct towards a pupil, and expressing his determination to prove their falsehood*

tion of young musicians seems to have begun by about 1625 (see Grassi's preface to A.9) and became widespread after about 1650. This is clearly one of the most historically important facets of his life and posthumous influence. Bernardo Pasquini's assiduous copying out and emulation of his works has long been known. Hammond (1983, p.95) has traced Frescobaldi's influence through Pasquini's pupil Gasparini to Gasparini's close associate Domenico Scarlatti. Schierning (1961) showed the presence of his works in south German manuscripts as early as the first half of the 17th century. His influence seems to have reached France chiefly through his pupil Froberger, whose toccata style was imitated explicitly by Louis Couperin. In England his music was known and emulated from at least 1627 (Hammond, 1983, p.96) and quoted by John Blow in his own toccatas. Riedel (1960, pp.54f and 117ff) pointed to Frescobaldi as being the most copied and influential of all keyboard composers in Germany during the second half of the 17th century. As regards northern Germany, Hedar and Riedel pointed to his influence on Buxtehude, and Bach as a young man owned the *Fiori musicali.* In the south the same collection became the touchstone of instrumental art in the circle around Fux (rather in the way that Palestrina was the ideal model of vocal art), and this situation obtained until well into the 19th century. Hawkins referred to Frescobaldi as the father of modern organ style (a judgment picked up by Gerber) and added that in 'fugue' he was 'without a rival'. Ambros gave perhaps the most resounding proclamation yet of Frescobaldi's importance and excellence, but, strangely enough, the 20th century has only recently begun to accord him the attention he deserves.

CHAPTER THREE

Works

I Youthful works

The three ensemble canzonas in A.1 were probably the first of Frescobaldi's works to be published. They were almost certainly in the hands of the printer or of a third person before he left Italy in the summer of 1607; indeed, as a still unknown composer, he was probably included in the print – which contains pieces by the most important composers of northern Italy (see Bartholomew, 1965) – through the efforts of Luzzaschi, who died that September.

The dedication of the fantasias (A.2) shows that he had composed at least some of them before he left Rome in 1607; he may have composed some of the others during his brief stay in the north. Since the northern style has several striking components not found in his own style and since all the basic procedures of the fantasias can be found in Italian music of the years preceding 1608, the current view is to discount the idea – originally proposed by Seiffert – of significant northern influence.

More recently, however, there has been a strong tendency to see the style of Frescobaldi's keyboard music, including this first print, as rooted in the Neapolitan school around Macque, Mayone and Trabaci (see Apel, 1938 and 1967, and Reimann, 1952). That there are shared elements of style between this school and

Frescobaldi's fantasias is certain. Recent research (summarized in Newcomb, Madison 1983) has uncovered a significant number of pieces from the shadowy late 16th-century school of composition in the Po valley which included Luzzaschi, Alessandro Milleville, Ercole Pasquini and a certain 'Giaches' (perhaps Brunel, perhaps Wert). The intellectual, rigorously contrapuntal nature of these pieces confirms the later remarks of Della Valle and Battiferri that the Ferrarese school inclined towards contrapuntal, intellectual music. Moreover, the existence of a partbook (not yet accessible to scholars) from a print of instrumental ricercares (1586) composed by Macque before he went to Naples reminds us that Macque first worked in Rome and had close ties with Ferrara; Macque's manuscript ricercares in the Biblioteca Nazionale, Florence, may be copies of these ricercares. Thus the imitative pieces of both the Neapolitan school and Frescobaldi should perhaps be seen as growing from a late 16th-century northern Italian style centred on a group of composers in the Po valley, perhaps also including Macque in Rome. For the closest stylistic ancestors of the fantasias of A.2 are the above-mentioned manuscript ricercares by Macque and those by 'Giaches' (discussed by Newcomb, 1978 and Madison 1983), which must have been composed before 1588, apparently in Ferrara, Mantua or Ravenna.

Frescobaldi's fantasias are rigorously intellectual and simultaneously austere and playful. They are written on each mode in turn. In their texture they are conservative, tending to ignore the dimensions of chordal harmony and functional tonality in favour of horizontal, contrapuntal manipulations. They show a tendency to derive almost all material from the subject or subjects, by means of a complicated process of rhythmic and melodic variation, often based on hexachord syllables (*inganni*). In those pieces that contain two or more subjects, Frescobaldi tended to introduce them all immediately and then to place them in varying contrapuntal combinations, rather than to expose them successively in separate sections like composers of the Venetian school. Frescobaldi, even at this early point in his career, was intensely preoccupied with contrapuntal technique. In the fantasias the result is perhaps somewhat lacking in contrast and even difficult to listen to when compared with his later work. The volume seems not to have enjoyed a large diffusion, for it was not reprinted; Grassi (in the preface to A.9) did not refer to it in his list of Frescobaldi's works; and Bernardo Pasquini seems to have had to copy it out by hand in order to obtain a copy for himself.

The madrigals of 1608, which, if one is to believe the dedication, were composed in Brussels in late 1607 and early 1608, reveal a similar tendency to virtuosity of technique. Here, however, one can much better discuss the roots of the style, for the Ferrarese madrigal style of the 1590s is by now reasonably well known. The close relationship between Frescobaldi's madrigals and the Ferrarese madrigal style of the mid-1590s, a style which Luzzaschi founded and Fontanelli and Gesualdo continued, is apparent at a glance. The clearest elements in common are the emphasis on polyphony rather than homophony; the nervous and constantly shifting textures; the frequency of cadences in which most of the voices drop out before reaching the tonal goal; the lack (in marked contrast to the madrigals of Marenzio and Monteverdi) of a firm bass line separate from the others in function and style; the nervous discontinuity of motion; and the imitation of quick rhythmic figures entering in very rapid succession. This last feature, almost a mannerism in Frescobaldi's madrigals, recalls Fontanelli more than anyone else. Indeed Frescobaldi tends to resemble more the two Ferrarese members of the triumvirate than he does its Neapolitan member, Gesualdo, whose harmonic boldness is nowhere to be found in his madrigals. His use of dissonance is in fact less adventurous than that of Luzzaschi, Fontanelli, Marenzio or Monteverdi, a facet of his style that can perhaps be ascribed to his years in Rome. His choice of texts suggests in part (Pocaterra and Rinaldi) the turn of the century in Ferrara and Mantua and in part (Marino) the first decade of the 17th century in Rome. The texts suggest the same combination of influences as the musical style: profound roots in the Ferrara of the 1590s, with tempering influences from the milder Roman style. Despite their occasional clumsiness and inappropriate treatment of text and despite their tendency to shortwindedness, these madrigals, especially in their contrapuntal detail, remain interesting and full of character.

II Works of first maturity, 1614–15

Before approaching that body of compositions by which Frescobaldi's reputation was chiefly made, at least for those who did not have the opportunity to hear him personally, it is necessary to make some general observations and distinctions. First, throughout his career Frescobaldi was extremely famous – probably predominantly so – as a performer; almost all the testimony to his fame in his own lifetime concerns his powers as a performer. Although the divorce between composer and performer is doubtless more keenly felt now (except in popular music) than it was in the early 17th century, there existed even then a distinction between the particular gifts of the performer – manual dexterity and rhythmic ability, for example – and those of the composer. Frescobaldi seems to have been richly endowed with both kinds of gift. Although his activity as a performer cannot be recaptured, the roles of performer and composer seem to come together in A.3–4, the toccatas of which suggest an attempt to capture in musical notation the inspired delivery of a particular performer; moreover, Frescobaldi saw fit to include in these volumes detailed instructions concerning style of performance. Nevertheless, close study of these toccatas shows them to be *res factae* disguised as improvisations – highly structured pieces in which a strong skeleton supports the luxuriant surface ornamentation (see Newcomb, Madison 1983). The ricercares and canzonas of A.5, no less structured, are more abstract in surface style.

A second possible dichotomy – that between traditional and innovatory elements – in Frescobaldi's art has often exercised commentators on his music. This dichotomy too is reflected in the pair of prints issued in 1614–15. Those elements of novelty that his contemporaries (e.g. Bonini) apprehended in his style seem to have been connected with his manner of harpsichord playing (probably his treatment of rhythm and ornamentation) and with the toccatas in particular among his printed pieces. His informative dedications to the toccatas again indicate that he was aware of this. He compared the style of the first book with 'i Madrigali moderni' (although one should remember that he was talking explicitly of tempo); he referred to the pieces of the second book as 'le presenti mie moderne fatiche' and remarked on their 'nuova maniera' and on the 'novità dell'artifitio'. Many elements of even the toccatas, however, are rather traditional. First, the title-page, like most of Frescobaldi's title-pages, reads more like a 16th-century than a 17th-century one. There are no fanciful titles, no new words for old forms; there is only a simple statement of the types of piece inside and the manner in which they are printed. Second, Frescobaldi's harmonic extravagances, which modern ears receive as progressive, refer back to the harmonic language of the Ferrarese and Neapolitan schools of the 1590s and early 1600s, a language that by 1615 had been replaced in most circles by a simpler and more tonal harmonic vocabulary. The truly progressive side of Frescobaldi's style was to be found in the new tonal focus with which he handled the traditional 16th-century contrapuntal techniques in A.5, and in the secondary dominants and carefully calibrated cadential deceptions and prolongations of A.3–4.

Of the two groups of pieces, the imitative pieces of A.5 are the more obviously conservative. They build on a tradition in Italian instrumental music going back 50–70 years and should be seen as one of the culminating exemplars of it. In fact, the type of piece represented especially by the ricercares of A.5 was rarely sent to the printer after 1610. Certain aspects of Frescobaldi's imitative pieces were particularly conservative, perhaps as a reflection of tendencies in both the Roman and the Ferrarese schools. These aspects are concentrated around the insistence on polyphonic workmanship (in contrast to the monodic style that was sweeping Italy at the time) and include both the requirement that organists maintain the ability to read a four-part open score and the constant posing and resolving of complicated problems of a polyphonic nature, sometimes explicitly stated as *oblighi* (on the Roman *obligo* tradition, see Durante, Madison 1983).

Finally, the areas of activity defined by A.3–4 and A.5 – especially the toccatas, the sets of variations on folk themes and the large four-part imitative forms – are basically those that preoccupied Frescobaldi for the rest of his life, and a glance at *SartoriB* provides sufficient evidence that he alone continued to explore these forms after the last prints of the Neapolitans in 1615. That his entire field of activity is remarkably like that of the Neapolitans Mayone and Trabaci is one of the strongest arguments for the direct influence on him of these composers. It would seem that in most of his output he was a traditionalist, who summed up the achievements of a century of Italian instrumental music. The grandest forms in which he worked – the large-scale toccata and the four-part imitative genres – virtually died with him; if they were continued or revived later in the 17th century, it was often with explicit reference to his example, as in the toccatas of Gottlieb Muffat and Froberger and the ricercares of Battiferri and Fabrizio Fontana.

Although the print A.3–4 includes toccatas, variation sets and dances, the toccatas receive the place of honour on the title-page and occupy most of the volume. These toccatas, together with those of A.7, are Frescobaldi's most personal creations; they are among the finest products of the intensity of feeling and freedom of fantasy that were the glories of the early Baroque era in Rome. Externally this print is modelled on Merulo's two books of toccatas, both in its title-page and in being engraved rather than printed by movable type. The form of Frescobaldi's pieces, however, is different in that he adopted only once Merulo's clearcut alternation between ornamented chordal sections and imitative sections. In addition he ranged far beyond Merulo in the bold and expressive nature of his ornamentation and harmony. The basic procedure of the toccata – throughout Frescobaldi's pieces and in Merulo's chordal sections – is a series of chords across which sweeps a flow of dazzling, virtuoso ornamentation. While Merulo's ornamentation is fairly even in motion and consistent in method within sections, Frescobaldi's is rhythmically and intervallically highly varied, agitated and full of individual character. In rhythm Frescobaldi is closer to Luzzaschi's madrigals of 1601 than he is to Merulo. It is to these pieces by Luzzaschi, to the manuscript capriccios of Macque, and to the variations and toccatas of Ercole Pasquini that one should look in order to understand the ancestry of Frescobaldi's toccatas. More than any of his predecessors, however, he was able to invest his nervous snatches of ornamentation with an emotional and motivic content that gives a vibrant, quasi-polyphonic life to his toccatas. Likewise, the variety of harmonic rhythm and the sureness with which he handled the secondary dominants and the cadential formulae of the proto-tonal vocabulary is his own achievement, only hinted at in Pasquini and Macque. It is because of this combination of textural intricacy and sureness of tonal control that these splendid, grandly rhetorical works have survived the death of their performer-creator and the passing of the short-lived stylistic context in which they were created.

A.5, printed five times during Frescobaldi's lifetime, seems to have been his most commercially successful collection. As has been remarked above, it is largely traditional. One finds in it no obvious drive to personal expression or to bold experimentation in rhythm, melody or harmony – tendencies which many commentators find characteristic of the early Baroque spirit in general and of Frescobaldi in particular. One does, however, find the continuance of a tendency to almost selfconscious virtuosity (already noted in B.2 and A.2) that is very characteristic both of Frescobaldi and of the early Baroque period. In the case of A.5 the virtuosity is compositorial: Frescobaldi delighted in difficult technical limitations. In one ricercare melodic movement is permitted only by leap; several others include an ostinato of some kind, either rigorously unvaried or varied according to a number of rigorous principles. As against this technical rigour, all the pieces are constantly informed with a playful spirit at once extrovert and engaging; this can be seen in witty rhythmic or melodic transformations of the themes or in the transposition on to another hexachord of only part of a theme based on solmization syllables, in such a way that the solmization of the theme remains constant while its melodic contour changes (*inganno*; see Harper, 1978–9, and Newcomb, 1978). These rhythmic and melodic transformational methods were all present in the fantasias as well, but the greater clarity of tonal shape and the opening up of the texture make the ricercares much easier than the fantasias to listen to and understand.

The canzonas are still more lively. Like the ricercares they are sectional pieces. Here, however, there is a clear formal scheme: they are in three to seven sections, and the even-numbered sections are in a contrasting metre. Contrast between sections is a basic principle in Frescobaldi's canzonas (Apel, 1967, saw this principle as originating with Trabaci). He sometimes, but not always, unified the various sections either by basing all of them on variations of a single theme or by bringing back the initial section at the end. The canzona was, like the capriccio later on, a nearly ideal field of activity for him, incorporating as it does variation, contrapuntal virtuosity and playful fantasy. Later canzonas even incorporate toccata-like cadenzas at the ends of sections.

The several vocal pieces by Frescobaldi appearing in anthologies between 1616 and 1625 are all of less importance and cannot help one to understand the considerable leap in style between his instrumental works of 1615 and those of 1624–8. These vocal works, which are for one to three voices and continuo, are in the simple style so characteristic of commercial anthologies of the time and against which Frescobaldi seems to have taken a firm stand in his instrumental music. They show none of the complexity of polyphonic thought, and little of the expressive intensity, of the keyboard works.

III Works of full maturity, 1624–7

With the capriccios of 1624 (A.6) the high plateau on which stands the remainder of Frescobaldi's instrumental production is reached. Like the ricercares and canzonas of A.5, the capriccios are sectional works, whose basic technical procedure is imitative counterpoint. In a sense they combine the worlds of the canzonas, the ricercares and the toccatas, for they have the abundant rhythmic vitality of the canzonas, the contrapuntal seriousness of the ricercares and the florid ornamentation of the toccatas in certain cadential sections. Since most of them (nine out of 12) treat a single theme, the principle of variation, specially prominent in the fantasias of A.2 and in the variation sets of A.3–4, is of primary importance here as well. The harmonic experiments, conspicuous in some of the toccatas of A.3–4 (especially no.12), are continued in the *Capriccio cromatico* and the *Capriccio di durezze*, both of which are short pieces concerned with a compositional problem rather than with a particular theme. The remainder of the capriccios are long, imitative pieces, considerably more ambitious than any of the ricercares in A.5 (as Frescobaldi pointed out in his introduction). In his choice of themes he followed tradition, choosing the venerable *la–sol–fa–re–mi* (used by Josquin among others), the ascending and descending hexachord (used as the basis for countless compositions in the 16th and 17th centuries) and the folktunes or musical recitation formulae that had been specially popular with the Neapolitans. Although the capriccios on a single theme touch the heights of Frescobaldi's contrapuntal art, they are far from arid exercises. As the word itself suggests, the pieces display an overwhelming freedom of invention. In addition a well-designed crescendo of both rhythmic momentum and intensity of accompanying ideas gives them dramatic sweep and unity. An excellent illustration of Frescobaldi's technical prowess is no.3, the capriccio on the cuckoo call, which, like ricercare no.10 of A.5, has an ostinato in the top part. In the capriccio the material is of the most uncompromising simplicity. The recurring figure *d″–b′* is put into a dazzling variety of contexts: it appears in a serious ricercare subject, in the quick motivic play of a canzona, in the triple-metre sections that were used for contrast in canzonas, as part of little dances, and surrounding toccata-like ornamental sweeps. Not even the *Sonata sopra 'Sancta Maria'* in Monteverdi's Vespers (1610) reaches such heights of ingenuity and virtuosity. Like the art of G. B. Marino and Bernini, the aim of this art is not only to delight the listener but also to make him marvel and admire. In the capriccios Frescobaldi took the great tradition of the Renaissance imitative forms and gave them their greatest and most characteristic statement of the early Baroque period.

The pieces in the second book of toccatas (A.7) are clearly more varied than those in the first; they look both backwards and forwards in Frescobaldi's production. On the one hand, one finds here the large-scale early Baroque toccata carried to its highest point of development (those of A.11 are much shorter and more restrained); one even finds an example of the anachronistic ornamental transcription practised by the Neapolitans. On the other hand, one finds the first liturgical pieces based on chant, the first toccatas for the organ and for the Elevation, and a more consistent use of the variation canzona. The toccatas and canzonas fill about two-thirds of the collection and are perhaps its most important part. The toccatas are of markedly greater complexity and virtuosity than those of the first book and carry to greater lengths the abrupt contrasts in rate and style of motion that had been an essential part of the earlier toccatas, now including the insertion of sections explicitly in dance-metres. Through the use of unifying pedal points, large-scale harmonic prolongations and motivic ostinato figures, some sections of them are given a sweep and continuity that, despite the contrasts just mentioned, are among their most arresting qualities. The ninth toccata is particularly remarkable for its difficult rhythmic proportions and its flashes of bright motivic play, alternating with both slow-moving chordal dissonance and magnificent washes of rapidly shifting dissonance caused by two or three simultaneous but independent ornamental flourishes. The canzonas of A.7, like those of A.5, are short, imitative, clearly sectional pieces. In A.7 the sections are often closed by toccata-like flourishes and related by variation. Frescobaldi's use of variation in these instances is not always as simple as the airy character of the pieces might suggest. His technique may, for example, embrace a device as complex and intellectual as the inversion of a characteristic internal phrase of the opening theme. When he does this, however, he is careful to bring the internal phrase to the listener's attention before submitting it to variation.

In 1628 Frescobaldi began his period of employment at the Medici court in Florence. From this period (1628–34) there are only the two books of *Arie musicali* (both of 1630). The books are remarkably similar in content. As in most such prints of the period, the majority of the pieces are for solo voice and give little scope to Frescobaldi's love of counterpoint and motivic play. This music, while by no means bad, is not on the level of the great instrumental prints of 1624 and 1627. Fortune (1953 and 1968) pointed out that scarcely any solo songs were composed in Florence after the early 1620s and that Frescobaldi's pieces in 1630 were already an anachronism. Hill, in a study of Frescobaldi's monodies published in the 1620s and 1630s (Madison 1983), has shown that they share the style and genres of the monodies in a series of manuscripts from the 1610s connected with the private music establishment of Cardinal Montalto (*d* 1623), a music-loving prelate with whose music establishment Frescobaldi is known to have been associated in the 1610s. It thus seems that in his two books of 1630 Frescobaldi was bringing back to Florence a Roman style of ten to 15 years before. Since the Roman style had, in its turn, originated in Florence in the first years of the century, perhaps his gesture was a form of flattery.

IV **Late works, 1628–37**

The instrumental canzonas of 1635 (A.10) are to a certain extent the reprint of a collection printed twice (in partbooks and in score) in 1628 (see A.8 and A.9) The contents of all three of these editions, however, differ from one another. Excluding the three compositions for spinettina included in A.9, 28 of the 48 different canzonas are to be found in all three editions, six are found in both A.8 and A.9, two in A.9 and A.10 and one each in A.8 and A.9 only, and ten are new to A.10. Although the texts of the canzonas common to A.8 and A.9 vary for the most part in small details only, none of the 30 canzonas from A.8 and A.9 that reappear in A.10 do so without alteration (Harper, 1975, Madison 1983). In the second versions there is greater expressive clarity, melodic motifs are more distinctive and rhythmic patterns more compelling, and the basso continuo is both simpler and less harmonically ambiguous. Moreover, in 16 canzonas there is substantial reworking, including the reordering or replacement of existing material and the addition of new material. The result is a greater tonal range as well as a stronger overall structure and more cogent metrical organization. But there is no fixed pattern, and, as with the keyboard canzonas, the sections of the instrumental canzonas, which are variable in length and number, are unified by Frescobaldi's flexible and many-sided use of melodic variation. They contain few academic devices or expressive stylistic extremes, nor do they include any of the idiomatic instrumental bravura to be found in the compositions of many of Frescobaldi's north Italian contemporaries. Yet for all their restraint and economy they are no less intense or convincing. Despite frequent shifts of metre, tempo and texture, each canzona forms a varied but unified whole, aided by the technique of evolving melodic variation and by the careful dovetailing of the sections. This dovetailing is often achieved by the addition or expansion of *adagio* links between sections, a feature that also appears in the canzonas of *Fiori musicali*.

The revision of the instrumental canzonas published in the three prints that mark Frescobaldi's departure from Rome and his return from Florence provides a link between the exuberant rhetorical style of the earlier keyboard prints and the intensity and economy of writing apparent throughout A.11 and in the additional pieces of A.12. Nonetheless, the entire question of his late style, from about 1630 on, still has to be thoroughly investigated. Besides the instrumental canzonas there are only two collections from this period – one of them of considerable size, the other quite small (A.11 and A.12). Most of the larger print is different enough in purpose from Frescobaldi's previous music for one to hesitate to make direct comparisons; much of the smaller one is made up of curiosities or miniatures. There is no firm proof of when the pieces in the posthumous A.13 were composed; their authenticity – or at least the authenticity of their readings – is not beyond question, since Frescobaldi himself did not prepare them for publication, and stylistically they are similar enough to the pieces of A.7 to suggest that they may come from ten to 20 years earlier. Thus there is very little definitely applicable evidence on which to base conclusions about the late style.

The larger print (A.11) has been since at least 1750 Frescobaldi's most famous collection. It is, however, unusual in his output in that, with the possible exception of the two final pieces, it is a collection of music for use in the Mass (there are only a few other liturgical pieces by Frescobaldi, in A.7). The arrangement of the pieces in A.11 as three organ masses (for Sundays, feasts of the Apostles and feasts of the Virgin Mary) follows a long-standing tradition (see Apel, 1967). But these masses exceptionally use only the Kyrie-Christe unit from the Ordinary, setting verses of the chant as organ versets. In addition each contains toccatas (before the Mass, before some ricercares and during the Elevation), and ricercares and canzonas as substitutes for some items in the Proper (such as the introit, gradual, offertory and communion).

The publication of organ pieces for performance at points in the Mass corresponding to certain items of the Proper can be traced back at least as far as Banchieri's *L'organo suonarino*, which first appeared in 1605. The practice of inserting organ pieces at these points is probably much older (see Bonta). The toccatas designated as belonging before a service (fig.7) or before a ricercare are very short, simple and clearly introductory in nature; those preceding a ricercare are among the few examples of the pairing of prelude and fugue in Italian organ music. The Elevation toccatas are considerably more developed. Because of the warmth and density of their harmonic palette they must be counted among the masterpieces of the period. The canzonas, which are sometimes variation canzonas and sometimes transform their material more radically, are like those of A.7, though they are simpler in form and texture and include explicit tempo markings (as do the canzonas of A.10). The ricercares, the first by Frescobaldi to be published since 1615, are marvels of concentration and complexity of thought. The usual feats of intellectual bravado abound: contorted chromatic subjects, long pedal points and an ostinato to be inserted *viva voce* by the organist, which goes beyond that in no.11 of A.6 in that he must now divine the proper points of entry. The ricercare with vocal ostinato has entrances on eight different stages of the circle of 5ths and bears the defiant inscription 'Let him who is able understand me; I understand myself' ('Intendomi [*recte* Intendami] chi puo che m'intend'io'). Did Frescobaldi consciously quote Petrarch's Canzone no.105, line 17 (albeit with a misprint)? The context is suggestive, for the canzone's previous line refers to St Peter. A.11 closes with two capriccios (the first of them is not so labelled), whose intended function, if any, in the preceding organ masses is not clear, since both are based on secular tunes, and the use of such tunes was officially excluded from the organ music in the mass. Both are works of major proportions that can be compared directly with the capriccios of 1624.

7. Girolamo Frescobaldi's 'Fiori musicali' (1635); the 'Toccata avanti la Messa della Madonna', in open score

The last works of Frescobaldi to be printed during his lifetime are those that he added to the third revision of the first book of toccatas (A.12). They include three capriccios; a succession of variations on the passacaglia and chaconne; and five groups of small pieces made up of one or two dances, as well as a small set of passacaglias or chaconnes (where there are two dances they are related by variation). The capriccio on the Ruggiero is a simple and melodious set of variations, more similar to the capriccio on *Or che noi rimena* (A.6, no.7) than to that on the Ruggiero in A.6, which in fact closely resembles in technique the *bergamasca* of A.11. Frescobaldi added fun and complexity to the simple variation form by inserting a second popular tune in unexpected contrapuntal combinations. The *Capriccio pastorale* is perhaps the earliest example of a type which later became so popular – the pastorale in rocking triple metre and major mode, with numerous pedal points and the broad, unornamented melodic gestures of many 17th-century Italian arias. The capriccio on *La battaglia* belongs to the long tradition of battle-pieces beginning in the early 16th century whose hammered chords, arpeggios and military rhythms tend to sound curiously naive to our ears. The string of variations on the passacaglia and chaconne, on the other hand, is certainly one of Frescobaldi's most impressive works. It is nothing more than a set of modulating strophic variations on a short harmonic pattern, and although Frescobaldi expressly said that one might play any variation separately as one wished, the rhythmic sweep and intensity of especially the last few variations leave the listener with the impression of a strong and solemn whole. Darbellay (*JAMS*, 1983) provides fascinating documentary evidence of the stages of Frescobaldi's struggle to make a convincing whole of this extended succession of diverse sections.

The foregoing paragraphs will have indicated how few pieces in A.11 and A.12 can appropriately be compared with those of ten years earlier (in A.6 and A.7). The toccatas for the Elevation and the canzonas in A.7 and A.11 are the most obvious examples. They are few, and their meaning is somewhat ambiguous. In discussing Frescobaldi's music published after 1634 it is customary to speak in general terms of a simpler, more balanced melodic and rhythmic style, of less exuberant forms and of simpler, more tonal harmonies. A comparison of the Elevation toccatas in terms of size, figuration and clarity of structure certainly tends to support this, as does a comparison of the capriccios in terms of harmony. Yet the harmony of the later Elevation toccatas is if anything more complex than that of the earlier, and the later variations on the passacaglia and chaconne are more complex in figuration, melody and harmony than the earlier ones.

Study of Frescobaldi has not progressed far enough for one to be able to say a great deal about his style during the last 15 years of his life (which include the years when his most famous pupil, Froberger, studied with him). There are indications that there was a considerable change at some time during this period. As noted above, Della Valle spoke of his new style ('another manner with more *galanterie* in the modern style'). It may be that the dances and the rather simple *Capriccio pastorale* of A.12 are examples of this style, or perhaps we do not even know any examples of it. Several contemporaries spoke of his many unpublished compositions. Modern scholarship has only just begun to work with the sizable body of manuscript keyboard music from the 17th century. Hammond (1983, pp.290–304) surveys the manuscripts with attributions to Frescobaldi, almost none of which can be accepted as solid. Some pieces attributed to Frescobaldi have been published (in CEKM, xxx), but much of the meticulous stylistic and palaeographical work of rejecting false attributions and identifying anonymous pieces still remains to be done; it has been well begun by Silbiger (*Italian Manuscript Sources*, 1980). Once this work is further under way, one will perhaps be able to speak more confidently of Frescobaldi's late style.

WORKS

Editions: *G. Frescobaldi: Opere complete*, ed. E. Darbellay, O. Mischiati and L. F. Tagliavini, Monumenti musicali italiani, i (Milan, 1975–) [O]
G. Frescobaldi: Sei madrigali, ed. F. Boghen (Florence, 1920) [B]
G. Frescobaldi: Canzoni a due canti col basso continuo, ed. H. T. David, Antiqua (Mainz and Leipzig, 1933) [D]
G. Frescobaldi: Orgel- und Klavierwerke, ed. P. Pidoux (Kassel, 1949–54) [P i–v]
G. Frescobaldi: Arie musicali (Florenz 1630), ed. H. Spohr, Musikalische Denkmäler, iv (Mainz, 1960) [S]
G. Frescobaldi: Canzonen, ed. F. Cerha, Diletto musicale, xlvi, xlix, lxxxvii–lxxxix (Vienna and Munich, 1962–6) [C]
G. Frescobaldi: Keyboard Compositions Preserved in Manuscripts, ed. W. R. Shindle, CEKM, xxx (1968) [Sh]
G. Frescobaldi: Ensemble Canzonas, ed. B. Thomas (London, 1975–) [T]
G. Frescobaldi: Toccatas, libro primo and libro secondo, ed. K. Gilbert (Padua, 1978) [G]

Numbers in right-hand margins denote references in the text.

INSTRUMENTAL

A.1 3 canzonas, a 4, 5, 8, 1608[24]; ed. in Bartholomew (1965); see also Hammond (1983), 306 — 104

A.2 Il primo libro delle [12] fantasie, a 4 (Milan, 1608); P i — 90, 104, 105–6, 112, 114

A.3–4 [12] Toccate e [3] partite d'intavolatura di cimbalo . . . libro primo (Rome, 1615 [Sartori 1615[a]]; rev. and enlarged 2/1616 [Sartori 1615–16[b]], with the variation sets altered, 1 variation set and 4 correnti added; 3/1616 [Sartori 1616[f] and 1615[a bis]]; 4/1628 as Il primo libro d'intavolatura di toccate di cimbalo et organo) O ii, P iii (from 1637 edn.), G i, orig. version of 3 variation sets in O ii and S; for dates of edns., see Darbellay (*JAMS*, 1983), n.1 — 84, 94, 108, 109, 110–12, 114, 115

A.5 [10] Ricercari, et [5] canzoni franzese fatte sopra diverse oblighi in partitura . . . libro primo (Rome, 1615/*R*1967; pubd with rev. of A.6, Venice, 1626); P ii [from 1626 edn.] — 94, 96, 108, 109, 110, 112–13, 114, 116

A.6 Il primo libro di [12] capricci fatti sopra diversi soggetti et arie in partitura (Rome, 1624; pubd with A.5 and without capriccio on Or che noi rimena, Venice, 1626); P ii [from 1626 edn., incl. capriccio missing from 1624 edn.]:
Bassa fiammenga: Cromatico di ligature al contrario; Il Cucho; Di durezze; La sol fa mi re ut; La sol fa re mi; Obligo di cantare le quinta parte, senza toccarlo; Or che noi rimena; Ruggiero; Spagnoletta; Un soggetto; Ut re mi fa sol la — 85, 95, 96, 113–15, 116, 120, 122, 123

A.7 Il secondo libro di [11] toccate, [6] canzone, [4] versi d'hinni, [3] Magnificat, [5] gagliarde, [6] correnti et altre [4] partite d'intavolatura de cimbalo et organo (Rome, 1627/*R*1978) (1 copy wrongly cited as autograph by Abbiati, pp.345, 351) [incl. ornamented version of madrigal by Arcadelt]; O iii, P iv [from 1637 edn.], G ii, Sh [only the 2 variation sets omitted from 1637 edn.] — 95, 97, 109, 110–11, 115–16, 119, 120, 123

A.8 Il primo libro delle [35] canzoni, a 1–4, bc, accomodate per sonare con ogni sorte de stromenti (Rome, 1628); C lxxxvii–lxxxix; D — 95, 96, 97, 117

A.9 In partitura, il primo libro delle [38] canzoni, a 1–4, bc, per sonare con ogni sorte di stromenti, con 2 toccate in fine (Rome, 1628) [contains 34 pieces from A.8, and 6 new works, incl. 2 for spinettina, 1 for spinettina, vn]; C xlvi, xlix; D;T; spinettina works in Sh:
L'Alessandrina; L'Altera; L'Altograndina; L'Ambitiosa; L'Arnolfinia; La Bernardina; La Bianchina; La Boccellina; La Bovisia; La Capponcina; La Capriola; La Cittadellia; La Diodata; La Donatina; La Franciotta; La Garzoncina; La Gualterina; L'Henricuccia; La Lamberta; La Lanciona; La Lievoratta; La Lipparella; La Lucchesina; La Marina; La Masotti; La Moricona; La Nicolina; La Nobile; La Plettenberger; La Rovellina; La Samminiata; La Sandoninia; La Sardina; La Tegrimuccia; La Todeschina; La Tromboncina; La Tuccina; La Vittoria (spinettina); 1 toccata (spinettina); 1 toccata (spinettina, vn) — 103, 106, 117

A.10 [40] Canzoni da sonare, a 1–4, bc, . . . libro primo (Venice, 1635/*R*1981) [contains 28 pieces from A.8 (of which 10 are rev.), 2 from A.9, and 10 new works]; D — 117–18, 120

A.11 Fiori musicali di diverse compositioni, toccate, kyrie, canzoni, capricci, e ricercari, in partitura, a 4 (Venice, 1635) [incl. 3 organ masses, 8 toccatas, 5 canzonas, 6 ricercares, 2 capriccios]; P v and other edns. — 98, 103, 115, 118–20, *121*, 122, 123

A.12 [12] Toccate d'intavolatura di cimbalo et organo, partite di diverse arie, e correnti, balletti, ciaconne, passacagli . . . libro primo (Rome, 1637/*R*1978) [contents as A.4, with 1 variation set on passacaglia and chaconne, 3 capriccios, several dance groups added]; P iii — 98, 118–19, 122, 123

A.13 [11] Canzoni alla francese in partitura . . . libro quarto, a 4 (Venice, 1645); P i: — 101, 119
La Bellerofonte; La Crivelli; La Gardana; La Paulini; La Pesenti; La Querina; La Rovetta; La Sabatina; La Scacchi; La Tarditi; La Vincenti

Many kbd works in MS; for full details see Silbiger (1980) and Hammond (1983); many ed. in Sh. 9, toccatas ed. in MMI, 1st ser., ii (1962)

SACRED VOCAL — 117

B.1 Liber secundus diversarum modulationum, 1–4vv (Rome, 1627) — 95
Works in 1616[1], 1618[3], 1621[3], 1625[1]; for modern edns., see Hammond (1983), 317–18 — 113

Angelus ad pastores, 3vv, bc, 1618[13]; Aspice Domine, lv, B.I; Ave virgo gloriosa, 4vv, B.1; Beatus vir qui suffert, 2vv, B.1; Benedicite Deum, 2vv, B.1; Benedicta tu mater, 2vv, B.1; Civitas Hierusalem noli flere, 4vv, B.1; Corona aurea super caput eius, 4vv, B.1; Decantabat populus Israel, 3vv, B.1; De ore prudentis procedit, 2vv, B.1; Deus noster refugium, 1v, B.1; Ego clamavi, 4vv, B.1; Ego flos campi, 3vv, B.1; Ego sum panis vivus, 3vv, bc, 1621[3]; Ego sum qui sum, 4vv, B.1; Exaudi nos Deus, 3vv, B.1; Exultavit cor meum, 1v, B.1; Exurge Domine, 2vv, B.1
Iesu flos mater virginis, 4vv, B.1; Iesu rex admirabilis, 3vv, 1625[1] (with bc), B.1 (2 settings); In te Domine speravi, 8vv, bc (autograph according to Haberl, 1887, p.82) authenticity doubtful, ed. I. Fuser (Padua, 1934); Iod. Manum suam, 1v, bc, *I-Bc*; Ipsi sum desponsata, 1v, B.1; O bone Jesu, 2vv, B.1; O Iesu mi dulcissime, 1v, B.1; O mors illa, 2vv, B.1; O sacrum convivium, 3vv, B.1; Peccavi super numerum, 3vv, bc, 1616[1]; Reminiscere miserationum, 2vv, B.1; Sic amantem diligite, 3vv, B.1; Sicut mater consolatur, 2vv, B.1; Tempus est ut revertar, 2vv, B.1; Tota pulchra es, 2vv, B.1; Vidi speciosam sicut columbam, 2vv, B.1; Viri sancti, 2vv, B.1; Vox dilecti mei pulsantis, 3vv, B.1

Missa sopra l'aria della monica, 8vv, bc, *I-Rsg*; O i
Missa sopra l'aria di Fiorenza, 8vv, bc, *Rsg*; O i
Magnificat secundi toni, 4 choruses; lost, cited in Waldner (1916), 134
Jod. Manum suam, lv, bc, *Bc*
In te Domine speravi, 8vv, *Bc*

SECULAR VOCAL — 117

B.2 Il primo libro de' [19] madrigali, 5vv (Antwerp, 1608) — 89, 106–7, 112
B.3 Primo libro d'arie musicali per cantarsi, 1–3vv, theorbo, hpd (Florence, 1630); S — 100, 116–17
B.4 Secondo libro d'arie musicali per cantarsi, 1–3vv, theorbo, hpd (Florence, 1630); S — 85, 100, 116–17
Works in 1621[14], 1621[15], 1622[10] — 13

Ahi bella, si, 5vv, B.2, ed. F. Boghen (London, 1922); Alla gloria, 1v, bc, 1621[14]; A miei pianti al fine, 1v, B.4, S 62; Amor perche fai tu, 5vv, B.2; Amor ti chiama il mondo, 5vv, B.2, ed. F. Boghen (London, 1922); A piè della gran croce, 1v, B.3, S 10; Ardo, e taccio il mio mal, 1v, B.3, S 4; Begli occhi, 2vv, B.3, S 33; Bella tiranna infida, 2vv, B.4, S 70; Ben veggio donna, 1v, B.4, S 48; Come perder poss'io, 5vv, B.2; Con dolcezza e pietate, 3vv, B.3, S 41; Corilla danzando, 3vv, B.3, S 39; Cor mio, 5vv, B.2; Così mi disprezzate, 1v, B.3, S 27

Da qual sphera, 5vv, B.2, ed. F. Boghen (London, 1922); Degnati, O gran Fernando, 1v, B.3, S 2; Deh, vien da me pastorella, 2vv, B.4, S 76; Deh, volate o miei voci, 3vv, B.4, S 73; Di licori un guardo, 1v, B.3 (2 settings), S 24; Doloroso mio core, 3vv, B.4, S 80; Donna, siam rei di morte, 1v, B.3, S 17; Dopo sì lungo error, 1v, B.3, S 8; Dove, dove ne'vai, 2vv, B.3, S 35; Dove, dove, Signor, 1v, B.3, S 7; Dove, dove sparir, 1v, B.4, S 55; Dunque dovrò, 1v, B.3, S 12; Era l'anima mia, 2vv, bc, 1622[10]; Eri già tutta mia, 2vv, B.3, S 37; Fortunata per me, 5vv, B.2, ed. F. Boghen (London, 1922)

Gioite, O selve, O venti, 2vv, B.4, S 68; Giunt'è pur Lidia, 5vv, B.2; Intro nave dorata, 1v, B.3, S 19; La mia pallida faccia, 1v, B.4, S 60; Lasso io languisco e moro, 5vv, B.2; Non mi negate, ohimè, 1v, B.3, S 23; Non vi partite, 2vv, B.4, S 66; O bell'occhi, 1v, bc, 1621[15]; Occhi che sete, 2vv, B.3, S 34; O dolore, O ferita, 3vv, B.4, S 81; Ohimè, che fur, che sono, 1v, B.4, S 53; O mio cor, dolce mia vita, 1v, B.4, S 63; Oscure selve, 1v, B.4, S 52; Perche fuggi, 5vv, B.2; Perche spess'a veder, 5vv, B.2, ed. F. Boghen (London, 1922)

Quanto più sorda sete, 3vv, B.4, S 74; Qui dunque oimè, 5vv, B.2; S'à la gelata mia, 5vv, B.2; Se la doglia, 5vv, B.2, ed. F. Boghen (London, 1922); Se l'aura spira, 1v, B.3, S 26; Se l'onde, ohimè, 1v, B.3, S 14; Se lontana voi sete, 5vv, B.2; Se m'amate io v'adoro, 2vv, B.3, S 31; Signor, c'ora fra gli-ostri, 1v, B.3, S 1; S'io miro in te, 5vv, B.2; So ch'aveste, 5vv, B.2; Soffrir non posso, 2vv, B.4, S 72; Son ferito, son morto, 1v, B.4, S 65; Ti lascio, anima mia, 1v, B.4, S 56; Troppo sotto due stelle, 1v, B.3, S 20; Tu pur mi fuggi, 5vv, B.2; Vanne, O carta amorosa, 1v, B.4, S 46; Vezzosissima filli, 5vv, B.2; Voi partite mio sole, 1v, B.3, S 25; Voi partite mio sole, 1v, B.4, S 59

BIBLIOGRAPHY

CATALOGUES AND BIBLIOGRAPHIES

SartoriB [1952, 2/1968]; *VogelB*

G. Gaspari: *Catalogo della biblioteca del Liceo musicale di Bologna* (Bologna, 1890–1905/*R*1961; 1943/*R*1970)

LETTERS

1. 25 June 1608, from Milan, not holograph (MS, *GB-Lcm*)
2. 26 June 1608, from Milan (MS, *US-NYpm*)
3. 29 July 1608, from Milan (MS, *D-Mbs*); transcr. and facs. in Cametti (1908), facing p.709, and in Abbiati (1941), 341
4. 1 July 1609, from Rome (MS, *GB-Lcm*) [dated in catalogue as 1 Dec 1609; see fig.6 above, p.102]
5. 15 July 1609, from Rome, ? in private collection; cited in Casimiri (1937 and 1942); frags. transcr. from a Berlin auction catalogue of 1930 in Casimiri (1942)

EitnerQ cites a letter of October 1609 in *GB-Lcm*; ?no.4 above

Ronga (1930), 297, cited a letter of 1609 in the library of the Sacred Harmonic Society whose collection went to *GB-Lcm* in 1883; this too is probably no.4

6. 19 September 1609, from Rome (MS, *I-FEd* Archivio Bentivoglio)
7. 13 December 1614, from Rome (MS, *I-MAs*)
8. 16 May 1615, from Rome (MS, *I-MAs*)
9. 5 September 1615, from Rome (MS, *I-MAs*); quoted and trans. in Hammond (1983), 347–8, n.24; quoted in *RIM*, xviii (1983), 210
10. 4 June 1624, from Rome (MS, *I-MOs*); transcr. and Fr. trans. in Prunières (1931)

Benvenuti (1931), 27, cited two letters in *I-MAs* (probably nos.7 and 8 above), one in London (? no.4) and one in Berlin (? no.5)

17TH-CENTURY DOCUMENTS

G. Diruta: *Il transilvano* (Venice, 1593–1609/*R*1978); ed. in BMB, 2nd ser., no.132 (n.d.)

A. Banchieri: *L'organo suonarino* (Venice, 1605, rev. 4/1638/*R*1969)

——: *Conclusioni nel suono dell'organo* (Bologna, 1609/*R*1968)

A. Superbi: *Apparato degli uomini illustri di Ferrara* (Ferrara, 1620)

A. Piccinini: *Intavolatura di liuto, et di chitarrone* (Bologna, 1623/*R* and transcr. 1962)

V. Giustiniani: *Discorso sopra la musica de' suoi tempo* (MS, 1628); Eng. trans., MSD, ix (1962), 63ff

B. Grassi: preface to A.9 (see Works and *SartoriB*)

A. Banchieri: *Lettere armoniche* (Bologna, 1628), 63

S. Bonini: *Prima parte de' discorsi e regole sopra la musica* (MS, n.d.); extracts in A. de la Fage: *Essais de diphtérographie musicale* (Paris, 1864); ed. M. A. Bonino (Provo, Utah, 1979)
W. Schonsleder: *Architectonice musices universalis* (Ingolstadt, 1631), 37; (2/1684)
M. Mersenne: *Harmonicorum libri* (Paris, 1635), ii, 109
A. Maugars: *Response faite à un curieux sur le sentiment de la musique d'Italie* [letter of 1 Oct 1639], ed. E. Thoinan (Paris, 1865/*R*1965)
P. Della Valle: *Della musica dell'età nostra* [letter of 10 Jan 1640], repr. in G. B. Doni: *Lyra Barberina*, ii, ed. A. F. Gori (Florence, 1763), 252f, and in A. Solerti: *Le origini del melodramma* (Turin, 1903/*R*1969), 158
G. B. Doni: letter of 20 July 1640 to M. Mersenne; extracts transcr. in Pirro (1925), 48
A. Vincenti: preface to A.13 (see Works and *SartoriB*)
G. B. Doni: *De praestantia musicae veteris* [before 1647], in G. B. Doni: *Lyra Barberina*, i, ed. A. F. Gori (Florence, 1763), 97
G. Scipione: letter dated 1652, pr. in *SartoriB*, 414
L. Battiferri: letter dated 1669, pr. in *SartoriB*, 456
L. Penna: *Li primi albori musicali*, iii (Bologna, 1672), 6; (4/1684/*R*1969, 5/1696)
A. Libanori: *Ferrara d'oro imbrunito* (Ferrara, 1665–74)
F. Fontana: letter dated 1677, pr. in *SartoriB*, 483f
A. Liberati: *Lettera scritta . . . in risposta ad una del Signor Ovidio Persapegi, 1684* (Rome, 1685); extract repr. in Gaspari, i, 85
F. Gasparini: *L'armonico pratico al cimbalo* (Venice, 1708), 14

BIOGRAPHY AND HISTORICAL STUDIES

BurneyH; *EitnerQ*; *GerberNL*; *HawkinsH*
G. Bentivoglio: *Memorie* [and letters], Biblioteca rara, ed. G. Daelli, xxxiii (Milan, 1864), 24
A. W. Ambros: *Geschichte der Musik*, iv (Leipzig, 1878), 435, 438; (rev. 3/1909 by H. Leichtentritt), 710, 715
F. X. Haberl: 'Giovanni Francesco Anerio', *KJb*, i (1886), 51
——: 'Hieronymus Frescobaldi', *KJb*, ii (1887), 67
——: introduction to *Collectio Musices Organicae ex operibus Hieronymi Frescobaldi* (Leipzig, 1889)
A. Solerti: *Ferrara e la corte estense nella seconda metà del decimosesto secolo* (Città di Castello, 1891, 2/1900)
M. Seiffert: *Geschichte der Klaviermusik* (Leipzig, 1899)
A. Solerti: *Musica, ballo e drammatica alla corte medicea dal 1600 al 1637* (Florence, 1905/*R*1968), 196
N. Bennati, ed.: *Ferrara a Girolamo Frescobaldi* (Ferrara, 1908)
A. Cametti: 'Girolamo Frescobaldi in Roma', *RMI*, xv (1908), 701–52

A. Pirro: 'Frescobaldi et les musiciens de la France et des Pays-Bas', *BSIM*, iv (1908), 1127

F. Waldner: 'Zwei Inventorien aus dem 16. u. 17. Jahrhundert', *SMw*, iv (1916), 128

G. Benvenuti: 'Noterella circa tre fughe attribuite al Frescobaldi', *RMI*, xxvii (1920), 133

A. Pirro: *Les clavecinistes* (Paris, 1925)

——: 'L'art des organistes', *EMDC*, II/ii (1926), 1250

A. Cametti: 'Girolamo Frescobaldi, sunta bio-bibliografico', *Bollettino bibliografico musicale*, ii/11 (1927), 1

L. Ronga: *Girolamo Frescobaldi* (Turin, 1930)

G. Benvenuti: 'Frescobaldiana', *Bollettino bibliografico musicale*, vi (1931), no.2, p.16; no.3, p.15

H. Prunières: 'Une lettre inédite de Frescobaldi', *ReM* (1931), no.119, p.232

R. Casimiri: 'Girolamo Frescobaldi, autore di opere vocali sconosciuti ad otto voci', *NA*, x (1933), 1–31

H. Prunières: 'Les musiciens du cardinal Antonio Barberini', *Mélanges de musicologie offerts a M. Lionel de la Laurencie* (Paris, 1933), 117

G. Frotscher: *Geschichte des Orgel-Spiels und der Orgel-Komposition* (Berlin, 1935–6, enlarged 3/1966)

R. Casimiri: 'Tre "Girolamo Frescobaldi" coetanei negli anni 1606–1609', *NA*, xiv (1937), 1

W. Apel: 'Neapolitan Links between Cabezón and Frescobaldi', *MQ*, xxiv (1938), 419

F. Abbiati: *Storia della musica*, ii (Milan, 1941), 339ff; (rev. 2/1967–8)

R. Casimiri: 'Girolamo Frescobaldi e un falso autografo', *NA*, xix (1942), 130

F. Morel: *Girolamo Frescobaldi, organista di S Pietro di Roma* (Winterthur, 1945)

M. F. Bukofzer: *Music in the Baroque Era* (New York, 1947)

J. Hedar: *Dietrich Buxtehudes Orgelwerke* (Stockholm, 1951)

A. Machabey: *Girolamo Frescobaldi: la vie, l'oeuvre* (Paris, 1952)

M. Reimann: 'Frescobaldi, Girolamo', *MGG*

N. Fortune: 'Italian Secular Monody from 1600 to 1635: an Introductory Survey', *MQ*, xxxix (1953), 171

H. F. Redlich: 'Girolamo Frescobaldi', *MR*, xiv (1953), 262

M. Reimann: 'Zur Deutung des Begriffs Fantasia', *AMw*, x (1957), 253

R. Lunelli: *L'arte organaria del rinascimento in Roma* (Florence, 1958)

F. W. Riedel: *Quellenkundliche Beiträge zur Geschichte der Musik für Tasteninstrumente in der 2. Hälfte des 17. Jahrhundert* (Kassel, 1960)

L. Schierning: *Die Überlieferung der deutschen Orgel- und Klaviermusik aus der ersten Hälfte des 17. Jahrhunderts: eine quellenkundliche Studie* (Kassel, 1961)

W. Apel: 'Die handschriftliche Überlieferung der Klavierwerke Frescobaldis', *Festschrift Karl Gustav Fellerer* (Regensburg, 1962), 40

A. Cavicchi: 'Contributo alla bibliografia di Arcangelo Corelli', *Ferrara* (Ferrara, 1962) [incl. list of organists and *maestri di cappella* of the Accademia della Morte, Ferrara]

F. Haskell: *Patrons and Painters: Art and Society in Baroque Italy* (New York, 1963, 2/1971)

C. V. Palisca: 'Musical Asides in the Correspondence of Emilio de' Cavalieri', *MQ*, xlix (1963), 339

R. Jackson: *The Keyboard Music of Giovanni Maria Trabaci* (diss, U. of California, Berkeley, 1964)

L. E. Bartholomew: *Alessandro Raverij's Collections of Canzoni per sonare, Venice, 1608* (Fort Hays, Kansas, 1965) [incl. transcrs.]

A. Cavicchi: introduction to *L. Luzzaschi: Madrigali per cantare e sonare a uno, due e tre soprani* (*1601*), MMI, 2nd ser., ii (1965)

F. Hubbard: *Three Centuries of Harpsichord Making* (Cambridge, Mass., 1965)

W. Apel: *Geschichte der Orgel- und Klaviermusik bis 1700* (Kassel, 1967; Eng. trans., rev. 1972)

——: 'Solo Instrumental Music', *NOHM*, iv (1968), esp. 646ff

N. Fortune: 'Solo Song and Cantata', *NOHM*, iv (1968), 178, 182

A. Newcomb: 'Carlo Gesualdo and a Musical Correspondence of 1594', *MQ*, liv (1968), 409

F. W. Riedel: 'Der Einfluss der italienischen Klaviermusik des 17. Jahrhunderts auf die Entwicklung der Musik für Tasteninstrumente in Deutschland während der ersten Hälfte des 18. Jahrhunderts', *AnMc*, v (1968), 18

S. Bonta: 'The Uses of the *Sonata da Chiesa*', *JAMS*, xxii (1969), 54–84

B. Cannon: 'Music in the Archives of the Basilica of Santa Maria in Trastevere', *AcM*, xli (1969), 199

A. Curtis: *Sweelinck's Keyboard Music: a Study of English Elements in Seventeenth-century Dutch Composition* (Leiden, 1969)

C. Terni: 'Girolamo Frescobaldi a Firenze (1628–33)', *Paragone*, xx (1969), 3

R. Jackson: 'On Frescobaldi's Chromaticism and its Background', *MQ*, lvii (1971), 255

E. Darbellay: 'Peut-on découvrir des indications d'articulation dans la graphie des tablatures de clavier de Claudio Merulo, Girolamo Frescobaldi et Michel-Angelo Rossi?', *IMSCR*, xi *Copenhagen 1972*, 342

W. Kirkendale: *L'Aria di Fiorenza, id est il Ballo del Gran Duca* (Florence, 1972)
——: 'Franceschina, Girometta, and their Companions', *AcM*, xliv (1972), 181–235
F. Hammond: 'Musicians at the Medici Court in the Mid-seventeenth Century', *AnMc*, xiv (1974), 151
S. Reiner: 'La vag'Angioletta (and others)', *AnMc*, xiv (1974), 26–88
E. Darbellay: 'Liberté, variété et "affetti cantabili" chez Girolamo Frescobaldi', *RdM*, lxi (1975), 197–243
——: 'Un manuscrit frescobaldien à Genève', *L'organo*, xiii (1975), 49
J. M. Harper: *The Instrumental Canzonas of Girolamo Frescobaldi: a Comparative Edition and Introductory Study* (diss., U. of Birmingham, 1975)
L. F. Tagliavini: 'L'arte di "non lasciar vuoto lo strumento": appunti sulla prassi cembalistica italiana nel Cinque- e Seicento', *RIM*, x (1975), 360
S. Wollenberg: 'A Note on Three Fugues Attributed to Frescobaldi', *MT*, cxvi (1975), 133
F. Hammond: 'Girolamo Frescobaldi in Florence', *Essays in Honor of Myron P. Gilmore* (Florence, 1977)
A. Newcomb: 'Girolamo Frescobaldi, 1608–1615', *AnnM*, vii (1964–77), 111–58
J. Harper: 'Frescobaldi's Early Inganni and their Background', *PRMA*, cv (1978–9), 1
J. Ladewig: *Frescobaldi's 'Ricercari et canzoni franzese' (1615): a Study of the Contrapuntal Keyboard Idiom in Ferrara, Naples, and Rome, 1580–1620* (diss., U. of California, Berkeley, 1978)
A. Newcomb: 'Form and Fantasy in Wert's Instrumental Polyphony', *Studi musicali*, vii (1978), 85
F. Hammond: 'Girolamo Frescobaldi and a Decade of Music in Casa Barberini', *AnMc*, xix (1979), 94–124
A. Newcomb: 'Il modo di far fantasia: an Appreciation of Luzzaschi's Instrumental style', *Early Music*, vii (1979), 34
——: *The Madrigal at Ferrara, 1579–1597* (Princeton, NJ, 1980)
A. Silbiger: *Italian Manuscript Sources of Seventeenth Century Keyboard Music* (Ann Arbor, 1980)
——: 'The Roman Frescobaldi Tradition, c. 1640–1670', *JAMS*, xxxiii (1980), 42–87
R. Hudson: *Passacaglia and Ciaccona: from Guitar Music to Italian Keyboard Variations in the Seventeenth Century* (Ann Arbor, 1981)
J. Ladewig: 'Luzzaschi as Frescobaldi's Teacher: a Little-known Ricercare', *Studi musicali*, x (1981), 241
E. Darbellay: 'L'énigme de la première édition (1624) des *Capricci* de Girolamo Frescobaldi', *Canadian University Music Review*, iii (1982), 123–57

Bibliography

F. Hammond: *Girolamo Frescobaldi* (Cambridge, Mass., 1983)

[*International Frescobaldi Conference:*] *Madison 1983* [incl. papers by Annibaldi, Darbellay, Durante, Harper, Hill, Newcomb and others]

[*International Frescobaldi Conference:*] *Ferrara 1983* [incl. papers by Annibaldi, Fabbris, Newcomb and others]

E. Darbellay: 'New Light upon the Chigi Manuscripts through an Investigation of the *Aggiunta* (1637) to the First Book of Toccate by Girolamo Frescobaldi', *JAMS*, xxxvii (1984)

FRANCESCO CAVALLI

Thomas Walker

CHAPTER ONE

Life

I Early years

Francesco Cavalli was born in Crema on 14 February 1602. His father, Giovanni Battista Caletti (or Caletto, or Caletti di Bruno), was a composer and *maestro di cappella* at Crema Cathedral, probably from the late 1590s and certainly by 1604. According to a contemporary account of Lodovico Canobio (see Sforza Benvenuti, 1888), Pietro (or Pier) Francesco, to give the boy his fuller name, received his earliest instruction in music from his father and was an unusually gifted boy soprano; he probably sang in the cathedral choir. His sweetness of voice and musical accomplishment brought him to the notice of Federico Cavalli, Venetian governor of Crema from July 1614 to March 1616, who with some difficulty (if this is not an embellishment of Canobio) persuaded Caletti to let him take the boy to Venice at the end of his term of office.

Doubtless under the protection of Federico Cavalli (whose name he later adopted: see below), Francesco entered the *cappella* of St Mark's, Venice, on 18 December 1616, as a soprano with an annual salary of 80 ducats, and on 18 February 1617 he was formally presented to the doge (as P. F. Bruni). His voice must have broken almost at once, but he is not mentioned as a tenor until 1 February 1627 (as F. Caletto); on 1 January 1635 his salary was raised to 100 ducats. (The fact that he was a tenor puts paid to a legend of jealous rivalry with Cesti based on Salvator Rosa's remark in a letter of 30 November 1652 about Cesti's success 'alla barba del basso che li voleva dar il naso in culo'.)

II Years at St Mark's

During the first quarter-century of Cavalli's activity at St Mark's the music was directed by Monteverdi, with whom he clearly enjoyed a close association, whether or not he ever formally studied with him. Moreover, he was probably the editor of Monteverdi's posthumously published *Messa a 4 voci et salmi* (Venice, 1650), which includes his own six-voice *Magnificat* setting. Traces of his hand and indeed of his music – the bass line of the opening sinfonia of *Doriclea* – occur in the Venetian manuscript of *L'incoronazione di Poppea*, prepared about the same time. In the *cappella* of St Mark's he also had the company of the slightly older Giovanni Rovetta and several other singer–composers. The breadth of musical life at Venice in his youth can be glimpsed in Leonardo Simonetti's *Ghirlanda sacra* (*RISM* 1625²), an anthology of solo motets by 26 composers, most of them Venetian, which includes his first known work. He is described as organist at the church of SS Giovanni e Paolo, a more distinguished position perhaps than that of singer at St Mark's, though less well-paid. He received the appointment on 18 May 1620, at which time he was living in the house of the nobleman Alvise Mocenigo, and he was given a salary of 30 ducats a year (see Arnold, 1965). His duties were not all that demanding, but even so they must have conflicted with those at St Mark's and involved him in the common practice of paying a substitute. Like all those who could, he further supplemented his income by playing or singing at church feasts. His participation in the patron saint's day celebration at the Scuola di S Rocco in 1627 for 26 lire (about four ducats), his organization of music for Pentecost at the Chiesa dello Spirito Santo in 1637 and his intervention as organist at S Caterina in 1646 are the documented fragments of what was probably a wide-ranging 'freelance' activity, partly engaged in together with the *cappella* of St Mark's.

Cavalli was dismissed, or acknowledged to have resigned, from SS Giovanni e Paolo on 4 November 1630, having not played the organ there since the preceding Lent. Venice was at that time in the throes of plague, and the church was in quarantine; however his departure was not, as has been supposed, due to these circumstances (the plague did not arrive until June) but, probably, to another: his marriage on 7 January 1630 to Maria Sozomeno, niece of the Bishop of Pula and widow of a well-to-do Venetian, Alvise Schiavina. Maria brought a dowry of more than 1200 ducats, together with a considerable amount of land and other capital. This advantageous marriage gave Cavalli some degree of financial independence and may explain his disinclination to travel and his early willingness to invest in operatic ventures. Also from about this time he began to use the name of his first patron: his earliest surviving aria (in *RISM* 1634^7) is ascribed to 'Francesco Bruni detto il Cavalli', while the motet *O quam suavis* (in *RISM* 1645^3) is signed 'Francesco Cavalli', but in official documents the distinction between his real and assumed names was nearly always made as 'Francesco Caletti detto il Cavalli'.

Cavalli won the competition for the post of second

organist at St Mark's on 23 January 1639, following the death of G. P. Berti, and received a salary of 140 ducats a year, rising in stages to the maximum of 200 in 1653. It is not surprising that when Monteverdi died in 1643 the senior and much published Rovetta, rather than Cavalli, should receive the post of *maestro di cappella*, but Massimiliano Neri's appointment as first organist in 1644 is more puzzling: Cavalli was the principal organist throughout the period, whatever his title, for he received a higher salary than Neri, and his playing was much praised by visitors, associates and propagandists. In 1647 Paul Hainlein compared him to Frescobaldi, complaining that he was too rarely heard. Ziotti (1655) commented that 'truly in Italy he has no equal' as a singer, organist and composer; similar remarks occur in G. B. Volpe's collection of his uncle Rovetta's madrigals (1645), which is dedicated to him. The date traditionally given for his promotion to first organist – 11 January 1665 – must have been an administrative adjustment following Neri's departure.

III **Operas, 1639–59**

Cavalli's début as an opera composer occurred the day after his election as organist at St Mark's and only two seasons after the introduction to Venice of musical theatre for paying audiences. His role was at first that of investor and organizer as well as composer. He was co-signatory of an agreement to produce 'accademie in musica' at the Teatro S Cassiano, Venice's first opera house, entered into with the librettist Orazio Persiani, the singer Felicita Uga and the dancing-master Giovanni Battista Balbi on 14 April 1638 (Uga and Balbi had been working there already: see Morelli and Walker,

1972). The first fruit of their collaboration was the 'opera scenica' *Le nozze di Teti e di Peleo*. Although the group was soon disrupted by financial difficulties, Cavalli wrote eight more operas for S Cassiano during the next decade. His only digression was in 1642, when he composed the 'favola' *Amore innamorato* for the Teatro S Moisè, where he again acted as some sort of impresario (see Pirrotta, 1966). Most of his operas during the 1640s were settings of librettos by Giovanni Faustini, beginning with *La virtù de' strali d'Amore* (1642) and *Egisto* (1643). *Egisto* enjoyed wide success as part of the repertory of travelling companies, which were instrumental in the spread of opera through Italy on the organizational model of the *commedia dell'arte*; it was even performed in Paris (1646) and possibly at Vienna (the only evidence for a performance is the presence of a score there). More successful still was Cavalli's setting of G. A. Cicognini's libretto *Giasone* (1649), with *Orontea* (also to a text by Cicognini, music by Cesti) the most enduringly popular opera in 17th-century Italy. They were the first works to turn completely to complex, fast-paced action and comic dexterity in place of the sophisticated atmosphere of Venetian literary academies that clung to opera in the 1640s.

Cavalli's activity in the 1650s reflects the many facets of the development of public opera more than any individual initiative. When Faustini took an interest in the Teatro S Apollinare in 1650, he followed him there, composing four operas in two years. After Faustini's death in December 1651, he worked for the Teatro SS Giovanni e Paolo, partly in association with the librettist Nicolò Minato, who was also his lawyer. In 1658–9 both were at the Teatro S Cassiano, which had been

8. Autograph MS containing the revision of the aria 'Se tal'or bramare il vedo' from Act 3 scene xiv of Cavalli's opera 'Hipermestra', composed 1654

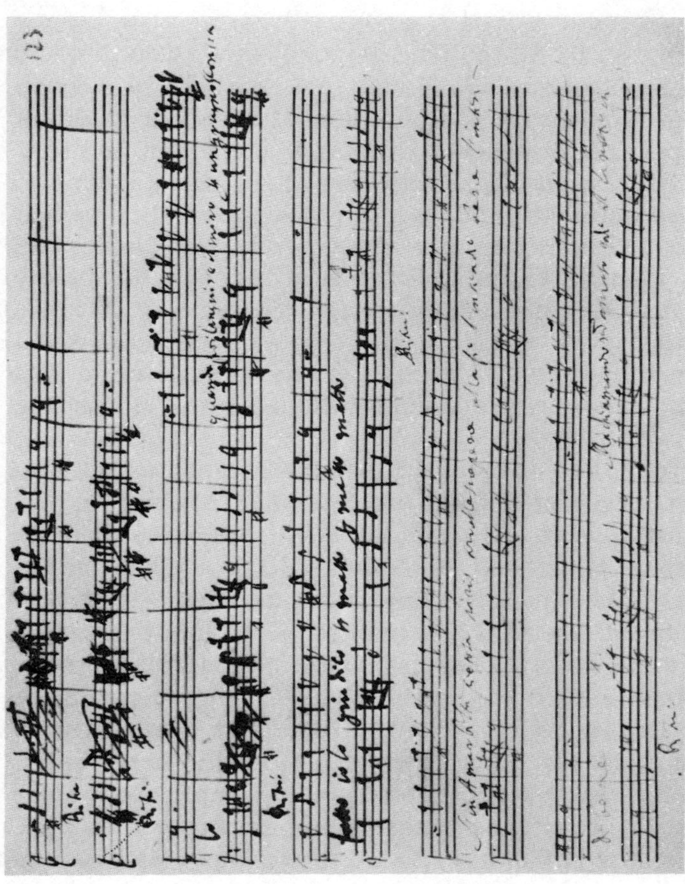

taken over by Marco Faustini, Giovanni's elder brother and another of Cavalli's lawyers. With Balbi, Cavalli contributed to the implantation of a regular tradition of opera performances at Naples, where in 1650 and 1651 *Didone*, *Giasone* and *Egisto* were staged, and a version of *L'incoronazione di Poppea*, in whose preparation he had a part. *Veremonda* was probably written for Naples and was given there on 21 December 1652, shortly before its first Venetian performance. In general Cavalli's works (above all *Egisto*, *Giasone*, *Xerse* and *Erismena*) were a mainstay of the repertory as opera gained a firm footing even in many smaller Italian towns during the 1650s and 1660s.

From 1647 until his death Cavalli rented a house on the Grand Canal from one Sebastian Michiel for 108 ducats a year. His wife died in 1652; they had no children. By her will, probated on 16 September, she left nearly all her property to him and testified to his zeal in caring for her family, including her children by her first marriage. In losing her Cavalli lost not only his marriage partner but also, it would seem, his principal music copyist (see Jeffery, 1980). Most of the operas written specifically for other cities date from the next period, and he may have considered seeking employment away from Venice after his release from family responsibilities, though he apparently did not travel then. As has been mentioned, *Veremonda* was performed at Naples at the end of 1652. In 1653 *Orione* was given at Milan to celebrate the election of Ferdinand IV, King of the Romans; the libretto had originally been offered to the Teatro S Moisè, Venice, in 1642 (see Pirrotta, 1966), but the music is certainly of the 1650s. *Hipermestra* was composed for Florence at the instance of Cardinal Gian

Carlo de' Medici; although it was used to celebrate the birth of the Spanish infante in 1658, Cavalli had sent the score in the autumn of 1654. Gian Carlo's patronage is confirmed in the dedication of the first of Cavalli's two publications, *Musiche sacre* (1656), which alluded to 'other compositions' already commissioned.

IV **Visit to France**

Following the Treaty of the Pyrenees between France and Spain (1659), the French prime minister, Cardinal Mazarin, laid plans for the celebration of the marriage of Louis XIV to Maria Theresia, daughter of the King of Spain, which would not hesitate to 'jetter l'argent par les fenêtres' in order to astound all Europe. So that he could stage the grandest possible spectacle he sent for the well-known Italian architect Gaspare Vigarani and commissioned him to build a large theatre in the Tuileries. Still in line with his long-standing cultural politics, he decided to mount an Italian opera with the aid of imported musicians. At the suggestion of Atto Melani, Cavalli was asked to compose it, but he reacted with some hesitation. In his letter of 22 August 1659 to the superintendent of Italian artists, Francesco Buti, he demurred on the grounds of age, obligation and aversion to travel; reduction of the original high salary offer was also a factor, perhaps the principal one. Buti proposed Cesti as a substitute, but Mazarin successfully used the French ambassador to Venice to secure Cavalli's acceptance, intervening with the procurators of St Mark's to ensure that his position as organist would be held for him and his salary paid even during his absence. The affair was not resolved until March 1660, but on 25 January the ambassador had a *Te Deum* sung at the church of SS Giovanni e Paolo in celebration of the French victory. Cavalli led it and was doubtless also its composer.

Cavalli left for France in April or May 1660 with an entourage of five, including two singers from the St Mark's *cappella*, the soprano Giovanni Caliari (or Calegari) and the tenor Giovanni Antonio Poncelli, and a boy, Giacomo da Murano, who may have been his copyist. On the way they visited the court at Innsbruck, where on 5 June a payment was recorded for the gift to Cavalli of 'guldne und silberne Trinkgeschirr' (the 'Pellicone d'argento indorato in forma di Struzzo' which he left to one of his executors). They may also have stayed at Munich, for it has been claimed (see Doglioni, 1671 edn.) that Cavalli was called to the Bavarian court. In July they arrived at Paris to find the theatre far from ready.

Cavalli spent nearly two years in Paris and must have been musically active throughout, but he left little trace of his presence; one French musician whose acquaintance he made was François Roberday, to whom he gave a fugue subject in August 1660. Beginning on 22 November *Xerse* was given as an interim measure in a temporary theatre built in the great picture gallery of the Louvre. A notable change from the Venetian version was the brutal octave transposition of the title role into the baritone range; the original three acts were redistributed into five and supplied with *entrées de ballet* by Lully. Accounts of the performance say nothing particularly good or bad about the music and in that respect are typical of 17th-century descriptions of opera, even in Italy. Cavalli probably composed the celebratory opera, *Ercole amante*, on Buti's libretto during his first 12 months in France. Mazarin's death on 9 March 1661 spelt the beginning of the end of Italian cultural prominence at the court, and the opera might not have been performed at all had not so much money already been spent on it. A supposed conspiracy against the Italian artists may have sabotaged Vigarani's machinery; but if Cavalli's music was not appreciated when *Ercole amante* was first performed on 7 February 1662, it was because no one could hear it, owing to the theatre's bad acoustics. The Venetian ambassador Grimani reported that 'The music was very fine and fitting; because of the vastness of the theatre it could not be enjoyed, but at the rehearsals at Mazarin's palace it always came off very well and to the complete satisfaction of the king and the court'. The spectacle lasted six hours and again included ballets by Lully, in which the king, queen and others of the court danced: little wonder that these received most of the attention in contemporary accounts.

V Last years in Venice

The last performance of *Ercole amante* took place on 6 May 1662, and by the summer, having meanwhile visited his birthplace, Cavalli was again in Venice, where he resumed his duties as organist. The fame that his visit to France gave him is indicated in the laudatory dedication to him (together with the other chief musicians of St Mark's) of Bonifazio Graziani's *Sacri concerti* (1668). Cavalli had left behind in Venice an unfulfilled contract for operas with Marco Faustini, but in a letter of 8 August he declared that he had left France resolved never to work for the theatre again. This statement has been interpreted as disillusionment over the reception of *Ercole amante*. It may just as well reflect his large financial reward from the French court (including a diamond ring 'bizzarramente e gentilmente lavorato': see Sforza Benvenuti, 1888), which would have freed him from any necessity to earn his living by the composition of operas, had he so chosen. He proposed to Faustini a Venetian performance of *Ercole amante*, but this came to nothing.

In the event, Cavalli set three more librettos by Minato, the first for Faustini at the Teatro SS Giovanni e Paolo, the others for the Teatro S Salvatore, in which, together with Minato, he seems to have had a financial interest. Two other operas composed for Venice were never performed: *Eliogabalo*, intended for Carnival 1668, and *Massenzio*, composed for Carnival 1673, were scrapped during rehearsals, the former possibly and the latter certainly because Cavalli's arias were not liked. *Coriolano*, his last new opera to be performed, was again a celebratory piece, written for the Farnese theatre at Piacenza (1669); he probably did not attend the performance. After his stay in France his life centred more on St Mark's than on the theatres. On 20 November 1668 he succeeded Rovetta as *maestro di cappella* and remained in the post until his death, confirming his attention to church music by a second publication, the eight-voice *Vesperi* of 1675; an inventory of the archive of St Mark's in 1720 records several other works now lost (see Caffi, 1854–5).

Cavalli died in Venice on 14 January 1676 and was buried in the church of S Lorenzo beside his sisters Diambra Caterina and Cecilia and his wife Maria and her uncle. He made provision for an elaborate requiem mass celebration to be put together for his funeral by the new *maestro di cappella* or, if one had not been selected, the *vicemaestro* (in either case this would have been Natale Monferrato). Twice a year thereafter Cavalli's own Requiem for two choirs was to be sung by the *cappella* and canons of St Mark's. He similarly combined piety with benefit by stipulating that the daily Mass paid for from his estate be celebrated by Caliari, whom he had raised and trained. His will and property inventory show that he was assiduous, if conservative, in building an estate. All his life he had fought off indebtedness and invested cautiously, even rejecting his father's estate in 1642 as being too encumbered by debts. He left more than 6000 ducats in interest-bearing accounts at the Venetian mint and salt office (about 1670 the doge's annual provision was just over 14,000 ducats, the entire budget for the *cappella* of St Mark's 5000), a good deal more land than he began with and an endless list of valuable objects, including paintings by his (unidentified) brother and a saucer with his coat-of-arms. A most important item was his collection of opera scores, which he gave to Caliari: shortly afterwards it passed to the Contarini collection (Biblioteca Nazionale Marciana, Venice), which now includes all his surviving operas. He had no direct heirs; after remembering friends and patrons he left the residuum of his estate to the nuns of S Lorenzo, with whom he and his wife had long had close relations. Two in particular, Fiorenza Grimani and Betta Mocenigo, he described as his pupils; both were children of noble houses with which he had been closely connected. Besides these two and Caliari and another youth whom he had taken on on a similar basis in the 1640s (see Morelli and Walker, 1972), his pupils included G. B. Volpe and Barbara Strozzi, who acknowledged her debt in her *Cantate*, op.2 (1651).

VI Reputation

Cavalli's growing fame and reputation in his later life and after his death were in contrast to his waning effectiveness as an opera composer. Visits by foreign musicians such as J. P. Krieger (1672) and possibly J. W. Franck were probably common in his old age. The survival of a score of *Erismena* in English translation argues that his reputation even reached England. Benedetto Ferrari, in justifying his own application at an advanced age for the post of *maestro di cappella* at Modena (1674) noted that Cavalli, who was then *maestro di cappella* at Venice, 'in età cadente fa colle sue virtù risplendere quella reggia' ('even in his failing years makes the republic shine with his virtues').

Publication of the first chronology of Venetian opera by his erstwhile collaborator Cristoforo Ivanovich (1681) made Cavalli seem an even more central figure than he was, for Ivanovich attributed to him most of the anonymous works from the first 15 years of public opera, and many of these attributions were taken up in later chronicles (Walker, 1972). In the 18th century he was on the margins of music historiography. Walther did not mention him; Mattheson (1740), who reported Krieger's visit to Venice, wished for him a more prominent place in lexica, and Scheibe (1745), who owned the score of one of his operas, praised the bold and affective character of his recitative. Burney judged *Erismena*, whose score (not the English-language one) he borrowed from 'Dr. Bever, the civilian', to be 'so deficient in poetical and musical merit that no perfection of performance could render it palatable' and full of airs which were 'psalmodic, monotonous and dull'. Fétis included several arias by Cavalli in his historical concerts in

Paris from 1832, and Vincent Novello gave him some attention in a lecture at the London Institute in 1840. The first critical treatment of his music was by Ambros (1878), who likened his position to that of Josquin; appreciation developed largely through the writings of Goldschmidt, Kretzschmar, Prunières and Wellesz.

Critical study and performance of Cavalli's music has largely followed on that of Monteverdi in both secular and sacred spheres. *Didone* was performed in Florence on the 350th anniversary of his birth in 1952. A seminal stage in the revival of his operas was the series of popular and controversial reconstructions (of *Ormindo*, *Calisto* and *Egisto*) by Raymond Leppard from 1967, the first two initially for Glyndebourne.

CHAPTER TWO

Works

I Operas

Cavalli produced music for the theatre during most of his working life. He composed nearly 30 operas for Venetian houses, and they run from the tentative beginnings of public opera to the firm establishment of Venice as a centre whose operas were imitated by, and exported to, cities throughout Italy. His works are central to that process of dissemination (see the detailed account by Bianconi in *DBI*, also Bianconi and Walker, 1975), and as only three operas by other composers (Monteverdi and Cesti) survive complete from before the late 1650s, his operas offer the only continuous view of musical style in Venetian opera over two decades. The absence of a development in his musical language has sometimes been overstated, but stability weighs more heavily than change. Such obvious external differences between operas as the number and placing and even the form of arias or the use of refrains, duets and choruses come directly or indirectly from the structure of the poem. Since Cavalli was first and foremost an evaluator and inventive translator of the affective moment, even differences of musical mood between operas (the lugubriousness of *Didone*, the rustic playfulness of *Calisto*) can be traced to the poetry.

Most free verse is set as recitative. This presents a more or less animated voice part over a slowly moving bass, usually giving no marked sensation of metre, though consistently notated in duple. However inventive, it rarely shows a clear melodic form. It usually consists of a succession of phrases, each ending in a clearly formulated and carefully approached cadence. Often the phrases are grouped into tonally closed paragraphs, corresponding to coherent sections of poetry. Another common technique of organization in the early operas is a long, slowly descending bass, over which any amount of melodic thread can be spun (e.g. *Gli amori d'Apollo e di Dafne*, Act 1 scene iii). The categories of gesture in Cavalli's recitative are by and large those of Monteverdi, but he handled them in a less extreme manner. If there are standard reactions to excited exclamation (rapid note values, word repetition) and to pathos (slow, descending lines, chromatic leading, usually of the bass), the details are always worked out afresh. His rhetoric is also responsive to syntax (questions, paragraphs) and sensitive and resourceful in the face of surprise. A casual madrigalism and symbolism of idea inform many passages (see ex.1, in particular at 'pianti', 'mi fuggi repente' and 'schernirmi'). Grosser instances of word-painting cover a range of emotion but are most commonly associated with passage-work (see ex.2).

In the later operas, rapid dialogue accounts for much of the poetry. This is reflected in the recitative primarily by faster cadence formulae. The semibreve and minim cadences that abound in operas of the 1640s are far outnumbered by those involving crotchets and quavers or in which the resolution of appoggiatura and dominant is left to the continuo (see ex.3). In some of the settings of librettos by Minato (*Orimonte*, *Xerse*, *Artemisia*)

Ex.1 *Gli amori d'Apollo e di Dafne,* Act 3 scene iv

Ex.2 *Gli amori d'Apollo e di Dafne*, Act 1 scene iv
Dell' al - ma li - ber - tà
le ve - - re lo - di.

much of the recitative dialogue is set out in open score, to accommodate overlapping between the parts. Lively argument is sometimes supported by a chain of 5ths in the harmony (e.g. *Scipione affricano*, Act 3 scene xviii).

Nearly all the recitative is 'semplice', accompanied only by continuo. Exceptional moments, rarely more than one per opera, may be underscored by string accompaniment in sustained chords, usually with no parts in the violin clef. In Zelemina's plea 'Invitta Veremonda' (*Veremonda*, Act 3 scene vii) and Misena's false quotation of Periandro 'Prendi quella corona' (*Eritrea*, Act 3 scene x) the two upper parts are called 'viole': it is not known whether these are 'da braccio' or 'da gamba'. Nerea's plea to Pluto (*Rosinda*, Act 1 scene vii) is a loosely strophic setting of two quatrains with a normal ritornello after the first, and Giuliano's exchange with

Eritea 'Deh manda quei singulti' (*Eliogabalo*, Act 2 scene iii) is a varied strophic recitative with four-part string accompaniment. Ercole's plaint 'Ma l'atroce mia doglia' (*Ercole amante*, Act 5) is exceptional in including violins in the five-part string ensemble, perhaps because the role is for bass.

In *Le nozze di Teti e di Peleo*, *Didone* and *Gli amori d'Apollo e di Dafne*, arioso passages – that is, recitative verse set lyrically – are infrequent. These passages usually involve either a shift to triple metre or a 'walking' bass in crotchets. In *Didone*, for example, the few ariosos are nearly all of the second type. From *La virtù de'*

strali d'Amore onwards, and particularly in settings of librettos by Faustini, arioso plays a much larger part and lends greater fluidity to the later operas. Occasionally it responds to lines of contrasting metre, but mostly it is motivated by text meaning or situation. Many ariosos are settings of aphoristic final lines or couplets, others are madrigalesque in impulse, still others reflect outbursts, festive or pathetic. The gestural content of arioso is similar to, if perhaps more limited than, that of aria. Most are short and simple, though melismatic writing and text repetition are part of the equipment, and emphasis may be given by an instrumental sinfonia, usually based on the preceding vocal material, as in 'Tu lieto intanto vivi' (*La virtù de' strali d'Amore*, Act 1 scene iv) or the end of Lesbo's speech in *Eritrea*, Act 3 scene v, the musical style of which is barely elevated over that of the preceding recitative.

Most poetry other than recitative verse in Cavalli's librettos is strophic, and it is this kind of verse on which most pieces that the sources call arias are based. The first three operas have a great quantity of such verse (between 20 and 25 poems). A majority of these poems use the same metres as recitative (lines of seven and 11 syllables); they may have up to nine strophes. They are always set as some sort of musical unit, whatever the internal changes of metre, rhythm or melodic character. All of the earliest operas include recitative settings of strophic poems, usually with the melody, but not the bass line, varied between the strophes. Some have their stanzas separated by a ritornello, as Ascanio's 'Son figlio di Enea' (*Didone*, Act 1 scene ii). Strophic recitative is an old-fashioned procedure, and examples in Cavalli's later operas are rare. It is significant that as early as *Ormindo* such pieces are uttered by gods (Destiny, Fortune). The inclusion of one in the prologue to *Elena* is exceptional, and the piece from *Eliogabalo* mentioned above is a curiosity: the texts of both operas are considerably earlier than their musical settings.

Most of Cavalli's arias are in triple metre. This is particularly true of the first operas, for example *Gli amori d'Apollo e di Dafne*, which apart from strophic recitatives has only three arias in duple time. Brief recitative interruptions such as in 'Maladette le guerre' (*Doriclea*, Act 1 scene iv) are frequent, however; sometimes they prepare the triple-time settings of a gnomic final line or couplet, as in the last strophe of 'Giovanetta che tiene' (*Gli amori d'Apollo e di Dafne*, Act 1 scene i). Varied strophes in triple metre also occur in the early operas, for example 'Padre, ferma i passi e l'armi' from *Didone* (Act 1 scene i). How rooted the idiom of aria composition is in the style of Monteverdi can be seen clearly in Cavalli's earliest surviving aria, *Son ancor pargoletta* (*RISM* 1634[7]). As with arioso, the other most common movement in aria writing is the 'walking' bass; it too can yield to recitative or alternate with triple metre in the same piece.

There is less plain strophic poetry in Faustini's librettos than in most others that Cavalli set before or after. By way of compensation they have many groups of lines of distinct poetic metre (four, five, six or eight syllables), which are generally composed in arioso fashion. These librettos also abound in refrains. Cavalli usually set them as large and highly articulated aria forms, complete with ritornello and sometimes with contrasts of musical metre, for example 'Udite, amanti' (*Doriclea*, Act 1 scene vi) or 'D'haver un consorte io son risoluta' (*Calisto*, Act 2 scene xiv). Other examples of dramatically or textually motivated structures larger and more elaborate than the simple aria are the several alternating pairs of strophes in *Egisto* ('Hor che l'Aurora', Act 1 scene i; 'E grato il penare', Act 3 scene i; 'Amanti, sperate', followed by a duet, Act 3 scene x); the prison scene in *Ormindo* Act 3 (also used in *Erismena*: see Rosand, 1975); the large duet sequence in Act 1 of *Orimonte*; the double varied strophic setting of *capitoli sdruccioli* at the beginning of Act 3 of *Veremonda* ('Né meste più, né più dolenti siano'), whose concluding duet is freely based on both sets of strophes; and the comic aria 'A chi voler fiori' from *Xerse* (Act 2 scene i), whose first lines punctuate the following dialogue in the manner of a refrain.

Cavalli's aria style, while essentially syllabic, makes use of melismatic flourishes; these are more often than not madrigalesque image portrayals, but their real function is increasingly that of 'bel canto' writing. Aria poems are set one or two lines at a time, with some kind of cadence but not necessarily a rhythmic hiatus at the end of each unit. Phrases tend to be asymmetrical and irregular in length and cannot in general be referred to preconceived patterns. The relationship of musical rhythm to poetic metre is highly variable. It is least predictable in settings of *versi sciolti* (lines of seven and 11 syllables), whereas it is almost tediously regular in the six-syllable verse much used by Faustini (see ex.4). A related special case are the five-syllable *sdruccioli* (lines with antepenultimate accent) widely used for rage, terror or invocation in 17th-century opera. The best-known example is Medea's incantation scene 'Dell'antro magico' (*Giasone*, Act 1 scene xv), but a related piece

Ex.4 Eritrea
(a) Act 1 scene ii
Dol - cis - si-me e ca- re fa - vil - le d'a-mor.
(b) Act 1 scene iv
Go - de - re fru - i - re con - ten- ti ci fà
(c) Act 1 scene vii
Oh oh bel- la fa-cel- la de l'a - ni-ma mi - a
(d) Act 2 scene x
Spe-ran-za spe-ran-za non gio-va non gio-va

occurs already in *Didone* (Ecuba's aria 'Tremulo spirito', Act 1 scene vii); on the margin of this category is 'Grandini, turbini' from *Orimonte* (Act 3 scene xi). The entire roles of Pane, Silvano and Satiretto in *Calisto* are composed of *sdruccioli*; the rustic comedy of this well-established poetic tradition is heightened by Cavalli's setting, which emphasizes the rhythmic peculiarity.

The operatic lament has its principal model in Monteverdi's *Arianna*; another model for Cavalli was the intervening lament repertory using stepwise descending ostinatos. Nearly all his operas include at least one lament, almost invariably in triple metre ('L'alma fiacca svanì', *Didone*, Act 1 scene iv, is exceptionally in duple) and the minor mode. Some are ostinato pieces, either chromatic ('Piangete, occhi dolenti', *Egisto*, Act 2 scene vi) or diatonic ('Al carro trionfale', *Statira*, Act 3 scene iv); 'Lasso io vivo e non ho vita' (*Egisto*, Act 2 scene i) has a descending tetrachord ritornello labelled 'passacalio'. Several have recitative interruptions ('Con infocati teli', *Doriclea*, Act 2 scene ii) or else dissolve into recitative ('Rivolgo altrove il piede', *Didone*, Act 2 scene ii). The straight ostinato went out of fashion in the 1650s (at least in Venice), and most of Cavalli's later pieces in this vein have a middle section in which the ostinato pattern is transposed to another key ('Misero cosi và', *Eliogabalo*, Act 1 scene xiii). Even many laments not actually using an ostinato begin with a descending bass line, simple or elaborated; one such is 'Ardo, sospiro e piango' (*Artemisia*, Act 1 scene xviii), which is also one of several with string accompaniment throughout. Pathetic chromaticism expressed either harmonically or melodically, rhythmically eccentric outbursts of passion and a sense of resignation conveyed by regularly cadencing phrases and descending lines are the common coin of his laments. Simple use of ostinato technique apart from the lament, such as in 'Vieni, vieni in questo seno' (*Rosinda*, Act 3 scene vi), is rare. 'Per me la vita' (*La virtù de' strali d'Amore*, Act 3 scene ii) uses a bass of the chaconne type in a traditional way, that of expressing carefree joy.

Cavalli responded less consistently to comedy than to pathos. Arias by comic characters may make their point by assertive repetition, as in 'Pazze voi che sdegnate' (*Egisto*, Act 1 scene vi), or, as in 'Che città' (*Ormindo*, Act 1 scene iii), by jagged rhythms taken over in the ritornello. Trivial melodies of regular phrase length, and jaunty use of the 'walking' bass (e.g. 'O sagace chi sa', *Ormindo*, Act 2 scene vi), are also associated with humorous contexts. Occasionally he used intentionally

Ex.5 *Eritrea*, Act 3 scene v

bizarre gestures, as in the falling-3rd cadences of 'Fleria la mia diletta' (*Orimonte*, Act 1 scene xii) or the image-motivated cross-rhythms of 'Sempre garisce e grida' (*Eritrea*, Act 3 scene v: see ex.5).

'Sempre garisce e grida' is representative of a formal

expansion and increase in range of gesture that mark his aria style from the early 1650s. Arias in duple metre (though still a minority) are more numerous than before, and they use means other than the 'walking' bass. Several pieces from *Oristeo* onwards, such as 'Quell'amante che vuole' (Act 2 scene xvi), have basses in quaver motion; the semiquaver bass line of 'Che non può lo stral d'Amore' (*Elena*, Act 2 scene xiii) is a device more often used by a younger generation of composers. Also in line with more modern taste are the motto openings of 'Bel sembiante' (*Rosinda*, Act 3 scene xi) and particularly 'Bella fede, ove sei gita' (*Veremonda*, Act 1 scene xi). Something of the same kind, in a more varied gestural context, is found in 'Vada pur dotto marito', from the same scene of *Veremonda*. The fleet vocality of 'La bellezza è un don fugace' (*Xerse*, Act 2 scene ix) is indicative of the increase in passage-work; less ostentatious but equally characteristic is the aria in triple metre 'Zeffiretti placidetti' from *Artemisia* (Act 1 scene xiii). *Artemisia* also includes the only example in Cavalli of an 'aria in eco' ('Fortunato, chi piegato', Act 2 scene vi), a double reducing echo added (after the fact) to phrase endings. There runs throughout the operas a tendency to use similar ideas in successive pieces, for example the relationship in *La virtù de' strali d'Amore* between 'Per me la vita' and 'Tu là di Cocito', which occur within a few pages of each other. It is probably less a quest for unity than a quirk of mind.

The librettos of Cavalli's later operas contain large numbers of two-strophe aria poems (*Scipione affricano*, for example, has 35), and they mostly fall into a few metrical patterns. They are usually set as *ABB′* forms (transposed and often otherwise modified repetition of

9. 'Camera' for Cavalli's 'Hipermestra' (Act 1 scene ix) designed by Ferdinando Tacca, Florence, Teatro degli Immobili, 1658: engraving by S. degli Alli from the libretto

the music for the final line or couplet) or as *ABA* (elementary da capo arias). In many of his arias from the last three dramas by Minato the musical rhythm rests directly on that of the poetry, with results that are not very striking. At the same time most of them are less obviously dance-like than those of some younger composers, and this may account for the failure of his last two Venetian operas to reach performance. The contrast of style is particularly evident between his *Eliogabalo* and the opera of the same title by Boretti which replaced it.

The amount of duet writing varies greatly from opera to opera, according to the structure of the libretto; it is concentrated in the dramas by Faustini. Although there are examples of duet recitative (*La virtù de' strali d'Amore* has several), the vast majority of duets are in triple metre and in a lightly imitative style. A common procedure is to spin out the imitations over a bass line that moves predominantly in dotted semibreves, as in 'O luci belle' from *Eritrea* (Act 1 scene viii). Less usual, though not less interesting, is the intricately imitative binary movement of 'Aure trecce inanellate', which begins Act 2 of *Ormindo*. Pieces for larger solo ensembles are demanded less often by the librettos. They are largely extensions of duet technique. Choral writing in most operas is brief and incidental, for instance the shout of 'Viva' that greets Pompeo in Act 2 scene vi of *Pompeo magno*. For obvious reasons of circumstance it is very much more extensive in *Ercole amante*, which includes in 'Dall'occaso' (Act 5) a genuine four-part continuo madrigal. The choruses of the earliest operas, such as 'Al cinghiale' in *Didone* (Act 3 scene ii), are probably best seen in the light of an earlier concertato tradition that asserts itself in, for example, Landi's *La morte d'Orfeo* (1619).

The principal function of Cavalli's orchestra is to provide ritornellos before and/or after the strophes of arias. The music of the ritornello is nearly always related to that of the aria, tending to use the beginning of the vocal line if it precedes the aria or the melody of the final line or couplet if it follows it. The material is often varied and concentrated with respect to the aria. Ritornellos may have one, two or three phrases; the commonest type has two of roughly equal length, each based on a point of imitation and often using sequence.

In nearly all the operas (*Orimonte* is an exception) some arias have more elaborate accompaniment, either phrase by phrase in antiphonal fashion, over the voice throughout (particularly in laments and pieces of related mood), or some combination of the two. *Gli amori d'Apollo e di Dafne* has one such aria, *Pompeo magno* nine.

Sinfonias also form part of all the operas. If they are attached to ariosos they differ from ritornellos only in not being repeated. Those at the beginnings of operas or acts most commonly are in duple metre with a *grave* minim movement, though some (including those that introduce most of the later operas) have more than one movement and use triple metre as well. Those of *Gli amori d'Apollo e di Dafne* (halved note values), *Egisto* (last phrase) and *Didone* (merely repeated) are transformed into the ritornello of the prologue. More descriptive orchestral music, usually of an extremely simple and rhythmic character, is provided by the 'sinfonia navale' of *Didone*, the 'sinfonia in battaglia' of *La virtù de' strali d'Amore* (one of several battle pieces in

Cavalli's operas), the 'infernale' of *Ercole amante* and, much more striking, the 'ballo de' tori' of *Veremonda*. There are also elements of *stile concitato* in several works, either as an independent orchestral movement (*Doriclea*) or as accompaniment to recitative (*La virtù de' strali d'Amore*), aria (*Doriclea*) or chorus (*Eliogabalo*). Apart from an occasional corrente (*Le nozze di Teti e di Peleo*, *Gli amori d'Apollo e di Dafne*, *La virtù de' strali d'Amore*) and a few balli, the dance music called for by the librettos is either notated for continuo alone or missing altogether from the scores. The orchestra is laid out in five, less often four, parts in nearly all full fair-copy scores, but the musical skeleton consists of two violins and bass, the combination found in all Cavalli's autographs. Wind instruments may have been used in the very first operas and *Ercole amante*; otherwise his orchestra certainly consisted of (solo) strings and continuo (lutes, theorbos, harpsichords), though one piece in *Elena* seems to call for trumpets in A.

Expressive indications are very few and far between, but one does meet 'piano' (*Xerse*, which also has an aria 'cantata in misura larga'), 'adagio' (*Hipermestra*), 'affettuoso' (*Hipermestra*, *Doriclea*) and 'altiero' (*Doriclea*).

II Sacred works

Cavalli's relatively modest quantity of extant sacred music is probably only a small part of a continuous production throughout his career. It is mostly in the tradition of the large concerted works fundamental to St Mark's, well represented by the Gabrielis and Monteverdi. Cavalli's earliest surviving piece, the solo motet *Cantate Domino*, is almost indistinguishable in style from Monteverdi, but most of his later works deliberately avoid extremes of gesture, even though a sensitivity to the imagery of the text remains the rule.

The Marian antiphons from the *Musiche sacre* (1656) illustrate writing for a small number of voices (from two to five). They obey a largely syllabic style, relieved by a few conventional or madrigalesque melismas. The rests of 'suspiramus' in *Salve regina* and the falling figure on 'cadente' in *Alma Redemptoris mater* reveal a close kinship to the rhetoric of secular text-setting. The opening of *Salve regina* uses a quotation from plainchant. All make use of light contrapuntal development. Although plain recitative is not an essential part of the style, there are moments of declamation which approach it.

The *Messa concertata*, also from *Musiche sacre*, is Venetian festive music on a grand scale, conceived for two choruses with instrumental accompaniment. Massive but also airy in construction, it uses a variety of vocal combinations, solo against tutti and choir against choir, with many orchestral interpolations used to set off one section from another. Its sections in triple metre use a fairly narrow range of figures; those in duple metre are more varied, with some arresting tunes. The Gloria and Credo have mock-fugal conclusions; the Sanctus and Agnus Dei are brief, in accordance with Venetian usage (see Bonta, 1969). Only in a few places is solo ornamentation clearly demanded.

The three *Magnificat* settings from the *Vesperi* (1675) are also for double choir, though without explicit instrumental parts except for continuo. Block harmony outweighs imitative textures, and sections for full chorus outnumber those for a reduced number of voices. They are set verse by verse, with fairly regular alternation between choirs. In the same tradition is the Requiem which Cavalli prepared as his own memorial. Solemn and full of *prima prattica* counterpoint, it seems closer to the spirit of the early seicento than to that of the 1670s.

The six instrumental works from the 1656 print, indiscriminately designated 'sonata' and 'canzone', were doubtless intended for liturgical use (see Bonta, 1969). They are close to Giovanni Gabrieli in style, if harmonically more modern, and only rarely partake of the idiomatic writing already present in many ritornellos of Cavalli's later operas. In the larger works – those in eight, ten and 12 parts – the instruments are handled polychorally; several pieces are in four sections with identical second and fourth movements in triple metre (see Selfridge-Field, 1975).

WORKS

Numbers in right-hand margins denote references in the text.

OPERAS

152–67

Dates are generally those of printed librettos. Titles of arias in MS are indicative rather than exhaustive. All performed in Venice unless otherwise stated.

Work	References
Le nozze di Teti e di Peleo (O. Persiani), Teatro S Cassiano, 24 Jan 1639, *I-Vnm*	141, 156, 167
Gli amori d'Apollo e di Dafne (G. F. Busenello), Teatro S Cassiano, 1640, *Vnm*, lib first pubd 1656 in Busenello's works; facs. in H. M. Brown, ed.: *Italian Opera 1640–1770* (New York, 1978)	153, 154, 155, 156, 158, 166, 167
Didone (Busenello), Teatro S Cassiano, 1641, *Vnm*, lib first pubd 1656 in Busenello's works, scenario only pubd 1641	144, 151, 152, 156, 157, 158, 160, 161, 165, 166
Amore innamorato (plot by G. F. Loredan, poetry P. Michiel, rev. G. B. Fusconi), Teatro S Moisè, 1 Jan 1642, music lost	141
La virtù de' strali d'Amore (G. Faustini), Teatro S Cassiano, 1642, *Vnm*	141, 156, 157, 161, 163, 165, 166, 167
Egisto (Faustini), Teatro S Cassiano, 1643, *A-Wn*, *I-Vnm*	141, 144, 151, 158, 159, 160, 161, 166
Ormindo (Faustini), Teatro S Cassiano, 1644, *Vnm*; ed. R. Leppard (London, 1969)	151, 158, 159, 161, 165
Doriclea (Faustini), Teatro S Cassiano, 1645, *Vnm*	138, 158, 161, 167
Titone (Faustini), Teatro S Cassiano, 1645, music lost, probably by Cavalli	
Giasone (G. A. Cicognini), Teatro S Cassiano, 5 Jan 1648/9, *A-Wn*, *B-Bc* (2 modern copies), formerly *D-Hs* (according to catalogue, 1876), *GB-Ouf*, *I-Fn*, *MOe*, *Nc*, *Rvat* Chigi, *Sc*, *Vnm*, *P-La*; 11 arias *I-Nc*, aria Dall'antro magico, *GB-Lbm*; part ed. in PÄMw, xi (1883)	141, 144, 159
Euripo (Faustini), ? Teatro S Moisè, 1649, music lost, ? by Cavalli	
Orimonte (N. Minato), Teatro S Cassiano, 20 Feb 1650, *Vnm*; arias Se giovinetti lascivetti, Amanti miserelli, *Vc*	153, 159, 160, 162, 166
Oristeo (Faustini), Teatro S Apollinare, 1651, *Vnm*	163
Rosinda (Faustini), Teatro S Apollinare, 1651, *Vnm*	155, 161, 163
Calisto (Faustini), Teatro S Apollinare, 1651/2, *Vnm*; ed. R. Leppard (London, 1975)	151, 152, 158, 160
Eritrea (Faustini), Teatro S Apollinare, 1652, *Vnm*	155, 157, 160, 162, 165
Veremonda l'amazzone di Aragona (rev. by L. Zorzisto [G. Strozzi] of G. A. Cicognini's Celio, orig. perf. Florence, 1646), Naples, Teatro del Palazzo Reale, 21 Dec 1652; Venice, Teatro SS Giovanni e Paolo, 28 Jan 1652/3, *Vnm*; aria Nella nave del core, *F-Pa*	144, 155, 159, 163, 167
Orione (F. Melosio), Milan, June 1653, *Vnm*, R. Leppard's private collection, London	144
Ciro (G. C. Sorrentino, rev. ? A. Aureli), orig. perf. Naples with music by Francesco Provenzale; Cavalli composed changes for perf. at Venice, Teatro SS Giovanni e Paolo, 30 Jan 1653/4, *MOe*, *Vnm* (1665 version with addl music by Mattioli); arias La speranza è un dolce inganno, In mezo alle schiere, Amanti fuggite lasciva [cadente] beltà, *F-Pa*, *Pn*	
Xerse (Minato), Teatro SS Giovanni e Paolo, 12 Jan 1654 [probably 1655], *Pn*, *I-Rvat* Chigi, *Vnm*; arias, incl. Che barbara pietà, Sete pazzi innamorarvi, La donna caduta, *F-Pa*, *Pn*	144, 146, 153, 159, 163, 167
Statira principessa di Persia (Busenello), Teatro SS Giovanni e Paolo, 18 Jan 1655 [?1656], *I-Mc*, *Vnm*; arias *Nc*	160
Erismena (Aureli), Teatro S Apollinare, 1655 [probably 1656], *Vnm* (2 versions), score in T. Bever's private collection in 18th century according to Burney, score with Eng. text in J. S. Cox's private collection, Guernsey; arias Pazzi amanti, 1656[4]; Faville d'amore, Son spezzati le catene, *GB-Lbm*; Vaghe stelle, *T*	144, 150, 159
Artemisia (Minato), Teatro SS Giovanni e Paolo, 10 Jan 1656 [probably 1657], *I-Vnm*	153, 161, 163
Hipermestra (G. A. Moniglia), Florence, Teatro degli Immobili, 12 June 1658, composed 1654, *Vnm*	*142–3*, 144, *164*, 167
Antioco (Minato), Teatro S Cassiano, 21 Jan 1658/9, music lost	
Elena (Faustini, completed Minato), Teatro S Cassiano, 26 Dec 1659, *Vnm*	158, 163, 167
Ercole amante (F. Buti), Paris, Tuileries, 7 Feb 1662, *Vnm*	146–7, 148, 156, 165, 167
Scipione affricano (Minato), Teatro SS Giovanni e Paolo, 9 Feb 1664, *Rvat* Chigi, *Sc*, *Vnm*, *P-La* (Act 3 only, with arias from other operas, incl. Donzelle fuggite lasciva beltà = Amanti fuggite lasciva beltà from Ciro); arias Amare e tacere, Zeffiretti qua correte, *F-Pn*, *I-Nc*; facs. in H. M. Brown, ed.: *Italian Opera 1640–1770* (New York, 1978)	155, 163

Mutio Scevola (Minato), Teatro S Salvatore, 26 Jan 1665, *Vnm*

Pompeo magno (Minato), Teatro S Salvatore, 20 Feb 1666, *D-AN*, *I-Vnm* 165, 166

Coriolano (C. Ivanovich), Piacenza, Teatro Ducale, 27 May 1669, music lost 148

Eliogabalo (anon., completed Aureli), composed for Teatro SS Giovanni e Paolo, 1668, but not perf., *Vnm* 148, 156, 158, 161, 165, 167

Massenzio (G. F. Bussani), composed for Teatro S Salvatore, 1673, but not perf., music lost 148

OPERAS OF DOUBTFUL AUTHENTICITY 150

(*attrib. Cavalli by Ivanovich unless otherwise stated; music lost*)

Narciso et Ecco immortalati (Persiani), Teatro SS Giovanni e Paolo, 30 Jan 1642, by M. Marazzoli and F. Vitali (see *ES*, ix, 1725)

Deidamia (S. Herrico), Teatro Novissimo, 5 Jan 1644

Il Romolo e 'l Remo (G. Strozzi), Teatro SS Giovanni e Paolo, 5 Feb 1645, by ? B. Strozzi

La prosperità infelice di Giulio Cesare dittatore (Busenello), intended for Teatro SS Giovanni e Paolo but possibly not perf.; lib pubd 1656 in Busenello's works

Torilda (P. P. Bissari), Teatro SS Giovanni e Paolo, 1648 [?1649]

Bradamante (Bissari), Teatro SS Giovanni e Paolo, 1650

Armidoro (B. Castoreo), Teatro S Cassiano, 20 Jan 1651, attrib. Cavalli by Bonlini (1730), attrib. G. Sartorio by Ivanovich

Helena rapita da Theseo (? G. Badoaro), Teatro SS Giovanni e Paolo, 1653

La pazzia in trono, overo Caligola delirante (D. Gisberti), Teatro S Apollinare, 1660, spoken drama with a little music, attrib. Cavalli by A. Groppo (1745); lib pubd 1675 in Gisberti's *Talia*

OTHER SECULAR

(*most attribs. doubtful; arias by Cavalli are probably from operas*)

Arias: Son ancor pargoletta, 1634[7], ed. K. Jeppesen, *La Flora* (Copenhagen, 1949); E rimedio al mal d'amore, 1656[4] (see also Erismena); Dolce colpo d'un sguardo amoroso, *F-Pn*; In amor non ho fortuna, *Pn*; O dolce servitù, *Pn*; Dolce amor, *GB-T*, probably the piece ed. J. Stainer, *Six Italian Songs for a Mezzo-soprano Voice* (London, 1897), and E. Rung, *Musica scelta di antichi maestri italiani* (Mainz, n.d.), almost certainly not by Cavalli 139, 158

Cantatas: Arm'il petto d'orgoglio, *Vc* (6 arias wrongly attrib. Cavalli in same MS); Chi non fa il giardinier, dated 1662 *MOe*; Ho un cor che non sa (Amante veridico), 1662 *MOe*; Levamiti davanti (Vanità in amore), 1662 *MOe*; Se laggiù negli abissi, *Nc*, ed. H. Riemann, *Kantaten-Frühling* (*1633–1682*) (Leipzig, 1912)

Arias ed.: F.-A. Gevaert, *Les gloires de l'Italie* (Paris, 1868); *Echi d'Italia* (?1880); A. Parisotti, *Arie antiche a una voce* (Milan, 1885–*c*1898/*R*1947); Goldschmidt (1893); Goldschmidt (1901); M. Zanon, *Francesco Cavalli: venti arie* (Venice, 1908); Prunières (1913); Wellesz (1913); Prunières, *Cavalli* (1931); Wolff (1937); Worsthorne (1954); Hjelmborg (1962); R. Leppard, *Francesco Cavalli: Five Operatic Arias* (London, 1966); Rosand (1975)

SACRED 167–9

Musiche sacre concernenti messa, e salmi concertati con istromenti, imni, antifone et sonate, 2–8, 10, 12vv, bc (Venice, 1656): 145, 168

Messa, 8vv, 2 vn, vc, other insts ad lib; ed. R. Leppard (London, 1966) 168

Alma Redemptoris mater, 2 S, A, T, B, ed. B. Stäblein, *Musica divina*, iv (Regensburg, 1950) 168

Ave maris stella, A, T, B, 2 vn, vc

Ave regina caelorum, T, B, ed. B. Stäblein, *Musica divina*, i (Regensburg, 1950)

Beatus vir, A. T. B, 2 vn, vc

Confitebor tibi Domine, 8vv, 2 vn, vc

Credidi, 2 S, A, T, B, 2 vn, vc

Deus tuorum militum, A, T, B, 2 vn, vc

Dixit Dominus, 8vv, 2 vn, vc, other insts ad lib

Domine probasti, S, A, B, 2 vn, vc

Exultet orbis, 4vv, 2 vn, vc

In convertendo, 2 S, A, T, B

Iste confessor, 2 S, 2 vn, vc

Jesu corona virginum, A, T, B, 2 vn, vc

Laetatus sum, A, T, B, 2 vn, 3 va, ed. R. Leppard (London, 1969)

Lauda Jerusalem, 8vv, 2 vn, vc, other insts ad lib

Laudate Dominum, 8vv, 2 vn, vc, ed. R. Leppard (London, 1969)

Laudate pueri, 2 S, A, T, B, 2 vn, vc

Magnificat, 8vv, 2 vn, vc, other insts ad lib, ed. R. Leppard (London, 1969)

Nisi Dominus, 4vv, 2 vn, vc

Regina caeli, A, T, B, ed. B. Stäblein, *Musica divina*, ii (Regensburg, 1950)

Salve regina, A, 2 T, B, ed. B. Stäblein, *Musica divina*, iii (Regensburg, 1950) — 168

Canzoni [sonate] a 3, 4, 6, 8, 10, 12; those a 6 and a 12 ed. R. Nielsen (Bologna, 1955) — 169

Vesperi, 8vv, bc (Venice, 1675): — 148, 168

Vespero della B. V. Maria: Dixit Dominus; Laudate pueri; Laetatus sum; Nisi Dominus; Lauda Jerusalem; Magnificat, ed. G. Piccioli (Milan, 1960)

Vespero delle domeniche: Dixit Dominus; Confitebor; Beatus vir; Laudate pueri; In exitu Israel; Laudate Dominum; Credidi; In convertendo; Domine probasti; Beati omnes; De profundis; Memento; Confitebor angelorum; Magnificat, ed. G. Piccioli (Milan, 1960)

Vespero delle cinque Laudate ad uso della cappella di S Marco: Laudate pueri; Laudate Dominum laudate eum; Lauda anima mea; Laudate Dominum quoniam bonus; Lauda Jerusalem; Magnificat, ed. G. Piccioli (Milan, 1960)

Cantate Domino, lv, bc, 1625[2]; ed. F. Vatielli, *Antiche cantate spirituali* (Turin, 1922) — 138, 167

O quam suavis, lv, bc, 1645[3] — 139

Magnificat, 6vv, 2 vn, bc, 1650[5] — 138

In virtute tua, 3vv, bc, 1656[1]

O bone Jesu, 2vv, bc, 1656[1]

Plaudite, cantate, 3vv, bc, 1656[1]

Missa pro defunctis [Requiem], 8vv, bc, *D-Bds*, *Dlb* — 149, 169

Il giuditio universale, oratorio, dated 1681, *I-Nf*, attrib. 'Cavalli' in MS but almost certainly not by Francesco Cavalli; attrib. 'Nicolas Cavalli' by Fétis, who incorrectly dated it as 18th-century

BIBLIOGRAPHY

BurneyH; *EitnerQ*; *FétisB*; *GerberL*; *GerberNL*; *RicordiE*; *SartoriB*

L. Goldioni [pseud. of G. N. Doglioni] and Z. Zittio [pseud of G. Ziotti]: *Le cose notabili et maravigliose della città di Venezia* (Venice, 1655), 206

N. Doglioni and others: *Le cose notabili et maravigliose della città di Venezia* (Venice, 1671), 207

C. Ivanovich: *Minerva al tavolino* (Venice, 1681, 2/1688)

G. C. Bonlini: *Le glorie della poesia e della musica* (Venice, 1730)

J. Mattheson: *Grundlage einer Ehren-Pforte* (Hamburg, 1740), 148; ed. M. Schneider (Berlin, 1910/*R*1969)

A. Groppo: *Catalogo di tutti i drammi per musica recitati ne' teatri di Venezia dall'anno 1637 ... sin all'anno presente 1745* (Venice, 1745)

J. A. Scheibe: *Der critische Musikus* (Leipzig, enlarged 2/1745/*R*1970)

L. Allacci: *Drammaturgia* (Rome, 1666; Venice, enlarged 2/1755/*R*1961)

G. Orloff: *Essai sur l'histoire de la musique* (Paris, 1822)

F. Caffi: *Storia della musica sacra nella già cappella ducale di San Marco in Venezia dal 1318 al 1797* (Venice, 1854–5, repr. 1931)

A. W. Ambros: 'Francesco Cavalli', *NZM*, lxv (1869), 313, 321

——: *Geschichte der Musik*, iv (Leipzig, 1878), 371ff; (rev. 3/1909 by H. Leichtentritt), esp. 635ff

L. N. Galvani [pseud. of G. Salvioli]: *I teatri musicali di Venezia nel secolo XVII (1637–1700): memorie storiche e bibliografiche* (Milan, 1879)

A. Ademollo: *I primi fasti della musica italiana a Parigi (1645–1662)* (Milan, 1884)

——: *I primi fasti del Teatro di Via della Pergola in Firenze (1657–1661)* (Milan, 1885)

C. Ricci: *I teatri di Bologna nei secoli XVII e XVIII: storia aneddotica* (Bologna, 1888/*R*1965), 330

F. Sforza Benvenuti: *Dizionario biografico cremasco* (Crema, 1888)

T. Wiel: *I codici musicali contariniani del secolo XVII nella R. Biblioteca di San Marco in Venezia* (Venice, 1888/*R*1969)

B. Croce: *I teatri di Napoli: secoli XV–XVIII* (Naples, 1891), 114

H. Kretzschmar: 'Die Venetianische Oper und die Werke Cavallis und Cestis', *VMw*, viii (1892), 1–76

H. Goldschmidt: 'Cavalli als dramatischer Komponist', *MMg*, xxv (1893), 45, 53, 61

L. Torchi: 'Canzoni ed arie ad una voce nel Seicento', *RMI*, i (1894), 581–656

R. Rolland: *Histoire de l'opéra en Europe avant Lully et Scarlatti* (Paris, 1895)
H. Goldschmidt: *Studien zur Geschichte der italienischen Oper im 17. Jahrhundert*, i (Leipzig, 1901/*R*1967)
A. Heuss: 'Die Venetianischen Opern-Sinfonien', *SIMG*, iv (1902–3), 404–77
R. Rolland: 'L'opéra populaire à Venise: Francesco Cavalli', *BSIM*, ii (1906), 1, 60, 151
H. Kretzschmar: 'Beiträge zur Geschichte der Venetianischen Oper', *JbMP 1907*, 71
W. Gurlitt: 'Ein Briefwechsel zwischen Paul Hainlein und L. Friedrich Behaim aus den Jahren 1647–48', *SIMG*, xiv (1912–13), 491
H. Prunières: *L'opéra italien en France avant Lulli* (Paris, 1913/*R*1975)
E. Wellesz: 'Cavalli und der Stil der Venetianischen Oper von 1640–1660', *SMw*, i (1913), 1–103
A. Pellegrini: *Spettacoli lucchesi nei secc. XVII–XIX*, i (Lucca, 1914), 132, 190
E. Schmitz: *Geschichte der weltlichen Solokantate* (Leipzig, 1914), 96; (rev. 2/1955), 84, 114f, 129
T. Wiel: 'Francesco Cavalli (1602–1676) e la sua musica scenica', *Nuovo archivio veneto*, 3rd ser., xviii (1914), 106–50; partial Eng. trans., *MA*, iv (1912–13), 1
H. Prunières: 'Notes sur une partition faussement attribuée à Cavalli: "L'Eritrea" (1686)', *RMI*, xxvii (1920), 267
R. Haas: *Die Musik des Barocks*, HMw (1928), 81, 133, 192
H. Prunières: *Cavalli et l'opéra vénitien au XVIIe siècle* (Paris, 1931)
——: 'Les opéras de Francesco Cavalli', *ReM* (1931), nos. 111–12, pp. 1–16, 125–47
A. Schlossberg: *Die italienische Sonata für mehrere Instrumente im 17. Jahrhundert* (Paris, 1935)
H. C. Wolff: *Die Venezianische Oper in der zweiten Hälfte des 17. Jahrhunderts* (Berlin, 1937, 2/1975)
A. Cametti: *Il teatro di Tordinona poi d'Apollo* (Tivoli, 1938), 62, 323
U. Rolandi: 'Le opere teatrali di Francesco Cavalli', *La scuola veneziana (secoli XVI–XVIII): note e documenti*, Chigiana, iii (1941), 15
B. Hjelmborg: 'Une partition de Cavalli: quelques remarques complémentaires aux recherches cavalliennes', *AcM*, xvi–xvii (1944–5), 39
M. Bukofzer: *Music in the Baroque Era* (New York, 1947)
D. J. Grout: *A Short History of Opera* (New York and London, 1947), 90
R. Giazotto: *La musica a Genova nella vita pubblica e privata dal XIII al XVIII secolo* (Genoa, 1951)

Bibliography

A. A. Abert: 'Cavalli', *MGG*

'Cavalli Opera Restored', *Musical Courier*, clxvi (1952), 5

A. A. Abert: *Claudio Monteverdi und das musikalische Drama* (Lippstadt, 1954)

W. Senn: *Musik und Theater am Hofe zu Innsbruck* (Innsbruck, 1954)

S. T. Worsthorne: *Venetian Opera in the Seventeenth Century* (Oxford, 1954/*R*1968)

N. Pirrotta: 'Cavalli, Pier Francesco', *ES*

W. Osthoff: 'Neue Beobachtungen zu Quellen und Geschichte von Monteverdis "Incoronazione di Poppea" ', *Mf*, xi (1958), 129

F. Bussi: *La messa concertata et la musique sacrée de Pier Francesco Cavalli* (Paris, 1960)

W. Osthoff: 'Antonio Cestis "Alessandro vincitor di se stesso" ', *SMw*, xxiv (1960), 13

H. S. Powers: '*Il Serse trasformato*', *MQ*, xlvii (1961), 481–92; xlviii (1962), 73–92

B. Hjelmborg: 'Aspects of the Aria in the Early Operas of Francesco Cavalli', *Natalicia musicologica Knud Jeppesen* (Copenhagen, 1962), 173

D. Arnold: ' "L'incoronazione di Poppea" and its Orchestral Requirements', *MT*, civ (1963), 176

R. Brockpähler: *Handbuch zur Geschichte der Barockoper in Deutschland* (Emsdetten, 1964)

W. Osthoff: 'Maske und Musik: die Gestaltwerdung der Opera in Venedig', *Castrum peregrini*, lxv (1964), 10–49; It. trans., *NRMI*, i (1967), 16

B. Hjelmborg: 'Om den venezianske arie indtil 1650', *DAM*, iv (1964–5), 91

D. Arnold: 'Francesco Cavalli: some Recently Discovered Documents', *ML*, xlvi (1965), 50

W. Osthoff: 'Francesco Cavalli', *LaMusicaE*

N. Pirrotta: 'Il caval zoppo e il vetturino: cronache di Parnaso 1642', *CHM*, iv (1966), 215

E. W. White: 'English Opera Research', *Theatre Notebook*, xxi (1966), 32 [incl. reproduction of page from English *Erismena* MS]

R. Leppard: 'Cavalli's Operas', *PRMA*, xciii (1966–7), 67

F. Bussi: 'La produzione sacra di Cavalli e i suoi rapporti con quella di Monteverdi', *RIM*, ii (1967), 229

G. F. Crain: 'Francesco Cavalli and the Venetian Opera', *Opera*, xviii (1967), 446

R. Giazotto: 'La guerra dei palchi', *NRMI*, i (1967), 245–86, 465–508

A. Mondolfi Bossarelli: 'Ancora intorno al codice napoletano della "Incoronazione di Poppea" ', *RIM*, ii (1967), 294

W. C. Holmes: 'Giacinto Andrea Cicognini's and Antonio Cesti's

Orontea', *New Looks at Italian Opera: Essays in Honor of Donald J. Grout* (Ithaca, NY, 1968), 108

N. Pirrotta: 'Early Opera and Aria', *New Looks at Italian Opera: Essays in Honor of Donald J. Grout* (Ithaca, NY, 1968), 39–107

H. S. Powers: '*L'Erismena travestita*', *Studies in Music History: Essays for Oliver Strunk* (Princeton, 1968), 259–324

D. Swale: 'Cavalli: the "Erismena" of 1655', *MMA*, iii (1968), 146

S. Bonta: 'The Uses of the *Sonata da chiesa*', *JAMS*, xxii (1969), 54–84

Y. F.-A. Giraud: *La fable de Daphné: essai sur un type de métamorphose végétale dans la littérature et dans les arts jusqu'à la fin du XVIIe siècle* (Geneva, 1969)

O. Jander: 'The Prologues and Intermezzos of Alessandro Stradella', *AnMc*, no.7 (1969), 87

J. Noble: 'Cavalli's "Ormindo" ', *MT*, cx (1969), 380 [review of the performing edn. by Raymond Leppard and of a gramophone record]

N. Pirrotta: 'Early Venetian Libretti at Los Angeles', *Essays in Musicology in Honor of Dragan Plamenac* (Pittsburgh, 1969/*R*1977), 233

R. L. Weaver: 'Opera in Florence: 1646–1731', *Studies in Musicology: Essays . . . in Memory of Glen Haydon* (Chapel Hill, 1969), 60

I. Bartels: 'Zum Problem des Instrumentalstückes in der frühvenezianischen Oper', *GfMKB, Bonn 1970*, 336

M. N. Clinkscale: *Pier Francesco Cavalli's 'Xerse'* (diss., U. of Minnesota, 1970)

A. Hicks: 'Cavalli and "La Calisto" ', *MT*, cxi (1970), 486

F. Testi: *La musica italiana nel Seicento* (Milan, 1970–72), i, 281–313, 457; ii, 291, 395

E. Rosand: *Aria in the Early Operas of Francesco Cavalli* (diss., New York U., 1971)

C. B. Schmidt: Review of gramophone record of Cavalli's *Erismena*, *JAMS*, xxiv (1971), 313

G. Morelli and T. R. Walker: 'Tre controversie intorno al San Cassiano', *Venezia e il melodramma nel Seicento: Venezia 1972*, 97

H. S. Powers: 'Il "Mutio" tramutato, i: Sources and Libretto', *Venezia e il melodramma nel Seicento: Venezia 1972*, 227

E. Rosand: 'Aria as Drama in the Early Operas of Francesco Cavalli', *Venezia e il melodramma nel Seicento: Venezia 1972*, 75

T. Walker: 'Gli errori di "Minerva al tavolino": osservazioni sulla cronologia delle prime opere veneziane', *Venezia e il melodramma nel Seicento: Venezia 1972*, 7

D. Arnold: 'A Background Note to Monteverdi's Hymn Settings', *Scritti in onore di Luigi Ronga* (Milan and Naples, 1973), 33

L. Bianconi: 'Caletti, Pietro Francesco, detto Cavalli', *DBI* [incl. detailed archival references]

J. Glover: 'Cavalli and "Rosinda" ', *MT*, cxiv (1973), 133
A. Chiarelli: *'L'incoronazione di Poppea* o *Il Nerone*: problemi di filologia testuale', *RIM*, ix (1974), 117–51
L. Bianconi and T. Walker: 'Dalla *Finta pazza* alla *Veremonda*: storie di Febiarmonici', *RIM*, x (1975), 379–454
J. Glover: 'The Peak Period of Venetian Public Opera: the 1650s', *PRMA*, cii (1975–6), 67
——: *The Teatro Sant'Apollinare and the Development of Seventeenth-century Venetian Opera* (diss., U. of Oxford, 1975)
J. Roche: 'Liturgical Music in Italy, 1610–60', *NOHM*, v (1975), 358, 361
E. Rosand: ' "Ormindo travestito" in *Erismena*', *JAMS*, xxviii (1975), 268
E. Selfridge-Field: *Venetian Instrumental Music from Gabrieli to Vivaldi* (Oxford, 1975)
H. C. Wolff: 'Italian Opera from the Later Monteverdi to Scarlatti', *NOHM*, v (1975), esp. 17ff
D. Arnold: 'Cavalli at St Mark's', *Early Music*, iv (1976), 266
F. Bussi: 'Storia, tradizione e arte nel *Requiem* di Cavalli', *NRMI*, x (1976), 49
J. Glover: 'Aria and Closed Form in the Operas of Francesco Cavalli', *The Consort*, xxxii (1976), 167
E. Rosand: 'Comic Contrast and Dramatic Continuity: Observations on the Form and Function of Aria in the Operas of Francesco Cavalli', *MR*, xxxvii (1976), 92
J. Glover: *Cavalli* (London, 1978)
R. Donington: 'Cavalli in the Opera House', *MT*, cxix (1978), 327
C. Sartori: *Primo tentativo di catalogo unico dei libretti italiani a stampa fino all' anno 1800* (Milan, n.d.) [incl. sources for Cavalli libs]
E. Rosand: 'Francesco Cavalli in Modern Edition', *CMc* (1979), no.27, p.73
E. R. Rutschman: 'Minato and the Venetian Opera Libretto', *CMc* (1979), no.27, p.84
G. Yans: *Un opéra de Francesco Cavalli pour la cour de Florence: L'Hipermestra* (Bologna, 1979)
D. Arnold: 'The Solo Motet in Venice (1625–1775)', *PRMA*, cvi (1979–80), 56
J. H. Moore: *Vespers at St Mark's, 1625–1675: Music of Alessandro Grandi, Giovanni Rovetta and Francesco Cavalli* (diss., U. of California, Los Angeles, 1979; Ann Arbor, 1980)
C. B. Schmidt: review of J. Glover: *Cavalli*, *JAMS*, xxxiii (1980), 196
P. Jeffery: *The Autograph Manuscripts of Francesco Cavalli* (diss., Princeton U., 1980)

J. H. Moore: 'The *Vespero delli cinque Laudate* and the Role of *salmi spezzati* at St Mark's', *JAMS*, xxxiv (1981), 249–78

G. Morelli, ed.: *Scompiglio e lamento (simmetrie dell'incostanza e incostanza delle simmetrie): L'Egisto di Faustini e Cavalli* (Venice, 1982)

ARCANGELO CORELLI

Michael Talbot

CHAPTER ONE

Life

I Early years

Arcangelo Corelli was born in Fusignano, a small town midway between Bologna and Ravenna, on 17 February 1653. The Corelli family were prosperous landowners, whose elevated social status undoubtedly contributed to the high regard in which the composer's future patrons were to hold both him and his family. Arcangelo was named after his father, who died a month before he was born. Together with four older children, Ippolito, Domenico, Giovanna and Giacinto, he was brought up by his mother Santa Corelli, née Raffini.

Corelli's childhood and early education have been the subjects of many fanciful anecdotes of doubtful veracity, but there is no reason to disbelieve the testimony of Crescimbeni (who as a leading member of the Arcadian Academy must have known Corelli well) that he first took music lessons from a priest in the nearby town of Faenza, continued his studies at Lugo, and finally went, in 1666, to Bologna. That city, which boasted one of the largest churches in Christendom in the basilica of S Petronio, was the home of a flourishing school of composers, whose outstanding figures included Cazzati, Perti, Colonna, G. B. Vitali and, nearer the end of the century, Torelli. Padre Martini claimed that here Corelli took violin lessons first from Giovanni Benvenuti and later Leonardo Brugnoli, both pupils of Ercole Gaibara, the doyen of Bolognese violinists. Burney, on the other hand, cited B. G. Laurenti as Corelli's teacher. Both accounts must be taken with some reservation, as 18th-century historians often named arbitrarily as teachers of the famous those whom they considered especially worthy of the responsibility. Hawkins's assertion that G. B. Bassani taught him, often dismissed in the past on the grounds of Corelli's supposed seniority, could well be true, as Bassani's date of birth is now believed to fall before 1650 and his activity as an organist in Ferrara to date from 1667. In 1670 Corelli, at the age of 17, was admitted to the Accademia Filarmonica of Bologna.

II **First years in Rome**

Corelli's presence in Rome is attested from 1675, the year in which he appeared as a violinist in the orchestra that was recruited for a series of Lenten oratorios at S Giovanni dei Fiorentini and, on 25 August, as the third of four violinists engaged to play for the annual celebration of the feast day of St Louis of France in the church named after the saint. His whereabouts during the four or so preceding years remain uncertain. Padre Martini stated that Corelli spent only four years in Bologna, but the initial appearance of his name in Roman payment books as 'Arcangelo bolognese' (confirming, incidentally, the nickname of 'Il Bolognese' on the title-pages of his opp.1–3) and his generally subordinate position among the orchestral violinists in 1675, and for some years after, suggest that he was a newcomer to Rome. Either this surmise is wrong, and Corelli arrived in Rome around 1671; or Padre Martini underestimated the length of his stay in Bologna; or

Corelli went to live elsewhere during the intervening years. There exists an anecdotal account, apparently originated by Rousseau, of a visit to France, where Corelli aroused Lully's jealousy. The dating of this visit is none too precise, and it has been assumed in modern times that the account is a garbled version of Cavalli's encounter with Lully. A subsequent visit to Spain mentioned by Padre Laurenti is still more nebulous.

In the next few years Corelli became one of the foremost violinists in Rome. In 1676 and the three following years he performed in Lenten oratorios in S Marcello, a church under the patronage of Cardinal Benedetto Pamphili. In 1676 and 1678 he was once again present in S Luigi dei Francesi on 25 August, playing second violin to Carlo Mannelli, whom he also partnered in an 'Esposizione delle 40 ore' at S Marcello on 20 September 1678. On 6 January 1679 he played at the inauguration of the Capranica theatre with Pasquini's *Dove è amore è pietà*. The earliest glimpse of the man behind this impressive series of public appearances comes from a letter he wrote on 13 May 1679 to Count Fabrizio Laderchi, an official of the Tuscan court. Corelli mentioned that he had entered the service of Queen Christina of Sweden as a chamber musician and was busy composing sonatas for her first 'academy'; these completed, he would supply the count with a sonata for violin and lute. In another letter to Laderchi of 3 June 1679 he reported the sending of the sonata, whose bass part could also be played on the cello. It has been suggested that this composition is the Corelli work included in an anthology of sonatas for violin and cello published in Bologna during the 1690s. In 1681 Corelli dedicated his first opus, 12 trio sonatas of the 'church' variety, to Queen Christina, describing them, perhaps with exaggeration, as the 'first fruits [*primitie*] of his studies'. Christina was before long replaced by Cardinal Pamphili as Corelli's most important patron, but she was still able to call on his services for special occasions. An *accademia per musica* by Pasquini performed in Christina's Palazzo Riario in honour of Roger Palmer (Earl of Castlemaine), James II's ambassador to the Holy See, by 150 string players led by Corelli and 100 singers on 2, 7 and 9 February 1687 evoked much admiration. In March 1689 Corelli directed a large band of players in two solemn masses, the first in Il Gesù and the second in Santa Casa di Loreto, to celebrate Christina's recovery from illness (a short-lived rejoicing, as she died the next month). Both ensembles included trumpets, and on the second occasion Corelli contributed 'a new sinfonia with trumpets'. This mention of a trumpet sinfonia increases the likelihood that the well-known trumpet sonata attributed to Corelli in a 1704 publication of Walsh and in various Italian and English manuscripts is a genuine work, whether or not identical with the sonata he is alleged to have composed for Mr Twiselton, trumpeter to the Duke of Aumont, in an advertisement in the *Daily Courant* of 16 March 1713.

Corelli's whereabouts between 3 June 1679 (the date of the second letter to Laderchi) and 30 April 1681 (the date of the dedication of op.1) are uncertain. One could easily believe that he remained in Rome were it not for reports of a visit to Germany around this time. The claim by the composer Caspar Printz, elaborated by J. A. Hiller, that Corelli visited the Bavarian court seems in part to result from a confusion of Corelli with

Giuseppe Torelli. Chrysander's mention of a visit to the Hanoverian court is no better substantiated. In 1682 Corelli reappeared at S Luigi, now as leader of ten violins. The second violin was Matteo Fornari, a pupil to whom he became devoted and who from then on was rarely to be absent from his side. On every subsequent 25 August up to and including the year 1708, when old age and failing health forced his retirement, Corelli paid his annual visit to the church. In 1684 he was inscribed, together with Alessandro Scarlatti, as a member of the Congregazione dei Virtuosi di S Cecilia, a body of whose instrumental section he became head in 1700. Also in 1684 he began to play regularly for musical functions organized by Fornari's employer Cardinal Pamphili, taking responsibility for the engagement and payment of the players. The academies held on Sundays at the cardinal's Palazzo al Corso were a focal point of Roman musical life, and it was perhaps at these that Corelli's first set of chamber trios, published in 1685 as op.2 and dedicated to Pamphili, were first heard. A sequential passage in the Allemanda of the third sonata (reproduced in *Grove 5*) gave rise to one of those acrimonious disputes concerning musical propriety so characteristic of the age. When first played in Bologna, where the sonatas had been brought out later that same year, these bars caused astonishment on account of a series of ostensible parallel 5ths between the first violin and the bass. At Colonna's instigation a certain Matteo Zani wrote a courteous letter to Corelli asking for his explanation. Corelli took the request in rather bad part: since, in his view, the 5ths were indirect and therefore legitimate, the Bolognese musicians must be ignorant of the rules of music. Thereupon the matter broadened into an inter-city dispute, each side enlisting support from local musicians, so that the correspondence continued for some months. It is unlikely that the Bolognese musicians, initially at least, were motivated by resentment at their former colleague's move to Rome, as has been hinted, for even now many will find the passage inherently contentious.

III Later years in Rome

On 9 July 1687 Cardinal Pamphili engaged Corelli as his music master at a monthly salary of ten Florentine piastres. Corelli went to live at the cardinal's palace, accompanied by his pupil Fornari and by a servant named Bernardino Salviati. Another musician employed by Pamphili was the Spanish cellist G. L. Lulier, often nicknamed by the Romans 'Giovannino del violone'. Corelli, Fornari and Lulier often performed together as a trio or, in the context of orchestral music, as a concertino of soloists. Lulier was also a composer, and a good example of the way in which his talents were harnessed to those of Corelli can be seen in the oratorio *S Beatrice d'Este*, which was performed early in 1689 in Pamphili's residence in honour of the visiting Cardinal Rinaldo d'Este. The music was by Lulier, and a very large orchestra under Corelli was mustered for the occasion, consisting of 39 violins, 10 violas, 17 cellos (*violoni*), 10 double basses, one lute, two trumpets and (presumably) one or more keyboard instruments – over 80 players, among whom were Pasquini and Francesco Gasparini. (A Roman orchestra of more typical size, such as the one Corelli directed at S Marcello in 1690, had a concertino supported by harpsichord, with a concerto grosso of four violins, two violas, one cello, two double basses and organ.) The oratorio was taken later that year to the d'Este court at Modena, and for this revival, if not already for the Roman performance, Corelli supplied an Introduzione (overture) and Sinfonia (probably the overture to the second part). The same division of labour between Corelli and the composer of the vocal music must often have occurred at Pamphili's court. On 20 September 1689 Corelli dedicated his third opus, 12 more *sonate da chiesa*, to Francesco II, Duke of Modena. It has been supposed that Corelli travelled to Modena then, but on slender evidence.

Pamphili's move for some years to Bologna in 1690 gave Cardinal Pietro Ottoboni, a rival Maecenas, an opportunity to assume the patronage of Corelli. The 22-year-old Ottoboni had been raised to the purple at the end of 1689 through an act of flagrant nepotism by his uncle, Pope Alexander VIII, and filled a succession of high ecclesiastical offices. Corelli went to live in his palace, the Cancelleria, where academies were regularly held on Monday evenings. Ottoboni acted towards the composer more like a friend than an employer, and his correspondence shows the affection he had for the entire Corelli family. Op.4, a second set of chamber trios, was dedicated to Ottoboni in 1694. Corelli continued to write sinfonias and concertos (the terminological distinction is often unclear). In 1693 he contributed some 'concerti' to an *Applauso musicale a quattro voci* by Lulier, and on 10 December 1700 was paid 30 scudi for composing a concerto and sinfonia for the Feast of the Translation of the Santa Casa di Loreto. These orchestral works attracted considerable notice. As early as 1682 Georg Muffat, a German composer who became acquainted with both Lully and Corelli, imitated them on his return from Rome in the sonatas of his *Armonico tributo*. In 1689 Angelo Berardi da S Agata wrote: 'Concertos for violins and other instruments are called "sinfonie", and today those of Signor Arcangelo Corelli, the famous violinist . . . the new Orpheus of our days, are prized and esteemed'.

Corelli also directed operatic performances at the Cancelleria and the Tordinona theatre. An interesting entry for 1 May 1702 in a Neapolitan diary records Corelli's arrival in Naples to play in the opera (possibly Scarlatti's *Tiberio, imperator d'Oriente*). Perhaps this brief visit, which cannot have been prolonged beyond the middle of August, is the one commemorated in Burney's famous anecdote: mistrusting the ability of the Neapolitan players, Corelli took with him Fornari and a cellist (possibly Lulier); to his surprise, his hosts played a concerto of his so well at sight that he exclaimed 'Si suona a Napoli' ('they play at Naples') to Fornari. The sequel to this episode was less fortunate: having agreed to direct the orchestra in an opera by Scarlatti, who was present, Corelli first found difficulty in executing a certain passage in a high register which the Neapolitans managed with ease, and then compounded his disgrace by making two false starts in C major to an aria in C minor.

On 26 April 1706 Corelli was admitted, with Pasquini and Scarlatti, to the Arcadian Academy, receiving the name of Arcomelo Erimanteo. There are records of Arcadian functions, unfortunately undated, in which he participated. Other engagements at the Pamphili and Ruspoli palaces brought him into contact with Handel. He played (none too successfully, according to Hawkins) in Handel's *Il trionfo del tempo e del disinganno* in May 1707, and led the orchestra in two performances of *La resurrezione* (9 and 10 April 1708).

After 1708 Corelli retired from public view. He busied himself with the composition, or more probably revision, of concerti grossi. A Christmas Concerto perhaps identical with op.6 no.8 had been composed as far back as 1690 for Ottoboni, and other concertos may well have matured for far longer, going back to the time of Muffat's visit or beyond. Possibly Corelli felt compelled to increase their quotient of virtuosity, converting what were originally sinfonias for church or theatre into more scintillating works able to stand comparison with the concertos of Torelli, Albinoni, Valentini and other pioneers, and profiting from the technical advances made in his op.5, the celebrated set of violin sonatas dedicated in 1700 to the Electress Sophie Charlotte of Brandenburg. In a notice concerning the papal contralto Matteo Simonelli, Adami da Bolsena observed in 1711 that Corelli (whom he claimed to be Simonelli's pupil) was just then perfecting his sixth opus, consisting of concertos, which he would shortly publish. A dedication was ready in December 1712, but Corelli was held back by a deterioration in his health. At the end of 1712 he moved out of the Cancelleria into the Palazzetto Ermini, a pied à terre normally occupied by his brother Giacinto, his nephew Arcangelo and the many possessions, including valuable paintings and musical instruments, he had accumulated. On 5 January he wrote his will, bequeathing to cardinals Ottoboni and Colonna one painting each, and to Matteo Fornari all his violins, his manuscripts, the plates of his op.4, and his future op.6. (Fornari dedicated the concertos, published by Estienne Roger of Amsterdam in the year after

Corelli's death, to the Elector Palatine Johann Wilhelm, an admirer to whom the composer had sent a *Concertino da camera* in 1708; the elector honoured Corelli posthumously with the Marquisate of Landenburg at Ottoboni's suggestion.) Corelli died on 8 January and was embalmed and buried in S Maria della Rotonda (the Pantheon). The anniversary of his death was marked for several years afterwards by solemn performances of his concertos in the Pantheon.

CHAPTER TWO

Reputation and influence

Hawkins's description of Corelli as 'remarkable for the mildness of his temper and the modesty of his deportment' sums up the impressions of contemporaries, who found those qualities admirable in one so famous and so rich. Contemporary portraits, of which the best known is one by the Englishman Hugh Howard (see fig. 10), who visited Italy during 1697–1700, emphasize the composer's archangel-like serenity. The style of his playing was in keeping –'learned, elegant and pathetic' – though one might not gather this from one witness, who claimed that 'it was usual for his countenance to be distorted, his eyes to become as red as fire, and his eyeballs to roll as if in an agony'. When directing string ensembles he was said to insist on unanimity of bowing among the players of each part, as Lully had done some years earlier. The number and eminence of his pupils make Corelli the most outstanding and influential violin teacher of his century. The Italians among them included Carbonelli, Castrucci, Gasparini, Geminiani and Somis (possibly also Bonporti, Locatelli, Mascitti and Mossi); the foreigners included the Frenchman Anet, the Spaniard Herrando, the German Störl and the English amateur Lord Edgcumbe.

Corelli's influence and reputation spread as much through the dissemination of his works, which coincided with the remarkable boom in music publishing around

10. Arcangelo Corelli: mezzotint by I. Smith Anglus after Hugh Howard (1675–1737)

1700, as through his teaching. The sheer number of reprints of his collections is unmatched before Haydn: op.1, for example, went through 35 known editions between 1681 and 1785 (not counting collective editions of opp.1–4 and innumerable arrangements, selections and pastiches for all manner of instruments and even voices). The most popular opus was the fifth, of which at least 42 editions had appeared by 1800. In England particularly his op.6 concertos were regarded as classics; they continued to be played, and preferred even to those of Handel, well into the 19th century. Some composers tried their hand at arranging Corelli's music. Geminiani's refashioning of six op.3 sonatas and the whole of op.5 as concerti grossi was a skilful, if misguided, effort, facilitated by the lack of any pronounced stylistic difference between Corelli's works for different media. Other composers used his music as a springboard for original composition: Bach borrowed the subject of the second movement of op.3 no.4 for an organ fugue (BWV579): F. M. Veracini left a set of *Dissertazioni sopra l'opera quinta del Corelli*, which elaborately reconstitute all 12 works; Tartini wrote a set of variations on the ever-popular Gavotte of the tenth solo sonata, entitled *L'arte dell'arco*. Rakhmaninov (using the folia theme in op.5 no.12) and Tippett have paid their homage more recently.

Corelli's own variation movements – the ciaconna forming by itself the final chamber sonata in op.2, and folia variations rounding off op.5 – were widely imitated. Dall'Abaco's sonata op.3 no.11 (1712) ends with a similar chaconne, while folia variations are found in T. A. Vitali's op.4 (1701), Albicastro's op.5 (1703), Vivaldi's op.1 (1705) and Reali's op.1 (1709, dedicated to Corelli). A *Suario o capriccio . . . all'imitationo* [sic] *del Corelli*, modelled on Corelli's folia, was composed by G. B. Tibaldi. Other composers besides Tibaldi deliberately aped Corelli's manner as a stylistic exercise: Bellinzani's trio sonatas 'ad imitazione d'Arcangelo Corelli', Galuppi's concerto 'sul gusto del Corelli' and Telemann's *Sonates Corellisantes* are all works of this kind.

The composers who slavishly imitated Corelli without acknowledgment were legion. John Ravenscroft (Giovanni Redieri) published at Rome in 1695 a set of trio sonatas so Corellian that Le Cène ventured to bring out nine of the works about 1730 as Corelli's 'op.7'. Other composers honoured Corelli more worthily by naming works or movements after him, either in an act of dedication, as in Valentini's sonata op.5 no.7, or in a stylistic evocation, as in Dandrieu's movement *La Corelli* (from his second harpsichord book, 1727) and Couperin's famous pair of programme works *Le Parnasse ou L'apothéose de Corelli*, in which Corelli's ascent to Parnassus is depicted, and *L'apothéose de Lully*, in which the respective champions of the French and Italian styles achieve reconciliation.

CHAPTER THREE

Style

If today Corelli's musical idiom often seems predictable, over-simple or even commonplace, it is paradoxically as a result of its very originality as perceived by his contemporaries, who, by appropriating and developing its most advanced features, turned what were once exciting novelties into dry clichés. His admission in the first letter to Laderchi that the sole purpose of his compositions was to 'show off' ('fare campeggiare') the violin may have been sincere, but does scant justice to the range of originality evident in opp. 1 and 2. The agile violin writing, already characterized by an abundance of broken-chord figuration, steers a happy course between Bolognese academicism, as typified by G. B. Vitali, and Venetian extravagance, as typified by Legrenzi. Extremes of register, which could detract from the cantabile quality, are avoided (the lowest string of the violin, made of unwound gut in Corelli's day, is rarely used, and the 3rd position is seldom exceeded, the *f'''* at bar 97 of the second concerto being the highest note he ever required). Conjunct upward or downward progressions of first-inversion chords, sometimes disguised by intervening chords, are already present in force; similarly, sequential progressions in which the roots of successive chords travel alternately a 5th in one direction and a 4th in the other. Both devices contribute to the notably modern sense of tonality, and are used to steer the music neatly into related keys as required. A memorable feature of Corelli's counterpoint is the 'leap-frogging' of the two violins, in which each part rises in turn by a 4th, having just fallen by step to resolve a suspension – the classic 18th-century method of producing a rising sequence in which the suspensions still resolve downwards. Corelli popularized certain rhythmical stereotypes, in particular the 'walking' or 'running' bass in which an inessential note is interposed between each two harmony notes. Ironically, the one device with which he is associated by name – the 'Corelli clash' (where the late resolution on to the leading note at a cadence coincides with the anticipation of the tonic note in the companion upper part) – is an asperity fashionable in dance music around 1680, but which hardly appears in his works outside op.2.

In formal matters, Corelli is often credited with the clearest exposition of the difference between the 'church' and 'chamber' varieties of sonata, and the establishment of four movements as the norm in both. These generalizations require much qualification. As early as opp.1 and 2 the first signs of convergence of the two varieties are apparent. All but three of the op.2 works have preludes (Corelli's term was taken up by many other composers) modelled on the opening slow movement of his typical church sonata, and nos.3 and 4 contain additional 'abstract' movements. In op.3 the church idiom comes closer to the chamber idiom in harbouring a greater proportion of movements in quick tempo and binary form, while the representation of abstract movements in the op.4 chamber sonatas shows a slight increase over op.2.

A further significant stage in the process of convergence is reached in opp.5 and 6: two of the finales of the ostensibly *da chiesa* works making up the first half of op.5 are styled 'Giga', while the penultimate sonata among the six *da camera* works has no dance titles at all for four out of its five movements. It was left to Corelli's successors to complete the amalgamation. The four-movement plan in church sonatas is merely an incipient tendency in op.1, but is virtually the norm in op.3. The chamber sonatas are as likely to be in three, or occasionally five, movements as four. Both the solo violin sonatas and the concertos (of which *da chiesa* works make up the first eight, and *da camera* works the rest) tend to observe a five-movement norm, the additional movement being in quick tempo. Not by coincidence are these the works in which solo display is most conspicuous: the extra movement is there to give the violinist (or the concertino) an opportunity to show a degree of technical dexterity that the more traditional contrapuntal movements cannot accommodate. Op.5 is a locus classicus of two types of movement that were much imitated: an opening slow movement which, as in the first work, is punctuated after each cadence by a passage of cadenza-like display writing, and a fugal movement in which the single violin simulates through double stopping the interplay of the upper parts in the trio medium. The slow movements, though they may appear statuesque as notated, were intended to be lavishly embellished. In 1710 Roger published a new edition of op.5 with embellishments, allegedly provided by Corelli himself to illustrate the correct manner of performance of the 12 slow movements in nos.1–6 (see

11. Part of the Adagio from 'Sonata a violino e violone o cimbalo di Arcangelo Corelli', 3rd edition, printed by Estienne Roger (Amsterdam, 1715), showing the written-out embellishments claimed to be Corelli's own

fig.11). There are seven other 18th-century sources giving ornamental versions of one or more movements, including some by Geminiani and Dubourg.

The medium chosen by Corelli for his concerti grossi was a favourite Roman one of the time, for which Stradella had already written a handful of instrumental works. The replacement of two violas by a second violin and a viola as the inner parts of a four-part layout, already seen in the final version of Stradella's *Il Danone* (1677), suited Corelli well, as it permitted him to reproduce the technique and style of his trio sonatas with little modification, although elements of the Bolognese trumpet sonata (e.g. the antiphony at the start of the second movement of the last concerto) and of the solo sonata were also included. The role of the orchestral violins is generally to double, or in virtuoso passages to reinforce, the concertino, producing a *chiaroscuro* effect not so different from the loud–soft alternation already exploited in the chamber works. As Corelli stated on the title-page, the orchestra ('concerto grosso') is optional. However, the viola's role is ambiguous. Since it may be duplicated, and never plays apart from the concerto grosso instruments, it clearly belongs with them; yet, since no concertino instrument is normally doubled by the viola, on the rare occasions when it presents important material (e.g. at the outset of the Largo of no.6) it can be omitted only at the price of having the cello of the concertino take over its line until it retreats into thematic anonymity – a poor makeshift. Perhaps this is the reason why Pepusch's score of the concertos places the viola in the concertino, and why Geminiani and Locatelli sometimes treated the viola in their similar concertos as a concertino instrument. As in some of the chamber sonatas, the first violin often dominates its partners, suggesting the solo concerto. A novelty for Corelli in these concertos is the adoption of French-style *saccadé* rhythms in nos.3 and 7. The form of the concertos proved less influential than their style, since newer, more dynamic formal concepts appeared from Torelli, Albinoni and Vivaldi even before op.6 was published. Only in conservative Rome and England were they accepted by some as a self-sufficient model. A combination of Corellian style and Vivaldian form may be seen in German concertos, including Telemann's.

The traditional view of Corelli is summed up by Newman in speaking of 'a remarkable sense of balance in the concentration and direction of all his musical forces'. Balance is not the most positive of virtues, and one can praise Corelli on other counts. His contrapuntal skill is most evident not in his fugues, which are admittedly sometimes too stiff when they are strict and too haphazard when free, but in a movement such as the Largo e puntato of op.1 no.12, where over a ground bass consisting of seven evenly spaced notes in a descending scale he wove ingenious patterns worthy of his contemporary Purcell. Ostinatos in his upper parts often create a splendidly abrasive harmonic effect against mobile bass lines. The instrumentation of his concertos has many happy touches: the bagpipe-like drone of the Pastorale appended to the eighth concerto is a worthy ancestor of the Polonaise in Handel's op.6, and the doubling of the concertino cello by the orchestral violins in the second Adagio of the fourth concerto is another imaginative stroke which makes it impossible to regard the concerti grossi merely as inflated trio sonatas. Few composers achieved so much so quickly, and with such economical means, as Corelli.

WORKS

Editions: *A. Corelli: Historisch-kritische Gesamtausgabe der musikalischen Werke*, ed. H. J. Marx, i–v (Cologne, 1976–) [M]
Les oeuvres de Arcangelo Corelli, ed. J. Joachim and F. Chrysander, Denkmäler der Tonkunst, iii (1871) [JC]

Numbers in right-hand margins denote references in the text.

PUBLISHED COLLECTIONS	
Sonate a tre [F, e, A, a, B♭, b, C, c, G, g, d, D], 2 vn, vle/archlute, org, op.1 (Rome, 1681), JC	182, 183, 184, 193, 195–6, 197, 200
Sonate da camera a tre [D, d, C, e, B♭, g, F, b, f♯, E, E♭, G], 2 vn, vle/hpd, op.2 (Rome, 1685), JC	182, 185–6, 193, 195–6
Sonate a tre [F, D, B♭, b, d, G, e, C, f, a, g, a], 2 vn, vle/archlute, org, op.3 (Rome, 1689), JC	182, 187, 193, 196, 197
Sonate a tre [C, g, A, D, a, E, F, d, B♭, G, c, b], 2 vn, vle, op.4 (Rome, 1694), JC	187, 189, 193, 196
Sonate [D, B♭, C, F, g, A, d, e, A, F, E, d], vn, vle/hpd, op.5 (Rome, 1700), JC	189, 193, 197, *198*, 199
Concerti grossi [D, F, c, D, B♭, F, D, g, F, C, B♭, F], 2 vn, vc (concertino), 2 vn, va, b (conc. grosso), op.6 (Amsterdam, 1714), JC; score of 2 movts, reputed autograph, *D-Bds*	189–90, 193, 197, 199–200

OTHER WORKS	
Ov. to S Beatrice d'Este (oratorio, G. C. Graziani or B. Pamphili), music by G. L. Lulier, 1689, *F-Pc*, M v	187
3 sonatas in [10] Sonate . . . composta da Arcangelo Corelli e altri autori, vn, bc (Amsterdam, 1697), M v (doubtful)	183
Sonata, A, vn, hpd (London, 1704), M v (doubtful)	
[6] Sonate a tre, 2 vn, bc, 'op. post' (Amsterdam, 1715), M v	
Sonata, D, tpt, 2 vn, bc, *I-Nc*; M v	184
2 sonatas, 2 vn, va, b, *Nc*; M v	
Fuga a quattro voci, *Fc*; M v (doubtful)	

BIBLIOGRAPHY

DOCUMENTATION, LETTERS

Original letters in Albi Rosenthal's private collection, London; *I-FOc*, *FZc*, *US-NYpm*; copies in *I-Bc*

M. Masseangeli: *Catalogo degli autografi lasciati alla Regia Accademia Filarmonica di Bologna* (Bologna, 1896), 83

C. Piancastelli: *In onore di Arcangelo Corelli: Fusignano ad Arcangelo Corelli nel secondo centenario dalla morte, 1913* (Bologna, 1914)

A. Cametti: 'Arcangelo Corelli à Saint-Louis-des-Français à Rome', *ReM*, iii/3 (1922), 25

E. J. Luin: 'Repertorio dei libri musicali di S. A. S. Francesco II nell'Archivio di Stato di Modena', *La bibliofilia*, xxxviii (1936), 420

A. Liess: 'Materialen zur römischen Musikgeschichte des Seicento: Musikerlisten des Oratorio San Marcello 1664–1725', *AcM*, xxix (1957), 137–71

——: 'Neue Zeugnisse von Corellis Wirken in Rom', *AMw*, xiv (1957), 130

H. Wessely-Kropik: 'Mitteilungen aus dem Archiv der Arciconfraternità di San Giovanni dei Fiorentini, detta della Pietà in Rom', *SMw*, xxiv (1960), 44

U. Kirkendale: 'The Ruspoli Documents on Handel', *JAMS*, xx (1967), 222–73

A. Savioli: 'Appunti "conterranei" per A. Corelli', *L'osservatore Romano* (9 Aug 1968)

C. Vitali: 'L'Opera III di Corelli nella diffusione manoscritta: apografi sincroni e tardi nelle biblioteche dell'Emilia-Romagna', *Nuovissimi studi corelliani: 3° congresso internazionale: Fusignano 1980*, 367

T. Walker: 'Due apocrifi corelliani', *Nuovissimi studi corelliani: 3° congresso internazionale: Fusignano 1980*, 381

F. Piperno: 'Le orchestre di Arcangelo Corelli: pratiche musicali romane: lettura dei documenti', *L'invenzione del gusto: Corelli e Vivaldi: mutazioni culturali, a Roma e Venezia, nel periodo post-barocco*, ed. G. Morelli (Milan, 1982), 42

F. Della Seta: 'I Borghese (1691–1731): la musica di una generazione', *NA*, new ser., i (1983), 139

LIFE

A. Berardi da S Agata: *Miscellanea musicale* (Bologna, 1689)

G. M. Crescimbeni: *L'Arcadia* (Rome, 1708)

A. Adami da Bolsena: *Osservazioni per ben regolare il coro* (Rome, 1711)

G. M. Crescimbeni: *Notizie istoriche degli Arcadi morti*, i (Rome, 1720)

G. B. Martini: *Cenni biografici manoscritti dei soci dell'Accademia Filarmonica di Bologna* (MS, *c*1750, *I-Baf*)

J.-J. Rousseau: *Lettre sur la musique françoise* (Paris, 1753)
J. A. Hiller: *Lebensbeschreibungen berühmter Musikgelehrten und Tonkünstler neuerer Zeit*, i (Leipzig, 1784)
F. Chrysander: *G. F. Händel* (Leipzig, 1858–67)
F. Pasini Frassoni: 'La famiglia di Arcangelo Corelli', *Rivista araldica*, v (1907), 83
A. Moser: 'Arcangelo Corelli und Antonio Lolli – zwei künstlerische Ehrenrettungen', *ZMw*, iii (1920–21), 415
F. Vatielli: *Arte e vita musicale in Bologna*, i (Bologna, 1927)
M. Pincherle: *Corelli* (Paris, 1933, enlarged 2/1954 as *Corelli et son temps*; Eng. trans., 1956)
L. De Angelis: 'Arcangelo Corelli nella direzione di un "Concerto e Sinfonia" in S. Maria di Loreto dei Marchigravi di Roma', *NA*, xvii (1940), 105
J. S. Deas: 'Arcangelo Corelli', *ML*, xxxiv (1953), 1
L. Montalto: 'A. Corelli nell'ambiente musicale romano fra il 1671–1703', *RMI*, liv (1954), 241
M. Rinaldi: *Arcangelo Corelli* (Milan, 1954)
L. Montalto: *Un mecenate in Roma barocca: il Cardinale Benedetto Pamphilj* (Florence, 1955)
F. S. Stillings: *Arcangelo Corelli* (diss., U. of Michigan, 1955)
A. Cavicchi: 'Notizie biografiche su Arcangelo Corelli', *Studi corelliani: 1° congresso internazionale: Fusignano 1968*, 131
C. F. Laurenti: 'Vita di Arcangelo Corelli di Fusignano', *Memorie storiche sopra l'isola di Fusignano* [MS, 1799–] (Fusignano, 1968)
R. Bossa: 'Corelli e il cardinal Benedetto Pamphili: alcune notizie', *Nuovissimi studi corelliani: 3° congresso internazionale: Fusignano 1980*, 211
F. Della Seta: 'La musica in Arcadia al tempo di Corelli', *Nuovissimi studi corelliani: 3° congresso internazionale: Fusignano 1980*, 123
F. Piperno: ' "Anfione in Campidoglio": presenza corelliana alle feste per i concorsi dell'Accademia del Disegno di San Luca', *Nuovissimi studi corelliani: 3° congresso internazionale: Fusignano 1980*, 151
M. Viale Ferrero: 'Arcangelo Corelli collezionista', *Nuovissimi studi corelliani: 3° congresso internazionale: Fusignano 1980*, 225

MUSICAL SOURCES

A. Moser: 'Zur Frage der Ornamentik in ihrer Anwendung auf Corellis op.5', *ZMw*, i (1918–19), 287
F. T. Arnold: 'A Corelli Forgery', *PMA*, xlvii (1920–21), 93
C. Sartori: 'Le quarantaquattro edizioni italiane delle sei opere di Arcangelo Corelli', *RMI*, lv (1953), 28
M. Tilmouth: 'Corelli's Trumpet Sonata', *MMR*, xc (1960), 217
N. Cherry: 'A Corelli Sonata for Trumpet, Violins, and Basso Continuo', *Brass Quarterly*, iv (1961), 103

A. Cavicchi: 'Contributo alla bibliografia di Arcangelo Corelli: l'edizione bolognese del 1700 dell'opera "quinta" e la ristampa del 1711', *Ferrara: Rivista del Comune*, ii/2 (1962), 3

——: 'Una sinfonia inedita di Arcangelo Corelli nello stile del concerto grosso 25 anni prima dell'opera VI', *Le celebrazioni del 1963 e alcune nuove indagini sulla musica italiana del XVIII e XIX secolo*, Chigiana, xx (1963), 43

M. Fabbri: '13 ignote composizioni attribute a Corelli in due manoscritti di Firenze e di Assisi', ibid, 23

H. J. Marx: 'Unveröffentlichte Kompositionen A. Corellis', *Studi corelliani: 1° congresso internazionale: Fusignano 1968*, 53

——: 'Ein neuaufgefundenes Autograph Arcangelo Corellis', *AcM*, xli (1969), 116

——: 'Some Corelli Attributions Assessed', *MQ*, lvi (1970), 88

D. D. Boyden: 'Corelli's Solo Violin Sonatas "Grac'd" by Dubourg', *Festskrift Jens Peter Larsen* (Copenhagen, 1972), 113

——: 'The Corelli "Solo" Sonatas and their Ornamental Additions by Corelli, Geminiani, Dubourg, Tartini, and the "Walsh Anonymous"', *Musica antiqua Europae orientalis III: Bydgoszcz 1972*, 591

H. J. Marx: 'Some Unknown Embellishments of Corelli's Violin Sonatas', *MQ*, lxi (1975), 65

WORKS

A. Schering: *Die Geschichte des Instrumental-Konzerts* (Leipzig, 1905, 2/1927/*R*1965)

W. S. Newman: 'Ravenscroft and Corelli', *ML*, xxxviii (1957), 369

A. Hutchings: *The Baroque Concerto* (London, 1961, rev. 3/1973)

S. H. Hansell: 'Orchestral Practice at the Court of Cardinal Pietro Ottoboni', *JAMS*, xix (1966), 398

N. Carrell: *Bach the Borrower* (London, 1967)

D. Arnold: 'The Corellian Cult in England', *Studi corelliani: 1° congresso internazionale: Fusignano 1968*, 81

A. Cavicchi: 'Aspetti didattici ed elementi di prassi esecutiva nell'opera di Corelli', *Studi corelliani: 1° congresso internazionale: Fusignano 1968*, 91

——: 'Corelli e il violinismo bolognese', *Studi corelliani: 1° congresso internazionale: Fusignano 1968*, 33

L. Finscher: 'Corelli als Klassiker der Trio-Sonate', *Studi corelliani: 1° congresso internazionale: Fusignano 1968*, 23

C. Gianturco: 'Corelli e Stradella', *Studi corelliani: 1° congresso internazionale: Fusignano 1968*, 55

O. Jander: 'Concerto Grosso Instrumentation in Rome in the 1660's and 1670's', *JAMS*, xxi (1968), 168

H. J. Marx: 'Die Musik am Hofe Pietro Kardinal Ottobonis unter Arcangelo Corelli', *AnMc*, no.5 (1968), 104–77

O. Mischiati: 'Aspetti dei rapporti tra Corelli e la scuola bolognese', *Studi corelliani: 1° congresso internazionale: Fusignano 1968*, 23

G. Morche: 'Corelli und Lully: über den Nationalstil', *Studi corelliani: 1° congresso internazionale: Fusignano 1968*, 65

G. Pestelli: 'Corelli e il suo influsso sulla musica per cembalo del suo tempo', *Studi corelliani: 1° congresso internazionale: Fusignano 1968*, 37

P. Petrobelli: 'Tartini e Corelli', *Studi corelliani: 1° congresso internazionale: Fusignano 1968*, 99

M. Pincherle: 'Corelli et la France', *Studi corelliani: 1° congresso internazionale: Fusignano 1968*, 13

M. G. White: 'F. M. Veracini's Dissertazioni sopra l'opera 5a del Corelli', *MR*, xxxii (1971), 1

S. Harris: 'Lully, Corelli, Muffat and the 18th-century String Body', *ML*, liv (1973), 197

D. Libby: 'Interrelationships in Corelli', *JAMS*, xxvi (1973), 263

D. L. Smithers: *The Music and History of the Baroque Trumpet before 1721* (London, 1973)

E. Selfridge-Field: *Venetian Instrumental Music from Gabrieli to Vivaldi* (Oxford, 1975)

O. Edwards: 'The Response to Corelli's Music in Eighteenth-century England', *SMN*, ii (1976), 51–96

H. J. Marx: Introduction and Kritischer Bericht to *A. Corelli: Historisch-kritische Gesamtausgabe der musikalischen Werke*, v (Cologne, 1976)

W. Apel: 'Studien über die frühe Violinmusik VIII: Die italienischen Hauptquellen von 1680 bis 1689', *AMw*, xxxvii (1980), 206

M. Baroni: 'Problemi di fraseggio nelle sonate a tre di Arcangelo Corelli', *Nuovissimi studi corelliani: 3° congresso internazionale: Fusignano 1980*, 71

R. Dalmonte: 'Procedimenti di chiusa nelle sonate a tre di Arcangelo Corelli', *Nuovissimi studi corelliani: 3° congresso internazionale: Fusignano 1980*, 97

W. D. Förster: 'Corelli e Torelli: Concerto Grosso e Sonata con tromba', *Nuovissimi studi corelliani: 3° congresso internazionale: Fusignano 1980*, 329

N. M. Jensen: 'The Performance of Corelli's Chamber Music Reconsidered: some Characteristics of Structure and Performance in Italian Sonatas for One, Two and Three Voices in the Decades preceding Corelli', *Nuovissimi studi corelliani: 3° congresso internazionale: Fusignano 1980*, 241

F. Noske: 'Corelli's "Ciacona": some Analytical Remarks', *Nuovissimi studi corelliani: 3° congresso internazionale: Fusignano 1980*, 15

C. Wintle: 'Corelli's Tonal Models: the Trio Sonata Op.III, no.1', *Nuovissimi studi corelliani: 3° congresso internazionale: Fusignano 1980*, 29

F. C. Ricci: 'Presenza di Corelli nell'opera violinistica di Francesco Maria Veracini: un caso di epignoismo progressivo', *L'invenzione del gusto: Corelli e Vivaldi: mutazioni culturali, a Roma e Venezia, nel periodo post-barocco*, ed. G. Morelli (Milan, 1982), 102

COLLECTIVE PUBLICATIONS

Studi corelliani: 1° congresso internazionale: Fusignano 1968

Nuovi studi corelliani: 2° congresso internazionale: Fusignano 1974

Nuovissimi studi corelliani: 3° congresso internazionale: Fusignano 1980

G. Morelli, ed.: *L'invenzione del gusto: Corelli e Vivaldi: mutazioni culturali, a Roma e Venezia, nel periodo post-barocco* (Milan, 1982)

ALESSANDRO SCARLATTI

Donald J. Grout

CHAPTER ONE

Life

I Early years

Alessandro Scarlatti was born in Palermo on 2 May 1660. Baptized as Pietro Alessandro Gaspare Scarlatti, he was the second of eight children of Pietro Scarlatti (*d* in or before 1678) and Eleonora d'Amato (Alessandro's older sister had died in infancy). The Scarlatti family (the name was also spelt Scarlata or Sgarlata) was a musical one (see family tree, fig.12). Four of Alessandro's siblings became musicians: his two sisters Anna Maria (1661–1703) and Melchiorra Brigida (1663–1736) and his brother Tommaso (*c*1669–1760) were professional singers, active mainly in Naples, while another brother, Francesco (1666–? after 1741), was a composer. Of Alessandro's own ten children, two were professional musicians: Pietro Filippo (1679–1750), an organist and composer, and, by far the most renowned, the composer and keyboard player Domenico (1685–1757, see pp.327–63).

At the age of 12, in June 1672, Alessandro Scarlatti was sent to Rome with his two young sisters, possibly to be cared for by relatives. Conditions of famine and turmoil in Palermo may have influenced the decision; but it was not uncommon for poor parents of large families to place talented children in surroundings where their gifts could develop (Pasquini had also gone to Rome at the age of 12).

12. The Scarlatti family tree

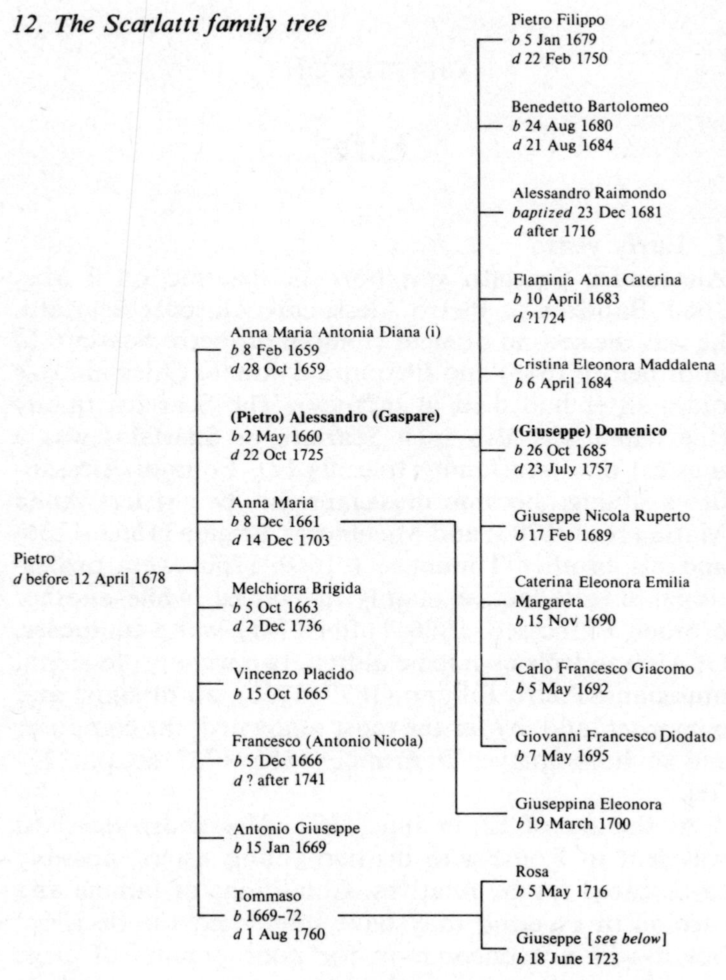

[relationship uncertain (?son of Tommaso, or ?nephew of Domenico): Giuseppe *b c*1718 (or 18 June 1723); *d* 17 Aug 1777]

Early years

Nothing is known about Scarlatti's early musical education. The conservatory at Palermo, founded in 1618, apparently did not offer musical training until towards the end of the century. Scarlatti may have been taught by his father or by a presumed relative of his mother, Vincenzo Amato, *maestro di cappella* at Palermo Cathedral. Upon moving to Rome he probably attended a choir school connected with a large church or seminary. Whatever formal discipline he may have had, at least as important to his education was the flourishing musical life to which he was exposed, and in which he certainly took part, during his formative years at Rome. There he attracted the attention of patrons on whose continuing favour his success depended, and with whom he carefully maintained connections all his life. In the private theatres, the two public opera houses, the numerous oratories, churches and academies of Rome, Scarlatti could have heard music by Cesti, Stradella, Pasquini, Sartorio and their contemporaries, performed under the best possible auspices. These years must have given him a comprehensive acquaintance with the music of his time and an initiation into the nature of a professional musical career.

The earliest known Roman document relating to Scarlatti is the record of his marriage, on 12 April 1678, to Antonia Anzalone, a native of Rome (though the surname was common in Sicily). They had seven sons and three daughters, but apparently only five children survived to maturity; provision for his offspring became one of his constant cares.

Scarlatti is first heard of as a composer early in 1679 when the Arciconfraternità del Ss Crocifisso commissioned him to write an oratorio, probably the one performed for them on 24 February. His earliest known opera *Gli equivoci nel sembiante* was a resounding success. Given repeatedly at Rome in 1679, it was soon produced at Bologna, Naples and Monte Filottrano, then at Vienna (Carnival 1681) and subsequently Ravenna and Palermo.

One of Scarlatti's first patrons was Queen Christina of Sweden, an important patron of arts and letters in Rome since 1655; she had founded at her palace two academies, one later to become the famous Arcadia. Stradella, Pasquini and Corelli were among her protégés. In the libretto of his second opera, *L'honestà negli amori* (1680), Scarlatti is described as her *maestro di cappella*, a title he held even after his departure for Naples in autumn 1683. At least three more operas and six oratorios, as well as many cantatas, date from his first Roman period. Among his influential protectors were two cardinals, Benedetto Pamphili and Pietro Ottoboni, both munificent patrons of the arts who maintained theatres in their palaces. Their virtual rivalry in promoting music was especially fortunate for opera, since the reigning Pope Innocent XI discouraged public theatrical spectacles.

II At Naples

Among the various influential figures at Rome who knew of Scarlatti and had heard his music was the Marquis del Carpio, Spanish ambassador to the Vatican. He became Viceroy of Naples in 1683; influenced probably by his friend the Duke of Maddaloni, he promptly invited Scarlatti to become his *maestro di cappella*. It is not clear why Scarlatti, who, in addition to the favour he enjoyed from his patrons, was also music director at S

Gerolamo della Carità, chose to leave Rome: one reason may have been the alleged marriage of one of his sisters with an ecclesiastic, which had brought the family under the disfavour of the papal authorities. A still more notorious scandal erupted at Naples. Scarlatti received his appointment from the viceroy in February 1684 on the death of P. A. Ziani; at the same time his brother Francesco Scarlatti, who had come to Naples as a child about ten years before, was named first violinist of the vice-regal chapel. Provenzale, honorary head of the chapel since 1680, had expected to succeed Ziani; on Scarlatti's appointment he resigned, and six singers left in sympathy. It was alleged that the Scarlattis owed their appointments to the intrigues of one of their sisters (probably Melchiorra rather than Anna Maria) with two court officials. The officials were discharged and the sister sent to a convent, but the brothers retained their posts; Alessandro remained head of the viceroy's musical establishment until 1702.

In the 1680s Naples was far from being the famous musical and operatic centre that it was soon to become. Opera had begun there with performances by a visiting troupe in 1650; at first the repertory was mainly Venetian, but there were also original operas by Neapolitan composers, including Provenzale. Scarlatti's *Gli equivoci nel sembiante* had been heard there in 1680; *Il Pompeo*, first given in Rome in 1683, was repeated at Naples in January 1684 under the composer's direction. For the next two decades over half the new operas heard in the city were by Scarlatti.

The principal patrons of opera were the viceroys, who maintained theatres in their palace and their summer residence at Posillipo and took an effective interest in the public theatres. Chief among these was the S Bartolomeo, where operas had been given since 1654; destroyed by fire in 1681, it was rebuilt two years later and provided with a permanent company of nine singers, five instrumentalists and a copyist, with Scarlatti as director. In 1696 the Duke of Medinaceli, the penultimate Spanish viceroy, enlarged S Bartolomeo to make room for more and bigger operatic 'machines'. As a rule, a new cantata or serenata would be performed privately for the viceroy and his guests; operas would be given first at the palace and then transferred to S Bartolomeo for the public.

Scarlatti's 18 years at Naples were a time of incessant labour. If *Lucio Manlio* (1705) was really, as he claimed, his 88th stage work, then the 40-odd known operas of 1684–1702 represent less than half his total output for those years. Ten serenatas, nine oratorios and 65 cantatas, figures again far below the actual total, are also datable from those years. Nor was Scarlatti's activity confined to Naples. In 1686 he was at the Palazzo Doria Pamphili in Rome for his new opera *La Rosmene*, and he often went to the city to superintend performances of his new cantatas and oratorios. One opera, *La Statira*, on a libretto by Cardinal Ottoboni, marked the reopening of the Tordinona Theatre there in January 1690; at the end of that same year *Gli equivoci in amore o vero Rosaura* was performed at the Palazzo della Cancelleria on the occasion of a double wedding involving the families of three of Scarlatti's patrons.

Serenatas and operas for Naples itself came from Scarlatti's pen at an increasing rate in the 1690s; many of the operas quickly made their way to other Italian

13. Alessandro Scarlatti: portrait by Lorenzo Vaccaro (1655–1706)

cities and even abroad. One of the best and most successful, *Il Pirro e Demetrio*, given at S Bartolomeo in 1694, was repeated within a few years at Rome, Siena, Florence, Milan, Brunswick (first in Italian and later in a German version) and probably Mantua and Leipzig. Florence heard it again as late as 1711, Fano in 1716; from 1708 to 1717 it ran for over 60 performances in London, with the words partly in English translation (his only opera given in England during his lifetime). Such international success was rare in Scarlatti's day. Almost equally widespread was the success of *La caduta de' Decemviri* (1697). This acclaim, however gratifying, brought no extra payment to composer or librettist.

By the late 1690s Scarlatti must have felt overwhelmed by the requirements of his Naples position: two or three new operas each year to be composed, rehearsed and conducted (at least at the first one or two performances), and repeated demands from the viceroy and other patrons for new serenatas, oratorios and cantatas; and, with all this, continuing anxiety about arrears of salary and the support of his family. Further, he was becoming discontented with the frivolous musical taste of the Neapolitans; every serious opera coming from Venice to Naples had to be decked out with comic scenes. Finally, by the turn of the century political unrest consequent upon the War of the Spanish Succession was beginning to undermine the privileged status of the nobility at Naples, rendering Scarlatti's situation precarious. In June 1702, having obtained a four-month leave of absence, he departed for Florence with his son Domenico.

III Late years

Prince Ferdinando de' Medici, son of the Grand Duke Cosimo III of Tuscany, was a keen musician and a distinguished patron of music in the years 1680–1710 and had already promoted a dozen of Scarlatti's operas at Siena, Livorno and Florence and in his own villa at Pratolino. Scarlatti had hoped, and continued to hope, for an appointment in the prince's service; but as that was not forthcoming he left Florence in October 1702, going briefly to Naples and Rome. During the next six years he sent Prince Ferdinando oratorios, church music (including one set of Lamentations and one of responsories) and at least four new operas. Of these last none of the music survives, or only doubtful fragments – a particularly unfortunate loss, since from Scarlatti's letters it is evident that he took special pains, explaining his ideas of composition and trying to adapt his style to the prince's requirements. Meanwhile, at the end of 1703 he had accepted a position in Rome as assistant music director at S Maria Maggiore and, probably at the same time, entered the service of his earlier patron Cardinal Ottoboni. His post at Naples was declared vacant in October 1704.

Prospects at Rome did not look favourable. Shortly after his arrival Scarlatti wrote to Prince Ferdinando: 'Rome has no shelter for Music, which lives here as a beggar'. His complaint was exaggerated, but it accurately reflected the situation as far as opera was concerned. The public theatres had been closed since 1700; private performances were few. Scarlatti's operatic output during these years was limited to the works he sent to Prince Ferdinando and two new operas which he supervised in Venice in 1707. The score of one, *Il Mitridate Eupatore*, is extant; although it is one of Scarlatti's greatest works, the Venetians did not like it and a cruel satirical poem was published about the composer. On his return journey to Rome Scarlatti spent nearly five months at Urbino, where his eldest son Pietro was music director at the cathedral.

The last years at Naples and those at Rome, especially 1704–6, were marked by a great efflorescence of cantatas, serenatas and oratorios, written for cardinals Ottoboni and Pamphili and other patrons, including Prince Francesco Maria Ruspoli, for whose palace concerts Scarlatti furnished oratorios and other works. His high professional standing was recognized by his election in 1706 to the Arcadian Academy, along with Pasquini and Corelli. In the following year he was promoted to *maestro di cappella* at S Maria Maggiore. The situation at Rome, however, could not be borne indefinitely. There may have been difficulties with Ottoboni; there was certainly a financial crisis in Scarlatti's affairs around 1707, when he appealed for help to Prince Ferdinando, who replied with a gift of money and a recommendation to the petitioner to commit himself to the care of divine providence. By the beginning of 1709 Scarlatti had accepted an invitation from Cardinal Grimani, the new Austrian Viceroy of Naples, to resume his former position there.

Scarlatti remained in Naples for ten years, assiduously maintaining contact with his Roman friends. A patent of nobility from Pope Clement XI in 1716 enabled him to sign his compositions with the title 'Cavaliere'. Of his 11 known operas for Naples in these years the most famous was *Il Tigrane*, first performed at

S Bartolomeo in 1715, repeated at Innsbruck in the same year and at Livorno in 1716. His last opera for Naples was *Il Cambise*, staged at S Bartolomeo in 1719; the composer was not present.

Two different aspects of Scarlatti's career became apparent at this later phase of his life. One was his interest in collaborating with other composers in revising or creating anew sacred and secular dramatic works. The extent of his involvement ranged from writing a few arias (*La Clotilda*, London, 1709) to composing an entire act for a pasticcio opera (*Giunio Bruto*, Act 3). Noteworthy among the composers sharing in these joint ventures were Antonio Caldara, Carlo Francesco Cesarini, Francesco Bartolomeo Conti, Francesco Gasparini and Antonio Lotti. His other new interest at this time was instrumental composition. The set of 12 *Sinfonie di concerto grosso* was begun in June 1715; probably much of his other orchestral and keyboard music dates from about the same period. Possibly this turn to instrumental music was a symptom of a psychological crisis. He had reached the height of his success and popularity in the 1690s. The collapse of his hopes with Prince Ferdinando, his failure at Venice, his discouragement at Rome, could all have been seen as signs pointing along a downward road. He was 55, an old man as such things were then reckoned. He may have felt unwilling, or unable, to adapt his style to the rising fashion for livelier, simpler, more superficially cheerful operatic music. He was subsiding into the status of an old master, admired and respected but unable to compete with younger composers in meeting new demands.

Once more Scarlatti obtained leave of absence from Naples. The 1718 carnival season found him at Rome to conduct his new opera *Telemaco* at the Capranica, a theatre of which Ruspoli was probably a supporting patron. On the same stage in 1719 came *Marco Attilio Regolo*, followed by revivals of two earlier works with revisions, and in 1721 *La Griselda*, Scarlatti's last surviving opera. These final operas were made possible by Scarlatti's loyal Roman patrons; they had no acclaim comparable to that which had greeted many of his earlier works. An oratorio, three masses and several cantatas are among the other compositions of this time.

Scarlatti's last years at Naples (1722–5) seem to have passed in tranquil retirement. The only compositions certainly from those years are four cantatas, a serenata for a royal marriage in 1723 and a set of sonatas for flute and strings (possibly a result of the composer's meeting with J. J. Quantz in 1724). Scarlatti died on 22 October 1725 and was buried in the Cecilia chapel at S Maria di Montesanto. The affectionate though conventionally fulsome Latin epitaph on his tomb, attributed to Ottoboni, calls him the greatest 'restorer' or 'renewer' of music of all ages.

CHAPTER TWO

Operas

Scarlatti's operas and cantatas are his most numerous and most characteristic compositions. These are the forms in which his genius spontaneously expressed itself and in which the traits of his musical style and the changes it underwent during his 40 years as a composer can best be observed.

The commonest designation in the librettos of Scarlatti's operas is *dramma per musica*, a term standing for a well-defined type of opera with a serious action and a happy ending. Personages are divided into rulers, their confidants and servants; the action deals with the rulers' love affairs, with all their attendant deceptions, jealousies and misunderstandings. With such librettos it is obvious that the 'dramma' exists only as a frame for the 'musica'. Unlike many Venetian operas of the middle and later 17th century, Scarlatti's *drammi per musica* seldom introduce mythological personages or call for elaborate stage machines. The characters, whether ostensibly historical or invented, are stylized. They have no inner life; not luminous in themselves, they may glow by reflection as the spotlight of a particular situation is turned on them, in the arias and duets, where action is suspended and music reigns supreme, but while the action goes on, in recitative, musical interest is minimal. Credible motivation and characterization are exceptional among Scarlatti's works. One of his best dramas is *Il Mitridate Eupatore*, called significantly a *tragedia per musica* and in five acts instead of the more usual three. In addition to his *drammi per musica*, Scarlatti wrote a few pastoral operas, some of them so designated, and several comedies, including the *commedia in musica* entitled *Il trionfo dell'onore*.

Scarlatti's style, already well established in *Gli equivoci nel sembiante* (1679), remained essentially consistent throughout his operas. It is misleading to think of the changes that took place between 1679 and 1721 in terms of 'progress'. Changes do of course occur; they involve dropping some of the early formal schemes, expanding the dimensions and clarifying the tonal plan of arias, enlarging the role of the orchestra, sharpening the pictorial outlines and (in exceptional instances) strengthening the dramatic impact. But the consistency and continuity are basic. In its way, *Gli equivoci nel sembiante* is as fine as any of the later operas. They vary in quality according to the circumstances under which the composer had to work. Like Mozart, Scarlatti had both readiness of musical invention to meet day-to-day requirements and the capacity to rise to great occasions.

Scarlatti inherited a tradition of opera which called for a large number of short arias distinctly set off from the recitatives. The performing time of an opera would have been little more than three hours. Allowing for the recitatives, overture, ballets, intermezzos and so on, and the fact that the score could include from 40 to 60 arias or other musical items, it is clear that many of the arias were very short. This is especially true of Scarlatti's early Roman operas and of many of those he wrote for Naples before 1702.

Some of the earliest arias rely for their structure on ostinato or quasi-ostinato bass patterns rather than on a clearly articulated design in the melody itself. A few show a fairly clear bipartite pattern, either *AB* or (less frequently) the 'seicento' form *ABB'*, with modifications. Much more common however are arias in which the first part is repeated, either entire or shortened, after a more or less contrasting middle section: when the first part returns complete the contrasting section is in the dominant (in major arias) or the relative major (in minor ones); when the reprise is shortened, the keys are more often the mediant minor and the dominant minor. A melody in any of the above forms may be repeated identically for a second strophe of text, usually with a short orchestral ritornello played between the strophes and possibly at the beginning or the end. Strophic arias disappeared only gradually from Scarlatti's operas; *Pirro e Demetrio* (1694) and *Massimo Puppieno* (1695) still have them. From the late 1690s onwards, however, the predominant, almost exclusive form is the full da capo aria *ABA* with *B* between a third and a half the length of *A*, similar to it in tempo and material but perhaps more lightly accompanied, modulating more widely and cadencing as a rule so as to define a tonal relationship with *A* of tonic major to mediant minor or tonic minor to dominant minor (or relative major).

The melodic range of an aria seldom exceeds a 9th or 10th. Prevailing movement is by step; wider intervals occur most often at the beginning of a phrase or section and towards the end, where leaps of a 3rd, a 4th, or more, commonly signal the approach of a cadence. The basic rhythm is quickly established, and there is considerable variety of motivic detail, overriding breaks in

14. Engraving after a stage design by Filippo Juvarra for Alessandro Scarlatti's 'Il Ciro', first performed at the Palazzo della Cancelleria, Rome, in 1712

the vocal line. After an opening phrase or two with periodic structure the melody spins out in phrases of irregular length embodying sequential patterns.

Immediate literal repetition of small units, a particular feature of Scarlatti's melody, occurs typically at the beginning of an aria where a concise subject is announced two or three times alternately in voice and accompaniment (not to be confused with the 'motto' or 'Devise', found for the most part in Scarlatti's late operas, an isolated short phrase for the voice which may even precede the instrumental introduction and may or may not be thematically related to the aria's first phrase). Another common place for repetition is at the end, where the closing phrase may be repeated as a gesture of finality. This device occurs most often in short arias in the early operas; in the longer later arias, the farewell gesture more often takes the form of a distinct, strongly dominant–tonic cadential figure in the voice, preceded usually by a fermata.

Another characteristic of Scarlatti's melody is chromatic inflection of the line at the approach to an important cadence, especially common in slow arias where the text has even the slightest hint of pathetic shading. In major keys the 3rd, and perhaps the 6th, may be made minor at such places, while in minor keys the 2nd may be lowered by a semitone, thus producing a 'Neapolitan 6th' in the harmony. Equally typical are melismatic passages, which even in short and otherwise simply syllabic arias may blossom out in the course of sequential development and lead decisively into a cadence. In longer arias, above all those expressing anger, resolution or martial ardour, the coloraturas are a natural projection of the mood and often motivated by some word or image in the text. They are also an important element of structure, being graduated in length and brilliance to correspond to the different levels of climax in the aria. Such passages call for a high degree of virtuosity, but their difficulties are essentially vocal; Scarlatti never made the awkward demands that Bach sometimes did. His is 'singers' music' in the best sense, and he took care to adapt his style to the capacities of particular performers.

In the early operas most arias have only continuo accompaniment. The relation between air and bass is essentially contrapuntal; the bass is an active line, not merely a foundation for the harmony, as it tended to become later, so that the harmonic rhythm is diversified and comparatively rapid. Orchestral accompaniments supply harmonic (but contrapuntally conceived) support, brief interjections or melodic echoes at pauses in the voice, and general thematic and rhythmic continuity. In the later operas, which have no continuo arias, the accompaniments are fuller and more diversified. The relation of instruments to voice in a Scarlatti aria is like that of ripieno to solo in a Baroque concerto. Sometimes, especially in the early operas, the orchestra participates only at the ritornellos; in others, it plays throughout the aria but with reduced instrumentation or the indication 'piano' while the voice is singing.

The string ensemble was basic, and on occasion Scarlatti called for other instruments, for example trumpets or horns for ceremonial scenes or martial arias, lutes for accompaniment, and (in the later operas) oboes. Obbligato horn parts appear in *Tigrane*, *Telemaco* and *Marco Attilio Regolo*; less common are obbligato parts for flutes, as in *Cambise* and *Griselda*.

Scarlatti's overtures have no thematic or other particular connection with the opera to follow. After about 1695 they settled into the standard three-movement Italian sinfonia form: a brilliant Allegro, often in D, for full orchestra; a short, tentative, transitional slow movement for reduced orchestra; and a bipartite finale in homophonic style and dance rhythm. Apart from the overtures the only orchestral numbers are short sinfonias, used typically to introduce scenes of splendour.

The extraordinary variety among the arias in Scarlatti's operas is the product of an inexhaustible flow of melodic invention coupled with great sensitivity to the rhythm, mood and imagery of a text. Variety is encouraged by the nature of the libretto. A dramatic situation may be implausible, a personage's reaction improbable or inconsistent, but none of these things matters; every aria is a self-contained world, psychologically as well as musically. There is a division into 'big' and 'little' arias: the former longer, more amply developed, usually with fuller orchestral accompaniment, apt to occur at points of strong conflict, and mostly assigned to the principal characters; the latter shorter, simpler in both thematic ideas and development, and apt to be pictorial or reflective. There are a few recurrent types of aria associated with certain keys: the martial-triumphal arias with trumpets (or trumpet-like figures in the strings), nearly always in D; a *deciso* type expressive of abrupt firm resolution, in C (or B♭); a great number of arias simply placid or cheerful, in G; arias typically assigned to the secondary lovers or to pastoral or other situations where no conflict is involved, in G or A (rarely D or E); and arias of sorrow, ranging from simple melancholy to wrenching grief,

15. Autograph MS of the opening of Act 1 scene v from Alessandro Scarlatti's opera 'La Griselda', first performed at the Teatro Capranica, Rome, 1721

most often in C minor but for special intensity sometimes in F minor. In serious arias of any type Scarlatti's imagination may seize on some visual image to generate an accompaniment figure that envelops the vocal melody in a nimbus of descriptive coloration. There are also comic arias and duets, lightly orchestrated, almost always in major keys, with rollicking tunes, and subject to sudden changes of mood and movement for quarrelsome outbursts, satirical interjections or parody.

Duets are few (one or two in each act), in the same style and form as arias and commonly designated 'aria à 2'. Often the voices, expressing congenial if not identical sentiments, alternate before forming parallel 3rds or 6ths at the cadences. Ensembles for more than two voices are uncommon until the late Roman operas, and even in these the trios and quartets are still essentially no more than da capo arias; they embody no marked contrast of personalities and do not advance the action. Larger ensembles and choruses are extremely rare (the 'septet' in *Eraclea* is merely a tiny three-section aria sung by seven singers in turn). Only at the close of an opera do all the singers and orchestra unite in what is usually a brief, perfunctory closing number.

Scarlatti's recitative differs in no salient respects from that in the operas of his contemporaries. In his early operas, in accordance with 17th-century practice, the *secco* style often shades into melodic arioso passages, particularly at the end of a recitative, thus forming a transition to the following aria. Some recitatives are accompanied by the full string orchestra *senza cembalo* (so marked, though occasionally continuo figures are written below the bass notes in the score); the upper string parts are written sometimes as long sustained notes, sometimes as full chords with the direction 'arpeggio'. Accompanied recitatives appear in operas from Scarlatti's first Neapolitan period; the earliest ones seem to be used mainly to establish atmosphere in nocturnal or dream scenes, a suggestion of the supernatural perhaps analogous to the use of string accompaniment for the Voice of God in Scarlatti's oratorio *Cain overo Il primo omicidio* or for the words of Christ in his *St John Passion*. In the operas from *La Statira* (1690) onwards, and notably in the late Neapolitan and Roman ones, accompanied recitative serves to bring into relief moments of high emotional tension, as in the closing scene of *Griselda*. In such recitatives the orchestra, as well as accompanying the voice, may intervene with interjections between the vocal phrases, as in *Marco Attilio Regolo*, Act 2 scene iv, or *Telemaco*, Act 1 scene xi.

By Scarlatti's time it was customary to end each scene with an aria followed by the exit of the singer; but the later 18th-century stereotype whereby a scene consisted simply of recitative and aria is not always valid for his operas. Not every scene has an aria; one may come at the beginning of a scene (especially if it is a solo scene), or in the middle of a scene between two sections of a recitative. On rare occasions two arias are juxtaposed without an intervening passage of recitative (*Il trionfo dell'onore*, Act 1). For the most part an aria comes at the end of a scene, rounding it off with a quasi-independent musical entity having no thematic or (necessarily) tonal connection with other similar entities in the opera. The principal personages, hence the most important artists, naturally have the most arias, and

Operas

Scarlatti paid due attention to variety in the type and placing of arias within each act; but attempts to find a tonal plan operating throughout a Scarlatti opera may be successful only in the seeker's imagination.

CHAPTER THREE

Other works

I Serenatas, oratorios and church music

The serenatas, unlike the operas, were written to order for celebration of special events in the households of Scarlatti's patrons. The mythological–pastoral texts consist mainly of alternating recitatives and arias. The effect as a whole is that of a picture or a design rather than of a drama; everything is stately and formal. Because of this, and because special performing resources were sometimes available, a good deal of the music in the serenatas is more elaborate than that in the operas. Recitatives, not being obliged to push ahead with a plot, are more leisurely and likely to expand into arioso or even coloratura. Most arias are in the usual da capo form, although strophic arias linger in the serenatas long after the type had disappeared from the operas. There are more duets and ensembles, a trio or quartet often being placed at both the beginning and end of a scene. The orchestra, especially in the later serenatas, is much more conspicuous than in the operas, and the writing includes unusual features such as concerto–ripieno distribution as well as considerable diversity of obbligato instruments and their combination in the accompaniments.

Most of Scarlatti's oratorios were written for Rome where they were performed either in one of the oratories or colleges or in the palaces of his patrons. Subjects include biblical stories, episodes from the lives of saints and allegorical actions or dialogues. The treatment ranges from the opera-like version of the combat between David and Goliath (Scarlatti's only extant Latin oratorio) to the purely internal drama of St Philip Neri's dying conversation with the personified figures of Faith, Hope and Charity. In their musical elements and general style the oratorios resemble the operas but, since the librettos are less stereotyped and not bound by requirements of stage scenery and action, the arias, recitatives and ensembles are combined more freely and Scarlatti could make more uniform use of all the voice ranges instead of principally sopranos. The 'coro' in these oratorios is not a chorus in the modern sense but an ensemble of all the soloists.

Scarlatti's liturgical music comprises motets and masses in both the so-called Palestrina style and the newer, 18th-century concertato style. Examples of the former are the two masses written for Pope Clement XI (1705, 1716); among the latter the St Cecilia Mass (1720) for five soloists, chorus and orchestra is an imposing large work of external splendour. One of Scarlatti's best liturgical works is the *St John Passion* (*c*1680), an austere, moving setting of the scriptural text. Roger of Amsterdam printed a collection of miscellaneous *Concerti sacri* (1707–8), brilliant in style; three motets for double choir, *Tu es Petrus*, *O magnum mysterium* and *Volo Pater* (*c*1707), are broad and dignified, and the little *Laetatus sum* for four voices is a model of counterpoint in Leo's manner.

II Cantatas

Scarlatti's enormous output of chamber cantatas reveals

perhaps more strikingly than any other class of his works his unbroken continuity with preceding phases of the Baroque era and his separation from the following period. With more than 600 known cantatas for which his authorship is reasonably certain and well over 100 others less reliably attributed to him he is clearly the most prolific composer of cantatas. These works crown the history of a genre which throughout more than a century of vigorous growth held a rank second only to opera; indeed contemporaries generally placed it above opera in refinement and regarded it as the supreme challenge to a composer's artistry. Scarlatti was among the last to contribute significantly to its literature.

A decisive majority of Scarlatti's cantatas are for solo voice, most for soprano but some for alto and a few for bass. A few are for two voices: two sopranos, soprano and alto, or soprano and bass. 90% are accompanied by continuo alone; the remainder, reflecting a contemporary trend, enlist various instrumental ensembles in addition to continuo, mostly strings but occasionally recorders or trumpet. They deal almost exclusively with love; heroic, comic or devotional subjects appear less often than in the past.

The most characteristic text is lyric, presenting in some imagined protagonist's monologue a series of contrasting reflections centred on some unifying thought. In most cantatas for two voices there is dialogue or an alternation between dialogue and lyric monologue. The protagonist is usually a shepherd or nymph, or may be drawn from mythology or history. Occasionally the monologue is introduced by an explicatory narrative or descriptive passage, and further narrative passages may thread the reflections together. The changes are normally paralleled by changes of poetic metre and rhyme pattern, and reflected too in changes in musical metre, tempo, rhythmic and melodic material, harmonic character, texture and the entire constellation of stylistic elements.

The cantata repertory in Rome in the 1670s included works not only by younger composers, such as Stradella, Pasquini and P. S. Agostini, but by composers of older generations too, including Cesti, Savioni, Carissimi and even Luigi Rossi (*d* 1653). Scarlatti drew comprehensively on this stylistic inheritance. The retrospective characteristics in his cantatas composed before about 1705 are striking. Musical refrains continue to appear as reflections of textual ones, either with periodic regularity or at irregular intervals. Exact or modified musical repetitions – occasionally only loose, imprecise correspondences – with new words reflect strophes in the texts. Not infrequently, however, a second strophe in the text is set to new music, preserving only a structural parallelism with that of the first; and a second strophe may be separated from the first by intervening sections. Responsiveness to his texts according to such procedures sometimes gives rise to forms that had flourished in earlier decades but had, it seems, been laid aside by Scarlatti's immediate predecessors, Pasquini and Agostini.

O dolce servitù, the verse of which is in part strophic, resembles in structure many cantatas of around the 1640s (like Rossi's *Da perfida speranza*): the first strophe consists of a 4/4 section in aria style, a short recitative and a 3/2 arioso. This entire complex is repeated, in part exactly, with the second strophe of the text. Sometimes only the first strophe's bass is repeated (only its pitches, its rhythm having been substantially altered) while the vocal line is in part newly composed: here Scarlatti reached back to the strophic variation, a structure prominent in the cantata's earliest history. An arrangement characteristic of the mid-century cantata survives in *Chi vedesse la ferita*: *ABCAB′C′A*, where *A* is a refrain in music and text while *B′C′* is a musical repetition of *BC* with a second strophe of its text (a similar arrangement is found in Carissimi's *Bel tempo per me*).

In most of Scarlatti's cantatas, late as well as early, diversification is especially conspicuous in composite structures comprising more or less discrete recitatives, arias and ariosos. In works composed before about 1705 they appear in the limitlessly varied combinations seen in the past, reflecting long, complicated poetic structures in which sections in various metres and rhyme patterns follow one another in unruly, wayward succession; these in turn reflect unruly successions of contrasting passions. Such arias continue to show the formal variety found in the past, including *ABB′* and related patterns (as old as Monteverdi), *AB*, ostinato arias, and the increasingly popular *ABA* and *ABA′*. Most have two strophes. In cantatas with instrumental ensemble many are continuo arias with ritornellos, resembling forms in contemporary operas. Recitatives continue to incorporate lyrical, expressive arioso, with refrains and other organizing devices. The integration of declamatory and aria-like elements often survives in Scarlatti's cantata recitatives. The 'curious mixture of air and recitative' with which *Solitudini amene, bersaglio* (1705) begins did not escape Burney's notice (*BurneyH*, ii, 630, 634).

A more orderly form, perhaps manifesting the spirit of the Age of Reason, became increasingly prominent in Scarlatti's cantatas in the 1690s: two (sometimes three) da capo arias contrasting in tempo and expressive character, each preceded by a recitative. Second strophes and refrains were laid aside. In his cantatas after 1704 significant deviations from this pattern are exceptional. A search for increased intensity of expression often gave rise to chromaticism, which is especially characteristic of recitatives, as is illustrated in the celebrated *Andate, o miei sospiri* ('Con idea inhumana', 1712). Notes in the most authoritative copies of this work suggest that Francesco Gasparini had presented Scarlatti with his setting as a token of friendship and that Scarlatti responded with two settings of his own, the first 'Con idea humana' and the second 'Con idea inhumana, ma in regolato Cromatico, non è per ogni Professore'. Both typify his mature style at its most beautiful, and the recitatives of the second are further distinguished by unusually daring chromaticisms.

Already singular in his time, Scarlatti's recitative frequently became even more alien through bold chromaticism, to a degree that his contemporaries could no longer accept. In 1728 J. D. Heinichen censured Scarlatti's 'extravagant and irregular harmony . . . as revealed in the vast production of his cantatas' (*Der General-Bass in der Composition*). Encumbrance with chromaticism, he protested, prevented their attaining the quality of 'rapid recitative'. His strictures reveal that a new conception of recitative had established itself, the rapid parlando, often characterized further by expressive impoverishment and flatness. Regarding this later conception as the norm, Heinichen rejected the impassioned Scarlattian form as 'unnatural and violent'. In the decade when the 'Neapolitan' style triumphantly conquered the European repertory, a contemporary saw Scarlatti not as the founder of any school but as a lonely eccentric, followed by no one except perhaps d'Astorga.

Scarlatti's cantatas for two voices appear in various forms. Most are composite structures. Usually a singer delivers on each entry a recitative followed by an aria. Some recitatives engage both singers in rapid dialogue. The concluding member is usually a duet aria or arioso, and most cantatas include additional duet arias. Some open with a duet aria and close with a repetition of it or with a repetition of its music set to the words of a second strophe; in some all members are duets. The duet arias rely chiefly on the trio texture developed by Monteverdi and basic to musical style throughout the Baroque era. The bass functions harmonically, but it is nevertheless active and melodically defined; it holds consistently apart, however, from the melody, imitations and parallels of the upper pair.

III Instrumental music

Scarlatti seems to have taken little or no interest in purely instrumental composition before 1715, the year in which he began composing his 12 *Sinfonie di concerto grosso*. But within the next ten years he produced other concerti grossi and chamber sonatas and a considerable number of toccatas and short harpsichord pieces. None of these shows him at his best. The orchestral and chamber works are conservative in form and style and singularly unexciting compared with those of his contemporary Corelli or the younger Vivaldi. Scarlatti's best and historically most important orchestral music is

16. Alessandro Scarlatti: portrait by an unknown artist

found in the overtures and ritornellos of his operas and serenatas. The keyboard toccatas, most in several short movements, show good feeling for the qualities of the instrument but are otherwise unremarkable except for one fine set of variations on the folia.

CHAPTER FOUR

Posthumous reputation

The legend that Scarlatti taught a whole generation of Neapolitan composers lacks supporting evidence. The only official teaching post he held was at the Conservatory of S Maria di Loreto for two months in spring 1689. No doubt he initiated Domenico, and presumably his other children, in the rudiments of music and it may be supposed that from time to time he assisted other young composers with advice or informal instruction. Hasse claimed to have been his pupil from 1722, but our only information comes from Hasse's conversations with Burney, 50 years later, and old men are apt to gild the recollections of their youth. The principal documents bearing on Scarlatti as teacher are the *Regole per principianti* prefixed to some manuscripts of his toccatas, which deal partly with fingering but chiefly with rules for the realization of figured basses; in neither respect are they literally 'for beginners'. More important for Scarlatti as theorist is the *Discorso sopra un caso particolare* (1717, but extant only in German translation in Kirnberger's *Die Kunst des reinen Satzes*, 1776–9), a detailed, tactfully worded but firm defence of principles governing the treatment of dissonance in strict counterpoint, with thoughtful observations on the relation of tradition to individual freedom in musical composition.

As for his historical position, there is a curious anomaly about Scarlatti's reputation in the 18th century.

The many copies of his operas, cantatas and arias in European libraries testify to an esteem more widespread than the limited success of most of his later operas would indicate; but his contemporaries towards the end of his life, while respecting his achievements, regarded him as an out-of-date composer. One senses this even in the words of his admirers Hasse, Quantz and Jommelli as reported by Burney. In the few 18th-century writings on music that mention Scarlatti he looms as a shadowy father-figure in the background of Vinci, Leo, Pergolesi and their successors of the 'Neapolitan school'. After the middle of the 19th century he is occasionally cited as the arch-villain whose bad example began the 'decline' of dramatic music, as in Emil Naumann's *Illustrierte Musikgeschichte* (1885) and more markedly in Romain Rolland's history of European opera (1895). Modern Scarlatti scholarship, with appreciation of his true qualities and historical position, began in 1905 with Edward J. Dent's *Alessandro Scarlatti*, followed in 1927 by Alfred Lorenz's studies of the early operas. Progress since then has continued at a modest pace. Some of the operas and oratorios have been made available in modern editions; important new details of his biography and of performances of his works have come to light. Among those areas that need further attention are Scarlatti's cantatas (as well as those of his predecessors and contemporaries).

Scarlatti was the outstanding composer of the late Italian Baroque period whose work marks the historical consummation of the era of Monteverdi, Cavalli, Cesti, Carissimi and Stradella. Typical for this orientation is Scarlatti's concentration on vocal composition in the forms of the *dramma per musica* and the cantata. Also typical are the stylistic features: the spun-out melodic lines, the basically contrapuntal texture, the sophisticated interplay of voice and orchestra and the characteristically Baroque relationship between drama and music in the operas. In many respects, and particularly in regard to those features of his music that can be most readily described in words, Scarlatti was a man of his time. He surpassed his contemporaries by virtue of superior genius and skill in the handling of a common musical language. He was no more a conscious innovator than Bach. As Bach worked in the comparative isolation of Lutheran Leipzig, so did Scarlatti in the intense but narrow worlds of the Neapolitan and Roman aristocracy; it is significant that Ottoboni lauded him as a 'friend of nobles and princes'. His music had little demonstrable direct influence on later 18th-century composers, Neapolitan or other (with the possible exception of Handel with respect to his 'borrowings'); but Dent was undeniably right in naming Mozart as his spiritual descendant.

WORKS

* *doubtful;* † *autograph*

Numbers in the right-hand column denote references in the text.

OPERAS

(3 acts unless otherwise stated; source information refers to complete scores unless otherwise stated) 221–31, 242

Edition: *The Operas of Alessandro Scarlatti*, ed. D. J. Grout, HPM, ix (1974–) [G]

DP *Rome, Palazzo Doria Pamphili* PR *Naples, Palazzo Reale* SB *Naples, Teatro S Bartolomeo*
SGG *Venice, Teatro S Giovanni Grisostomo* TC *Rome, Teatro Capranica* VM *Pratolino, Villa Medicea*

Title, Genre	*Libretto*	*First Performances, Remarks*	*Sources, Edn.*	
Gli equivoci nel sembiante, dramma	D. F. Contini	Contini's private theatre, Rome, Feb 1679; as L'errore innocente, Bologna, 1679; as Amor non vuole inganni, Vienna, carn. 1681; as Gl'amori fortunati negl'equivoci, Venice, aut., 1690	*A-Wn* (Act 1 only), *B-Bc*, *I-Bc*, *MOe*, *Rsc*, *Vnm*; ed. in G vii	212, 213, 222
L'honestà negli amori, dramma	G. F. Bernini	Rome, Palazzo Bernini, 6 Feb 1680	*MOe*, *Rc* (?autograph)	212
Tutto il mal non vien per nuocere, commedia	G. D. de Totis	Rome, Palazzo Rospigliosi, 1681; as Dal male il bene, Naples, 1687	*D-Bds*, *I-MC* (partly autograph); *Nc*	
*Il Lisimaco, dramma	G. Sinibaldi	Rome, Palazzo Bernini, 1681	—	
Il Pompeo, dramma	N. Minato	Rome, Teatro Colonna, 25 Jan 1683	*B-Br*; ed. J. Roberts (New York, in preparation)	213
La guerriera costante	F. Orsini	Rome, palace of Duchess of Bracciano, carn. 1683	*I-Rvat*	
L'Aldimiro o vero Favor per favore, dramma	de Totis	PR, 6 Nov 1683	arias *GB-Lbm*, *Och*, *I-Bc*, *Rvat*	
La Psiche o vero Amore innamorato, dramma	de Totis	PR, 21 Dec 1683	recit and aria *PAVu*	
*Il Fetonte, dramma	de Totis	PR, 22 Nov 1685	—	
Olimpia vendicata, dramma	A. Aureli	PR, 23 Dec 1685; as Amor vince lo sdegno o vero L'Olimpia placata, TC, 1692, with new music by Scarlatti and F. Gasparini	*F-Pn*, *GB-Lbm*, *I-Vnm*	
*L'Etio, dramma	A. Morselli	PR, carn. 1686	aria *MC*, *Nc*	
La Rosmene o vero L'infedeltà fedele, melodramma	de Totis	DP, carn. 1686	*D-BD*, *MÜs*, *F-Pn*, *I-Fc* (Acts 1 and 2)	214
Clearco in Negroponte, dramma	A. Arcoleo	PR, 21 Dec 1686	*MOe*	
La santa Dinna, commedia	B. Pamphili	DP, carn. 1687, Act 1 by Alessandro Melani, Act 2 by B. Pasquini, Act 3 by Scarlatti	—	

Il Flavio, dramma	M. Noris	PR, ?14 Nov 1688	arias *GB-Och*, *I-Fc*, *MOe*, *Nc*	
*La Dori, dramma	A. Apolloni	PR, 18 Jan 1689	arias *MOe*, *Nc*	
L'Anacreonte tiranno, melodramma	G. F. Bussani	SB, 9 Feb 1689	aria *Nc*	
*La serva favorita, dramma	C. Villifranchi	VM, 1689	—	
L'Amazzone corsara [guerriera] o vero L'Alvilda, dramma	G. C. Corradi	PR, 6 Nov 1689	*D-Mbs*, *I-MC*	
La Statira, dramma	P. Ottoboni	Rome, Teatro Tordinona, 5 Jan 1690	*D-Mbs*, *GB-CDp*, *Lbm*, *I-MOe*; ed. in G ix	214, 230
Gli equivoci in amore o vero La Rosaura, melodramma	G. B. Lucini	Rome, Palazzo della Cancelleria, Dec 1690; as La Rosaura, ?Florence, 1692	*A-Wn*, *D-WD*, *F-Pc* (Acts 1 and 2), *GB-Lbm*; facs. of Acts 1 and 2 ed. R. Eitner (New York, 1966)	214
L'humanità nelle fiere o vero Il Lucullo, dramma		SB, 25 Feb 1691	—	
La Teodora augusta, dramma	Morselli	PR, 6 Nov 1692	*Och*, *I-Fc*	
Gerone tiranno di Siracusa, dramma	Aureli	PR, 22 Dec 1692	*GB-Och*	
L'amante doppio o vero Il Ceccobimbi, melodramma		PR, April 1693	—	
Il Pirro e Demetrio, dramma	Morselli	SB, 28 Jan 1694; as La forza della fedeltà, Florence, carn. 1712	*B-Br*, *I-Nc*	216, 223
Il Bassiano o vero Il maggior impossibile, melodramma	Noris	SB, spr. 1694	—	
La santa Genuinda, o vero L'innocenza difesa dall'inganno, dramma sacro	Pamphili	DP, 1694, Act 1 by G. L. Lulier, Act 2 by Scarlatti, Act 3 by C. F. Cesarini (or C. F. Pollarolo)	*D-Mbs*, *F-Pc*, *GB-Lbm*	
Le nozze con l'inimico o vero L'Analinda, melodramma		SB, 1695; as L'Analinda overo Le nozze col nemico, Florence, carn. 1702	*F-Pn*	
Nerone fatto Cesare, melodramma	Noris	PR, 6 Nov 1695	arias and duets *I-Nc*	
Massimo Puppieno, melodramma	Aureli	SB, 26 Dec 1695	*MC*; ed. in G v	223
Penelope la casta, dramma	Noris	SB, ?23 Feb 1696; ? perf. Palermo, 1694	arias *Nc*	
La Didone delirante, opera drammatica	F. M. Paglia, after A. Franceschi	SB, 28 May 1696	arias *Bc*, *Bsp*, *Nc*, *Os*, *Rvat*	
Comodo Antonino, dramma	Paglia, after Bussani	SB, 18 Nov 1696	arias *F-Pthibault*	
L'Emireno o vero Il consiglio dell'ombra, opera drammatica	Paglia	SB, 2 Feb 1697	*A-Wn*, *I-Nc*; comic scenes *D-Dlb*	
La caduta de' Decemviri, dramma	S. Stampiglia	SB, 15 Dec 1697	*B-Br*, *C-Mc*, *GB-Lbm*, *I-Nc*, *US-I*, *PO*; comic scenes *D-Dlb*; ed. in G vi	216

Title, Genre	*Libretto*	*First Performances, Remarks*	*Sources, Edn.*	
La donna ancora è fedele, dramma	Contini (rev.)	SB, 1698	*I-Nc*; comic scenes *D-Dlb*	
Il prigioniero fortunato, dramma	Paglia	SB, 14 Dec 1698	*GB-Lbm*, *I-Nc*; comic scenes *D-Dlb*	
Gl'inganni felici, dramma	A. Zeno (except for comic scenes)	PR, 6 Nov 1699; as L'Agarista ovvero Gl'inganni felici, with intermezzi Brenno e Tisbe, Florence, carn. 1706	arias *Nc*; comic scenes *D-Dlb*	
L'Eraclea, dramma	Stampiglia	SB, 30 Jan 1700	items in *A-Wn*, *B-Br*, *D-Dlb*, *F-Pn*, *GB-Cm*, *Lbm*, *I-Nc*; ed. in G i	229
Odoardo (with intermezzi Adolfo e Lesbina), dramma	?Zeno	SB, 5 May 1700	arias *F-Pc*, *I-Nc*; comic scenes *D-Dlb*	
Dafni, favola boschereccia	Paglia, after E. Manfredi	Naples, Casino del Vicerè a Posillipo, 5 Aug 1700; as L'amore non viene dal caso, Iesi, carn. 1715	*GB-Cfm*; comic scenes *D-Dlb*	
Laodicea e Berenice, dramma	Noris (adapted)	SB, April 1701	*F-Pn*	
Il pastor[e] di Corinto, favola boschereccia	Paglia	Naples, Casino del Vicerè a Posillipo, 5 Aug 1701	*B-Br*; comic scenes *D-Dlb*	
Tito Sempronio Gracco (with intermezzi Bireno e Dorilla), dramma	Stampiglia	SB, ?carn. 1702	arias *D-MÜs*, *F-Pc*, *I-Nc*; comic scenes *D-Dlb*	
Tiberio imperatore d'Oriente, dramma	G. D. Pallavicino	PR, 8 May 1702	arias *F-Pc*, *I-Fc*, *Nc*	188
Il Flavio Cuniberto, dramma	Noris	VM, Sept 1702 (? not 1st perf.)	*GB-Och*	
Arminio, dramma	A. Salvi	VM, Sept 1703	—	
Turno Aricino, dramma	Stampiglia	VM, Sept 1704	arias *D-MÜs*, *F-Pc*	214
Lucio Manlio l'imperioso, dramma	Stampiglia	VM, Sept 1705	—	
Il gran Tamerlano, dramma	Salvi, after N. Pradon	VM, Sept 1706		
Il Mitridate Eupatore, tragedia (5 acts)	G. Frigimelica Roberti	SGG, carn. 1707	*B-Br*, *D-Bds*, *F-Pn*	218, 222
Il trionfo della libertà, tragedia (5 acts)	Frigimelica Roberti	SGG, carn. 1707	arias *A-Wn*, *B-Br*, *I-Rvat*	
Il Teodosio, dramma	? V. Grimani	SB, 27 Jan 1709	—	
L'amor volubile e tiranno, dramma	G. D. Pioli, G. Papis	SB, 25 May 1709; as La Dorisbe ó L'amor volubile e tiranno, Rome, carn. 1711; as La Dorisbe, Genoa, aut. 1713	*B-Bc*, *D-Dlb*	
La principessa fedele, dramma	A. Piovene (rev. ? D. A. Parrino)	SB, 8 Feb 1710	*B-Br* (inc.), arias *D-MÜs*; ed. in G iv	
La fede riconosciuta, dramma pastorale	? B. Marcello	SB, 14 Oct 1710	†*GB-Cfm*	
Giunio Bruto o vero La caduta dei Tarquini, dramma	?Sinibaldi	planned for Vienna, 1711, perf. cancelled; Act 1 by C. F. Cesarini, Act 2 by A. Caldara, Act 3 by Scarlatti	*A-Wn*	219

Il Ciro, dramma	Ottoboni	Rome, Palazzo della Cancelleria, carn. 1712	†*B-Bc*, *US-Wc*	*224*
Scipione nelle Spagne (with intermezzi Pericca e Varrone), dramma	Zeno, N. Serino; intermezzi by ?Salvi	SB, 21 Jan 1714; intermezzi perf. as La dama spagnola ed il cavalier romano, Bologna, carn. 1730	*B-Br*, *GB-Lbm*, *I-Bu*, *MC* (Act 1 and intermezzi)	
L'amor generoso (with intermezzi Despina e Niso), dramma	Papis, Stampiglia	PR, 1 Oct 1714	*GB-Lbm*, *US-Wc*	
Il Tigrane o vero L'egual impegno d'amore e di fede, dramma	D. Lalli	SB, 16 Feb 1715	*GB-Bu*, *Lbm*, *I-Fc*, *Nc*; ed. in G viii	218, 226
Carlo re d'Allemagna (with intermezzi *Palandrana e Zamberlucco), dramma	F. Silvani	SB, ?26 Jan 1716	*Bu*	
La virtù trionfante dell'odio e dell'amore, dramma	Silvani	PR, 3 May 1716		
Telemaco, dramma	C. S. Capece	TC, carn. 1718	†*A-Wn*, *D-MÜs*, *F-Pc*; ed. H. Brown (New York, 1978)	220, 226, 230
Il trionfo dell'onore, commedia	F. A. Tullio	Naples, Teatro dei Fiorentini, 26 Nov 1718	*GB-Lbm*, *US-Wc*; ed. H. Williams (New York, 1982)	222, 230
Il Cambise, dramma	Lalli	SB, 4 Feb 1719	*I-Nc* (?autograph)	219, 226
Marco Attilio Regolo (with intermezzi Leonzio e Eurilla), dramma	?Noris (adapted)	TC, carn. 1719	†*GB-Lbm*, *US-Wc*; ed. in G ii	220, 226, 230
La Griselda, dramma	after Zeno	TC, Jan 1721	*B-Bc*, *D-Bds*, *MÜs*, †*GB-Lbm* (Acts 1 and 3); ed. in G iii; ed. D. Drechsler (Kassel, 1960)	220, 226, *228*, 230

CONTRIBUTIONS TO OTHER COMPOSERS' OPERAS

DP – *Rome, Palazzo Doria Pamphili* PR *Naples, Palazzo Reale* SB *Naples, Teatro S Bartolomeo*

Title (genre, libretto)	*Composer(s)*	*Performance*	*Scarlatti's contribution*	*Sources*
L'Idalma o vero Chi la dura la vince (dramma, G. D. de Totis)	B. Pasquini	DP, 1682	reworking of Act 1	—
L'Arsate	—	?Rome, 1683	arias	*I-Nc*, *Rsc*
Il Giustino (dramma, N. Beregan)	G. Legrenzi	PR, 6 Nov 1684	?prol	—
L'amico dell'amico, e nemico di se stesso	—	?Naples, 1693	arias	*Bc*, *Rvat*
L'Odoacre (dramma, N. Bonis)	G. Varischino	SB, 5 Jan 1694	arias	—
L'Arione (dramma, O. d'Arles)	C. Valtolina, D. Erba and 25 others	Milan, 9 June 1694	aria, Mio povero core	—

Title (genre, libretto)	Composer(s)	Performance	Scarlatti's contribution	Sources	
*La forza della virtù (dramma, D David)	C. F. Pollarolo and others	before 1699; rev. as Creonte tiranno di Tebe, SB, spr. 1699	arias	—	
La Semiramide (dramma, F. M. Paglia)	G. Aldrovandini	PR, 19 Dec 1701	?prol, arias	*Nc*	
L'Ariovisto (dramma)	G. A. Perti, Magni, Ballarotti	Florence, aut. 1702	arias	arias *D-MÜs*	
La pastorella (opera pastorale)	C. F. Cesarini, G. L. Lulier, G. Bononcini	Rome, Palazzo Venezia, 1705; as Love's Triumph, London, 1708	arias	arias *GB-Lbm*; pubd (London, 1709)	
Thomyris Queen of Scythia (opera, P. A. Motteux)	[pasticcio]	London, Drury Lane, 1 April 1707	arias	arias *Lbm*; pubd (London, 1707)	
Il figlio delle selve (dramma, C. S. Capece)	C. Bani	Palazzo Zuccari, 17 Jan 1709	?arias	*F-Pc*	
La Clotilda (dramma)	F. B. Conti	London, Haymarket, 2 March 1709	arias	arias *GB-Lbm*; pubd (London, 1709)	219
Lo Petracchio scremmetore (opera comica, A. Capis)	F. Scarlatti	Aversa, 1711	?15 arias	—	
Il Porsenna (dramma, A. Piovene)	A. Lotti	SB, 19 Nov 1713	arias	*Lbm*, *I-MC* (Act 2)	
Giove in Argo (A. M. Luchini)	Lotti	Dresden, Schlosstheater, 25 Oct 1717	intermezzi: Vespetta e Milo (2 by Scarlatti, 1 by F. Conti)	—	

SERENATAS 214, 216, 218, 232–3, 240

CV *Naples, Casino del Vicerè a Posillipo*
DP *Rome, Palazzo Doria Pamphili*
PR *Naples, Palazzo Reale*
TC *Rome, Teatro Capranica*

Title (incipit)	Libretto	Scoring	Performance	Sources
Diana ed Endimione (Voi solitarie piante)		2vv, insts	c1679–85	?*F-LYc*, *Pn*, *I-MC*, *US-Wc*
L'Olimpo in Mergellina			Mergellina, 25 Aug 1686	—

*Serenata in honour of James II of England			DP, 1688	—
Serenata		4vv, insts	Naples, house of Scipione Giuvo, 8 Oct 1691	—
Venere, Adone et Amore (Dal giardin del piacere)	F. M. Paglia	3vv, insts	CV, 15 July 1696; rev. Rome, Aug 1706	*GB-Och*, *I-MC*; *D-MÜs*
Il trionfo delle stagioni	Paglia		Piazza, PR, 26 July 1696	—
Il Genio di Partenope, la Gloria del Sebeto, il Piaçere di Mergellina (Venticelli soavi che con ali)		3vv, insts	Mergellina, 5 Aug 1696	*I-MC*
Venere ed Amore (Del mar Tirreno in su l'amena sponda)		2vv, insts	?CV, *c*1695 1700	*B-Br*; ed. A. Tirabassi (Brussels, 1921)
Clori, Lidia e Filli (Già compito il suo giro)		3vv, insts	*c*1700	*Bc*
Serenata			Naples, Palazzo della Posta, 2 June 1701	—
Serenata (based on Tiberio imperatore)			PR, 19 April 1702	—
Clori, Dorino e Amore (Cari lidi, amene sponde)		3vv, chorus, insts	PR, 2 May 1702	*D-Bds*, *MÜs*
Serenata for Queen Maria Casimira	P. Ottoboni		Rome, in front of Palazzo Zuccari, 9 Aug 1703	—
Serenata for the Spanish Ambassador		2vv	Rome, Palazzo di Spagna, 4 Oct 1703	—
Venere e Adone: Il giardino d'amore (Care selve, amati orrori)		2vv, insts	*c*1700–05	*Bds*, *MÜs*; ed. O. Drechsler (Frankfurt, 1963)
Endimione e Cintia (Sento un'aura che dolce)		2vv, insts	?Rome, 1705	*B-Bc*, *D-Bds*, *MÜs*
Clori e Zeffiro (Vaga, auretta soave)	G. Buonaccorsi	2vv, insts	Rome, 14 Sept 1705	*B-Bc*, *D-Bds*, *MÜs*
Amore e Virtù ossia Il trionfo della virtù (No, che non voglio più)		2vv, insts	?Rome, 1706	*Bds*; ed. A. Tirabassi (Brussels, 1923)
Fileno, Niso e Doralbo: Serenata a Filli (Tacete, aure, tacete)		3vv, insts	?Rome, 1706	*MÜs*
Sole, Urania e Clio: Le muse Urania e Clio lodano le bellezze di Filli (O mie figlie canore)		3vv, insts	?Rome, 1706	*MÜs*
Venere, Amore e Ragione: Il ballo delle ninfe (Cerco Amore, Amor che fa?)	S. Stampiglia	3vv, insts	Rome, 1706	*Bds*, *MÜs*, *E-Mn*; ed. H. Williams (Clinton, NY, 1982)
Cupido e Onestà: Il trionfo dell'Onestà (Puote si poco)		2vv, insts	?Rome, Sept 1706	*D-MÜs*

Title (*incipit*)	Libretto	Scoring	Performance	Sources	
Le glorie della Bellezza del Corpo e dell'Anima (In sì bel giorno che il Gran Natale), for the birthday of Queen Elizabeth of Spain	G. Papis	6vv, choruses, insts	Piazza, PR, 28 Aug 1709		
Pace, Amore e Providenza (Al fragor di lieta tromba)	Papis	3vv, choruses, insts	PR, 4 Nov 1711	*B-Bc*, *D-Bds*, *MÜs*	
Serenata for coronation of Charles III as King of Hungary (*olim* Il genio austriaco)			PR, 19 June 1712	—	
Il genio austriaco: Il Sole, Flora, Zeffiro, Partenope e Sebeto (Dia la Fama il suo fiato)	Papis	6vv, choruses, insts	Piazza, PR, 28 Aug 1713	—	
Serenata in honour of the vicereine, Donna Barbara d'Erbenstein			PR, 4 Dec 1715	—	
La gloria di primavera (Nato è già l'Austriaco Sole)	N. Giovo	5vv, chorus, insts	Naples, Palazzo di Nicola Gaetano d'Aragona, 20–23 May 1716; London, King's Theatre, 28 March 1721	*A-Wn*, *D-Mbs*, *GB-Lbm*, *I-Nc*	
Filli, Clori e Tirsi (Dalle fiorite arene)		3vv, insts	PR, 4 Dec ?1716; rev. Rome, 1721, as La ninfa del Tago (Dalle dorate arene)	*D-Bds*, *MÜs*	
Partenope, Teti, Nettuno, Proteo e Glauco (Chi al vasto ondoso)		5vv, chorus, insts	PR, 4 Nov 1718	*US-Wc*	
La virtù negli amori (Dolce sonno, obliò dei mali)	G. Lemer	6vv, chorus, insts	TC, 16 Nov 1721	—	
Erminia (Ove smarrita, e sola), for the wedding of the Prince of Stigliano		4vv, chorus, insts	Naples, Palazzo Stigliano, 13 June 1723	*GB-Lcm*, *I-MC* (Part I), *I-Nc* (Part I) (Part II lost); ed. T. E. Griffin (MA thesis, Los Angeles, 1975)	220
*Diana, Amore, Venere (Bel piacere ch'è la caccia)		3vv, insts		*Mc* (?by P. Scarlatti)	

ORATORIOS, LARGE SACRED WORKS

(*Italian oratorios unless otherwise stated*)

Edition: *Gli oratorii di Alessandro Scarlatti*, ed. L. Bianchi (Rome, 1964–) [B]

212, 214, 216, 217, 218, 220, 232–3, 242

Title (genre)	*Text*	*Scoring*	*Performance*	*Sources, Edn.*	
?(Lat. oratorio)			Rome, Oratorio del Ss Crocifisso, 24 Feb 1679	—	211
?(Lat. oratorio)			Rome, Oratorio del Ss Crocifisso, 12 April 1680	—	
Passio Domini Nostri Jesu Christi secundum Joannem (Lat. Passion)	Bible	A, B, SATB, str, bc	*c*1680	*I-Nc*, *Nf*; ed. E. Hanley (New Haven, 1955); ed. O. Deffner (Stuttgart, 1966)	230, 233
?(Lat. oratorio)			Rome, Oratorio del Ss Crocifisso, 20 Feb 1682	—	
Agar et Ismaele esiliati	G. D. de Totis	3S, A, B, str, bc	Rome, ?Palazzo Pamphili, 1683; as L'Abramo, Palermo, 1691; as Ismaele soccorso dall'angelo, Rome and Florence, 1695; as Il sacrificio di Abramo, Rome, 1703	*A-Wn*; ed. in B ii	
Il trionfo della gratia	B. Pamphili	2S, A, str, bc	Rome, 1685; as La Maddalena pentita, Modena, 1686; as La conversione di S Maria Maddalena, Florence, 1693	*D-Dlb*, *GB-Cfm*, *I-MOe*, *Rli* (parts), *Rw*	
Il martirio di S Teodosia		S, A, T, B, str, bc	Modena, 1685; as S Teodosia vergine e martire, Florence, 1693	*A-Wn*, *B-Br*, *F-Pn*, *I-MOe*, *Rli* (parts)	
I dolori di Maria sempre vergine		S, A, T, B, str, bc	Naples, S Luigi di Palazzo, 1693; in Lat. as La concettione della beata vergine, Rome, 1703	*F-Pn*	
La Giuditta (i)	Pamphili	2S, A, T, B, str, tpt, trbns, 2 fl, bc	Naples, 1693	*I-Nc*, St Elizabeth College, Morristown, NJ, USA; ed. in B i	
Samson vindicatus (Lat. oratorio)	Pamphili		Rome, Oratorio del Ss Crocifisso, 25 March 1695	—	
Cantata . . . per la notte di natale	?P. Ottoboni	4vv	Rome, Palazzo Apostolico, 24 Dec 1695	—	
Il martirio di S Orsola		2S, A, T, B, str, tpt, lute, bc	?Lyons, *c*1695–1700	*F-LYm*	

Title (genre)	Text	Scoring	Performance	Sources, Edn.	
La Giuditta (ii)	A. Ottoboni	S, A, T, str, bc	c1697–1700	*GB-Ckc*; ed. in B iii	
Davidis pugna et victoria (Lat. oratorio)		2S, A, T, B, SATB, SATB, str, bc	Rome, Oratorio del Ss Crocifisso, 5 March 1700 (probably not 1st perf.)	*F-LYm*; ed. in B v	233
L'assunzione della Beata Vergine Maria	P. Ottoboni	2S, 2A, str, bc	Rome, Collegio Clementino, 1703; as La sposa dei sacri cantici, Naples, 1710	*A-Wn, D-MÜs, F-Pc, US-STu*	
*S Maria Maddalena de' pazzi	Pamphili		Rome, Collegio Clementino, 1705	—	
S Michaelis Arcangelis cum Lucifer pugna et victoria (Lat. oratorio)	?Pullioni		Rome, Oratorio del Ss Crocifisso, 3 April 1705	—	
Il regno di Maria assunta in cielo	P. Ottoboni	4vv	Rome, Palazzo della Cancelleria, 23 Aug 1705		
S Casimiro, Re di Polonia		3S, A, T, str, bc	Florence, Compagnia della Purificazione di Maria Vergine e di S Zenobi detta di S Marco, 1705	*A-Wgm, Wn, E-Mn*	233
S Filippo Neri		S, 2A, T, str, tpt, lute, bc	Rome, Collegio Clementino, 1705	*B-Br, D-MÜs*; ed. R. Giazotto and G. Piccioli (Milan, 1960)	
Qual di lieti concenti (Serenata for Tirsi e Fileno) (Christmas cantata)			Rome, ?Palazzo Apostolico, c1705	*MÜs*	
Il Sedecia, Re di Gerusalemme	F. O. Fabbri	2S, A, T, B, chorus, str, 2 ob, 2 tpt, timp, lute, bc	?Urbino, 1705	*A-Wn, B-Bc, D-B, Dlb, Hs, Mbs, I-Rc*; ed. G. Guerini (Milan, 1961)	
Abramo il tuo sembiante (Christmas cantata)	S. Stampiglia	2S, A, T, B, chorus, str, 2 ob, bc	Rome, Palazzō Apostolico, 24 Dec 1705	*D-MÜs*	
Il trionfo della Ss Vergine assunta in cielo	P. Ottoboni	2S, 2A, str, fl, 2 ob, tpt, lute, bc	Florence, Compagnia della Purificazione di Maria Vergine e di S Zenobi detta di S Marco, 1706	*MÜs*	
S Francesco di Paola			Urbino, Chiesa della Communità, 1706	—	
Humanità e Lucifero		S, T, str, tpt, pic, bc	?1706	*MÜs*	
Il martirio di S Susanna	Stampiglia		Florence, Chiesa dei Filippini, 1706	—	
Alcone, ove per queste (Christmas cantata)	Fabbri	3vv, ?insts	Rome, Palazzo Apostolico, 24 Dec 1706	—	
Cain overo Il primo omicidio		2S, 2A, T, B, str, bc	Venice, Lent 1707	†*US-SFsc*; ed. in B iv	230

Title	Librettist	Scoring	First performance	Sources
Il giardino di rose: La Ss Vergine del Rosario		2S, A, T, B, str, 2 tpt, 2 fl, 2 ob, bn, lute, bc	Rome, 24 April 1707	*D-MÜs*
Serafini al nostro canto (Christmas cantata)	M. S. Mirandolano	3vv, ?insts	Rome, Palazzo Apostolico, 24 Dec 1707	—
Il martirio di S Cecilia	?P. Ottoboni		Rome, Lent, 1708	
La Ss Annunziata	?P. Ottoboni	3S, A, T, str, bc	Rome, Palazzo Ruspoli, 25 March 1708 (?1st perf. 1700)	*B-Br*, *D-MÜs*
Oratorio per la Passione di Nostro Signore Gesù Cristo (Passion oratorio)	P. Ottoboni	2S, A, str, 4 tpt, trbn, timp, bc	Rome, Palazzo della Cancelleria, 4 April 1708; in Lat. as Culpa, Poenitentia et Gratia, Rome, 1725	*Dlb*, *WD*
La vittoria della fede	C. S. Capece		Rome, Palazzo Zuccari, 12 Sept 1708	—
Il trionfo del valore		5vv, ?insts	Naples, Palazzo Reale, 19 March 1709	—
La Ss Trinità			Naples, May 1715	Fondazione Bravi, Brescia; ed. G. Piccioli (Bologna, 1953)
[La vergine addolorata]		2S, A, T, str, fl, ob, tpt, bc	Rome, 1717	*B-Bc*, *GB-Lwa*, *I-Nf*
La gloriosa gara tra la Santità e la Sapienza		3vv	Rome, 13 June 1720	—

Also arias in pasticcio oratorios: I trionfi di Giosuè (G. P. Berzini), Florence, Compagnia di S Marco, 1703, and as Giosuè in Gabaon, Florence; Sara in Egitto (D. Canavese), Florence, Compagnia di S Marco, 1708

CANTATAS

212, 214, 216, 218, 220, 233–8, 242

Arranged alphabetically by incipit, titles given in parentheses; for S, bc, unless otherwise stated; for sources see Hanley, 1963, and Pagano, Bianchi and Rostirolla, 1972

A battaglia, pensieri, S, A, 2 vn, vc, db, tpt, mandola, bc, 1699; Abbandonar Fileno dovea, S/A, bc; Abbandonato e solo (Il Nerone), S/A, bc; *A chi t'inganna, bella tiranna, S/A, bc; Ad altro uso serbate; Agitato mio core, dove ti volgi?, 1704; Agitato sen cade (La Sofonisba); Ah ben lo vedi, o core; *Ah che pur troppo è vero; Ah fuggi, sì, mio core; Ahi che sarà di me? (Floro e Tirsi), 2S, bc, 2 Sept 1707; Ah Mitilde vezzosa, 29 July 1712; Alba che neghittosa; *Al fin diviene amante

*Al fine, o Clori amata; Al fin m'ucciderete, S/A, bc, 20 July 1705; Alle troiane antenne (Didone abbandonata), 18 Sept 1705; *Allor che stanco il sole, S, 2 vn, bc; Allor ch'il Dio di Delo (La Gelosia), 26 Feb 1705; *Allor ch'il fier leone; Al mare, al bosco, al rio; Alma, tu che dal cielo (D. A. Ottoboni), S, 2 vn, bc, 12 Sept 1709; Alme voi che provaste; Al mormorio dell'onda; *Al mormorio d'un vago ruscelletto; Al pensiero, miei sguardi, July 1706; Al seren di si bel giorno, 26 Oct 1704; Al voler del bene amato (Devesi amare per servire); *Amai, dolce mia vita, A, bc; *Amanti, anch'io son preso, S, 2 vn, bc

Amica, hora che Aprile (Filli e Clori), 2S, 2 vn, bc, ?1694; Amici s'è vinto (Amor perduto e ritornato) (D. A. Ottoboni), before 1710; Ammore brutto figlio de pottana, T, bc; Amo e godo d'amare; *Amo, e negar nol posso, Dec 1704; Amo, ma l'idol mio, A/S, bc, 9 June

1701; *Amo, peno, e languisco, Mez, bc; Amo, peno, gioisco (Amante timido di spiegarsi alla sua dama); *Amor che fia di noi (Cantata grave); Amor con l'idol mio, 3 April 1702; Amore, o mi togli le fiamme; Amor, fabro ingegnoso; Amor, Mitilde è morta (La morte di Mitilde); *Amor, o crudo amor, sempre in tormenti; Amor, tu che si bella fiamma accendesti

Andate, o miei sospiri (i), 10 March 1712; Andate, o miei sospiri (ii), 237
1712; A piè d'un faggio ombroso; A piè d'un verde colle; *Api industri che volate (Paragone amoroso); *A placar la mia bella, T, bc; Appena chiudo gl'occhi (Il sogno), S, vn, bc; Appena giunse al forte campo (Oloferne), B, 2 vn, bc (inc.); A privarmi del bel; Ardea per Coridone Clori; Arder per due pupille (Bella dama contenta), 1704; Ardo d'amore e impatiente; *Ardo e del nobil foco; Ardo, è ver, per te d'amore, S, fl, bc (inc.); Ardo tacito amante, S/A, bc, 30 Aug 1706; Arse felice un tempo; A soffrire impara, o core

Assiso in verde prato; A te, Lisa gentile, A, bc; Augelletti semplicetti che girate (La rete d'amore); Augellino prigioniero, ferma oh Dio; Augellin, sospendi i vanni (i) (B. Pamphili), S, 2 vn, bc; Augellin, sospendi i vanni (ii) (Pamphili); Augellin vago e canoro, S, 2 fl, bc, 16 June 1699; Aure io son di voi geloso, S/A, bc; A voi che l'accendeste (F. M. Paglia), *c*1692; Balze alpestri e romite (Amante che gode la beatitudine alpestre); Barbara ingrata Fille, S/A, bc, 18 Sept 1706; Bei prati, freschi rivi (Il disperato); Bei prati, verdi colli, 5 Nov 1704; Bel Dorino–Amata Clori, S, B, 2 vn, bc

Bella, dunque n'andrai; *Bella madre dei fiori, S, 2 vn, bc; Bella onda che mormori, S, ?2 vn, bc, 1694, lost; Bella, per te d'amore, S/A, bc; Bella quanto crudel spietata Irene, June 1717; Bella rosa adorata (La rosa), Sept 1704; Bella se quella face; *Belle faci del cielo, A, 2 vn, tpt, bc; *Belle pupille care, e chi (attrib. Francesco Scarlatti in *GB-Mp*, Q544 Bk51); Benchè o sirena bella; Benchè porti nel volto; Benchè vezzosa Irene; Ben folle e chi non parte; Ben mio quel verme alato (Paglia), S, 2 vn, bc; Biondi crini ch'in fronte; *Boschi amati che cingete col silenzio

Cara sempre agl'occhi miei; *Care pupille belle, belle se mi lasciate; *Care selve, a voi ritorno; Care selve gradite; Caro amor, quant'è gradita; Caro Fileno mio, quanto mi spiace; *Caro laccio, dolce nodo, S/A, bc, 1695; Celinda è la mia vita; Cerca nel cor di Mille, A/S, bc, 10 Aug 1706; Cerco, né so trovar beltà fedel; Che fai, mio cor?, S/A, bc; Che le dolcezze estreme, before 1698; Che mai sarà di me?; Che più farai, arciero Amor? (Clori e Dorino), S, B, bc; *Che più tardi, o ninfa bella?; *Che pretendi, o tiranna?; Che rispetti, che, mondo?; *Che Sisifo infelice, 25 July 1706

*Chi batte al mio core? (F. Melosio); Chi m'insegna ov'è quel bene?; Chi m'insegna un tetto?; *Chi mi toglie a riposi?; Ch'io da te mi divida, A, bc; *Ch'io scopri il mio affetto, before 1694; *Ch'io ti manchi di fede; *Chiudea presso d'un fonte; Chiudetevi per sempre e di pianger cessate; Chiusa tra fosche bende; Chi vedesse la ferita; Chi 236
vidde mai o chi provo?; Cinta dei più bei fiori; *Cinta di rai splendea; *Cleopatra la bella, la Venere d'Egitto (Lamento di Cleopatra); Cleopatra, mia reina (Marc'Antonio e Cleopatra), S, A, bc; *Clori, adorata Clori, o quante pene; Clori, allor ch'io ti vidi, 17 April 1701

Clori bell'idol mio, Clori mia vita; Clori, bell'idol mio, sai tu qual è il desio?, 1 July 1705; Clori, io tacqui a bastanza; Clori, mia cara Clori, moro; Clori mia, Clori bella, ah non più, S, fl, bc, 18 June 1699; Clori mia–Dorino caro (Dorino e Clori), S, B, bc; *Clori mia, se t'amo (Risoluzione di Tirsi) (Paglia), lost; Clori, mi sento al seno; Clorinda [Mitilde] è bella e sempre è più vivace; *Clori spietata, mio crudel tesoro; Clori superba, e come mai?; Clori vezzosa e bella, A, bc; Colui che fisso mira, S/A, bc, April ?1696; Come il foco alla sua sfera; *Come potesti mai; Come può non esser bella?, 15 Feb 1701

Come volubil gira la ruota; *Con la speme di godere; Con non inteso affanno; Contentati mio core, A, bc; Con trasparente velo, 13 Dec 1702; Cor di Bruto, e che risolvi?, B, bc; Coronate il bel crine; Correa nel seno amato, S, 2 vn, bc, before 1694; Cruda Filli spietata; *Crudelissimo amore, A, bc (probably by Albinoni); *Crudel, mira quest'occhi; Crudel, perchè privarmi?, 2S, bc; Crudo Amor, che vuoi da me?; Crudo Amor, empie stelle, iniqua sorte, before 1702; Crudo Amor, empie stelle, Irene ingrata; Crudo Amor, saper vorrei; Da che Tirsi mirai; Dagli strali d'amore, 3 Sept 1701; *Da l'arco d'un bel ciglio, A, bc (published in Albinoni's op.4, 1702)

Dal bel volto d'Irene, 4 Jan 1705; Dal colle al pian discesa; *Dal crudele Daliso (published in G. B. Bassani's op.3, 1682); Dal dì ch'Amor m'accese; Dal dì che l'empio fato; *Dal giorno fortunato ch'io vidi (Paglia); Dal grato mormorio; *Dalisa, e come mai, A, bc; Dalla fida compagna abbandonata; Dalla nativa sfera scese, 5 Oct 1704; Dalla speme deluso (Paglia); Dalle pene amorose; Dalle tirrene sponde parti Filli; Dall'oscura magion dell'arsa Dite (L'Orfeo), S, 2 vn, bc; Dammi, amore, un altro cor; Da qual parte celeste, 20 Oct 1701; Da quel dì che Mitilde; Da quell'hora fatale (i); Da quell'hora fatale (ii), 1716

Da sventura a sventura, ?1690; Da turbini di pene; *Da voi parto, amati rai, B, bc; *Deh, per mercè l'ignudo Dio; Deh torna, amico sonno (Il sonno); Del faretrato nume amor tiranno; Del lagrimoso lido (Euridice dall'Inferno), 17 June 1699; Della spietata Irene fur l'accese pupille; *Delle patrie contrade; Del mio seno la costanza, S/A, bc; Del Tebro in su le sponde; Del Tirreno a le sponde (Cantata di lontananza); Del Tirreno sul lido, A, bc, Dec 1697; Dentro il sen della mia Irene; *Dentro un orrido speco; *Di che havete paura?; Di cipresso funesto (Querele e morto di Tirsi per Clori ingrata), before 1694; *Di colore de' cieli (Occhi azurri); *Di due vaghe pupille nere

Diedi a Fileno il core (Amor corrisposto), A/S, bc, 1705; Di me che sarà?; Dimmi che pensi, o Amore, before 1702; Dimmi, Clori superba (Clori superba), S/A, bc, 1704; *Dimmi, crudel, e quando, S, A, bc; Dimmi, mio ben, perchè; Dipende da te solo la pace, 1v, bc; Di pensiero in pensier, A, bc; *Disperate pupille, hor, sì, piangete (Disperatione amorosa), S, B, bc; Dispettoso pensiero; *Dolci istinti d'amore; *Dopo lungo penar (i); Dopo lungo penar (ii), B, bc; Dorisbe, i miei lamenti (Eurillo sdegnato); Dormono l'aure estive, S/A, bc, 10 Jan 1705; Dove alfin mi traeste? (L'Arianna); Dov'è Filli, dov'è?

Dove fuggi, o bella Clori? (i), S, A, bc, lost; Dove fuggi, o bella Clori? (ii) (Lidio e Clori), S, A, 2 vn, bc; Dove fuggo, a che penso?, S, vn, bc; *Dove l'eneta Dori alla reggia; Dove una quercia annosa (Beltà bruna) (Paglia); Dove xestu, cor mio?, lost; Dov'io mi volga o vada; Due nemici tiranni, 1722; D'un platano frondoso; Dunque ingrato spergiuro, S/A, bc; Dunque perchè lontano; Dunque sperar non lice; Ebra d'amor fuggia (L'Arianna), S, 2 vn, bc; Ecco ch'a voi ritorno (after F. de Lemene), 2 versions; E come, oh Dio, lontana?, before 1707; *E come, o Dio, tacito e fido?; E come, ohime, poss'io?, 11 Feb 1714

E con qual core, oh Dio (i); *E con qual core, oh Dio (ii); E con qual core, oh Dio (iii), S, 2 vn, bc; *E gran pena l'amare; E la speme un desio tormentoso, 16 Oct 1704; Elitropio d'amor, S/Mez, bc, 1694; E lungi dal mio bene; *Entro a più foschi horrori; Entro romito speco; E penar degg'io ancora, S/A, bc; E pure il gran tormento, S/A, bc; *E pur è vero che alletti; E pur odo e non moro; E pur tenti il ritorno (G. Monaci); E pur vuole il cielo e amore (D. Benigni), S, A, bc, before 1706; E quando, ingrata Nice?; E quando mai cessate?; *Era già l'alba e in cielo (Europa rapita da Giove in forma di toro)

Era giunta quell'ora, 29 Nov 1704; Era l'oscura notte e d'ogni intorno di fosco ammanto, S, 2 vn, bc; Era l'oscura notte e d'ogni intorno le tremolanti stelle; E satio ancor non sei; E sia pur vero, S/A, bc; E sino a quando, Amor?; E sino a quando, o stelle?; *Essere innamorato e non poterlo dir; Eurilla all'or che sei cinta; Eurilla, amata Eurilla, before 1698; Eurilla, io parto, a Dio; Eurilla, oh Dio, nel seno palpita; *E viva al diletto la mia rimembranza; Facile sembra a un core l'amar; Farfalla che s'aggira (La pazzia, overo La stravaganza), 11 Aug 1706; Farfalletta innocente se correndo

Fatto d'amor seguace, S/A, bc; Ferma omai, fugace e bella, A, 2 vn, va, bc, Dec 1724; Fiamma ch'avvampa; Fida compagna, del tuo alato amante (Lontananza), S, 2 vn, bc; Fiero acerbo destin dell'alma mia; Filen, mio caro bene (Filli che esprime la sua fede a Fileno), A, 2 vn, fl, bc; Fileno, oh Dio, Fileno, di quest'anima amante, S, 2 vn, bc; Fileno, ove t'en vai? (Clori abbandonata), 11 Oct 1704; Fileno, quel Fileno, tutto fe', S, 2 vn, bc; Filla mia, perchè piangi?; Fille, dolente Fille; Fille, mia cara Fille, 18 Nov 1704; Fille, tu parti, oh Dio, S/A, bc, 12 March 1722

Filli adorata, ah ben comprendo (Chiese Fileno come stasse in gratia di Fille: ella rispose, 'ne ben, ne male'); Filli adorata e cara, Filli che fosti, 23 April 1705; Filli adorata e cara, io parto (Partenza: Fileno giura fedeltà a Filli), 22 Sept 1706; Filli altera e spietata; *Filli che del mio core, May 1700; Filli che fra gl'orrori (Cantata . . . notturna), S, 2 vn, bc, 1706; Filli crudel, dunque tu parti?; Filli, di questro cor parte più cara; Filli, già volge l'anno; *Filli, la lontananza homicida, 1695; Filli, la tua bellezza, 27 June 1702; Filli mia, Filli cara (Descrittore di bella donna), 15 Jan 1702

*Filli mia, tu mi consoli; Filli, mio ben, mia vita, May 1704; *Filli, sei bella, è ver; Filli, tu sai s'io t'amo (Sconsolato rusignolo), S, 2 fl, bc, April 1701; Fiumicel che del mio pianto; *Fiumicel cui l'onde chiare, A, bc; *Flagellava nel cielo (Il Narciso); Fonte d'ogni dolcezza, 12 March 1709; Fonti amiche, erbe care; Forse di Sirio ardente; Fra liete danze; Fra mille semplicetti augei canori, 14 Aug ?1701; Frangi l'arco e lo stral, 27 Aug 1706; Fra tante pene, e tante, 23 June 1706; Fu d'oro il primo dardo; *Fuori di sua capanna, S, vn/fl, bc

*Giacea d'un mirto all'ombra; *Giacea presso alla sponda; Già di trionfi onusto (Il Germanico) (Pamphili), before Oct 1691; Già lusingato appieno da zeffiri, S, 2 vn, bc; Già per lunga stagion bersaglio (Lo strale d'amore); Già sepolto è fra l'onda, S, 2 vn, va, va da gamba, bc; Già sorge l'alba (Dorisbe cacciatrice); Già sul carro dorato (Occhi neri); Già vicina è quell'ora, S/A, bc, 15 June 1699; Giù di Vulcan nella fucina eterna, A, bc, 1698; Giunto è il fatal momento (Partenza), 1705; *Goderai sempre crudele, 1695 (inc.); Ha l'umore stravagante; Ho una pena intorno al core; I celesti zaffiri, 19 Aug 1701, lost; Il centro del mio core

Il ciel seren, le fresche aurette (La primavera: Clori e Lisa compagne), 2S, bc; *Il cor che vive oppresso; Il fulgido splendor d'un ciglio arciero, 14 March 1705; Il genio di Mitilde, S/A, bc; Il mio sol non è più meco, 31 Oct 1704; *Il più misero amante, A, bc; Il rosignolo se scioglie il volo (i), A/S, bc, 19 Dec 1698; Il rosignolo se scioglie il volo (ii), 26 Aug 1700; Il timido mio core (Immagini d'orrore); Imagini d'orrore, B, 2 vn, bc, 16 July 1710; In amorosi ardori; In bel sonno profondo; In che giammai t'offesi?, 8 Aug 1706; In due vaghe pupille; Infelice mio core, che ti valse?

Infelice mio core, giunse alfin; *In fra notturni orrori (published in A. Marcello, 12 cantate a voce sola, 1708); Ingiustissimo amor, tu che sovvente; In placida sembianza; In questa lacrimosa orrida valle (Tantalo sitibondo); In solitaria soglia; *In traccia del suo bene (published in G. B. Bassani's op.2, 1680); In vano, amor tiranno tenta; Io ben so che siete arciere, 1704; Io che ad un tronco; *Io che con aurea luce; Io che dal cor di Fille, S/A, bc; *Io credei che felice; Io m'accendo a poco a poco; Io morirei contento; Io non v'intendo, o stelle; *Io per Dori mi struggo, before 1694

Io son Neron l'imperator del mondo (Il Nerone), 1698; Io son pur solo; *Io t'amerò e nel mio petto; Io ti vuò dir, Dorisbe, Aug 1700; Io vengo, o Filli, 20 Sept 1706; Irene, idolo mio, in questo a me, 12 July 1705; Irene, idolo mio, se per te vivo; La beltà ch'io sospiro (Pamphili), 16 Aug ?1701; La cagion delle mie pene; Là dell'Arno su l'onde; Là dove al sonno in braccio (Paglia), 1v, insts, lost; Là dove al vivo argento; Là dove a Mergellina, 1725; La face d'amore ch'il core m'arde (D. A. Ottoboni), before 1710; La fortuna di Roma (Il Coriolano) (Pamphili), S/A, bc, ?1694; La gran madre d'amore (Innamoramento di Venere et Adone)

La gratia, la sembianza della tua pastorella, 22 Feb 1702; *Lagrime dolorose dagl'occhi miei, T, 2 vn, bc; Là nel ben sen della regal Sirena; Là nel campo de fiori (inc.); Là nell'arcadic spiagie, 1700; Langue Clori vezzosa; L'armi crudeli e fiere, A, bc; Lascia, deh lascia al fine; Lascia di tormentarmi, amor tiranno, 1709; Lasciami alquanto piangere, May 1716; Lasciami sospirar, io voglio piangere (Dorindo e Fileno), S, B, bc; Lascia omai di tormentarmi, o memoria; Lascia più di tormentarmi, rimembranza, 1688; Lasciate ch'io v'adori (Preghiera amorosa), 19 Oct 1705; Lasciate, homai lasciate di tormentarmi più; Lasciato havea l'adultero superbo (Lucretia Romana) (Pamphili), before 1691; *La speranza che lusinga (A. Colombi)

*L'augellin che sciogle il volo, A, bc; La vezzosa Celinda; Leandro, anima mia (Ero e Leandro), A/S, bc; *Leggi, de' leggi, o Clori, A, bc; L'empio mio destin brama la morte, 2 vv, bc; Le vaghe tue pupille (Bella donna crudele); *L'huom che segue una speranza (Tormento della Speranza e della Fortuna), A, bc; Libertà del mio cor; Lidio, in van mi condanni (Bella donna rimproverata a torto nel partire del suo vago così risponde); Liete, placide e belle acque, 1709; Lieti boschi, ombre amiche, A/S, bc, 18 Aug 1704; *Lilla, mi parto, addio, S/A, bc; Lisa, del foco mio (Clori e Lisa compagne), 2S, bc, 28 Feb 1706

Lontananza, che fai?, 27 Nov 1701; Lontananza crudele, deh perchè? (Lontananza), 4 Oct 1713; Lontananza crudele, tu mi trafiggi, before 1694; Lontananza non risana, A, bc; Lontananza tiranna che da te mi divide; Lontan da la sua Clori; Lontan dall'idol mio, S/A, bc, 1699; *Lontan dal suo tesor; Lontan dal tuo bel viso (Paglia), S/A, bc; Lontano dal suo bene; Lo sa il ciel, sallo amore; Lo so ben io; Luci care al mondo sole; *Luci, siete pur quelle, S/A, bc; Lumi ch'in fronte (Ama e non spera godere), 4 Dec 1703; Lumi, dolenti lumi, chiudetevi, S/A, bc; Lunga stagion dolente, 3 June 1706; Lungi dal ben ch'adoro

Lungi dalla cagion per cui sospiro (Lontananza), 20 Dec 1704; Lungi dall'idol mio, A, bc; *Mal fondati sospetti, 1685; Mal sicuro è il fior nel prato (D. A. Ottoboni), before 1710; Mentre affidan al mar di Cupido; Mentre al sonno chiudea; *Mentre Clori la bella presso un ruscel, S, 2 vn, bc; Mentre Clori la bella sotto l'ombre d'un mirto, S, 2 fl, bc; Mentre da questo monte; Mentre Eurillo fedele [infelice], before 1694; *Mentre in un dolce oblio; Mentre mesto e piangente, A, bc; Mentre sul carro aurato (Clori e Mirtillo), S, A, bc; Mentre un zeffiro altero; Mentre un zeffiro arguto, S/B, 2 vn, bc, ?before 1694

Mesto, lasso e ramingo, June 1704; M'ha diviso il cor dal core (D. A. Ottoboni), A, bc, before 1710; *Mia bella Clori, ascolta; Mia bellissima Clori quando i lumi; Mia Climene adorata se mai occhio, 1710; Mia Dorinda, mia vita, S, vn, bc, 1706; *Mi contento cosi, T, 2 vn, bc; Mie speranze fallaci; Mi nasce un sospetto (Amante insospettito);

*Mio cor, dov'è la bella libertà?, A, vn, bc; Mi parto, Eurilla, a Dio, A, bc; Mira, o Filli, quella rosa (La rosa); Mirtillo, anima mia, già che parti (Partenza), S, 2 vn, bc; Mitilde, addio poichè di nuovo amante; Mitilde, alma mia, se udiste mai, 3 July 1720

Mitilde, anima mia, conforto di mie pene; Mitilde, mio tesor, così veloce; Mitilde, mio tesoro, e dove sei? (Mitilde); *Mitilde, oh quanto dolce e lusinghiero; Mi tormenta il pensiero (i), 10 March 1701; Mi tormenta il pensiero (ii) (Amante parlando con il pensiero), A/B, bc; Mondo, non più, lost; Morirei disperato se credessi (Paglia), before 1694; *Mostri, deh non temete; Nacqui a' sospiri e al pianto, S, 2 vn, bc, ? before 1693; Nei languidi respiri; Nel centro oscuro di spelonca; Nel dolce tempo in cui ritorno, 27 May 1712; Nella stagione appunto che il pianeta (Paglia), S, 2 vn, bc

Nella tomba di Gnido (Paglia), S, 2 vn, bc; Nelle arene del Tago, A, bc, 24 July 1698; Nell'estiva stagione; Nel mar che bagna al bel Sebeto il piede, B, bc; Nel mar che bagna a Mergellina il piede; Nel profondo del mio core; Nel sen degl'antri; Nel silentio commune, S, 2 vn, va, bc; Nel suo fido caro nido; Ne' tuoi lumi, o bella Clori (Begl'occhi), 1704; Nice mia, un solo istante; Ninfa crudel, deh vieni, A, bc; Non è come si dice, 20 Aug ?1701; Non è facile ad un core (La catena d'amore), 4 Dec 1704; *Non mi credi, deh perchè?; No, non deggio, è troppo cara, 1709; No, non è ver ch'altro amore, 26 Aug 1706

No, non lasciar, canora e bella, 20 Nov 1704; No, non posso fingere (D. A. Ottoboni), before 1710; No, non ti voglio, Cupido, S, A, bc; No, non vorrei vivere fra le catene; Non per pioggia del cielo, 1720; Non più contrasti, no (Amore e rispetto), 6 Oct 1721; Non posso già ne voglio; Non sdegnar bella Clori; *Non si parli di ventura; Non so qual più m'ingombra (Cantata pastorale), S, 2 vn, bc, Dec 1716; *Non temo disastri; Non v'è simile al mio core (Paglia), 1v, insts, lost; Notte cara a un cor che langue, 1705; Notte cara, ombre beate, before 1694; Notte ch'in carro d'ombre, S, 2 vn, bc

Notte placida e lieta, 13 Sept 1706; Occhi miei ch'al pianto avvezzi, A, bc; Occhi miei che pagaste, 24 Nov 1705; O che mostro, o che furia (D. A. Ottoboni), 20 July 1709; O che pena è la mia (Fedeltà non creduta), S/A, bc, 1704; *O chi ridir potrebbe?; O Clori, ahi, bella Clori; O come bello con onde chiare (Tirsi e Clori), 2 S, bc, before 1702; O de' pastori diletto stuolo (L'agnellino); *O de' regni di Dite Eumenidi spietate; O di fere e d'augelli che ti ricetti; O dolce servitù; *O Fileno, crudele ingrato; O generoso eroe, 11 Dec 1702, lost; Ogni affanno crudele

235–6

Oh di Betlemme altera povertà (Cantata pastorale per la nascità di Nostro Signore), S, 2 vn, va, vc, lute; Oh Dio, che viene amore; *Omai dal cielo al più sublime punto; Ombre romite e solitarie piante, S, A, bc; Ombre tacite e sole, S, 2 vn, va, bc, 31 Oct 1716; O Mitilde, fosti meco tiranna, 1711; O Mitilde, o del core, 9 Dec 1708; O pace del mio cor (i), S/A, bc; O pace del mio cor (ii); *O penosa lontananza–O felice lontananza, S, B, bc; Ora che 'l verno riede, A, bc; Or che a me ritornasti (i), S/A, bc; Or che a me ritornasti (ii); *Or che barbara sorte; Or ch'in petto d'Eurilla (Eurilla placata)

Or [Hor] che di Febo ascosi, S, 2 vn, bc, 1704; *Or che disciolto è il nodo; Or che di te son privo; Or che di Teti in seno; Or [Hor] che graditi horrori copron del dì (i); Or [Hor] che graditi orrori copron del dì (ii); Or (Hor) che l'aurato Nume, S, 2 vn, bc; Or [Hor] che lungi son io (2 versions); *Or che su legno aurato; *Or per pietà del mio crudel destino, S, A, bc; O sol degl'occhi miei (D. A. Ottoboni), 31 Dec 1704; O sventurata Olimpia; Ove al Sebeto in riva; Ove fuor del mio seno (Il sospiro); Ove il fiorito impero mostra; Ove in grembo a la pace (Desio di solitudine)

*Ove placido e cheto; *O v'ingannate a fe'; O voi di queste selve habitatrici, S/A, bc, 1717; Parla mia pena omai, S/A, bc; *Parte da me Cupido; *Pastor d'Arcadia, è morta Clori; Pastorella innamorata; Pastori amici, amiche pastorelle; Peno, e del mio penar (Costanza), 28 Aug 1705; Pensier che in ogni parte, S/A, bc; Pensier che sei inflessibile, 12 Feb 1702; Pensieri, oh Dio, qual pena; Penso che non ho core (Piangi la lontananza della sua donna [bella]), ?1705; *Per celeste bellezza arde il mio cor; Perchè mai, luci amorose?, April 1700; Perchè sospiri, o Niso? (Doralba e Niso), S, A, bc; Perchè tacete, regolati concenti?, A, 2 vn, bc

Perde al vostro confronto, S, 2 vn, bc, ? before 1696; *Per destin d'ingrat' amore, T, bc; Perdono, Amor, perdono (i), A, bc, 6 June ?1702; Perdono, Amor, perdono (ii), 29 Oct 1704; Per farmi amar da tutte (D. A. Ottoboni), before 1710; Perfida Filli ingrata (Costanza), 27 July 1705; *Per formare la bella che adoro (Ritratto di Clori); *Per l'ondoso sentiero, S, 2 vn, bc; Per prova di mia fede, A, bc; Per queste dell'antica Alba famosa; Per saettar un seno (i); Per saettar un seno (ii); Per te, Florida bella, July 1708; Per tormentarmi il core

Per un momento solo (Lo sfortunato), S/A, bc; Per un vago desire (La lezione di musica); *Per un volto di gigli e di rose (probably by Albinoni); Piagge fiorite, ameni prati; Piagge fiorite e amene, io parto,

28 Aug 1716; *Piangea, un di piangea Fileno, S/A, bc; *Piangete o miei pupille, S, 2 vn, bc; Piangi la tua sventura, 1 July 1706; Piango ogn'ora del mio core; Piango, sospiro, e peno (i); Piango, sospiro, e peno (ii), A, 2 vn, bc, before 1693; Più che penso all'idol mio; Più non risplende, 2S, str, bc, before 1696; Più non si puote amar; Più veggio Lidia mia; Poi che a Tirsi infelice

Poi che cessano al fin; Poi che la bella Clori (Amante schernito), ?1699; *Poi che legge fatal; Poi che l'Ercole argivo (Lisimaco, Re di Traccia); *Poi che riseppe Orfeo; *Porto il cor incatenato; Potesse almen, 1v, vn, bc, before 1696, lost; Preparati, o mio core, A, bc; Presso a un limpido fonte (Fileno disingannato), 2 Sept 1706; Presso il balcon dell'incostante Nisa, 15 June 1699; *Pria che desto ai nitriti spaventate dal ciel; Prima d'esservi infedele (Clori fedele), S, 2 vn, bc; Primavera, sei gentile; Pur al fine la vincesti; Qual bellezza divina?; Quale al gelo s'adugge, 25 Jan 1705

Qualora io veggio la vezzosa Irene, S, 2 vn, bc; *Qualor io vi passeggio; Qualor l'egre pupille; Qualor miro la bella; Qualor tento scoprire (after F. de Lemene), A/B, bc; Quando Amor vuol ferirmi; Quando che ti vedrò; Quando credeva il core, 16 Oct ?1701; *Quando Lidia amorosa; Quando l'umide ninfe, 8 Nov 1704; Quando mai troverò d'Amor nel regno, 7 Jan 1705; Quando satia sarai?; Quando stanche dal pianto; *Quando un eroe che s'ama, 2S, bc; Quando veggio un gelsomino; Quante le grazie son, A, bc, 4 June 1703; Quanti affanni ad un core (Pene amorose per lontananza), S/A, bc; Quanto io v'ami o luci, A, bc

*Quanto mi sdegni più; Quanto, o Filli, t'inganni?, 10 March 1701; Quanto piace agl'occhi miei; Quanto vezzosa e quanto adorna; Quel cor ch'a te già diede; Quel Fileno infelice, 24 Sept 1705; Quella che chiudo in sen fiamma amorosa, 25 Feb 1705; Quella pace gradita, S, fl, vn, vc, bc; Quel pastor si gentile, S, 2 vn, bc (inc.); Quel piacer che nell'amarti, 26 Oct 1704; Quel ruscelletto, o Clori; Questa, quest'è la selva, S/A, bc; Questa vermiglia rosa, 30 Jan 1705; Quest'è il giardin felice; Queste torbide e meste onde, 1717; Questo di bei giacinti serto, S/A, bc

Questo silenzio ombroso (Il sonno), S, A, or 2S, bc, 17 Sept 1707; Qui dove alfin m'assido (Il rosignuolo); Qui dove a piè d'un colle; Qui dove aure ed augelli, 15 Jan 1705; *Qui dove in aspre balze, A, bc; Qui vieni, ingrata Fille; *Radamisto, è portento che Zenobia; Regie soglie, alte moli, 18 Oct 1720; *Ritardati momenti, egre dimore (published in G. B. Bassani's op.3, 1682); *Rondinella torna al lido (i), 1701; Rondinella torna al lido (ii); S'accinge Eurillo al canto; Sanno, o Filli adorata, 24 Aug 1716, lost; Sarà pur vero, o stelle?; Sarei troppo felice (Pamphili), 30 April ?1701; Sazio di più soffrire, S/B, bc; *Scherza col onda del caro lido; Sciolgo in lagrime amare; Sciolta da freddi amplessi (Marito vecchio, sposa giovane), 1 May 1704

Scompagnata tortorella (La tortorella); Scorgo il fiume e scorgo il rio (La primavera), S/A, bc, 8 June 1704; Scuote di fronte all'Appennin nevoso; *Sdegno fiero ed amore; Se a goder torna il mio core; Se amassi da dovero (L'infedeltà); Se amor con un contento; Se a quel fiero dolor (L'amante non corrisposto lascia d'amare), S/A, bc; *Se credete all'amor mio; *Se dalla cruda Irene, A/S, bc; Se d'Elisa spietate il bel sembiante; Sedeva Eurilla un giorno (Esagerationi d'Eurilla) (Paglia); Se mai Clori gentile; *Se nell'amar Coriste

Senti, bella crudele; Senti, bell'idol mio (Bella donna prega ad essere amata), 1705; *Sentite, o tronchi, o sassi, S/A, bc, before 1715; Sento nel core certo dolore (S'allontana per non innamorarsi), S/A, bc; Senz'alma, senza cor; *Se per amor quest'alma; *Serba il mio cor costante; *Se tu parti io morirò (published in G. B. Bassani's op.2, 1680); Se vagheggio nel mattino, 1709; Siamo in contesa la bellezza ed io (Pamphili), 4 May ?1701; Si, conosco, o Mitilde; Siete unite a tormentarmi, A, 2 vn, bc; Silenzio, aure volanti, S, 2 vn, bc; S'io t'amo, s'io t'adoro, June 1704; Si, t'intendo, tu vuoi ch'io non pensi (Non può scordarsi della sua dama), S/A, bc

So che non lice, 1v, bc, before 1696, lost; Solitudini amene, apriche collinette, S, fl, bc; Solitudini amene, bersaglio d'empia sorte, 15 236
April 1705; Solitudini care, in voi spera; Son contenta di soffrire; Son io, barbara donna, A, bc; Son le nere pupillette, A, bc, 12 March 1702; Sono amante e m'arde il core, A, bc, before 1694; *Sono un alma tormentata; *Son pur care le catene, S, A, bc; Son quest'ultimi momenti (Cantata di lontananza), S/A, bc, before 1714; Sopra le verdi sponde che la Brenta, before 1694; Sopra le verdi sponde del Sebeto, 2 Feb 1712; Sorge l'alba; Sorta fin da le piume, 8 Jan 1702

Sotto l'ombra d'un faggio, piangente e sospirante, B, vn, bc; Sotto l'ombra d'un faggio, sul margine d'un rivo (Paglia), S, 2 vn, bc; Sovente amor mi chiama, A, bc; *Sovra carro stellato, S, 2 vn, bc; Sovra il margine erboso; Sovra questi fecondi ameni colli, 3 Nov 1704; Speranze mie, addio, Mez, bc, 1694; Spero ch'havrò la pace (D. A. Ottoboni), before 1710; *Spesso suol l'alma mia (Amore e gelosia); Spiega l'ali il mio pensiero (Lontananza), ?1702; Splendeano in bel sembiante, B, bc (inc.); *Stanca l'afflitta Clori, S/A, bc; Stanco di più soffrire a voi ritorno; Sta presente il mio tesoro

Strali, facelle, amore, A, bc; Stravagante è l'amor (Fileno amante di Clori, Irene, e Nice), 1720; Stravagante non è l'amore, 1720; *Stravaganza d'amore accade in noi (Paglia); Su bel seggio di fiori, 21 May 1705; Su la morbida erbetta, lost; Su la sponda del mare (L'Olimpia), S, 2 vn, va, bc; *Su la sponda fiorita di limpido ruscello, 20 Aug ?1718; Su la sponda fiorita d'un rio pargoleggiante (L'Adone); Su le fiorite sponde di un vago ruscelletto, 2 Aug 1712; Su le rive dell'Elba; Su le sponde d'Abbido (Il Leandro), 1693; Su le sponde del Reno

Su le sponde del Tebro, S, 2 vn, tpt, bc; Sul margine d'un rio dove l'onde fugaci (Elpino tradito), S/A, bc; Sul margine d'un rivo cui facevan ricamo, S, 2 vn, bc; Sul margine fiorito d'un limpido [tumido] ruscello, 4 Dec 1704; *Sul margine fiorito d'un placido torrente; Su l'ora appunto che col carro d'oro (La fenice), S, 2 vn, bc, 1703; Sventurati miei pensieri; Taccio e tacendo moro, A, bc; Taci, infedele [infelice] amore, 1720; Talor per suo diletto, 28 April ?1718; Tanti affanni e tante pene; Tanto strano è l'amor mio, April 1697; Temo d'amarti poco

Tenebrose foreste erme; *The Beautious Melissa; Tiranna ingrata, che far dovrò?, B, 2 vn, bc; *Tiranno di mia fe'; *Tirsi, mentr'io dormiva; Tirsi pastore amante (Pastorello innamorato che va in traccia della sua ninfa), S, 2 vn, bc; Ti vorrei credere speranza; Tormentatemi pur, furie d'amore, S/A, bc; *Torna al sen dolce mia pace; Torna il giorno fatale (Anniversario amoroso) (?Pamphili), ?S, bc, June 1710, lost; Tra le pompe fiorite, A, bc; *Tra l'ombre più secrette; Tra queste ombrose piagge, 1709; Tra solitarie balze; Tra speranza e timore, B, vn, bc; *Tra verdi piante ombrose

Troppo care, troppo belle (Amante contento); Troppo ingrata Amaranta; Troppo oppressa dal sonno; Tu che una dea rassembri, S, 2 vn, bc; Tu mi chiedi s'io t'amo, 5 Feb 1709; Tu mi lasciasti, o bella, April 1698; Tu parti, idolo amato (i) (Cantata di lontananza), S/A, bc, 1702; Tu parti, idolo amato (ii) (Amante che parte a bella donna che resta), 21 April 1706; Tu resti, o mio bel nume (i), B, 2 vn, bc; Tu resti, o mio bel nume (ii) (Bella donna che parte al suo amante che resta), 22 April 1706; Tu sei quella che al nome (Bella dama di nome santa), A, 2 vn, fl, bc

*Tutto acceso d'amore, S/A, bc; *Udite, o selve, o fiume; Una beltà ch'eguale (Amante sventurato); *Un cervello frenetico ch'amò; Un dì Tirsi l'amante; Un giorno Amor la benda si disciolse, 1709; Un incredula speranza; Un sol guardo di Clori, A, bc; Un sospiro d'un amante (La luccioletta) (Pamphili); Un spietato destino, A, bc; Un Tantalo assetato; Vaga Elisa, la tua rimembranza, June 1708; Vaghe selve beate (Mitilde ritirata in solitudine); Vaghe tende adorate; Vaghe fonti di luce (Occhi neri); *Vago il ciel non saria; Va pur lungi da me, 8 Oct 1704

Vedi, Eurilla, quel fior (Cantata per camera per l'ecc.mo Duca di Maddaloni), S, 2 vn, va, bc, Jan 1725; Vedi, Fille, quel sasso; Veggio l'idolo mio; Venite, amici, e con ghirlande (G. Ansaldi); Venne ad amor desio, 29 April 1705; . . . ver per un diletto ma senza amor (inc.); Vi comanda un cenno solo (D. A. Ottoboni), before 1710; *Viddi un giorno un fiumicello; Vieni, o caro Mirtillo, A, bc, June 1708; *Viva, viva mia libertà, 2S, bc; Voi ben sapete, o di romito bosco

*Voi che dell'alma mia havete il vanto, lost; Voi dell'idolo mio care treccie, A, bc; Voi giungeste, o vaghi fiori (I fiori), A, bc; *Voi mi dite tu sei bella; Vola, Cupido, dal cor mio fido, ? before 1696; *Vo narrando a quel ruscello; Vorrei, Filli adorata, farti palese, S/A, bc, 21 Nov 1705; *Vuoi che mora incenerito; *Vuoi ch'io spiri tra i sospiri (Amante desideroso di morire per liberarsi dall'amore), 20 Sept 1699; *Vuoi più, Filli crudele? A, bc; *Zeffiretti che spirate, A, bc; Zeffiretto che indrizzi il tuo volo, 14 Dec 1702

MADRIGALS

(*ed. J. Jürgens, Frankfurt am Main, 1980*)

Arsi un tempo e l'ardore (G. Marino), SSATB, *A-Wgm*

Cor mio, deh, non languire, SSSSA, *D-Bds*, *Mbs*, *MÜs*, *GB-Cfm*, *Lbm*, *T*, *I-Bc*, *Gi(l)*, *Nc*, *Rc*, *USSR-KA*

Intenerite voi, lacrime mie (O. Rinuccini), SATTB, *GB-Lbm*

Mori, mi dici (Marino), SSATB, *I-Nc*

O morte, agli altri fosca, a me serena, SSATB, *A-Wgm*

Or che da te, mio bene, SATB, *I-Nc*

O selce, o tigre, o ninfa, SSATB, *GB-Lbm*

Sdegno la fiamma estinse (O. Tavaletta), SSATB, *Lbm*

MASSES, MASS MOVEMENTS (*complete sources only*) 220, 233

Missa Clementina (i), SSATB, Rome, Dec 1705, *A-Wn, B-Br, D-Bds, DS, Mbs, MÜs, SWl, GB-Cfm, Lbm, I-Fc, Rvat, USSR-KA* 233

Messa a quattro voci, SATB, Rome, 1706, *D-MÜs, F-Pc, GB-Lbm, I-Rf, Rvat*

Messa per il natale di Nostro Signore Gesù Cristo, SSATB, SATB, 2 vn, bc, Rome, 1707, lost

Missa Clementina (ii), SSATB, Rome, 1716, *D-Bds, Mbs, I-Mc, Nc, Rvat* 233

Missa pro defunctis, SATB, 1717, *B-Bc, D-Bds, Mbs, MÜs, F-Pc, †I-BGi*

Messa di S Cecilia, S, S, A, T, B, SSATB, 2 vn, va, bc, Rome, Oct 1720, *Rc*; ed. J. Steele (London, 1968) 233

Missa ad usum cappellae pontificiae, SATB, 1721, *F-Pc, GB-Lbm, I-Rsc*

Missa ad canonem, SATB, *A-Wn, D-Bds, MÜs, F-Pc, I-Nc*

Missa in IV tono, SSATB, org, *D-MÜs*

Messa tutta in canone di diverse specie, SSATB, *A-Wn, D-Bds, F-Pc, GB-Cfm, I-Bc, Fc*

*Credo, S, A, T, B, SATB, 2 ob, 2 hn, str, org, *Nc*

*Credo breve, SATB, 2 vn, bc, *F-Pn*

*Gloria, SATB, 2 vn, va, 2 ob, 2 hn, bc, *D-Dkh, Dl*

MOTETS 233

Concerti sacri, motetti . . . e Salve regina, 1–4vv (Amsterdam, 1707–8; Naples, 1702, lost, as Motetti sacri, 1–4vv, vns, op.2) [CS] 233

Ad amantem cordis, S, 2 vn, bc, *I-Nf*

Ad Dominum cum tribularer, SATB, ?1708, *Baf, US-U*

Adorna thalamum tuum Sion, SATB, Jan 1708, *D-MÜs, GB-Lbm*

Ad te Domine levavi, SATB, ?1708, *I-Baf, US-U*

Audi filia, et inclina aurem, SSATB, ob, 2 vn, va, org, Oct 1720, †*I-Rc*; ed. J. Steele (London, 1968)

Ave maris stella, SATB, bc, *D-Bds, I-Nc*

Ave regina coelorum, SS, bc, 1722, *Nc*

Beatus vir qui timet, SSATB, org, *D-MÜs*

Benedicta et venerabilis es, S, SATB, 2 vn, va, bc, 4 July 1720, *MÜs*

Cantantibus organis Cecilia, S, ob, 2 vn, va, bc, Oct 1720, *MÜs*

Caro mea vere est cibus, STB, org, 31 Dec 1707, *I-Rvat*

Confitebor tibi Domine, SSATB, org, *D-MÜs*

Constitues eos principes, SAB, org, 1716, *A-Wn, D-MÜs, US-U*

Date sonum, date cantum, S, bc, 24 Nov 1705, *I-Nf*

De tenebroso lacu, A, 2 vn, va, bc, *GB-Lbm*

Dextera Domini fecit virtutem, SSB, org, 1715, *A-Wn, D-MÜs, US-U*

Diffusa est gratia, SS, org, *D-MÜs*

Diligam te, SAT, 2 vn, bc, CS

Dixit Dominus (i), SSATB, org, *Dl, MÜs*

Dixit Dominus (ii), SSATB, ob, 2 vn, va, bc, *I-Mc*

Dixit Dominus (iii), SSATB, org, *D-MÜs*

Dixit Dominus (iv), S, A, T, B, SATB, 3 vn, bc, *I-Mc*

Domine in auxilium meum, SATB, ?1708, *Baf, US-U*

Domine refugium factus es nobis, SSATB, *A-Wn, D-Mbs, MÜs*

Domine vivifica me, SATB, ?1708, *I-Baf, US-U*

Egli è ver che mi consolo, A, bc, 24 Nov 1705, *I-Nf*

Est dies trophei, SATB, 2 vn, bc, CS

Exaltabo te Domine quoniam, SATB, ?1708, *Baf, US-U*

Exultate Deo adjutori, SATB, *A-Wn, D-Dl, Mbs, MÜs, I-Baf, Nc*

Exurge Domine non prevaleat, SATB, ?1708, *Baf, US-U*

Infirmata, vulnerata, A, 2 vn, bc, *I-Nf* (dated 16 Oct 1702), CS

In hoc mundo inconstante, S, 2 vn, bc, 24 Nov 1705, *Nf*

Inni e Improperi per la Missa Praesanctificatorum della Parasceve, S, A, SATB, 2 vn, bc, Florence, ?1708: Vexilla regis prodeunt (even-numbered verses); Populc meus; Crux fidelis–Pange lingua gloriosi; Vexilla regis prodeunt (odd-numbered verses): *Baf*

Intellige clamorem meum, SATB, ?1708, *Baf, US-U*

Iste est panis, SATB, *D-MÜs* (inc.)

Jam sole clarior, S, 2 vn, bc, *GB-Lcm*, CS

Jesu corona virginum, S, A, T, SATB, 2 vn, va, bc, Oct 1720, †*I-PLcon, Rsc*

Justitiae Domini rectae, SATB, ?1708, *Baf, US-U*

Laetatus sum (i), SATB, *A-Wn, D-Mbs, GB-Lbm* 233

Laetatus sum (ii), SATB, *I-Rc* (inc.)

Laetatus sum (iii), SSATB, 2 vn, bc, 1688, *Nf*

Laetatus sum (iv), SSATB, 2 vn, va, bc, Aug 1721, †*D-Bds*

Lamentazioni per la Settimana Santa, Florence, ?1708: Incipit lamentatio Jeremiae prophetae, S, 2 vn, va, bc; Jod–Manum suam misit hostis, S, 2 vn, va, bc; De lamentatione Jeremiae prophetae, S, 2 vn, va, bc; Lamed–Matribus suis dixerunt, S, 2 vn, va, bc; De lamentatione Jeremiae prophetae, S, 2 vn, bc; Aleph–Quomodo obscuratum est, T, 2 vn, bc: *I-Baf* 217

Lauda Jerusalem Dominum, SATB, org, *D-MÜs*
Laudate Dominum omnes gentes, SATTB, 2 vn, 2 va, vc, bc, *Bds*, *MÜs*
Laudate Dominum quia benignus, SSB, org, *MÜs*
Laudate pueri Dominum (i), SSATB, bc, *Dl*, *MÜs*
Laudate pueri Dominum (ii), S, SATB, 2 vn, bc, *MÜs* (inc.)
Magnificat (i), primo tono, SSATB, org, *MÜs*
Magnificat (ii), D, SSATB, insts, *MÜs* (inc.)
Memento, Domine, David, SATB, *Bds*, *Dl*, *Mbs*, *MÜs*, *F-Pc*, *GB-Lbm*, *T*, *I-Bc*, *Mc*, †*Nc*
Miserere mei Deus, miserere, SATB, *Baf*
Miserere mei Deus, secundum (i), SATB, SSATB, 1680, *Rvat*
Miserere mei Deus, secundum (ii), e, S, SSATB, 2 vn, va, bc, 1705, *D-Bds*, *MÜs*, *I-Baf*, *US-U*
Miserere mei Deus, secundum (iii), c, S, SSATB, 2 vn, va, bc, ?1715, *D-Bds*, *MÜs*, *I-Baf*, *US-U*
*Miserere mei Deus, secundum (iv), a, SATB, bc, 1721, *BE*
Mortales non auditis, S, A, 2 vn, bc, CS
Nisi Dominus aedificaverit (i), S, A, SATB, 2 vn, bc, *A-Wn*, *D-Bds*, *Dl*, *GB-Lbm*
Nisi Dominus aedificaverit (ii), SATB, org, *D-MÜs*
O magnum mysterium, SATB, SATB, 1707, *Dl*, *MÜs* 233
Properate fideles, SATB, 2 vn, bc, CS
Quae est ista, SAT, 2 vn, bc, CS
[27] Responsori per la Settimana Santa, S, A, T, B, SATB, bc, Florence, ?1708: Aestimatus sum; Amicus meus; Animam meam dilectam; Astiterunt reges terrae; Caligaverunt oculi mei; Ecce quomodo moritur; Ecce vidimus eum; Eram quasi agnus; Ierusalem surge; In Monte Oliveti; Jesum tradidit impius; Judas mercator pessimus; Omnes amici mei; O vos omnes; Plange quasi virgo; Recessit pastor noster; Seniores populi; Sepulto Domino; Sicut ovis; Tamquam ad latronem; Tenebrae factae sunt; Tradiderunt me; Tristis est anima mea; Una hora; Unus ex discipulis; Velum templi; Vinea mea electa: *I-Baf* 217
Rorate coeli dulcem, S, 2 vn, bc, *GB-Lcm*, CS
Sacerdotes Domini incensum et panes, SAT, org, *A-Wn*, *D-MÜs*, *US-U*

Salve regina (i), SA, 2 vn, bc, *I-Mc*, *Nc*
Salve regina (ii), SATB, Feb 1703, *A-Wn*
Salve regina (iii), S, 3 vn, bc, *I-Nf*
Salve regina (iv), SATB, 2 vn, bc, *B-Br*, *D-Mbs*, *F-Pn*, CS
Salve regina (v), S, 2 vn, va, bc, *D-Mbs*
Salvum fac populum tuum, SATB, ?1708, *I-Baf*
Sancti et justi in Domino gaudete, SATB, SATB, *D-MÜs* (inc.)
Spirate, aure, spirate, A, 2 vn, bc, *I-Nf*
Stabat mater, SA, 2 vn, bc, *Fc*, *Rsc*
Super solium gemmis ornatum, S, 2 vn, bc, *Nf*
Te Deum, SSATB, 2 ob, 2 vn, va, bc, *Rc*
Totus amore languens, A, 2 vn, bc, CS
Tu es Petrus, SATB, SATB, org, *A-Wn*, (?†)*B-Bc*, *D-Bds*, Singakademie, Berlin, *Dl*, *Mbs*, *MÜs*, †*DK-Kk*, *F-Pc*, *GB-Cfm*, *Lbm*, *T*, *I-Bc*, *Mc*, *Nc*, *USSR-KA* 233
Tui sunt coeli et terra, SSB, org, *A-Wn*, *D-MÜs*, *US-U*
Unam petii a Domino, SATB, ?1708, *I-Baf*
Valerianus in cubiculo, A, ob, 2 vn, va, bc, *D-MÜs*
*Veritas mea et misericordia, SATB, *MÜs*
Vexilla regis prodeunt, SS, 2 vn, bc, †*I-MOe*
Volo Pater ut ubi ego sum, SATB, SATB, org, *D-MÜs* 233

KEYBOARD 238, 240, 241

Toccate per cembalo, *I-MC*
Dieci partite sopra basso obbligato, 1716, *D-MÜs*, *I-Nc*
Primo e secondo libro di toccate (G, a, G, a, G, d, d, a, G, F), *A-Wn*, *I-Nc*
Due sinfonie per cembalo, 16 June 1699, *D-MÜs*
Toccata per studio di cembalo, 1716, *I-Nc*
Toccata d'intavolatura per cembalo ò pure per organo d'ottava stesa, *PLcon*
Tre toccate, ognuna seguita da fuga e minuetto, 1716, *Nc*
Variations on 'La follia', 1715, *GB-Lbm* 240
Other keyboard works in *D-MÜs*, *GB-Lbm*, *I-Gi(l)*, *Mc*, *MOe*, *Nc*, *Tn*, *Tci*, *Rsc*, *P-C*, *US-NH*

OTHER INSTRUMENTAL 238–9

12 sinfonie di concerto grosso, begun 1 June 1715, †*GB-Lbm*: F, 2 vn, va, vc, 2 fl, bc; D, 2 vn, va, vc, fl, tpt, bc; d, 2 vn, va, vc, fl, bc; e, 2 vn, va, vc, fl, ob/vn, bc; d, 2 vn, va, vc, 2 fl, bc; a, 2 vn, va, vc, fl, bc; g, 2 vn, va, vc, fl, bc; G, 2 vn, va, vc, fl, bc; g, 2 vn, va, vc, fl, bc; a, 2 vn, va, vc, fl, bc; C, 2 vn, va, vc, fl, bc; c, 2 vn, va, vc, fl, bc 219, 238

VI Concertos in Seven Parts (London, *c*1740) (f, c, F, g, d, E), 2 solo vn, solo vc, 2 vn, va, bc, *D-Bds*, *GB-Cu*, *Ob*, *I-Rsc*, *US-NYp*

*Six Concertos for Keyboard and Orchestra (C, A, e, c, G, E♭), *GB-Lbm* (inc.)

Quattro sonate a quattro (f, c, g, d), 2 vn, va, vc, *D-MÜs*, *F-Pc*

Sette sonate per flauto e archi (D, a, c, a, A, C, g), fl, 2 vn, vc, bc, 1725, *I-Nc* 220

Sonata (F), fl, 2 vn, bc, *D-MÜs*

*Sonata (D), fl, 2 vn, bc, *I-Bc*

Sonata (A), 2 fl, 2 vn, bc, *D-MÜs*

Sonata (F), 3 fl, bc, *MÜs*

Suite (F), fl, bc, 16 June 1699, *MÜs*

Suite (G), fl, bc, June 1699, *MÜs*

THEORETICAL AND PEDAGOGICAL

Regole per principianti, *c*1715, *GB-Lbm*, *I-MC* 241

Discorso sopra un caso particolare in arte, April 1717, lost; Ger. trans. in J. P. Kirnberger, *Die Kunst des reinen Satzes in der Musik* (Berlin and Königsberg, 1776–9), ii, 143 241

Canons: Tenta la fuga ma la tenta invano, *NT*; Voi sola, 3S, *GB-Y*; Commincio solo, 3S, *Y*; 2 canons a 2, *Lbm*

15 fugues a 2, *I-Nc*, *Ria*

Studio a quattro sulla nota ferma, *GB-Lbm*

Varie partite obligate al basso, *I-MC*

Varie introduttioni per sonare e mettersi in tono delle compositioni, ?1715, *GB-Lbm*

BIBLIOGRAPHY

BurneyH
G. M. Crescimbeni: *L'arcadia*, vii, prosa V (Rome, 1711)
G. Grossi: *Biografia degli uomini illustri del Regno di Napoli* (Naples, 1819)
F. Florimo: *La scuola musicale di Napoli e i suoi conservatorii*, ii (Naples, 1882/*R*1969)
E. J. Dent: 'The Operas of Alessandro Scarlatti', *SIMG*, iv (1902–3), 143
——: 'The Earliest String Quartets', *MMR*, xxxiii (1903), 202
——: 'Alessandro Scarlatti', *PMA*, xxx (1903–4), 77
J. S. Shedlock: 'The Harpsichord Music of Alessandro Scarlatti', *SIMG*, vi (1904–5), 160, 418
E. J. Dent: *Alessandro Scarlatti: his Life and Works* (London, 1905, rev. 2/1960 with additions by F. Walker)
G. Piccini ['Jarro']: 'Alessandro Scarlatti; studio aneddotico su documenti originali', *La lettura*, xiv (1914), 929
H. Junker: 'Zwei *Griselda* Opern', *Festschrift zum 50. Geburtstag Adolf Sandberger* (Munich, 1918), 51
C. van den Borren: *Alessandro Scarlatti et l'esthétique de l'opéra napolitain* (Brussels and Paris, 1921)
P. Strüver: *Die Cantata da camera Alessandro Scarlattis* (diss., U. of Munich, 1923)
U. Prota-Giurleo: *Alessandro Scarlatti 'il Palermitano'* (Naples, 1926)
A. Lorenz: 'Alessandro Scarlattis Opern und Wien', *ZMw*, ix (1926–7), 86
——: *Alessandro Scarlattis Jugendoper* (Augsburg, 1927)
A. Bonaventura: 'El Stabat Mater de Alessandro Scarlatti', *Revista de musica*, ii (1928), 145
A. Cametti: 'Carlo Sigismondo Capeci (1652–1728), Alessandro e Domenico Scarlatti e la Regina di Polonia a Roma', *Musica d'oggi*, xiii (1931), 55
P. Dotto: 'Gaspare Alessandro Scarlatti il Palermitano', *Musica d'oggi*, xvii (1935), 383
U. Rolandi: 'Il 'Cain', sconosciuto oratorio di Alessandro Scarlatti', *NA*, xiii (1936), 176
Gli Scarlatti (*Alessandro – Francesco – Pietro – Domenico – Giuseppe*): *note e documenti sulla vita e sulle opere*, Chigiana, ii (1940)
D. de' Paoli: '*Diana ed Endimione* di Alessandro Scarlatti', *RaM*, xiii (1940), 139
C. Sartori: 'Il *Dafni* di Alessandro Scarlatti', *RMI*, xlv (1941), 176
——: '*Dori* e *Arione*, due opere ignorate di Alessandro Scarlatti', *NA*, xviii (1941), 35

E. Zanetti: '*Gli inganni felici* in una sconosciuta raccolta di arie di Alessandro Scarlatti', *RaM*, xiv (1941), 416
C. Sartori: 'Gli Scarlatti a Napoli', *RMI*, xlvi (1942), 374
E. J. Dent: 'A Pastoral Opera by Alessandro Scarlatti', *MR*, xii (1951), 7
U. Prota-Giurleo: 'Breve storia del teatro di corte e della musica a Napoli nei secoli XVII e XVIII', *Il teatro di corte del Palazzo reale di Napoli* (Naples, 1952), 19–146
E. Hanley: 'Current Chronicle', *MQ*, xxxix (1953), 241 [on the *St John Passion*]
R. G. Pauly: 'Alessandro Scarlatti's *Tigrane*', *ML*, xxxv (1954), 339
L. Ronga: 'Motivi critici su Alessandro Scarlatti', *RMI*, lvi (1954), 125
L. Montalto: *Un mecenate in Roma barocca* (Florence, 1955)
J. A. Bank: 'De kerkmuziek van Alessandro Scarlatti', *St Gregoriusblad*, lxxx (1956)
L. Ronga: *Arte e gusto nella musica* (Milan and Naples, 1956), 92–126
C. Sartori: 'Una Arianna misconosciuta: La Laodice di A. Scarlatti', *La Scala* (1956), no.79, p.4
J. Edmunds: 'Chamber Cantatas: the Mastery of Alessandro Scarlatti', *Tempo* (1956–7), no.42, p.24
G. Confalonieri: 'Nota su *Varrone e Pericca* di Alessandro Scarlatti', *Immagini esotiche nella musica italiana*, Chigiana, xiv (1957)
A. Liess: 'Materialien zur römischen Musikgeschichte des Seicento', *AcM*, xxix (1957), 137–71
A. Garbelotto: 'Alessandro Scarlatti', *Archivio storico siciliano*, 3rd ser., x (1959), 239
A. Liess: 'Die Sammlung der Oratorienlibretti (1679–1725) und der restliche Musikbestand des Fondo San Marcello der Biblioteca Vaticana in Rom', *AcM*, xxxi (1959), 63
P. Taylor Lee: *The Keyboard Style of Alessandro Scarlatti* (diss., Yale U., 1959)
M. Fabbri: 'Le musiche di Alessandro Scarlatti "per il tempo di penitenza e di tenebre" ', *I grandi anniversari del 1960 e la musica sinfonica e da camera nell'Ottocento in Italia*, Chigiana, xvii (1960), 17
G. A. Pastore: 'Nuove cantate di Alessandro Scarlatti', *Il San Carlo* (Naples, 1960), 32
Celebrazione del terzo centenario della nascita di Alessandro Scarlatti (n.p., 1960) [RAI publication]
M. Fabbri: *Alessandro Scarlatti e il Principe Ferdinando de' Medici* (Florence, 1961)
R. Pagano: 'Alexander Scarlatti, civitatis Panormi', *Conservatorio di musica Vincenzo Bellini, Palermo, annuario 1960–61* (1962), 11

Bibliography

A. Garbelotto: 'Contributo per un catalogo aggiornato delle opere di Alessandro Scarlatti', *Archivio storico siciliano*, 3rd ser., xiii (1963), 239–344

E. Hanley: *Alessandro Scarlatti's Cantate da Camera: a Bibliographical Study* (diss., Yale U., 1963)

——: 'Scarlatti, Alessandro', *MGG*

O. M. Henry: *The Doctrine of Affections in Selected Solo Cantatas of Alessandro Scarlatti* (diss., Ohio State U., 1963)

C. Terni: 'Stile e armonie di Alessandro Scarlatti per un dramma liturgico', *Le celebrazioni del 1963 e alcune nuove indagini sulla musica italiana del XVIII e XIX secolo*, Chigiana, xx (1963), 115–54

M. Boyd: 'Form and Style in Scarlatti's Chamber Cantatas', *MR*, xxv (1964), 17

C. R. Morey: *The Late Operas of Alessandro Scarlatti* (diss., Indiana U., 1965)

M. Fabbri: 'Torna alla luce la partitura autografa dell'oratorio *Il primo omicidio* di Alessandro Scarlatti', *Chigiana*, xxiii (1966), 245

U. Kirkendale: 'The Ruspoli Documents on Handel', *JAMS*, xx (1967), 222–73

L. Bettarini: 'Appunti critici sulle Sette sonate per flauto e archi di Alessandro Scarlatti', *Chigiana*, xxv (1968), 239

D. J. Grout: 'La *Griselda* di Zeno e il libretto dell'opera di Alessandro Scarlatti', *NRMI*, ii (1968), 207

J. López-Calo: 'L'intervento di Alessandro Scarlatti nella controversia sulla Messa *Scala aretina* di Francisco Valls', *AnMc*, no.5 (1968), 178

H. J. Marx: 'Die Musik am Hofe Pietro Cardinal Ottobonis unter Arcangelo Corelli', *AnMc*, no.5 (1968), 104–77

D. J. Poultney: *The Oratorios of Alessandro Scarlatti: their Lineage, Milieu, and Style* (diss., U. of Michigan, 1968)

B. Trowell: 'Scarlatti and Griselda', *MT*, cix (1968), 527

J. A. Westrup: 'Alessandro Scarlatti's *Il Mitridate Eupatore* (1707)', *New Looks at Italian Opera: Essays in Honor of Donald J. Grout* (Ithaca, 1968), 133

L. Bianchi: *Carissimi, Stradella, Scarlatti e l'oratorio musicale* (Rome, 1969)

P. Brandvik: *Selected Motets of Alessandro Scarlatti* (diss., U. of Illinois, 1969)

M. Boyd: 'Scarlatti's *La Statira*', *MT*, cxi (1970), 495

J. E. Shaffer: *The Cantus Firmus in Alessandro Scarlatti's Motets* (diss., George Peabody College for Teachers, Nashville, 1970)

P. R. Piersall: *The Bass Cantatas of Alessandro Scarlatti* (diss., U. of Oregon, 1971)

A. Mondolfi Bossarelli: 'Riesumazione di uno sconosciuto Scarlatti', *Conservatorio di musica S. Pietro a Majella, annuario 1965–1971* (Naples, n.d.), 37

R. Pagano, L. Bianchi and G. Rostirolla: *Alessandro Scarlatti* (Turin, 1972) [reviewed by R. Strohm, *RIM*, xi (1976)]

G. Pestelli: 'Haendel e Alessandro Scarlatti: problemi di attribuzione nel MS A.7b.63 della biblioteca del Conservatorio "Nicolo Paganini" di Genova', *RIM*, vii (1972), 103

M. Robinson: *Naples and Neapolitan Opera* (London, 1972)

G. Rose: 'Two Operas by Scarlatti Recovered', *MQ*, lviii (1972), 420

E. H. Alton: 'The Recorder Music of Alessandro Scarlatti (1660–1725)', *Recorder and Music Magazine*, iv (1973), 199

M. Fabbri: 'Il dolore e la morte nelle *voci in solitudine* di Alessandro Scarlatti', *Scritti in onore di Luigi Ronga* (Milan and Naples, 1973), 127

J. Jürgens: 'Die Madrigale Alessandro Scarlattis und ihre Quellen', *Scritti in onore di Luigi Ronga* (Milan and Naples, 1973), 279

E. Krist: 'Alessandro Scarlatti's *Messa di Santa Cecilia*', *American Choral Review*, xv (1973), 3

G. Pestelli: 'Le toccate per strumento a tastiera di Alessandro Scarlatti nei manoscritti napoletani', *AnMc*, no.12 (1973), 169

D. Poultney: 'Alessandro Scarlatti and the Transformation of Oratorio', *MQ*, lix (1973), 584

J. Steele: '*Dixit Dominus*: Alessandro Scarlatti and Handel', *SMA*, vii (1973), 19

E. Badura-Skoda: 'Ein Aufenthalt Alessandro Scarlattis in Wien im Oktober 1681', *Mf*, xxvii (1974), 204

D. J. Grout: 'The Original Version of Alessandro Scarlatti's *Griselda*', *Essays on Opera and English Music in Honour of Sir Jack Westrup* (Oxford, 1975), 103

Colloquium Alessandro Scarlatti: Würzburg 1975

R. Strohm: 'Hasse, Scarlatti, Rolle', *AnMc*, no.15 (1975), 221–57

——: 'Italienische Opernarien des frühen Settecento (1720–1730)', *AnMc*, no.16 (1976) [whole vol.]

M. T. Inkeles: *A Study, Realization, and Performance of Unpublished Cantatas for Soprano and Basso Continuo ca. 1690–1706 of Alessandro Scarlatti* (diss., Columbia U. Teachers College, 1977)

H. E. Smither: *A History of the Oratorio*, i: *The Oratorio in the Baroque Era: Italy, Vienna, Paris* (Chapel Hill, 1977)

G. Jones: 'Alessandro Scarlatti's *Il Ciro*', *Studien zur Barockoper*, ed. H. Marx, *Hamburger Jahrbuch für Musikwissenschaft*, iii (Hamburg, 1978)

L. Lindgren: 'Le opere drammatiche "romane" di Francesco Gasparini (1689–1699)', *Francesco Gasparini (1661–1727): atti del primo convegno internazionale: Camaiore 1978*, 167

D. J. Grout: *Alessandro Scarlatti: an Introduction to his Operas* (Berkeley, 1979)

R. Strohm: *Die italienischen Oper im 18. Jahrhundert* (Wilhelmshaven, 1979)

C. Troy: *The Comic Intermezzo: a Study in the History of Eighteenth-Century Italian Opera*, Studies in Musicology, no.9 (Ann Arbor, 1979)

C. K. Van de Kamp Freund: *Alessandro Scarlatti's Duet Cantatas and Solo Cantatas with Obbligato Instruments* (diss., Northwestern U., Evanston, 1979)

S. Durante: 'La *Guida armonica* di Giuseppe Ottavio Pitoni', *Nuovissimi studi: atti del terzo congresso internazionale: Fusignano 1980*, 285

E. Harris: *Handel and the Pastoral Tradition* (New York and London, 1980)

M. Lindley: 'An Introduction to Alessandro Scarlatti's *Toccata prima*', *Early Music*, x (1982), 333

T. Griffin: *The Late Baroque Serenata in Rome and Naples: a Documentary Study with Emphasis on Alessandro Scarlatti* (diss., U. of California, Los Angeles, 1983)

W. Holmes: *'La Statira' by Pietro Ottoboni and Alessandro Scarlatti: the Textual Sources, with a Documentary Postscript* (New York, 1983)

F. D'Accone: *Alessandro Scarlatti's 'Gli equivoci nel sembiante': the History of a Baroque Opera* (New York, in preparation)

L. Lindgren: 'Musical Drama in Rome during the Career of Alessandro Scarlatti (1660–1725)', *Roma e il teatro nel '700*, ed. Istituto della Enciclopedia Italiana (Rome, in preparation)

ANTONIO VIVALDI

Michael Talbot

CHAPTER ONE

Life

I Early years

Antonio (Lucio) Vivaldi was born in Venice on 4 March 1678. His father, Giovanni Battista, a baker's son, was born in Brescia about 1655. He moved with his widowed mother in 1666 to Venice, where for a while he worked as a barber before becoming a professional violinist in early adulthood. Eight children, of whom Antonio was the eldest, are known to have been born to his union with Camilla Calicchio, a tailor's daughter, whom he married in June 1676.

None of Antonio's brothers and sisters became musicians, although Francesco (*b* 1690) emulated his elder brother's entrepreneurial spirit by adding to his main calling of wigmaker those of paving contractor and publisher. On 23 April 1685 Giovanni Battista was engaged as a violinist at St Mark's under the surname of Rossi. This suggests that red hair, which was to earn Antonio the sobriquet of 'il prete rosso' ('the red priest'), was a family characteristic. In the same year Giovanni Battista became a founder-member of the Sovvegno dei Musicisti di S Cecilia. From 1689 to 1693 he served, under the name 'Giovanni Battista Vivaldi detto Rosetto', as director of instrumental music at the Mendicanti. He became sufficiently esteemed as a violinist to be listed alongside his celebrated son in Coronelli's *Guida de' forestieri*. There are hints that he was from time to time involved in operatic management. He may have been a composer as well: *La fedeltà sfortunata*, an opera attributed to one G. B. Rossi, was performed at an unidentified Venetian theatre in 1688 (or possibly 1689). In November 1729 he was granted one year's leave of absence from St Mark's in order to accompany a son (presumably Antonio) to Germany. He did not rejoin the orchestra on his return and died on 14 May 1736. He no doubt exerted a strong influence on Antonio, who outlived him by a mere five years. Father and son lived together, with various other family members, in three successive apartments in different parts of Venice between 1711 and 1736.

Antonio was baptized officially on 6 May 1678. Because the life of the newborn infant was thought to be in danger the midwife had performed an emergency baptism on the day of his birth; a possible cause was the earthquake which shook Venice on 4 March, but it is more likely that the ailment which the composer claimed to have afflicted him from birth was already showing itself. This condition ('strettezza di petto' was how Vivaldi described it) has tentatively been identified as a type of bronchial asthma. Although Vivaldi as an adult was evidently determined not to let it prevent him from undertaking frequent and arduous journeys, even if that meant maintaining a large and expensive entourage, its physical and particularly its psychological effect on him should not be underestimated.

Between 18 September 1693 (the date of his tonsure) and 23 March 1703 (the date of his ordination) Vivaldi was trained for the priesthood by the Fathers of S Geminiano and those of S Giovanni in Oleo while continuing to live with his family in the district of S

Martino. At least once during this period (at Christmas 1696) he is known to have been engaged as an additional violinist at St Mark's. The only extant report of his accompanying on the harpsichord comes from near the end of his life, but it can be assumed that he mastered that instrument early on. Soon after his ordination he ceased for good to say Mass. A clue to the date of this renunciation is the termination, in August 1705, of a benefice worth 80 ducats annually that he had enjoyed at the Pietà since the beginning of his employment there, and which required him to say Mass daily. In 1737, while under censure for conduct unbecoming to a priest, he blamed his failure on his ailment – probably quite truthfully, for in the light of his lifelong devotion to money, it is hard to imagine any other sufficiently compelling reason. The case is strengthened by a fanciful 18th-century report of his temporary retirement to the sacristy during celebration of Mass (if one chooses to discount the explanation that his purpose was to write down a fugue). His reputation for extreme piety, even bigotry, was well earned. The religious motto 'Laus Deo' (abbreviated as L.D.) and an expanded version 'LDBMDA', usually found as a monogram and possibly standing for 'Laus Deo Beataeque Mariae Deiparae Amen', occur with great frequency at the head of his scores – strange to say, particularly those of operas. From Goldoni's account of a meeting with Vivaldi in 1735 we glimpse the composer taking refuge from a rather unwelcome confrontation in mechanical recitation from his breviary, and in a legal wrangle of 1739 with the scenographer Antonio Mauro, Vivaldi thunderingly calls down the wrath of God on his adversary.

II Appointment at the Pietà

In September 1703 Vivaldi obtained his first official post, becoming *maestro di violino* at the comfortable but unremarkable annual salary of 60 ducats at the Pio Ospedale della Pietà, one of four Venetian institutions devoted to caring for foundlings or orphans and specializing in the musical training of the girls among them who showed aptitude. Services – one might almost call them concerts – at the Pietà were a focal point in the social calendar of the Venetian nobility and foreign visitors, and it was essential to ensure both the competent instruction and rehearsal of the young singers and instrumentalists and the regular supply of new works for them. Vivaldi owed his appointment to a request made earlier that year by the Pietà's *maestro di coro* (musical director) Francesco Gasparini that violin and oboe masters be engaged. In August 1704, 40 ducats were added to his salary in consideration of his teaching of the *viole all'inglese* – a family of variously sized instruments similar to *viole d'amore* in having sympathetic strings. To Vivaldi fell in addition the task of acquiring new string instruments for the orchestra and maintaining those already in use.

The governors of the Ospedale della Pietà renewed his post annually until February 1709, when a majority voted on a second ballot against retaining him. It seems less probable that Vivaldi was dismissed from his post on grounds of incapacity or misconduct, or through personal animosity, than that the post itself was temporarily discontinued, perhaps in the interests of economy. The orchestra would certainly be left in capable hands for the pyramidically organized structure of teaching at the Pietà was headed by a group of older girls and women with the rank of *maestra*, under the supreme direction of two *maestre di coro*; these were the foremost performers among the girls, and some of them (for example, the Anna Maria commemorated in the title of several of Vivaldi's concertos) attained fame beyond the Pietà. Ironically, his very success in producing seasoned performers may have contributed to his redundancy. That explanation gains support from the fact that the comparable post of teacher of wind instruments was left unfilled for long periods, and that during his lifetime no other violin teacher was ever appointed, although teachers of the cello, beginning with a certain Rev. Antonio Vandini (often confused, even in the Pietà's records, with Vivaldi – whose name did however appear anagramatically as Lotavio Vandini in the libretto of *Aristide*), were employed between 1720 and 1728.

Meanwhile, Vivaldi was seeking recognition as a composer. The earliest extant edition of his op.1, a set of 12 chamber sonatas in the trio medium, is that by Sala dated 1705 and dedicated to Count Annibale Gambara, a Venetian nobleman. That edition describes Vivaldi on the title-page as 'Musico di violino, professore veneto', making no mention of his appointment at the Pietà but acknowledging his status as a priest by use of the title 'Don'; it could be a reprint of a lost original edition dating from 1703, though the inclusion of a letter of dedication implies otherwise. His op.2, consisting of violin sonatas, was dedicated in 1709 to Frederick IV of Denmark, who is reported to have attended a service at the Pietà under Vivaldi's direction on 30 December 1708, the day after his arrival in Venice. By then Vivaldi was writing concertos, which circulated in manuscript; copies of some of his cello concertos made by

17. Antonio Vivaldi: caricature (1723) by Pier Leone Ghezzi

the musician Franz Horneck while staying in Venice during the Carnival season of 1708–9 have survived in the library of the Counts of Schönborn.

Vivaldi was voted back into his former post at the Pietà in September 1711 and was reappointed against steadily mounting opposition every year until March 1716, when the required majority of two-thirds was not obtained. Surprisingly, in May 1716 he was appointed to a position of greater responsibility, *maestro de' concerti.* It is worth noting, however, that long before this time Vivaldi had allowed himself to be styled *maestro de' concerti* on title-pages and in opera librettos. The departure, in April 1713, of Gasparini on a sick leave from which he never returned gave Vivaldi an opportunity to write sacred music, for Pietro Scarpari (Dall'Oglio), the singing master and interim *maestro di coro*, was a poor replacement as a composer. The governors were so pleased with Vivaldi's efforts that in June 1715 they gave him a special payment of 50 ducats for 'an entire mass, a vespers, an oratorio, over 30 motets and other labours'. In November 1716 Vivaldi followed his *Moyses Deus Pharaonis* with a new oratorio, *Juditha triumphans*, which contained patriotic references to Venice's war against the Turks.

In 1711 Estienne Roger, the Amsterdam publisher, brought out what was to become the most influential music publication of the first half of the 18th century: Vivaldi's *L'estro armonico* op.3, dedicated to Ferdinand, Grand Prince of Tuscany; it comprised 12 concertos divided equally into works for one, two and four solo violins. The change to Roger from local publishers, which several other eminent Italian composers made about the same time, reflected not only the superiority of the engraving process over the printing from type still normally used in Italy (a superiority acknowledged in Vivaldi's preface to *L'estro armonico*) but also the enormous growth in demand for the latest Italian music in northern Europe. Nowhere was the enthusiasm for Vivaldi's concertos stronger than in Germany. Bach transcribed several of them (including five from op.3) for keyboard, and his royal master Prince Johann Ernst of Saxe-Weimar wrote concertos in Vivaldi's style. German musicians visiting Venice such as Stölzel (1713–14), Heinichen (1713–16) and Pisendel (1716–17) sought him out. Pisendel, who is known to have taken lessons from him, copied out several of his sonatas and concertos and also received autograph scores of many works directly from the master, who continued to have close relations with the Saxon court. Quantz, who first heard Vivaldi's concertos at Pirna in 1714, gave him credit in his *Anweisung* for having reformed the concerto (together with Albinoni); the formula for composing a concerto set out by Quantz conforms in every particular to Vivaldi's normal practice.

La stravanganza op.4, a set of 12 violin concertos, was dedicated in about 1714 to Vettor Delfino (Dolfin), a young pupil of Vivaldi from the Venetian nobility. The next three publications (opp.5–7, comprising six sonatas and 18 concertos), belonging to the years *c*1716–17, were left undedicated: apparently Roger ordered them from the composer and had them engraved at his own expense, which shows Vivaldi's exceptional popularity – this procedure, later in the century to become normal, was still rather rare.

During the 1710s Vivaldi followed his father into the turbulent world of opera. Already in 1708 he had composed the serenata *Le gare del dovere*, which employed fully operatic musical resources. Although his ealiest known opera, *Ottone in Villa*, was performed at the summer resort of Vicenza in May 1713 (at the same time as his earliest known oratorio, *La vittoria navale*), he first established

L' ESTRO ARMONICO
CONCERTI
Consacrati
ALL' ALTEZZA REALE
DI
FERDINANDO III
GRAN PRENCIPE DI TOSCANA
Da D. Antonio Vivaldi
Musico di Violino e Maestro de Concerti del
Pio Ospidale della Pieta di Venezia
OPERA TERZA
LIBRO PRIMO.

A AMSTERDAM
Aux depens D'ESTIENNE ROGER Marchand Libraire
Chez qui l'on trouve un assortiment general de toute sorte de
Musique, dont on peut avoir chez lui le Catalogue.
N°.50

18. Title-page of Vivaldi's 'L'estro armonico' op.3 (Amsterdam: Roger, 1711) himself, as both a composer and an impresario, at the Venetian theatre of S Angelo. In the Carnival (winter season) of 1714 Vivaldi wrote the dedication of the libretto by G. Braccioli for M. A. Gasparini's *Rodomonte sdegnato*, as he did again a year later for *Luca Papirio*, set to music by Predieri. It was possibly Predieri's opera that the Frankfurt lawyer J. F. A. von Uffenbach heard on 4 February 1715, when he noted in his diary that Vivaldi was the 'entrepreneur' (mistakenly believing him also to be the composer). Vivaldi's own *Orlando finto pazzo* opened the 1714–15 season, and a pasticcio (*Nerone fatto Cesare*) and two new operas followed up to 1717. Between 1716 and 1718 he also wrote three operas for the S Moisè theatre; in addition, there were some revivals.

III **Years of travel**

In April 1718 Vivaldi took his recent opera *Armida al campo* to Mantua, staying until 1720. During that time he wrote three operas for performance in the 1719 and 1720 Carnival seasons. The Governor of Mantua (for the Habsburgs) was Prince Philipp of Hessen-Darmstadt, a noted music lover. Vivaldi became his *maestro di cappella da* (or *di*) *camera*, a curiously worded title he retained after leaving Mantua. Several secular vocal works were written for the Mantuan court.

Having briefly returned to Venice, Vivaldi was soon off to Rome, where, according to two letters of 1737 to Guido Bentivoglio, he spent three Carnival seasons and was invited twice to play before the pope. Three operas performed in Rome during the 1723 and 1724 Carnival seasons are known, and it is possible that the other season of which Vivaldi wrote was that of 1720, when he contributed one act to *Tito Manlio* (RV778, not to be confused with the Mantuan opera of the same title, RV738, of which Vivaldi was the sole composer). Pier Leone Ghezzi's famous caricature of Vivaldi (fig.17) was drawn during Carnival 1723 when *Ercole su 'l Termodonte* was being staged. While in Rome, or perhaps during the cardinal's visit to Venice in 1726, Vivaldi almost certainly came into contact with Pietro Ottoboni, Corelli's former patron; a handsome volume of violin sonatas in Manchester can be traced back to Ottoboni's library. Another patron was Princess Maria Livia Spinola Borghese, to whom he was recommended by Alessandro Marcello. It is uncertain whether Vivaldi lived continuously in Rome between 1723 and 1725. In July 1723 the Pietà governors agreed to ask him to supply the orchestra with two concertos every month (at one sequin each), sending them by post if necessary, and to direct three or four rehearsals of them when in Venice. As a composer Vivaldi was evidently still a major asset to the Pietà, notwithstanding his incessant travelling, which ruled out a teaching post.

It was around this time that Vivaldi's association with the contralto Anna Giraud (or Girò) must have begun. She was the daughter of a wigmaker of French origin and became his singing pupil. Between 1724 and 1747 she appeared regularly on the operatic stage, especially in Venice. Some librettos describe her as 'Mantovana'; that may mean not that she originated from Mantua but that she had a connection with the Mantuan court. She was also known as 'Annina della Pietà', either through having been educated at the Pietà or through her friendship with Vivaldi. Goldoni thought her voice weak but conceded that she was a good actress and had an attractive appearance. The alterations made by Goldoni at Vivaldi's instance to Zeno's original libretto show for *Griselda* that Vivaldi was aware of his pupil's limitations. Both Anna Giraud and her sister Paolina (who, it is suggested, acted as the composer's nurse) were loyal members of his entourage. Tongues inevitably wagged, and it was widely believed that the Giraud sisters, and particularly Anna, were Vivaldi's mistresses, despite his denial.

From 1726 to 1728 Vivaldi was again active as a composer and impresario at S Angelo. At the same time his instrumental works were continuing to spread his reputation. *Il cimento dell'armonia e dell'inventione* op.8 (opening with the four concertos portraying the seasons) appeared by 1725 and was dedicated to the Bohemian Count Wenzeslaus von Morzin (a distant relative of the Morzin who employed Haydn), of whom Vivaldi claimed to be the *maestro in Italia*. *La cetra* op.9 was dedicated to Emperor Charles VI, whom Vivaldi was reported by the Abbé Antonio Conti in a letter to Madame de Caylus to have met in autumn 1728, possibly in Trieste, and from whom he allegedly received much money, a golden chain and medallion, and a knighthood. (The 12 different concertos also entitled *La cetra* and dated 1728 in a manuscript in Vienna may commemorate that meeting; the published *La cetra* appeared earlier, in 1727.) The pioneering flute concertos of op.10 and the string concertos of opp.11 and 12 were issued by Le Cène before the end of the decade. Although the publisher bore the costs of all five collections, Vivaldi was evidently dissatisfied with the financial returns, for in 1733 he told the English traveller Edward Holdsworth of his decision not to have any more concertos published as it inhibited his more profitable trade in manuscripts, for which the current price was a guinea per concerto; and indeed no work of his published after op.12 appeared with his proven consent (op.13, *Il pastor fido*, is a clever pasticcio incorporating fragments of concertos by Meck and G. M. Alberti as well as Vivaldi, while a presumably spurious op.14 was announced but never appeared).

Between late 1729 and early 1733 Vivaldi travelled widely. Perhaps the invitation to Vienna cited in a letter of 1737 relates to this period. He may well have visited Prague (where since 1725 an operatic company headed by the Venetian singer Antonio Denzio had been active at the court of Count Sporck), as two new operas were given there in autumn 1730 (*Argippo*) and spring 1731 (*Alvilda*). By his own account, Vivaldi liked to oversee productions of his new operas, so the dates and places of their premières afford valuable clues to his movements.

During 1733–5 he wrote several operas for S Angelo and the Grimani theatre of S Samuele to which Goldoni was attached. His entrepreneurial activities in Venice seem to have ended; instead, he increasingly promoted opera in smaller mainland centres like Verona, Ancona, Reggio and Ferrara. From *L'Adelaide* (Verona, 1735) onwards Vivaldi styled himself *maestro di cappella* of Francis Stephen, Duke of Lorraine and (from 1737) Grand Duke of Tuscany, the future Emperor Francis I. The title was doubtless little more than honorific. Meanwhile, he was reinstated at the Pietà as *maestro di cappella* in August 1735. The governors now wished to take a firmer line on his travelling, and his renewed absences probably contributed to his failure to gain reappointment in March 1738. His links were not severed, however: when Friedrich Christian, Crown Prince of Saxony-Poland, visited the Pietà on 21 March 1740 Vivaldi was asked to supply and direct the performance of three concertos (RV540, 552, 558) and one sinfonia (RV149); the scores, mostly autograph, were taken back to Dresden.

Vivaldi was on close terms with Marquis Guido Bentivoglio d'Aragona, a resident of Ferrara. He enlisted Bentivoglio's support to stage operas at Ferrara during the Carnival seasons of 1737, 1738 and 1739; 13 letters by Vivaldi to Bentivoglio and copies of several replies by the marquis, most of which are in the Bentivoglio archives, provide among other things an illuminating record of these three essays (all of them less than successful, alas) in operatic promotion. In 1737 there were wrangles over a singer's contract and the choice of operas, and an unseemly attempt by Vivaldi to exact the full payment. In 1738 Tomaso Ruffo, Cardinal-Archbishop of Ferrara (a papal domain), forbade Vivaldi to enter Ferrara, ostensibly on account of his relationship with Anna Giraud and his refusal to say Mass, so that he was compelled to put the enterprise in the hands of local impresarios in whom he had little confidence. This contretemps allowed him to travel to Amsterdam to direct the musical performances celebrating the centenary of the Schouwburg theatre, for which he wrote the concerto RV562*a*, on 7 January 1738. In 1739 Vivaldi, who was in Venice presumably supervising the performances of his *Feraspe* and *Tito Manlio*, paid dearly for his absence from Ferrara. The first opera, *Siroe*, was criticized for faults in its recitatives (because, Vivaldi bitterly claimed, of alterations arbitrarily introduced by the harpsichordist, P. A. Berretta) with the result that the theatre's patrons refused to mount *Farnace*, the second opera. Bentivoglio was sympathetic but too politic to intervene.

De Brosses, who met Vivaldi in autumn 1739, found his stock low with the Venetian public. That may be one reason why Vivaldi was persuaded to undertake his last, mysterious journey in 1740 (the ground for which may have been prepared by Anna Giraud's visits to Graz in 1739 and 1740 to sing in the opera). On 29 April (not August) 1740 the Pietà governors, having got wind of his imminent departure, rejected a motion to buy 'a certain portion of concertos' from him; they must have relented, however, as on 12 May he was paid for 20 concertos. Vivaldi had reached Vienna by 28 June 1741, the date of the receipt for the sale of several concertos to Count Antonio Vinciguerra di Collalto. On 28 July he died in a house owned by the widow of a Viennese saddler named Waller and was given a pauper's burial on the same day at the Hospital Burial Ground (Spettaler Gottesacker), confirming a note in a contemporary Venetian manuscript (*Commemoriali Gradenigo*) that states that Vivaldi, who had once earned 50,000 ducats (presumably annually) died in poverty through his prodigality.

CHAPTER TWO

Reputation

Antonio Vivaldi was so unconventional as both man and musician that he was bound to elicit much adverse comment in his lifetime. His vanity was notorious: he boasted of his fame and illustrious patrons, and of his fluency in composition, asserting before De Brosses that he could compose a concerto in all its parts more quickly than it could be copied. In many cases these claims were clearly exaggerated. He told Holdsworth, for example, that 17 (not 12) collections by him had been published, rather deceitfully counting double each opus divided into two books. His claim to Bentivoglio in 1739 that he had composed 94 operas (fewer than 50 are known) needs to be interpreted in this light. Along with his vanity went an extreme sensitivity to criticism, which comes out even in the dedications of his opp.1 and 4, where one sees a phrase such as 'i miei sudori forse malignati dalla critica' ('my efforts, which are perhaps spoken ill of by the critics'). His preoccupation with money was excessive by any standards: it is a subject that surfaces continually in his letters to Bentivoglio. Holdsworth and De Brosses found that Vivaldi drove a hard bargain with foreign visitors. Yet the sheer zest of the man compelled admiration. De Brosses wrote of his 'furie de composition', and Goldoni painted a charming picture of the old man's enthusiasm on seeing the aria text his visitor had penned before his very eyes. His egotism must have been redeemed by higher qualities for him to have retained the loyalty of the Giraud sisters and several patrons. If the well-known engraving of him by François Morellon La Cave (and its imitation by Lambert) conveys all too successfully his self-satisfaction, the anonymous painting in Bologna of an unnamed violinist believed to be Vivaldi shows a more sympathetic, pensive side.

Vivaldi was praised more readily by his contemporaries as a violinist than as a composer, though few went as far as Goldoni, who categorized him as 'excellent joueur de violon et compositeur médiocre'. Uffenbach's report of his ending the accompaniment to an operatic aria with 'a fantasy [i.e. cadenza] which really terrified me, for such has not been nor can ever be played; he came with his fingers within a mere grass-stalk's breadth of the bridge, so that the bow had no room – and this on all four strings with imitations and at incredible speed' vividly captures his predilection for extremely high positions, cadenza-like passages and multiple stopping. Such pyrotechnics undoubtedly hindered his acceptance as a serious composer. Avison found his compositions 'equally defective in various harmony and true invention', an opinion found too sweeping by William Hayes who, attributing the composer's faults 'to his having a great command of his instrument, being of a volatile disposition (having too much mercury in his constitution) and to misapplication of good parts and abilities', nonetheless thought that the 11th concerto in *L'estro armonico* (RV565) gave evidence of his 'capacity in solid composition'. Hawkins admitted the 'peculiar force and energy' of his concertos, though he found them 'wild and irregular' and disparaged their part-writing.

Quantz had turned against Vivaldi by the time his *Anweisung* appeared in 1752, reproaching him for too much routine composing and for falling under the bad influence of opera. Further, many of Quantz's criticisms directed towards particular features of the contemporary Italian style, such as its fondness for simple, functional bass parts thematically unrelated to the upper parts, apply *a fortiori* to Vivaldi, their originator or popularizer. C. P. E. Bach taxed 'a certain master in Italy' (obviously Vivaldi) with initiating the custom of writing the bass in a high register and assigning it to violins, a usage already deplored by Marcello. Vivaldi's kindest German critic was the italophile Mattheson, who commended him for his observation of the distinction between apt vocal and instrumental writing (the first avoiding the leaps of the second). Ironically, Tartini was reported by De Brosses to have instanced Vivaldi as one of those men gifted in instrumental composition who met with failure when they essayed opera – perhaps a case of sour grapes, for Goldoni wrote that most of Vivaldi's operas were successful.

A few decades passed, and Vivaldi fell into virtual oblivion, except among a few music historians and lexicographers – to be rescued, like so many of his contemporaries, via Bach scholarship. The influence of Vivaldi on Bach had been acknowledged by Forkel; now Rühlmann and Waldersee unearthed the Vivaldi originals of the Bach transcriptions and made their comparisons – always, at that time, to the Italian's disadvantage. His unequivocal importance to the history of the concerto was first demonstrated by Arnold Schering in 1905. The steady growth of interest in him received a tremendous spur from the discovery by Alberto Gentili in the 1920s of what can only have been Vivaldi's personal collection of scores (the great variety of genres, both sacred and secular, and the preponderance of autograph scores make it unlikely that the collection originally belonged to the Pietà, as some have suggested): the Foà and Giordano manuscripts, now in the Biblioteca Nazionale, Turin. These were already in the library of the Venetian bibliophile Jacopo Soranzo by 1745, and subsequently became, before their arbitrary division as a legacy into two collections, the property of Gluck's renowned patron Count Giacomo Durazzo (1717–94), intendant of the Vienna Opera and the imperial Ambassador in Venice from 1764 to 1784. The seal was set on Vivaldi's rehabilitation by the inauguration in 1947 by Ricordi of a collected edition of his instrumental works and the appearance of Marc Pincherle's famous study in the following year.

The cataloguing of Vivaldi's large and diverse output has proved a difficult task, especially as works having thematic incipits in common often prove on closer examination to be different. With the rapid progress of Vivaldi research in recent years the demerits of older catalogues have come increasingly to outweigh their merits: of the two catalogues most in use at the time of writing, that by Pincherle (published as the second volume of his study) offers a system of numbering independent of original opus numbers for the orchestral works alone, and suffers from innumerable inaccuracies and omissions, while Fanna's catalogue (in which works are classified according to their instrumentation), is designed for use in conjunction with the Ricordi collected edition, and omits incomplete or lost works as well as all the vocal music. Rinaldi's catalogue classifies the instrumental works by opus numbers, supplementing Vivaldi's own with additional ones and assigning a group of like works to each; his system is now little favoured. As the most complete, accurate and rationally organized catalogue that has so far appeared, Ryom's *Verzeichnis der Werke Antonio Vivaldis* has many advantages. The volume numbers of Ricordi's edition of the instrumental works (a new, critical edition has recently begun to appear from the same publisher) naturally retain their usefulness as a means of guiding the inquirer directly to the music.

CHAPTER THREE

Works

I Instrumental music

No brief description can do justice to the variety of form, scoring and imagination in Vivaldi's 500-odd concertos. If he did not invent ritornello form – in which varied restatements in different keys of a ritornello (refrain), usually for the full ensemble, alternate with modulating episodes of free thematic character, where a soloist (if present) predominates – he was at least the first composer to use it regularly in the fast movements of concertos, so providing his contemporaries with the models they were seeking. The same is true of the standard three-movement plan. Several occasional features of Vivaldi concertos were taken further and made normative by his successors: the northern Italians, including Tartini and Locatelli, copied his reference to the ritornello opening at the start of the first solo episode, the infiltration of solo writing into the ritornello, and the provision of a cadenza; the Germans, notably Bach, developed his techniques of thematic integration – the reprise of the first solo idea in the final episode and the use of ritornello fragments to accompany the soloist. Very often, Vivaldi has a double statement of the ritornello in the tonic at the end of the movement (which facilitates the matching of the openings of the first and last episodes) or a single statement of the ritornello interrupted by one or more solo excursions generally either reminiscent of earlier solo material or in the nature of a cadenza. G. M. Alberti and Telemann were among the composers who often copied this feature. One Vivaldian idiosyncrasy – the tendency to make ritornello restatements progressively shorter and less complete, while the length of episodes increases – was not taken over by his imitators, who preferred more symmetrical proportions. This peculiarity was accentuated by Vivaldi's impulsive way of composing: certain ideas in the opening ritornello, it seems, captured his imagination and recur almost automatically, while others, equally fertile in possibilities, are passed over, allowing the ritornello to become whittled down by a process akin to natural selection. It also happens that spontaneous modifications devoid of specific purpose are made to the ritornello in the act of writing it out again, as if the composer disdained to refresh his memory by consulting earlier pages. A simplified version of ritornello form is often used in slow movements, though binary form or through-composed form (sometimes employing a ground bass) also occur. Binary and variation form are occasionally found in finales.

Roughly 350 concertos are for one solo instrument and strings, over 230 of them for violin. Other solo instruments are (in descending order of frequency) bassoon, cello, oboe, flute, viola d'amore, recorder (including the so-called 'flautino') and mandolin. There are 40-odd double concertos, mostly for two similar instruments but including such rare combinations as viola d'amore and lute (RV540). Ensemble concertos, in which three or more soloists participate, number over 30 and introduce, among other instruments, clarinets (making one of their earliest orchestral appearances), salmoè (chalumeaux), theorbos, horns and timpani. A very important group of works is constituted by nearly 60 *concerti ripieni* (or string concertos without soloist), stylistically very close to operatic sinfonias, with which they were virtually interchangeable; some of them demonstrate an impressive sense of thematic economy and a flair for fugal writing that should give pause to those who consider Vivaldi an arch-instigator of the 'flight from counterpoint'. Over 20 concertos are for a small group of solo instruments without string ripieno; the tutti is formed by the united soloists, as in Bach's Brandenburg Concerto no.3. Finally, there are a small number of works for double string orchestra with soloists, continuing an old Venetian tradition which had by now spread beyond St Mark's.

Many of the concertos received descriptive titles of various kinds. Some refer to the original performer or performers (e.g. *Il Carbonelli* RV366), while others recall the particular feast (as in the concertos 'per la Solennità di S Lorenzo') on which the work was performed. Some allude to an unusual technical feature; in *L'ottavina* (RV763), for instance, all the solos are directed to be played in the upper octave. Other titles (e.g. *L'inquietudine* RV234) characterize the pervading mood of the work. Lastly, some programmatic or onomatopoeic concertos have appropriate titles (e.g. *Il gardellino* RV90, 428; *La tempesta di mare* RV98, 433, 570). In these, the elements in the 'programme' which remain constant (e.g. the huntsmen in the finale of the 'Autumn' concerto from the 'Four Seasons') are, quite logically, incorporated in the ritornello, while transitory events (e.g. the death of their quarry) are depicted in individual episodes. The slow movements

19. Autograph score of the opening of Vivaldi's Concerto in C minor for strings and continuo RV*120*

are mostly static tableaux in which instrumentation is sometimes skilfully used to differentiate parts of the scene: in the central movement of the 'Spring' concerto, for instance, we hear simultaneously a sleeping shepherd (solo violin), a rippling brook (orchestral violins) and a vigilant sheepdog (viola).

Vivaldi was a deft and enterprising orchestrator. In general, the number of real parts is reduced and the texture lightened in solo passages, but the ways in which that is achieved are so varied as to defy enumeration. Single-line accompaniments on continuo or ripieno violins are the most common. He employed many special colouristic effects, such as muting and pizzicato, and paid exceptional attention for his time to the nuances of string articulation and bowing. The well-known passage in op.3 no.10 (RV580) where each of the four solo violins arpeggiates in a different manner is a representative instance. In particular, Vivaldi was fond of syncopated bowing in which the change of bow occurs on a note off the beat. Occasionally he seems to call for a true crescendo or diminuendo, anticipating early Classical style.

His approximately 90 sonatas are by comparison conservative in form and style, reflecting the special role of the genre in Italy as the repository of traditional technique. The trio sonatas of opp.1 and 5 are firmly in the chamber style, paying due homage to Corelli, while the solo sonatas, variously for violin, cello and wind instruments, are mostly in a composite church–chamber style where *da camera* elements have the upper hand, as shown by the supremacy of binary form, even in slow movements. The most interesting sonatas are perhaps a group of four for two violins performable without bass support (RV68, 70, 71, 77), which probably antedate Leclair's op.3 duets.

In his instrumental music Vivaldi was an uninhibited self-borrower. The extent to which material, including whole movements, was not merely re-used in works of the same genre but even transferred from one genre to another is remarkable. The slow movement of a solo sonata (RV12) can reappear in a solo concerto (RV582). A binary sonata finale (RV755) can be converted into ritornello form and used in a concerto (RV229). More subtly, the opening of the Allemanda finale of RV3 supplies the material of the episodes in the first movement of RV101 and its later version RV437. In those cases the sequence of borrowing is fairly clear, but in many others guesses are hazardous on present evidence. Vivaldi was also prone to modify existing works when they were required for new purposes; it is unlikely that he would ever have considered any version definitive.

II Vocal music

Vivaldi's sacred music, less well known outside Italy, was subject to the operatic influences of his age, although many individual movements remain close to the *stile osservato*. The numerous solo motets are patently modelled on the opera scena. It is noticeable how often the principal melodic interest in choral movements is allotted to the violins, leaving the choir to declaim homophonically in the background (as in the outer movements of the Credo RV591), thus anticipating the symphonic mass of Haydn's generation. Alongside operatic influence that of the concerto is rarely absent. An extreme case is the *Beatus vir* RV598, conceived as a vast span of 420 bars in ritornello form; here the vocal soloists are heard in the episodes and the choir fulfils tutti and solo functions by turns. In his church music Vivaldi succeeded admirably in conveying the general sense of the text, but his word-setting can be cavalier (as, indeed, in his secular vocal music) and his attentiveness to the individual word or phrase slight. It is the factor of a strong musical personality rather than artistic finesse that has brought popularity in recent times to the Gloria RV589, the *Magnificat* RV610 and 611, and the oratorio *Juditha triumphans*.

His cantatas and serenatas are written in the style often misleadingly termed 'Neapolitan' after Alessandro Scarlatti. Their backbone is a series of two or more da capo arias, with which recitatives alternate. Over three-quarters of his cantatas are for solo voice (soprano or alto) and continuo alone, the favoured combination of the time. They constitute the least innovatory portion of his output, but by no means the least expertly written. There is a hint in one cantata (*Nel partir da te mio caro* RV661) that Vivaldi sometimes wrote the poetic text himself, for whereas three rejected openings of one recitative there have one text, the successful fourth version has a similar but not identical text. (If so, could he not have also written the *sonetti dimostrativi* accompanying the 'Four Seasons'?) The serenatas are more extended works, intermediate in style between cantata and opera and commissioned to celebrate an event or eulogize some person. Lacking the length and bombast of the operas, while furnishing more interesting sonorities than the cantatas, they fully deserve revival.

The scores of 21 operas, some lacking one or more acts, have survived. They include his first opera (*Ottone in Villa*) and one of his last (*Rosmira*). Viewed dramatically, the operas merely supply what was expected of a composer working within narrow and at the time universal conventions; that apart, the music is as vital and imaginative as any he wrote. Obbligato instruments are introduced from time to time: for example, *Armida* calls for a solo violin, *Giustino* a psaltery and *L'Olimpiade* a horn. It is interesting that some of the later scores include a few arias by Leo, Hasse, Handel, Pergolesi and other composers of the moment. Vivaldi may have wished to lend a veneer of fashionability to the operas, no longer confident of his ability to satisfy public taste; or perhaps he borrowed simply for convenience.

III **Points of style**

Vivaldi's musical language is so distinctive that a few of its peculiarities are worthy of note. His melody shows a penchant for Lombardic rhythms (which, according to Quantz, he first introduced) and syncopation – betraying, perhaps, Venice's connections with Dalmatia and the Slavonic hinterland. His treatment of the variable sixth and seventh degrees of the minor scale was amazingly flexible, admitting the augmented 2nd as a melodic interval even in an ascending line. Compound intervals, including the octave, could take an expressive melodic value hitherto barely exploited. He took ideas from the major into the minor mode (and vice versa) with almost Schubertian freedom. He formed melodies from mere cadential fragments (a phenomenon well described by Kolneder as 'Kadenzmelodik'). His harmony abounds in 7th chords, and he used the higher dominant discords (9th, 11th, 13th) over pedals with near recklessness. He can modulate extremely abruptly, often through a VII–I rather than V–I progression. Juxtapositions of very slow and very fast harmonic rhythms are frequent. His phrasing often includes irregular groups (e.g. of one and a half bars' length). His two violins frequently toss a pair of contrapuntally contrasted motifs back and forth over several bars, either at one pitch (producing a quasi-canonic effect) or at different pitches in a sequential pattern; sequence, incidentally, was a device whose attractiveness to Vivaldi could be dangerous in his more facile moments. Ostinato phrases in one part which contradict the changing harmonies of the other parts are typical.

It is rare that such an individualist attracts many followers. Yet during the period 1710–30 Vivaldi's influence on the concerto was so strong that some established composers older than him like Dall'Abaco and Albinoni felt obliged to modify their style in mid-career. In most of Italy, and in France after about 1725, the Vivaldian model was enthusiastically adopted. Only in conservative Rome and certain other parts of Europe (notably England) where the Corellian style had taken firm root was its hegemony resisted, and even then a Vivaldian spirit informs many concertos whose form is more Corellian than Vivaldian. Because the influence of the concerto permeated all forms of composition Vivaldi can legitimately be regarded as a most important precursor of G. B. Sammartini and the Bach sons in the evolution of the Classical symphony. Equally, he can be seen as a harbinger of musical Romanticism, not just on account of the pictorialism in certain programmatic concertos, but in more general terms because of the higher value he placed on expression than on perfection of detail.

WORKS

Catalogues: P. Ryom: *Verzeichnis der Werke Antonio Vivaldis: kleine Ausgabe* (Leipzig, 1974, 2/1979) [RV] 289
M. Pincherle: *Inventaire thématique* (Paris, 1948) [vol.ii of *Antonio Vivaldi et la musique instrumentale*] [P page/no.] 289
Editions: *Le opere di Antonio Vivaldi*, ed. G. F. Malipiero and others (Rome, 1947–72) [M] [italic nos. indicate vol. containing notably spurious versions or incorrect reproductions of musical texts] 289, 280
Principal MS sources *I-Tn* Foà and Giordano, *D-Dlb* and *GB-Mp*; for details see RV, P and M 281, 289

Numbers in right-hand margins denote references in the text.

SOLO SONATAS 281

(*with bc; for vn unless otherwise stated*)

Sources: Sonate, vn, hpd (Venice, 1709); as op.2 (Amsterdam, 1712–13) 275
VI sonate, vn/2 vn, bc, op.5 [numbered consecutively with op.2] (Amsterdam, 1716) [printed nos. given] 278, 295
VI sonates, vc, bc (Paris, 1740)

RV	*Key*	*P*	*M*	*Sources and remarks*	
1	C	2/6	399	op.2 no.6	
2	C	5/2	*369*	2nd, 4th movts in RV4	
3	C	6/2	366		296
4	C	—	—	2nd, 4th movts in RV2, inc.	
5	c	5/9	368		
6	c	5/5	372		
7	c	—	—	inc.	
8	c	2/7	400	op.2 no.7	
9	D	3/1	404	op.2 no.11	
10	D	5/10	364		
11	D	6/8	—	inc.; also Breitkopf catalogue, see Brook	
12	d	6/1	365		296
13	d	—	—	doubtful	
14	d	2/3	396	op.2 no.3	
15	d	5/8	367		
16	e	2/9	402	op.2 no.9	
17	e	—	—	inc.	
17a	e	—	—	complete version, different 3rd movt	
18	F	3/3	430	op.5 no.13	
19	F	6/11	491		
20	F	2/4	397	op.2 no.4	
21	f	2/10	403	op.2 no.10	
22	G	—	—		
23	G	2/8	401	op.2 no.8	
24	G	—	529	doubtful	
25	G	5/4	*371*		
26	g	5/6	373		
27	g	2/1	394	op.2 no.1	
28	g	6/4	356		
29	A	5/3	370		
30	A	3/4	431	op.5 no.14	
31	A	2/2	395	op.2 no.2	
32	a	3/2	405	op.2 no.12	
33	B♭	3/5	432	op.5 no.15	
34	B♭	5/7	374		
35	b	3/6	433	op.5 no.16	
36	b	2/5	398	op.2 no.5	
37	b	—	—	inc.	
754	C	—	—		
755	D	—	—		296
756	E♭	—	—		
757	g	—	—		
758	A	—	—	formerly RV746 (withdrawn)	
759	B♭	—	—		
760	b	—	—		
776	G	—	—	probably unauthentic pastiche	

38	d	5/1	—	vc, lost; Breitkopf catalogue, see Brook	
39	E♭	6/9	504	vc	
40	e	4/9	477	vc, VI sonates, no.5	
41	F	4/6	474	vc, VI sonates, no.2	
42	g	—	530	vc	
43	a	4/7	475	vc, VI sonates, no.3	
44	a	6/10	503	vc	
45	B♭	4/8	476	vc, VI sonates, no.4	
46	B♭	4/10	478	vc, VI sonates, no.6	
47	B♭	4/5	473	vc, VI sonates, no.1	
48	C	—	490	fl	
49	d	7/9	517	fl	
50	e	—	—	fl, doubtful	
51	g	—	—	fl	
52	F	7/10	501	rec	
53	c	6/3	375	ob	

OTHER SONATAS

Source: Il pastor fido sonates, musette, vielle, fl, ob, vn, bc, 'op.13' (Paris, 1737), doubtful — 283, 295

54	C	3/9	467	op.13 no.1	
55	C	4/3	471	op.13 no.5	
56	C	3/10	468	op.13 no.2	
57	G	4/1	469	op.13 no.3	
58	g	4/4	472	op.13 no.6	
59	A	4/2	470	op.13 no.4	
779	C	—	—	vn, ob, org (obbl), salmoè (opt.)	

TRIO SONATAS
(*with bc; for 2 vn unless otherwise stated*)

Sources: Suonate da camera a 3, 2 vn, vle/hpd, op.1 (Venice, 1705) — 193, 275, 286, 295

VI sonate, vn/2 vn, bc, op.5 [numbered consecutively with op.2] (Amsterdam, 1716) [printed nos. given] — 278, 295

60	C	—	528	doubtful	
61	C	1/3	384	op.1 no.3	
62	D	1/6	387	op.1 no.6	
63	d	1/12	393	op.1 no.12, variations on 'La Follia'	
64	d	1/8	389	op.1 no.8	
65	E♭	1/7	388	op.1 no.7	
66	E	1/4	385	op.1 no.4	
67	e	1/2	383	op.1 no.2	
68	F	7/6	57	bass opt.	295–6
69	F	1/5	386	op.1 no.5	
70	F	7/4	58	bass opt.	295–6
71	G	7/5	17	bass opt.	295–6
72	g	3/8	435	op.5 no.18	
73	g	1/1	382	op.1 no.1	
74	g	—	—		
75	A	1/9	390	op.1 no.9	
76	B♭	3/7	434	op.5 no.17	
77	B♭	7/7	24	bass opt.	295–6
78	B♭	1/10	391	op.1 no.10	
79	b	1/11	392	op.1 no.11	
80	G	—	—	2 fl	
81	g	—	—	2 ob	
82	C	7/3	63	trio; vn, lute	
83	c	7/1	20	vn, vc	
84	D	6/5	355	fl, vn	
85	g	7/2	75	trio; vn, lute	
86	a	7/8	18	rec, bn	

SONATAS FOR MORE THAN TWO INSTRUMENTS

779	C	—	—	vn, ob, org (obbl), chalumeau (opt.)	

CHAMBER CONCERTOS
(*for several insts, bc*) — 293

87	C	81	155	rec, ob, 2 vn	
88	C	82	143	fl, ob, vn, bn	
89	D	—	—	fl, 2 vn	
90	D	—	42	'Il gardellino', fl/rec/vn, ob/vn, vn, bn/vc; see RV428	293
91	D	206	149	fl, vn, bn	

RV	Key	P	M	Sources and remarks	Pages
92	D	198	39	rec, vn, bn/vc	
93	D	209	62	lute, 2 vn	
94	D	207	144	rec, ob, vn, bn	
95	D	204	154	'La pastorella', rec/vn, ob/vn, vn, bn/vc	
96	d	6/7	354	fl, vn, bn	
97	F	286	248	va d'amore, 2 hn, 2 ob, bn	
98	F	—	—	'La tempesta di mare', fl, ob, vn, bn; see RV433 and RV570	293
99	F	323	147	fl, ob, vn, bn; see RV571	
100	F	322	106	fl, vn, bn	
101	G	—	52	rec, ob, vn, bn; see RV437	296
102	G	—	—	fl, 2 vn; doubtful	
103	g	402	23	rec, ob, bn	
104	g	—	33	'La notte', fl/vn, 2 vn, bn; see RV439	
105	g	403	103	rec, ob, vn, bn	
106	g	404	41	fl, vn, bn, or 2 vn and vc	
107	g	6/6 = 360	40	fl, ob, vn, bn	
108	a	77	44	rec, 2 vn	

CONCERTOS AND SINFONIAS FOR STRINGS AND CONTINUO (*S in P column = sinfonia*) 293

Source: 6 concerti, solo vn, 2 vn, va, org, vc, op.12 (Amsterdam, 1729) 282, 283

RV	Key	P	M	Sources and remarks	Pages
109	C	67	185	conc.	
110	C	61	200	conc.	
111	C	95	—	conc.; RV717 with different 2nd movt	
111a	C	S15	—	sinfonia; RV717 with different 2nd movt	
112	C	S23	507	sinfonia	
113	C	94	509	conc.	
114	C	27	493	conc.	
115	C	63	309	conc. ripieno	
116	C	S2	506	sinfonia	

RV	Key	P	M	Sources and remarks	Pages
117	C	64	308	conc.; RV693, 1st sinfonia, with different 2nd movt	
118	c	438	32	conc.	
119	c	422	177	conc.	
120	c	427	30	conc.	*294*
121	D	175	246	conc.	
122	D	S7	*362*	sinfonia	
123	D	191	114	conc.	
124	D	157	464	conc., op.12 no.3	
125	D	S14	—	sinfonia, inc.	
126	D	197	113	conc. [3 movts]	
127	d	280	176	conc.	
128	d	294	251	conc.	
129	d	86	36	'Concerto madrigalesco'	
130	E♭	441	21	'Sonata al Santo Sepolcro'	
131	E	S19	161	sinfonia	
132	E	S13	515	sinfonia, doubtful	
133	e	113	492	conc.	
134	e	127	56	sinfonia and conc.	
135	F	S5	*363*	sinfonia	
136	F	279	59	conc.	
137	F	S17	516	sinfonia	
138	F	313	288	conc.	
139	F	—	—	conc.; see RV543	
140	F	S4	242	sinfonia and conc.	
141	F	291	241	conc.	
142	F	292	6	conc.	
143	f	443	289	conc.	
144	G	145	512	'Introdutione'; by G. Tartini (withdrawn)	
145	G	123	252	conc.	
146	G	S8	361	sinfonia/conc.	
147	G	S6	—	sinfonia	
148	G	S12	*360*	sinfonia; by D. Gallo (withdrawn)	
149	G	S3	321	sinfonia	284
150	G	114	290	conc.	

151	G	143	49	'Concerto alla rustica'	
152	g	371	226	conc. ripieno	
153	g	394	*287*	conc.	
154	g	362	310	conc.	
155	g	407	11	conc.; solo vn in 3rd and 4th movts	
156	g	392	115	conc.	
157	g	361	182	conc.	
158	A	235	8	conc. ripieno	
159	A	231	5	conc.; 2 vn, solo vcs in 3rd movt	
160	A	230	184	conc.	
161	a	60	201	conc.	
162	B♭	S11	*359*	sinfonia	
163	B♭	410	9	'Conca', conc.	
164	B♭	363	50	conc.	
165	B♭	378	172	conc.	
166	B♭	398	7	conc.	
167	B♭	400	190	conc.	
168	b	S22	518	sinfonia	
169	b	S21	22	'Sinfonia al Santo Sepolcro'	
741	C	25	—	sinfonia, ?ens, lost	
—	D	—	—	sinfonia, *I-Vč* (inc.)	

SOLO VIOLIN CONCERTOS 292
(*with str, bc*)

Sources: L'estro armonico (2 bks), op.3 (Amsterdam, 1711)	277, 278, *279*
La stravaganza (2 bks), op.4 (Amsterdam, *c*1714)	278, 286
VI concerti a 5 stromenti, 3 vn, va, bc, op.6 (Amsterdam, 1716–17)	278
Concerti a 5 stromenti, 3 vn, va, bc (2 bks), op.7 (Amsterdam, *c*1716–17)	278
Il cimento dell'armonia e dell'inventione (2 bks), op.8 (Amsterdam, 1725)	282
La cetra (2 bks), op.9 (Amsterdam, 1727)	282
6 concerti, solo vn, 2 vn, va, org, vc, op.11 (Amsterdam, 1729)	282
6 concerti, solo vn, 2 vn, va, org, vc, op.12 (Amsterdam, 1729)	282, 283

170	C	20	379	
171	C	66	194	
172	C	19	322	
172a	C	—	—	different 3rd movt, addl 2nd movt, inc.
173	C	11	465	op.12 no.4
174	C	—	—	Ringmacher catalogue, lost
175	C	93	508	2 solo vn in several movts
176	C	26	495	
177	C	21	160	
178	C	8	85	op.8 no.12; see RV449
179	C	14	—	see RV581
179a	C	—	—	different 3rd movt, inc.
180	C	7	81	'Il piacere', op.8 no.6
181	C	9	—	
181a	C	9	122	op.9 no.1, 3rd movt from RV183
182	C	68	195	
183	C	38	256	see RV181a
184	C	22	328	
185	C	4	424	op.4 no.7; 2 vn, solo vcs in several movts
186	C	88	13	
187	C	62	311	
188	C	5	443	op.7/i no.2
189	C	29	376	
190	C	59	120	
191	C	39	259	
192	C	S20	162	sinfonia; 2 solo vn in 1st movt
192a	C	—	—	different 3rd movt, inc.
193	C	—	—	Rheda catalogue, lost
194	C	40	167	
195	C	12	481	
196	c	413	427	op.4 no.10
197	c	431	173	
198	c	—	—	
198a	c	416	133	op.9 no.11, different 2nd movt
199	c	419	4	'Il sospetto'
200	c	—	—	Pirnitz catalogue, lost

RV	Key	P	M	Sources and remarks
201	c	426	230	
202	c	417	461	op.11 no.5
203	D	160	—	inc.
204	D	149	428	op.4 no.11; in printed sources 2 solo vn in 1st movt
205	D	173	331	
206	D	177	497	
207	D	156	188	op.11 no.1
208	D	—	314	= BWV594
208a	D	151	452	op.7/ii no.5, different 2nd movt
209	D	193	286	
210	D	153	84	op.8 no.11
211	D	182	261	
212	D	—	—	'Concerto fatto per la Solennità della S Lingua di S Antonio in Padova 1712'
212a	D	165	312	different versions of 1st and 3rd movts, different 2nd movt
213	D	163	347	
213a	D	—	—	different 3rd movt, inc.
214	D	152	453	op.7/ii no.6; also attrib. D. Gallo
215	D	194	305	
216	D	150	439	op.6 no.4
217	D	201	69	
218	D	196	307	
219	D	167	335	
220	D	158	482	
221	D	179	203	'per violino in tromba'
222	D	192	294	
223	D	174	494	see RV263a, 762
224	D	161	343	
224a	D	—	—	different 2nd movt
225	D	186	174	
226	D	170	302	
227	D	211	513	
228	D	162	345	
229	D	171	*117*	

296

RV	Key	P	M	Sources and remarks
230	D	147	414	op.3 no.9; = BWV972
231	D	199	31	
232	D	200	68	
233	D	195	306	
234	D	208	37	'L'inquietudine'
235	d	293	258	
236	d	259	—	op.8 no.9; see RV454
237	d	277	325	
238	d	260	131	op.9 no.8
239	d	254	441	op.6 no.6
240	d	269	324	
241	d	270	336	
242	d	258	82	op.8 no.7
243	d	310	45	'con violino senza cantin'
244	d	263	463	op.12 no.2
245	d	276	333	
246	d	272	285	
247	d	312	296	
248	d	316	74	
249	d	253	425	op.4 no.8
250	E♭	425	227	
251	E♭	428	254	
252	E♭	418	349	
253	E♭	415	80	'La tempesta di mare', op.8 no.5
254	E♭	429	38	
255	E♭	—	—	Pirnitz catalogue, lost
256	E♭	—	502	'Il ritiro'
257	E♭	439	193	
258	E♭	430	169	
259	E♭	414 = 355	437	op.6 no.2
260	E♭	421	352	
261	E♭	437	304	2 solo vn in 1st movt
262	E♭	420	340	
263	E	—	—	
263a	E	242	123	op.9 no.4; 3rd movt from RV223
264	E	245	166	

293

265	E	240	417	op.3 no.12; = BWV976	
266	E	247	180		
267	E	243	327		
268	E	244	29		
269	E	241	76	'La primavera', op.8 no.1	282, 295, 297
270	E	248	15	'Il riposo – per il Santissimo Natale'	
270a	E	—	—	different 2nd movt, inc.	
271	E	246	297	'L'amoroso'	
272	e	110	—	by J. A. Hasse (withdrawn)	
273	e	125	164		
274	e	—	—		
275	e	109	484		
275a	e	—	—	different 2nd movt; see RV430	
276	e	108	480		
277	e	106	459	'Il favorito', op.11 no.2	
278	e	144	93		
279	e	98	419	op.4 no.2	
280	e	101	440	op.6 no.5	
281	e	126	168		
282	F	325	87		
283	F	314	301		
284	F	251	426	op.4 no.9	
285	F	275	346		
285a	F	255	446	op.7/i no.5, different 1st movt	
286	F	290	70	'per la Solennità di S Lorenzo'	293
287	F	317	187		
288	F	324	66		
289	F	296	165		
290	F	—	—	Pirnitz catalogue, lost	
291	F	252	479	op.4 no.6 in the Walsh edn.	
292	F	271	357		
293	F	257	78	'L'autunno', op.8 no.3	282, 293, 297
294	F	—	—	'Il ritiro'	
294a	F	256	451	'Il ritiro', op.7/ii no.4, different 2nd movt	
295	F	315	303		
296	F	295	158		
297	f	442	79	'L'inverno', op.8 no.4	282, 297

298	G	100	429	op.4 no.12	
299	G	102	449	op.7/ii no.2; = BWV973	
300	G	103	124	op.9 no.10	
301	G	99	420	op.4 no.3	
302	G	112	358		
303	G	121	228		
304	G	—	—	Pirnitz catalogue, lost	
305	G	—	—	Ringmacher catalogue, lost	
306	G	136	186		
307	G	124	255		
308	G	107	460	op.11 no.4	
309	G	—	—	'Il mare tempestoso', Pirnitz catalogue, lost	
310	G	96	408	op.3 no.3; = BWV978	
311	G	117	202	'per violino in tromba'	
312	G	122	247		
313	G	138	156	'per violino in tromba'	
314	G	111	192		
314a	G	—	—	different 2nd movt	
315	g	336	77	'L'estate', op.8 no.2	282, 297
316	g	—	—	= BWV975, lost	
316a	g	328	423	op.4 no.6, different 3rd movt	
317	g	343	462	op.12 no.1	
318	g	330	438	op.6 no.3	
319	g	351	351		
320	g	399	—	inc.	
321	g	395	292		
322	g	348	—	inc.	
323	g	352	329		
324	g	329	436	op.6 no.1	
325	g	372	253		
326	g	332	444	op.7/i no.3	
327	g	374	257		
328	g	357	178		
329	g	354	334		
330	g	408	92		
331	g	393	295		
332	g	337	65	op.8 no.8	
333	g	379	175		

RV	Key	P	M	Sources and remarks
334	g	339	127	op.9 no.3; see RV460
335	A	219	487	'The Cuckow', RV518 with different 2nd movt
335a	A	—	—	'Il rosignuolo', different 2nd movt
336	A	216	191	op.11 no.3
337	A	—	—	Pirnitz catalogue, lost
338	A	217	485	attrib. J. Meck (withdrawn)
339	A	232	496	
340	A	228	323	
341	A	227	330	
342	A	221	489	
343	A	229	100	
344	A	223	339	
345	A	214	126	op.9 no.2
346	A	237	229	
347	A	213	422	op.4 no.5
348	A	215	129	op.9 no.6
349	A	225	293	
350	A	234	245	
351	A	—	—	Ringmacher catalogue, lost
352	A	236	16	
353	A	239	313	
354	a	6	445	op.7/i no.4
355	a	92	519	
356	a	1	411	op.3 no.6
357	a	3	421	op.4 no.4
358	a	10	128	op.9 no.5
359	B♭	340	130	op.9 no.7
360	B♭	347	—	inc.
361	B♭	345	466	op.12 no.6
362	B♭	338	83	'La caccia', op.8 no.10
363	B♭	350	348	'Il corneto da posta'
364	B♭	346	483	
364a	B♭	—	—	different 2nd movt
365	B♭	376	163	
366	B♭	358	332	'Il Carbonelli'

RV	Key	P	M	Sources and remarks
367	B♭	405	1	
368	B♭	396	291	
369	B♭	356	157	
370	B♭	349	199	
371	B♭	375	262	
372	B♭	370	284	
373	B♭	335	450	op.7/ii no.3, doubtful
374	B♭	333	447	op.7/i no.6
375	B♭	373	86	
376	B♭	377	170	
377	B♭	364	499	
378	B♭	380	—	inc.
379	B♭	344	183	op.12 no.5
380	B♭	409	64	
381	B♭	327	514	see RV528 and RV383a; = BWV980
382	B♭	412	511	
383	B♭	353	377	
383a	B♭	327	418	op.4 no.1; different 1st movt, see RV381
384	b	168	326	
385	b	178	498	
386	b	183	260	
387	b	202	179	
388	b	172	378	
389	b	184	96	
390	b	185	171	
391	b	154	125	op.9 no.12
752	D	—	—	Sonsfeld catalogue, lost
761	c	—	—	
762	E	—	—	see RV223
763	A	—	—	'L'ottavina'
764	B♭	—	—	see RV548
768	A	—	—	see RV396
769	d	—	—	see RV393
770	d	—	—	see RV395
771	c	—	—	inc.

772	D	—	—	inc.	
773	F	—	—	inc.	
742	D	—	—	frag.	
743	f	—	—	?conc. mentioned in Vivaldi's autograph thematic catalogue, lost	
744	A	—	—	frag., end of 1st and 2nd movts only	
745	B♭	397	—	3rd movt only	

OTHER SOLO CONCERTOS 292
(*with str, bc*)

Sources: Concerti a 5 stromenti, 3 vn, va, bc (2 bks), op.7 (Amsterdam, 1716–17) 278
Il cimento dell'armonia e dell'inventione (2 bks), op.8 (Amsterdam, 1725) 282
VI concerti, fl, 2 vn, va, org, vc, op.10 (Amsterdam, *c*1728) 282
6 concerti, solo vn, 2 vn, va, org, vc, op.11 (Amsterdam, 1729) 282

392	D	166	337	va d'amore	
393	d	289	198	va d'amore; see RV769	
394	d	288	196	va d'amore	
395	d	287	—	va d'amore; see RV770	
396	A	233	189	va d'amore; see RV768	
397	a	37	341	va d'amore	
398	C	31	218	vc	
399	C	33	211	vc	
400	C	30	204	vc	
401	c	434	19	vc	
402	c	—	527	vc	
403	D	181	235	vc	
404	D	176	500	vc	
405	d	—	524	vc	
406	d	282	212	vc, see RV481	
407	d	—	523	vc	
408	E♭	424	206	vc	
409	e	119	137	vc	
410	F	285	243	vc	
411	F	284	233	vc	
412	F	283	221	vc	
413	G	120	231	vc	
414	G	118	317	vc, see RV438	
415	G	—	522	vc	
416	g	—	526	vc	
417	g	369	234	vc	
418	a	35	244	vc	
419	a	32	220	vc	
420	a	—	521	vc	
421	a	34	232	vc	
422	a	24	205	vc	
423	B♭	—	525	vc	
424	b	180	219	vc	
425	C	134	98	mand	
426	D	—	—	fl	
427	D	203	102	fl	
428	D	155	456	fl, 'Il gardellino', op.10 no.3; see RV90	293
429	D	205	153	fl	
430	e	—	—	fl, see RV275a	
431	e	139	—	fl, inc.	
432	e	142	—	fl, inc.	
433	F	261	454	fl, 'La tempesta di mare', op.10 no.1; see RV98 and RV570	293
434	F	262	—	fl, op.10 no.5; see RV442	
435	G	104	457	fl, op.10 no.4	
436	G	140	151	fl	
437	G	105	458	fl, op.10 no.6; see RV101	296
438	G	118	138	fl, see RV414	
		141	—	fl, ?inc., different version of 1st movt	
439	g	342	455	fl, 'La notte', op.10 no.2; see RV104	
440	a	80	148	fl	
441	c	440	159	rec	
442	F	—	46	rec, see RV434	
443	C	79	105	flautino	

RV	Key	P	M	Sources and remarks
444	C	78	110	flautino
445	a	83	152	flautino
446	C	—	—	ob
447	C	41	216	ob, see RV448
448	C	43	217	ob, see RV470 and RV447
449	C	8	—	ob, op.8 no.12; see RV178
450	C	—	283	ob, see RV471
451	C	44	222	ob
452	C	91	520	ob
453	D	187	279	ob
454	d	259	2	ob, op.8 no.9; see RV236
455	F	306	14	ob
456	F	264	488	ob
457	F	—	315	ob, see RV485
458	F	—	—	ob
459	g	—	—	ob, inc.
460	g	—	—	ob, op.11 no.6; see RV334
461	a	42	215	ob
462	a	—	—	ob
463	a	—	316	ob, see RV500
464	B♭	334	448	ob, op.7/ii no.1, doubtful
465	B♭	331	442	ob, op.7/i no.1, doubtful
466	C	51	274	bn
467	C	48	239	bn
468	C	55	—	bn, inc.
469	C	49	237	bn
470	C	43	281	bn, see RV448
471	C	50	282	bn, see RV450
472	C	45	238	bn
473	C	90	118	bn
474	C	69	47	bn
475	C	56	267	bn
476	C	57	277	bn
477	C	46	224	bn
478	C	71	34	bn
479	C	52	272	bn
480	c	432	225	bn
481	d	282	67	bn, see RV406
482	d	303	—	bn, inc.
483	E♭	433	273	bn
484	e	137	71	bn
485	F	318	109	bn, see RV457
486	F	304	268	bn
487	F	298	236	bn
488	F	299	240	bn
489	F	305	266	bn
490	F	307	278	bn
491	F	300	271	bn
492	G	128	275	bn
493	G	131	276	bn
494	G	130	300	bn
495	g	384	269	bn
—	G, D	—	—	2 fl concs., Eisenstadt catalogue, lost
—	e, B♭	—	—	2 vc concs., *I-Vc* (inc.)
496	g	381	214	bn
497	a	72	72	bn
498	a	70	28	bn
499	a	47	223	bn
500	a	89	119	bn, see RV463
501	B♭	401	12	bn, 'La notte'
502	B♭	382	270	bn
503	B♭	387	298	bn
504	B♭	386	299	bn

DOUBLE CONCERTOS 292
(*with str, bc*)

Sources: L'estro armonico (2 bks), op.3 (Amsterdam, 1711) 277, 278, *279*
La cetra (2 bks), op.9 (Amsterdam, 1727) 282

RV	Key	P	M	Sources and remarks
505	C	65	181	2 vn
506	C	18	342	2 vn
507	C	23	112	2 vn

508	C	17	116	2 vn	
509	c	436	48	2 vn	
510	c	435	60	2 vn	
511	D	190	89	2 vn	
512	D	189	108	2 vn	
513	D	159	486	2 vn	
514	d	281	209	2 vn	
515	E♭	423	210	2 vn	
516	G	132	27	2 vn	
517	g	366	207	2 vn	
518	A	—	—	(withdrawn)	
519	A	212	410	2 vn, op.3 no.5	
520	A	220	—	2 vn, inc.	
521	A	224	344	2 vn	
522	a	2	413	2 vn, op.3 no.8; = BWV593	
523	a	28	140	2 vn	
524	B♭	390	107	2 vn	
525	B♭	389	145	2 vn	
526	B♭	15	—	2 vn, inc.	
527	B♭	365	208	2 vn	
528	B♭	—	—	2 vn, see RV381	
529	B♭	391	111	2 vn	
530	B♭	341	132	2 vn, op.9 no.9	
764	B♭	—	—	2 vn; see RV548	
765	F	—	—	2 vn; see RV767	
531	g	411	61	2 vc	
532	G	133	104	2 mand	
533	C	76	101	2 fl	
534	C	85	139	2 ob	
535	d	302	264	2 ob	
536	a	53	263	2 ob	
537	C	75	97	2 tpt	
538	F	320	91	2 hn, solo vc in 2nd movt	
539	F	321	121	2 hn	
540	d	266	320	va d'amore, lute	284, 292
541	d	311	95	vn, org	
542	F	274	353	vn, org	
543	F	301	265	vn, ob, see RV139	
544	F	308	135	'Il Proteo o sia Il mondo al rovescio', vn, vc; see RV572	
545	G	129	280	ob, bn	
546	A	238	146	vn, vc; later version vn, vc all'inglese	
547	B♭	388	35	vn, vc	
548	B♭	406	73	vn, ob; see RV764	
766	c	—	—	vn, org, *Mp*, see RV510	
767	F	—	—	vn, org, *Mp*, see RV765	
774	C	—	—	vn, org, inc.	
775	F	—	—	vn, org, inc.	
—	G	—	—	vn, vc, *I-Vc* (inc.)	

MULTIPLE CONCERTOS (*with str, bc*) 292

Source: L'estro armonico (2 bks), op.3 (Amsterdam, 1711) 277, 278, *279*, 287

549	D	146	406	4 vn (vc in 1st movt), op.3 no.1	
550	e	97	409	4 vn, op.3 no.4	
551	F	278	88	3 vn	
552	A	222	319	'Concerto con violino principale con altro violino per eco in lontano', vn and 3 solo vn	284
553	B♭	367	134	4 vn	
554	C	36	250	vn, org/vn ad lib, ob	
554a	C	36	—	vn, org/vn ad lib, vc	
555	C	87	142	3 vn, ob, 2 rec, 2 va all'inglese, chalumeau, 2 vc, 2 hpd [2 tpt, 2 vle, in 3rd movt]	
556	C	84	54	'per la Solennità di S Lorenzo'; 2 ob, 2 cl, 2 rec, 2 vn, bn [lute in 2nd movt]	293
557	C	54	90	2 vn, 2 ob, bn [2 rec, bn in 2nd movt]	
558	C	16	318	2 vn 'in tromba marina', 2 rec, 2 mand, 2 chalumeaux, 2 theorbos, vc	284
559	C	74	10	2 cl, 2 ob	
560	C	73	3	2 cl, 2 ob	
561	C	58	53	vn, 2 vc	
562	D	169	380	vn, 2 ob, 2 hn	
562a	D	444	—	vn, 2 ob, 2 hn, timp; different 2nd movt	284

RV	Key	P	M	Sources and remarks	
563	D	210	510	vn, 2 ob	
564	D	188	99	2 vn, 2 vc	
564a	D	—	—	2 vn, 2 ob, bn [doubtful version]	
565	d	250	416	2 vn, vc, op.3 no.11; = BWV596	287
566	d	297	213	2 vn, 2 rec, 2 ob, bn	
567	F	249	412	4 vn, vc, op.3 no.7	
568	F	267	338	vn, 2 ob, 2 hn, bn	
569	F	273	43	vn, 2 ob, 2 hn, bn [vc in 3rd movt]	
570	F	—	150	'La tempesta di mare', fl, ob, bn [vn solo in 1st movt], see RV98 and RV433	293
571	F	268	350	vn, 2 ob, 2 hn, vc, bn, see RV99	
572	F	—	—	'Il Proteo o sia Il mondo al rovescio', 2 fl, 2 ob, vn, vc, hpd; see RV544	
573	F	265	—	2 ob, 2 hn, 2 bn, lost	
574	F	319	94	vn, 2 trombon da caccia, 2 ob, bn	
575	G	135	26	2 vn, 2 vc	
576	g	359	249	vn, ob, 2 rec, 2 ob, bn	
577	g	383	25	'per l'orchestra di Dresda', vn, 2 ob, 2 rec, bn	
578	g	326	407	2 vn, vc, op.3 no.2	
579	B♭	385		'Concerto funebre'; vn, ob, chalumeau, 3 va all'inglese	
580	b	148	415	4 vn, vc, op.3 no.10; = BWV1065	295
751	D	—	—	2 fl, 2 vn, 2 bn; Sonsfeld catalogue, lost	
				CONCERTOS WITH DOUBLE ORCHESTRA (*solo inst(s) with 2 str orch, bc*)	293
581	C	—	55	solo vn, Assumption BVM, see RV179	
582	D	164	141	solo vn, Assumption BVM	296
583	B♭	368	136		
584	F	309	—	vn, org; solo parts inc.	
585	A	226	381	2 vn, 2 rec [vc in 3rd movt], 2 vn, 2 rec, org [vc in 3rd movt]	
				OTHER INSTRUMENTAL	
750	—	—	—	miscellaneous inst works listed in 18th-century catalogues, of which insufficient information is given	

MASSES, MASS SECTIONS

RV	Key		
586	C	Sacrum (mass: Ky, Gl, Cr, San, Ag), doubtful	
587	g	Kyrie, 2 choirs	
588	D	Gloria with introduzione, see RV639; last movt arr. from G. M. Ruggieri's Gloria, 1708, see RV Anh.23	
589	D	Gloria, last movt arr. from Ruggieri's Gloria, 1708, see RV Anh.23	297
590	D	Gloria, Prague catalogue, lost	
591	e	Credo	296
592	G	Credo, doubtful	
		PSALMS ETC	
593	G	Domine ad adiuvandum me (response), 2 choirs	
594	D	Dixit Dominus (Ps cx), 2 choirs	
595	D	Dixit Dominus (Ps cx)	
596	C	Confitebor tibi Domine (Ps cxi)	
597	C	Beatus vir (Ps cxii), 2 choirs	
598	B♭	Beatus vir (Ps cxii)	296
599	B♭	Beatus vir (Ps cxii), Prague catalogue, lost	
600	c	Laudate pueri Dominum (Ps cxiii)	
601	G	Laudate pueri Dominum (Ps cxiii)	
602	A	Laudate pueri Dominum (Ps cxiii), 2 choirs	
602a	A	[different 7th movt and variation in 9th movt]	
603	A	[modified version of RV602]	
604	C	In exitu Israel (Ps cxiv)	
605	C	Credidi propter quod (Ps cxvi), see RV Anh.35	

RV	Key	Title	Page
606	d	Laudate Dominum (Ps cxvii)	
607	F	Laetatus sum (Ps cxxii)	
608	g	Nisi Dominus (Ps cxxvii)	
609	e	Lauda Jerusalem (Ps cxlvii), 2 choirs	
610	g	Magnificat	297
610a	g	[double chorus version of RV610, alterations to 7th movt and ensemble]	
611	g	Magnificat, 4 movts from RV610 replaced by 5 new movts	297
	B♭	Confitebor tibi Domine (Ps cxi), *I-Vc* (inc.)	

HYMNS, ANTIPHONS ETC

RV	Key	Title	Page
612	C	Deus tuorum militum, hymn	
613	B♭	Gaude mater ecclesia, hymn	
614	F	Laudate Dominum omnes gentes, off, doubtful	
615	?C	Regina coeli, ant, inc.	
616	c	Salve regina, ant, 2 choirs	
617	F	Salve regina, ant	
618	g	Salve regina, ant	
619	—	Salve [regina], ant, lost	
620	C	Sanctorum meritis, hymn	
621	f	Stabat mater, hymn	
622	—	Te Deum, anthem, cited in *Mercure de France* (1727), lost	

MOTETS AND INTRODUCTIONS 296

RV	Key	Title	Page
623	A	Canta in prato	
624	G	Carae rosae respirate	
625	F	Clarae stellae	
626	c	In furore giustissimae irae	
627	G	In turbato mare	
628	G	Invicti bellate	
629	g	Longe mala umbrae terrores	
630	E	Nulla in mundo pax	
631	E♭	O qui coeli terraeque	
632	F	Sum in medio tempestatum	
633	F	Vestro Principi divino	
634	A	Vos aurae per montes	
635	A	Ascende laeta (Dixit)	
636	G	Canta in prato (Dixit)	
637	B♭	Cur sagittas (Gloria)	
638	c	Filiae mestae (Miserere)	
639	D	Jubilate o amoeni chori (Gloria RV588), A	
639a	D	[version for S]	
640	g	Longe mala umbrae terrores (Gloria)	
641	F	Non in pratis (Miserere)	
642	D	Ostro picta (Gloria)	
748	?G	Aria per la communione, Prague catalogue, lost	

ORATORIOS

RV	Title	Page
—	La vittoria navale, Vicenza, 1713, lost	278
644	Moyses Deus Pharaonis, Venice, 1714, lost	277
645	Juditha triumphans devicta Holofernes barbarie (J. Cassetti), Venice, 1716	277, 297
646	L'adorazione delli tre re magi, Milan, 1722, lost	

OTHER SACRED VOCAL
(*also known as opera arias*)

RV	Title	Page
646	Ad corda reclina, F ['Concertus italicus']	
647	Eja voces plausum date, E♭ ['Aria de Sanctis']	
648	Ihr Himmel nun, E ['Concertus italicus']	

SOLO CANTATAS 297
(*with bc*)

RV	Title	Page
649	All'ombra d'un bel faggio, S	
650	All'or che lo sguardo, S	
651	Amor hai vinto, S, same text as for RV683	
652	Aure voi più non siete, S	
653	Il povero mio core, S	
654	Elvira, Elvira anima mia, S	
655	Era la notte, S	
656	Fonti di pianto piangete, S	
657	Geme l'onda che parte, S	
658	Del natio suo rigore, S	
659	Indarno cerca la tortorella, S	
660	La farfalletta s'aggira, S	
661	Nel partir da te mio caro, S	297

RV		
662	Par che tardo, S	
663	Scherza di fronda, S	
664	Seben vivono senz'alma, S	
665	Sì levi dal pensier, S	
666	Sì sì luci adorate, S	
667	Sorge vermiglia in ciel, S	
668	T'intendo sì mio cor, S	
669	Tra l'erbe, i zeffiri, S	
670	Alla caccia, alla caccia, A	
671	Care selve amici prati, A	
672	Filli di gioia, A	
673	Ingrata Lidia hai vinto, A	
674	Perfidissimo cor!, A	
675	Piango, gemo, sospiro, A	
676	Pianti, sospiri, A	
677	Qual per ignoto, A	
747	Candida Lylia, cantata/?motet, Prague catalogue, lost	
753	Prendea con man di latte, S	

SOLO CANTATAS
(*with inst(s), bc*)

RV		
678	All'ombra di sospetto, S, fl	
679	Che giova il sospirar, S, str	
680	Lungi dal vago, S, vn	
681	Perchè son molli, S, 2 solo vn, 2 vn	
682	Vengo à voi luci adorate, S, str	
683	Amor hai vinto, A, str; same text as for RV651	
684	Cessate omai cessate, A, str	
684a	[variant version, inc.]	
685	O mie porpore più belle, A, str	
686	Qual in pioggia dorata, A, 2 hn, str	

OPERAS — 280, 288, 297–8

RV		
729	Ottone in Villa (D. Lalli), Vicenza, delle Grazie, May 1713	278, 297
727	Orlando finto pazzo (G. B. Braccioli), Venice, S Angelo, aut. 1714	280
724	Nerone fatto Cesare (M. Noris), Venice, S Angelo, carn. 1715 [only 12 arias by Vivaldi], lost	280
706	La costanza trionfante degl'amori e de gl'odii (A. Marchi), Venice, S Moisè, carn. 1716, lost; as Artabano, Re de' Parti, Venice, S Moisè, carn. 1718, lost; as L'Artabano, Mantua, carn. 1725; parts of music used in Die über Hass und Liebe siegende Beständigkeit, Hamburg, 1719, RV Anh.57; parts of music used in La Tirannia gastigata, Prague, Sporck, 1726, RV Anh.55; arr. A. Galeozzi as L'odio vinto dalla costanza (Marchi and B. Vitturi), Venice, S Angelo, carn, 1731, lost RV Anh.51; as Doriclea, Prague, Sporck, carn. 1732, lost	
700	Arsilda Regina di Ponto (Lalli), Venice, S. Angelo, aut. 1716; sinfonia also in RV736	
719	L'incoronazione di Dario (A. Morselli), Venice, S Angelo, carn. 1717	
737	Tieteberga (A. M. Lucchini), Venice, S Moisè, aut. 1717, lost; rev. with 9 new arias, Venice, aut. 1717	
732	Scanderbeg (A. Salvi), Florence, della Pergola, 22 June 1718, lost	
699	Armida al campo d'Egitto (G. Palazzi), Venice, S Moisè, carn. 1718, Acts 1 and 3 only extant; sinfonia also in RV710; as Gl'inganni per vendetta, Vicenza, delle Grazie, 1720, lost	280, 298
736	Teuzzone (Zeno), Mantua, Arciducale, carn. 1719; sinfonia also in RV700	
738	Tito Manlio (Noris), Mantua, Arciducale, carn. 1719	281, 284
704	La Candace o siano Li veri amici (F. Silvani and Lalli), Mantua, Arciducale, carn. 1720, lost	
739	La verità in cimento (Palazzi and Lalli), Venice, S Angelo, aut. 1720	
778	Tito Manlio (pasticcio), Rome, della Pace, 1720, collab. G. Boni and C. Giorgio	281
715	Filippo Re di Macedonia (Lalli), Venice, S Angelo, carn. 1721, collab. G. Boneveni, lost	
734	La Silvia (dramma pastorale, E. Bissaro), Milan, Ducale, 26 Aug 1721, lost	
710	Ercole su 'l Termodonte (G. F. Bussani), Rome, Capranica, 23 Jan 1723, lost; sinfonia also in RV699	281

717 Giustino (N. Berengani), Rome, Capranica, carn. 1724; sinfonia also in RV111 and 111a 298

740 La virtù trionfante dell'amore e dell'odio overo Il Tigrane (Silvani), Rome, Capranica, carn. 1724, collab. B. Micheli and N. Romaldi [also called Mitridate]

721 L'inganno trionfante in amore (Noris and G. M. Ruggieri), Venice, S Angelo, aut. 1725, lost

707 Cunegonda (A. Piovene), Venice, S Angelo, carn. 1726, lost

712 La Fede tradita e vendicata (Silvani), Venice, S Angelo, carn. 1726, lost; rev. as Ernelinda (pasticcio, Silvani), Venice, S Cassiano, *c*1750, other music by F. Gasparini and B. Galuppi

709 Dorilla in Tempe (Lucchini), Venice, S Angelo, aut. 1726; sinfonia also in RV711

722 Ipermestra (Salvi), Florence, della Pergola, carn. 1727, lost

735 Siroe, Re di Persia (Metastasio), Reggio, Pubblico, May 1727, lost 284

711 Farnace (Lucchini), Venice, S Angelo, aut. 1727; sinfonia also in RV709 285

728 Orlando [furioso] (Braccioli), Venice, S Angelo, aut. 1727

730 Rosilena ed Oronta (Palazzi), Venice, S Angelo, 17 Jan 1728, lost

702 L'Atenaide o sia Gli affetti generosi (Zeno), Florence, della Pergola, 29 Dec 1728

697 Argippo (Lalli), Prague, Sporck, aut. 1730, lost 283

696 Alvilda, Regina de' Goti, Prague, Sporck, spr. 1731, lost; recits and arie bernesche not by Vivaldi 283

714 La fida ninfa (S. Maffei), Verona, Filarmonico, 6 Jan 1732, ed. R. Monterosso (Cremona, 1965); rev. as Il giorno felice, RV777

733 Semiramide (Zeno), Mantua, Arciducale, carn. 1732, lost

723 Motezuma (G. Giusti), Venice, S Angelo, aut. 1733, lost

725 L'Olimpiade (Metastasio), Venice, S Angelo, carn. 1734 298

695 L'Adelaide (?Salvi), Verona, Filarmonico, carn. 1735 [version of L'Atenaide], lost 283

718 Griselda (Zeno, adapted by C. Goldoni), Venice, S Samuele, May 1735 282

698 Aristide ('drama eroi-comico', Goldoni), Venice, S Samuele, May 1735 [music by 'Lotavio Vandini', anagram of Antonio Vivaldi], lost 275

703 Bajazet (Piovene), Verona, Filarmonico, carn. 1735; music compiled by Vivaldi from several composers [also called Tamerlano]

716 Ginevra, Principessa di Scozia (Salvi), Florence, della Pergola, Jan 1736, lost

Anh.67 Didone, London, April 1737, with arias by Vivaldi, lost

705 Catone in Utica (Metastasio), Verona, Filarmonica, May 1737, Acts 2 and 3 only extant

777 Il giorno felice, Vienna, 1737, lost; rev. of RV714

731 Rosmira [fedele] (S. Stampiglia), Venice, S Angelo, carn. 1738, music compiled by Vivaldi from several composers 297

726 L'oracolo in Messenia (Zeno), Venice, S Angelo, carn. 1738, lost

713 Feraspe (Silvani), Venice, S Angelo, aut. 1739, lost 284

749 Miscellaneous arias not belonging to known operas

SERENATAS 297

688 Le gare del dovere, 5vv, Rovigo, 1708, music lost 278

687 Dall'eccelsa mia Reggia (Gloria e Himeneo), 1725

692 Questa, Eurilla gentil, 4vv, Mantua, 31 July 1726, music lost

694 L'unione della Pace e di Marte (A. Grossatesta), 3vv, Venice, 1727, music lost

693 La Sena festeggiante (Lalli), 3vv, ?Venice, 1726; 1st sinfonia, RV117 with different 2nd movt

691 Il Mopso (egloga pescatoria, E. Nonnanuci [G. Cendoni]), Venice, Pietà, *c*1738, music and text lost

689 Le gare della Giustizia e della Pace (G. B. Catena), Venice, music and text lost

690 Mio cor povero cor, 3vv

WORKS INCORRECTLY ATTRIB. VIVALDI

Conc., C, RV Anh.2, P446, by P. Locatelli or A. W. Solnitz; conc., d, RV Anh.3, P445, anon.; conc., A, RV Anh.5, P447, by G. Sammartini; vn conc., D, RV Anh.9, Fanna I, no.237, by F. Veracini; conc., RV Anh.10 = BMV979, by G. Torelli; conc., e, RV Anh.11, P116, by Johann Ernst of Saxe-Weimar; conc., G, RV Anh.12, P115, probably by Johann Ernst of Saxe-Weimar; conc., A, RV Anh.14, P218, by Veracini; conc., a, RV Anh.15, P13, anon.; vn conc., B♭, RV Anh.16 = BWV974, by A. Marcello; conc., c, RV Anh.17, Fanna XII, no.53, by G. P. Telemann; conc., C, RV Anh.62, transcr. for vn, pf, by F. Kreisler; conc., e, RV Anh.64, formerly RV272 (withdrawn), by J. Hasse; conc., e, solo vn, 2 vn, bc, RV Anh.64a, attrib. A. M. Scaccia, different 2nd movt from RV Anh.64, *GB-Mp*; conc., RV Anh.65, formerly RV338 (withdrawn), by J. Meck; conc., C, ob, fl, bn, hpd, RV Anh.66, by Vivaldi or Handel; sinfonia, G, RV Anh.4, PS1, by Hasse; sinfonia, RV Anh.68, formerly RV 148 (withdrawn), by D. Gallo, *GB-Mp*; sinfonia, RV Anh.70, formerly RV 144 (withdrawn), by G. Tartini

Gloria, D, for 2 choirs, 9 Sept 1708, RV Anh.23, by G. M. Ruggieri, last movt used in RV588 and 589; Lauda Jerusalem, C, RV Anh.35, anon., music used in RV605; Te Deum, g, RV Anh.38, anon., inc.; Alessandro nell'Indie, RV Anh.40, not by Vivaldi; Demetrio, RV Anh.44, not by Vivaldi; L'odio vinto dalla costanza, RV Anh.51, see RV706; La Tirannia gastigata, RV Anh.55, see RV706; Die über Hass und Liebe siegende Beständigkeit oder Tigrane, RV Anh.57, see RV706; Il vinto trionfante del vincitore, Venice, 1717, RV Anh.58, doubtful contribution by Vivaldi; 7 cantatas, RV Anh.61, ?formerly *F-Pn*, lost

BIBLIOGRAPHY

CATALOGUES AND DOCUMENTATION

A. Fuchs: *Thematisches Verzeichniss über die Compositionen von Antonio Vivaldi* (MS, *D-Bds*, 1839); facs. with commentary ed. P. Ryom in *Vivaldi Informations*, i (1971–2), 43

W. Altmann: 'Thematischer Katalog der gedruckten Werke Antonio Vivaldis', *AMw*, iv (1922), 262

A. Gentili: 'La raccolta di rarità musicali "Mauro Foà" alla Biblioteca nazionale di Torino', *Accademie e biblioteche d'Italia* (1927), 36

——: 'La raccolta di antiche musiche "Renzo Giordano" alla Biblioteca nazionale di Torino', *Accademie e biblioteche d'Italia* (1930), 117

M. Rinaldi: *Catalogo numerico tematico delle composizioni di Antonio Vivaldi* (Rome, 1945)

M. Pincherle: *Inventaire thématique* (Paris, 1948) [vol.ii of *Antonio Vivaldi et la musique instrumentale*]

W. Kolneder: 'Zur Frage der Vivaldi-Kataloge', *AMw*, xi (1954), 323

H. R. Jung: 'Die Dresdener Vivaldi-Manuskripte', *AMw*, xii (1955), 314

B. S. Brook, ed.: *The Breitkopf Thematic Catalogue, 1762–1787* (New York, 1966)

K. Heller: 'Die Bedeutung J. G. Pisendels für die deutsche Vivaldi-Rezeption', *GfMKB, Leipzig 1966*

P. Damilano: 'Inventario delle composizioni musicali manoscritte di Antonio Vivaldi esistenti presso la Biblioteca nazionale di Torino', *RIM*, iii (1968), 109–79

A. Fanna: *A. Vivaldi: Catalogo numerico-tematico delle opere strumentali* (Milan, 1968) [catalogue of the Ricordi edn.]

P. Ryom: 'Le recensement des cantates d'Antonio Vivaldi', *DAM*, vi (1968–72), 81

R. Eller: 'Über Charakter und Geschichte der Dresdener Vivaldi-Manuskripte', *Vivaldiana* (1969), 57

G. Gentili Verona: 'Le collezioni Foà et Giordano della Biblioteca nazionale di Torino', *Vivaldiana* (1969), 30

P. Ryom: 'Etude critique des catalogues et nouvelles découvertes', *Vivaldiana* (1969), 69–113

K. Heller: *Die deutsche Überlieferung der Instrumentalwerke Vivaldis* (Leipzig, 1971)

N. Ohmura: *A Reference Concordance Table of Vivaldi's Instrumental Works* (Tokyo, 1972)

P. Ryom: 'Le premier catalogue thématique des oeuvres d'Antonio Vivaldi', *Festskrift Jens Peter Larsen* (Copenhagen, 1972), 127

——: 'Un nouveau catalogue des oeuvres d'Antonio Vivaldi', *IMSCR*, xi *Copenhagen 1972*, 633

——: *Antonio Vivaldi: table de concordances des oeuvres* (Copenhagen, 1973)

——: 'Inventaire de la documentation manuscrite des oeuvres de Vivaldi: I. Biblioteca nazionale di Torino (première partie: le fonds Foà)', *Vivaldi Informations*, ii (1973), 61–112

——: *Verzeichnis der Werke Antonio Vivaldis: kleine Ausgabe* (Leipzig, 1974, rev. 2/1979)

M. Fechner: 'Neue Vivaldi-Funde in der Sächsischen Landesbibliothek Dresden', *Vivaldi-Studien: Referate des 3. Dresdner Vivaldi-Kolloquiums: mit einem Katalog der Dresdner Vivaldi-Handschriften und -Frühdrucke: Dresden 1978*, 42

E. Garbero: 'Drammaturgia vivaldiana: regesto e concordanze dei libretti', *Antonio Vivaldi da Venezia all'Europa*, ed. F. Degrada and M. T. Muraro (Milan, 1978), 111

O. Landmann: 'Katalog der Dresdener Vivaldi-Handschriften und -Frühdrucke', *Vivaldi-Studien: Referate des 3. Dresdner Vivaldi-Kolloquiums: mit einem Katalog der Dresdner Vivaldi-Handschriften und -Frühdrucke: Dresden 1978*, 101

A. Girard and G. Rostirolla: 'Catalogo delle composizioni di Antonio Vivaldi', *RMI*, xiii (1979), 210–89

P. Ryom: 'Le manuscrit perdu du fonds de Dresde', *Informazioni e studi vivaldiani: Bollettino dell'Istituto Italiano Antonio Vivaldi*, i (1980), 18

A. L. Bellina, B. Brizi and M. G. Pensa: *I libretti vivaldiani: recensioni e collazione dei testimoni a stampa* (Florence, 1982)

M. Talbot: 'A Vivaldi Discovery at the Conservatorio "Benedetto Marcello" ', *Informazioni e studi vivaldiani: Bollettino dell'Istituto Italiano Antonio Vivaldi*, iii (1982), 3

M. Grattoni: 'Una scoperta vivaldiana a Cividale del Friuli', *Informazioni e studi vivaldiani: Bollettino dell'Istituto Italiano Antonio Vivaldi*, iv (1983), 3

GENERAL

HawkinsH

E. Holdsworth: letters of 13 Feb, 16 July 1733, 4 May 1742 to Charles Jennens (MS, *GB-BENcoke*)

P. Gradenigo: *Commemoriali* (MS, *I-Vmc*)

J. Mattheson: *Der vollkommene Capellmeister* (Hamburg, 1739/*R*1954)

C. Avison: *An Essay on Musical Expression* (London, 1752)

[W. Hayes]: *Remarks on Mr. Avison's Essay on Musical Expression* (London, 1753)

J. J. Quantz: 'Lebenslauf', in F. W. Marpurg: *Historisch-kritische Beyträge zur Aufnahme der Musik*, i (Berlin, 1754/*R*1970), 197–250

C. Goldoni: Introduction to *Commedie*, xiii (Venice, 1761)
——: *Mémoires de M. Goldoni pour servir à l'histoire de sa vie, et à celle de son théâtre*, i (Paris, 1787), 286
C. de Brosses: *Lettres historiques et critiques sur l'Italie*, i (Paris, 1799), 297
F. Caffi: *Storia della musica teatrale in Venezia* (MS, *I-Vnm*, *c*1850)
F. Stefani: *Sei lettere di Antonio Vivaldi veneziano* (Venice, 1871)
A. Salvatori: 'Antonio Vivaldi (il prete rosso)', *Rivista della città di Venezia*, vi (1928), 325
M. Pincherle: 'Antonio Vivaldi, essai biographique', *RdM*, xi (1930), nos.33–6, pp.161, 265
——: 'Vivaldi and the *Ospitali* of Venice', *MQ*, xxiv (1938), 300
R. Gallo: 'Antonio Vivaldi, il prete rosso: la famiglia, la morte', *Ateneo Veneto* (1938), Dec
——: 'L'atto di morte di Antonio Vivaldi', *La scuola veneziana (secoli XVI–XVIII): note e documenti*, Chigiana, iii (1941), 58
M. Abbado: *Antonio Vivaldi* (Turin, 1942)
M. Rinaldi: *Antonio Vivaldi* (Milan, 1943)
M. Pincherle: *Antonio Vivaldi et la musique instrumentale* (Paris, 1948/*R*1968)
E. Preussner: *Die musikalischen Reisen des Herrn von Uffenbach* (Kassel and Basle, 1949)
F. Zobeley: *Rudolf Franz Erwein Graf von Schönborn (1677–1734) und seine Musikpflege* (Würzburg, 1949)
M. Pincherle: *Vivaldi* (Paris, 1955; Eng. trans., 1958)
G. F. Malipiero: *Antonio Vivaldi, il prete rosso* (Milan, 1958)
D. Arnold: 'Instruments and Instrumental Teaching in the Early Italian Conservatoires', *GSJ*, xviii (1965), 72
R. Giazotto: *Vivaldi* (Milan, 1965)
W. Kolneder: *Antonio Vivaldi: Leben und Werk* (Wiesbaden, 1965; Eng. trans., 1970)
D. Arnold: 'Orchestras in Eighteenth-century Venice', *GSJ*, xix (1966), 3
R. de Candé: *Vivaldi* (Paris, 1967)
A. Cavicchi: 'Inediti nell'epistolario Vivaldi–Bentivoglio', *NRMI*, i (1967), 1–34
'Fac-similé et traductions de cinq lettres de Vivaldi à Bentivoglio', *Vivaldiana* (1969), 117
H. Pabisch: 'Neue Dokumente zu Vivaldis Sterbetag', *ÖMz*, xxvii (1972), 82
R. Giazotto: *Antonio Vivaldi* (Turin, 1973) [with catalogue of works by A. Girard and discography by L. Bellingardi]
A. Hicks: 'An Auction of Handeliana', *MT*, cxiv (1973), 892

F. Fano: 'Una traccia prossima alla prima origine della raccolta di musiche vivaldiane conservata alla Biblioteca Nazionale di Torino', *Medioevo e umanesimo*, xxiv (1976), 83
T. Antonicek: 'Vivaldi in Österreich', *ÖMz*, xxxiii (1978), 128
D. Arnold: 'Vivaldi's Motets for Solo Voice', *Vivaldi Veneziano Europeo: Venezia 1978*, 37
B. Brizi: 'Domenico Lalli librettista di Vivaldi?', *Vivaldi Veneziano Europeo: Venezia 1978*, 183
F. Degrada: 'Vivaldi e Metastasio: note in margine a una lettura dell' *Olimpiade*', *Vivaldi Veneziano Europeo: Venezia 1978*, 155
C. Gallico: 'Vivaldi dagli archivi di Mantova', *Vivaldi Veneziano Europeo: Venezia 1978*, 77
K. Heller: 'Vivaldis Ripienkonzerte: Bemerkungen zu einigen ausgewählten Problemen', *Vivaldi-Studien: Referate des 3. Dresdner Vivaldi-Kolloquiums: mit einem Katalog der Dresdner Vivaldi-Handschriften und -Frühdrucke: Dresden 1978*, 1
H. Hucke: 'Vivaldis Stabat Mater', *Vivaldi Veneziano Europeo: Venezia 1978*, 49
W. Kolneder: 'Musikalische Symbolik bei Vivaldi', *Vivaldi Veneziano Europeo: Venezia 1978*, 13
L. Moretti: 'Dopo l'insuccesso di Ferrara: diverbio tra Vivaldi e Antonio Mauro', *Vivaldi Veneziano Europeo: Venezia 1978*, 89
——: 'Le inconvenienze teatrali: documenti inediti su Antonio Vivaldi impresario', *Antonio Vivaldi da Venezia all'Europa*, ed. F. Degrada and M. T. Muraro (Milan, 1978), 26
M. Rinaldi: 'Vita, morte e risurrezione di Antonio Vivaldi', *Studi musicali*, vii (1978), 189
R. Strohm: 'Bemerkungen zu Vivaldi und der Oper seiner Zeit', *Vivaldi-Studien: Referate des 3. Dresdner Vivaldi-Kolloquiums: mit einem Katalog der Dresdner Vivaldi-Handschriften und -Frühdrucke: Dresden 1978*, 81
M. Talbot: 'Charles Jennens and Antonio Vivaldi', *Vivaldi Veneziano Europeo: Venezia 1978*, 67
——: 'Ungewöhnliche Tonleiterformen bei Vivaldi', *Vivaldi-Studien: Referate des 3. Dresdner Vivaldi-Kolloquiums: mit einem Katalog der Dresdner Vivaldi-Handschriften und -Frühdrucke: Dresden 1978*, 73
——: *Vivaldi* (London, 1978, 2/1984)
——: *Vivaldi* (London, 1979)
G. Vio: 'Precisazioni sui documenti della Pietà in relazione alle "Figlie del coro" ', *Vivaldi Veneziano Europeo: Venezia 1978*, 101
M. Abbado: 'Antonio Vivaldi nel nostro secolo con particolare referimento alle sue opere strumentali', *NRMI*, xiii (1979), 79
W. Kolneder: *Antonio Vivaldi: Dokumente seines Lebens und Schaffens* (Wilhelmshaven, 1979)

N. Ohmura: 'I "concerti senza orchestra" di Antonio Vivaldi', *NRMI*, xiii (1979), 119

G. Corti: 'Il teatro La Pergola e la stagione d'opera per il carnevale 1726–1727: lettere di Luca Casimiro degli Albizzi a Vivaldi, Porpora ed altri', *RIM*, xv (1980), 182

W. Kolneder: 'Gibt es einen Vivaldistil?', *Informazioni e studi vivaldiani: Bollettino dell'Istituto Italiano Antonio Vivaldi*, i (1980), 9

L. Moretti: 'Un cembalo per la Giro', *Informazioni e studi vivaldiani: Bollettino dell'Istituto Italiano Antonio Vivaldi*, i (1980), 58

G. Vio: 'Antonio Vivaldi prete', *Informazioni e studi vivaldiani: Bollettino dell'Istituto Italiano Antonio Vivaldi*, i (1980), 32

B. Brizi: 'Gli *Orlandi* di Vivaldi attraverso i libretti', *Antonio Vivaldi: teatro musicale, cultura e società: Venezia 1981*, 315

F. Della Seta: 'Documenti inediti su Vivaldi a Roma', *Antonio Vivaldi: teatro musicale, cultura e società: Venezia 1981*, 521

G. F. Folena: 'La cantata e Vivaldi', *Antonio Vivaldi: teatro musicale, cultura e società: Venezia 1981*, 131

K. Heller: 'Anmerkungen zu Vivaldis Opernsinfonien', *Antonio Vivaldi: teatro musicale, cultura e società: Venezia 1981*, 207

H. Hucke: 'Vivaldi und die vokale Kirchenmusik des Settecento', *Antonio Vivaldi: teatro musicale, cultura e società: Venezia 1981*, 191

M. G. Pensa: 'L'*Atenaide* di Apostolo Zeno adattata per la musica di Vivaldi', *Antonio Vivaldi: teatro musicale, cultura e società: Venezia 1981*, 331

E. Selfridge-Field: 'Vivaldi's *Te Deum*: Clue to a French Patron?', *Informazioni e studi vivaldiani: Bollettino dell'Istituto Italiano Antonio Vivaldi*, ii (1981), 44

R. Strohm: 'Vivaldi's Career as an Opera Producer', *Antonio Vivaldi: teatro musicale, cultura e società: Venezia 1981*, 11

M. Talbot: 'Vivaldi and a French Ambassador', *Informazioni e studi vivaldiani: Bollettino dell'Istituto Italiano Antonio Vivaldi*, ii (1981), 31

——: 'Vivaldi's Serenatas: Long Cantatas or Short Operas?', *Antonio Vivaldi: teatro musicale, cultura e società: Venezia 1981*, 67

C. Timms: 'The Dramatic in Vivaldi's Cantatas', *Antonio Vivaldi: teatro musicale, cultura e società: Venezia 1981*, 97

G. Vio: 'Antonio Vivaldi violinista in S. Marco?', *Informazioni e studi vivaldiani: Bollettino dell'Istituto Italiano Antonio Vivaldi*, ii (1981), 51

R.-C. Travers: *La maladie de Vivaldi* (Poitiers, 1982)

——: 'Une mise au point sur la maladie de Vivaldi', *Informazioni e studi vivaldiani: Bollettino dell'Istituto Italiano Antonio Vivaldi*, iii (1982), 52

G. Vio: 'Una nuova abitazione di Vivaldi a Venezia', *Informazioni e studi vivaldiani: Bollettino dell'Istituto Italiano Antonio Vivaldi*, iii (1982), 61

R. Wiesend: 'Vivaldi e Galuppi: rapporti biografici e stilistici', *Antonio Vivaldi: teatro musicale, cultura e società*, ed. L. Bianconi and G. Morelli (Florence, 1982), 233

G. Vio: 'Antonio Vivaldi e i Vivaldi', *Informazioni e studi vivaldiani: Bollettino dell'Istituto Italiano Antonio Vivaldi*, iv (1983), 82

WORKS

J. J. Quantz: *Versuch einer Anweisung die Flöte traversiere zu spielen* (Berlin, 1752, 3/1789/*R*1952; Eng. trans., 1966)

C. P. E. Bach: *Versuch über die wahre Art das Clavier zu spielen* (Berlin, 1753/*R*1957; Eng. trans., 1949, 2/1951)

A. Schering: *Geschichte des Instrumental-Konzerts* (Leipzig, 1905, 2/1927/*R*1965)

W. Kolneder: 'Die Klarinette als Concertino-Instrument bei Vivaldi', *Mf*, iv (1951), 185

——: 'Vivaldi als Bearbeiter eigener Werke', *AcM*, xxiv (1952), 45

W. S. Newman: 'The Sonatas of Albinoni and Vivaldi', *JAMS*, v (1952), 99

W. Kolneder: *Aufführungspraxis bei Vivaldi* (Leipzig, 1955, 2/1973)

R. Eller: *Vivaldis Konzertform* (diss., U. of Leipzig, 1956)

——: 'Geschichtliche Stellung und Wandlung der Vivaldischen Konzertform', *Kongressbericht: Wien Mozartjahr 1956*, 150

H. R. Rarig: *The Instrumental Sonatas of Antonio Vivaldi* (diss., U. of Michigan, 1958)

L. E. Rowell: *Four Operas of Antonio Vivaldi* (diss., U. of Rochester, 1958)

W. S. Newman: *The Sonata in the Baroque Era* (Chapel Hill, 1959, rev. 2/1966/*R*1972)

R. Eller: 'Die Entstehung der Themenzweiheit in der Frühgeschichte des Instrumentalkonzerts', *Festschrift Heinrich Besseler* (Leipzig, 1961), 323

A. Hutchings: *The Baroque Concerto* (London, 1961, rev. 3/1973)

W. Kolneder: *Die Solokonzertform bei Vivaldi* (Strasbourg and Baden-Baden, 1961)

D. Higbee: 'Michel Corrette on the Piccolo and Speculations regarding Vivaldi's "Flautino" ', *GSJ*, xvii (1964), 115

D. D. Boyden: *The History of Violin Playing from its Origins to 1761* (London, 1965)

W. Kolneder: 'Vivaldis Aria-Concerto', *DJbM*, ix (1965), 17

T. Volek and M. Skalická: 'Vivaldis Beziehungen zu den böhmischen Ländern', *AcM*, xxxix (1967), 64

H. C. Wolff: 'Vivaldi und der Stil der italienischen Oper', *AcM*, xl (1968), 179

P. Damilano: 'Antonio Vivaldi compose due vespri?', *NRMI*, iii (1969), 652

M. M. Dunham: *The Secular Cantatas of Antonio Vivaldi in the Foà Collection* (diss., U. of Michigan, 1969)

D. Lasocki: 'Vivaldi and the Recorder', *Recorder and Music Magazine*, iii (1969), 22

M. Talbot: 'The Concerto Allegro in the Early Eighteenth Century', *ML*, lii (1971), 8, 159

——: 'Albinoni and Vivaldi', *Vivaldi Informations*, i (1971–2), 23

D. Arnold: 'Vivaldi's Church Music: an Introduction', *Early Music*, i (1973), 66

W. Kolneder: *Melodietypen bei Vivaldi* (Berg am Irchel and Zurich, 1973)

I. Farup: *Vivaldis anvendelse af fløjteinstrumenter* (diss., U. of Copenhagen, 1974)

H. Maurer: *The Independent Arias of Antonio Vivaldi in Foà 28* (diss., Indiana U., 1974)

E. Selfridge-Field: *Venetian Instrumental Music from Gabrieli to Vivaldi* (Oxford, 1975)

R. Strohm: 'Zu Vivaldis Opernschaffen', *Venezia e il melodramma nel settecento: Venezia 1975*, 237

——: *Italienische Opernarien des frühen Settecento (1720–1730)*, AnMc, no.16 (Cologne, 1976)

P. Ryom: *Les manuscrits de Vivaldi* (Copenhagen, 1977)

H. E. Smither: *A History of the Oratorio*, i: *The Oratorio in the Baroque Era: Italy, Vienna, Paris* (Chapel Hill, 1977)

P. Avanzi: 'Sulla realizzazione del basso continuo nell'opera 2 di Antonio Vivaldi', *Ricerche musicali*, ii (1978), 113

E. Cross: 'Vivaldi as Opera Composer: "Griselda"', *MT*, cxix (1978), 411

——: 'Vivaldi's Operatic Borrowings', *ML*, lix (1978), 429

J. W. Hill: 'Vivaldi's Griselda', *JAMS*, xxxi (1978), 53

E. Selfridge-Field: 'Vivaldi's Esoteric Instruments', *Early Music*, vi (1978), 332

M. Talbot: 'Vivaldi's "Manchester" Sonatas', *PRMA*, civ (1977–8), 20

——: 'Vivaldi's Op.5 Sonatas', *The Strad*, xc (1979–80), 678

E. Cross: *The Late Operas of Antonio Vivaldi, 1727–1738* (Ann Arbor, 1980)

M. Talbot: 'Vivaldi e lo chalumeau', *RIM*, xv (1980), 153

——: 'Vivaldi's Four Seasons', *Music Teacher*, lix (1980), 16

C. Vitali: 'Una lettera di Vivaldi perduta e ritrovata, un inedito monteverdiano del 1630 e altri carteggi di musicisti celebri, ovvero splendori e nefandezze del collezionismo di autografi', *NRMI*, xiv (1980), 404

M. Talbot: 'A Vivaldi Sonata with Obbligato Organ in Dresden', *Organ Yearbook*, xii (1981), 81
K. Heller: *Concerto ripieno und Sinfonia bei Vivaldi* (diss., U. of Rostock, 1982)
F. Tammaro: 'Contaminazione e polivalenze nell' *Orlando finto pazzo*', *RIM*, xvii (1982), 71
K. Heller: 'Über die Beziehungen zwischen einigen Concerto- und Sinfonia-Sätzen Vivaldis', *Informazioni e studi vivaldiani: Bollettino dell'Istituto Italiano Antonio Vivaldi*, iv (1983), 41
K. Hortschansky: 'Arientexte Metastasios in Vivaldis Opern', *Informazioni e studi vivaldiani: Bollettino dell'Istituto Italiano Antonio Vivaldi*, iv (1983), 61
R. Wiesend: 'Die Arie "Gia si sa ch'un empio sei": von Vivaldi oder von Galuppi?', *Informazioni e studi vivaldiani: Bollettino dell'Istituto Italiano Antonio Vivaldi*, iv (1983), 76

SPECIALIST PERIODICALS AND COLLECTIONS

Antonio Vivaldi: note e documenti sulla vita e sulle opere, Chigiana, i (1939)
La scuola veneziana (secoli XVI–XVIII): note e documenti, Chigiana, iii (1941)
Fac-simile di un autografo di Antonio Vivaldi, Quaderno dell'Accademia chigiana, xiii (Siena, 1947)
Fac-simile del Concerto funebre di Antonio Vivaldi, Quaderno dell'Accademia chigiana, xv (Siena, 1947)
Vivaldiana (Brussels, 1969)
Vivaldi Informations (Copenhagen, 1971–)
F. Degrada and M. T. Muraro, eds.: *Antonio Vivaldi da Venezia all'Europa* (Milan, 1978)
Vivaldi-Studien: Referate des 3. Dresdner Vivaldi-Kolloquiums: mit einem Katalog der Dresdner Vivaldi-Handschriften und -Frühdrucke: Dresden 1978
Vivaldi Veneziano Europeo: Venezia 1978
NRMI, xiii/1 (1979) [special Vivaldi issue]
Informazioni e studi vivaldiani: Bollettino dell'Istituto Italiano Antonio Vivaldi (Milan, 1980–)
Antonio Vivaldi: teatro musicale, cultura e società: Venezia 1981

VIVALDI AND BACH

J. Rühlmann: 'Antonio Vivaldi und sein Einfluss auf Joh. Seb. Bach', *NZM*, lxiii (1867), 393, 401, 413
P. Waldersee: 'Antonio Vivaldi's Violinconcerte unter besonderer Berücksichtigung der von Johann Sebastian Bach bearbeiteten', *VMw*, i (1885), 356

Bibliography

A. Schering: 'Zur Bach-Forschung', *SIMG*, iv (1902–3), 234; v (1903–4), 565

E. Praetorius: 'Neues zur Bach-Forschung', *SIMG*, viii (1906–7), 95

M. Schneider: 'Das sogenannte "Orgelkonzert d-moll von Wilhelm Friedemann Bach" ', *BJb*, viii (1911), 23

R. Eller: 'Zur Frage Bach–Vivaldi', *GfMKB, Hamburg 1956*, 80

——: 'Vivaldi–Dresden–Bach', *BMw*, iii (1961), 31

P. Ryom: 'La comparaison entre les versions différentes d'un concerto d'Antonio Vivaldi transcrit par J. S. Bach', *DAM*, v (1966–7), 91

H.-G. Klein: *Der Einfluss der Vivaldischen Konzertform im Instrumentalwerk Johann Sebastian Bachs* (Baden-Baden, 1970)

J. T. Igoe: 'Bachs Bearbeitungen für Cembalo solo: eine Zusammenfassung', *BJb*, lvii (1971), 91

H.-J. Schulze: 'Johann Sebastian Bachs Konzertbearbeitungen nach Vivaldi und anderen: Studien- oder Auftragswerke?', *DJbM*, xviii (1973–7), 80

——: 'Neue Ermittlungen zu J. S. Bachs Vivaldi-Bearbeitungen', *Vivaldi-Studien: Referate des 3. Dresdner Vivaldi-Kolloquiums: mit einem Katalog der Dresdner Vivaldi-Handschriften und -Frühdrucke: Dresden 1978*, 32

DOMENICO SCARLATTI

Joel Sheveloff

CHAPTER ONE

Life

Domenico Scarlatti was born in Naples on 26 October 1685, the sixth of ten children of Alessandro Scarlatti (see p.209) and Antonia Anzalone. Though baptized Giuseppe Domenico, he appears to have used only his second Christian name, which became altered during his years in the Iberian peninsula to Domingo, and the surname to Escarlati (or Escarlatti). The lives and works of the Scarlattis constantly intertwine; for example, Domenico has often been confused with Giuseppe Scarlatti (*c*1718–1777), who was probably his nephew (see family tree, p.210).

It is not known how, where and from whom Domenico Scarlatti received his musical training. His name appears on no conservatory roster, and the assertions that Francesco Gasparini, Gaetano Greco, Bernardo Pasquini or any of the elder Scarlattis were his actual teachers are not verifiable (though he learnt a great deal from the compositions of all of those men, among others). On 13 September 1701 he was appointed organist and composer of the Naples royal chapel, of which Alessandro Scarlatti was *maestro*; no compositions from the period of this employment are extant. In the following year, father and son obtained four months' leave to travel to Florence where Alessandro hoped to secure more favourable working conditions in the private theatre of Ferdinando de' Medici. Whether

Domenico met the keyboard instrument maker Bartolomeo Cristofori at this time has long been a subject of speculation; it is known that Cristofori supplied Ferdinando's harpsichords and was experimenting with the hammer action of his *gravicembalo col piano e forte*. Scarlatti returned to his post in Naples, probably with his father, within the four months allotted to him or shortly after that. He wrote music for two Neapolitan opera productions in 1703 and drastically rewrote Carlo Francesco Pollarolo's *Irene* in 1704.

In spring 1705 Alessandro, wielding the full force of parental authority, ordered his son to go from Naples to Venice, through Rome and Florence, in the company of the celebrated castrato Nicolo Grimaldi. It is worth quoting Alessandro's letter of recommendation to Ferdinando de' Medici, where he described his feelings about his son's growing ability with a warmth and precision generally lacking in documents on Domenico's life:

I have forcibly removed him from Naples where, though there was scope for his talent, it was not the kind of talent for such a place. I am removing him from Rome as well, because Rome has no shelter for music, which lives here as a beggar. This son of mine is an eagle whose wings are grown; he must not remain idle in the nest, and I must not hinder his flight. Since the virtuoso Nicolino of Naples is passing through here on the way to Venice, I thought fit to send Domenico with him, escorted only by his own ability. He has advanced much since he was able to be, together with me, in a position to enjoy the honour of serving Your Highness personally, three years ago. He sets forth to meet whatever opportunity may present itself for him to make himself known – opportunity for which one waits in vain in Rome today.

Nothing is known of the four years Scarlatti spent in Venice. In 1709 he entered the service of Maria Casimira in Rome; his renown grew under the patronage of this exiled Polish queen. (A generation earlier his father had enjoyed a similar situation in Rome under the sponsorship of the exiled Swedish Queen Christina.) The private court of Maria Casimira, which had papal permission to present 'decent comedies', was graced by the composition of at least one cantata, one oratorio and seven operas by Scarlatti.

An important meeting-place of musical people in Rome during those years was the establishment of Cardinal Pietro Ottoboni, at whose weekly recitals of chamber music (known as the Accademie Poetico-musicali) Scarlatti met virtuosos and composers including Corelli, Handel and a young Englishman, Thomas Roseingrave. Roseingrave became a personal friend and ardent admirer of Scarlatti; from 1718 onwards he was the key figure in the dissemination of Scarlatti's vocal and keyboard music in Britain. At this time Handel and Scarlatti allegedly had a contest in virtuosity at the organ and harpsichord, in which Handel is said to have prevailed on the organ, Scarlatti on the harpsichord; but the only source of this tale is Mainwaring's account in his biography of Handel, written more than a half-century later.

On 19 November 1713 Scarlatti took up the post of assistant *maestro di cappella* of the Cappella Giulia at St Peter's; he succeeded Tommaso Baj as *maestro di cappella* on 22 December 1714. Earlier that year, soon after Maria Casimira left Rome, he received a similar appointment with the Marquis de Fontes, Portuguese ambassador to the Vatican. He thus provided music for both sacred and secular employers. But he was still apparently unable to free himself from the interference of a domineering father until legal independence was enforced in a document of 28 January 1717; there are

20. Engraving by Charles-Joseph Flipart after Jacopo Amiconi's portrait (1752) of King Fernando VI, Maria Barbara and the Spanish royal household; Domenico Scarlatti and Farinelli can be seen front right of the musicians' gallery

indications that Alessandro continued to exert as much influence over Domenico as he could even after that time.

In August 1719 Scarlatti resigned his positions in Rome. His movements during the ensuing 12 months are unaccounted for, but he may have spent some time in Palermo, where a 'Dominicus Scarlatti' was admitted to the Unione di Santa Cecilia in April 1720 (see Pagano). By September 1720 he was in Portugal serving as *mestre* of the increasingly opulent patriarchal chapel in Lisbon. Details about his arrival and sojourn in Lisbon are few; much of the documentation pertaining to his eight or nine years in Portugal was apparently destroyed in the earthquake of 1 November 1755 in which the city was nearly obliterated. But we do know from other sources of three visits he made to Italy, apparently on leave from Lisbon. In 1724 he travelled to Rome, meeting Quantz and possibly Farinelli. The following year he went to Naples to pay his final respects to his rapidly failing father; there he probably met the protégé of Alessandro's last years, Hasse. In 1728 he returned to Rome to marry 16-year-old Maria Catarina Gentili, the mother of his first five children. There is no convincing evidence that Domenico ever left the Iberian peninsula after 1728. The Scarlattis who in later years appeared in Austria, France, England or Ireland were other members of this numerous clan.

Scarlatti's duties in Lisbon included the musical education, particularly the training at the keyboard, of King John V's talented daughter, the Infanta Maria Barbara, and his younger brother Don Antonio. With the former Scarlatti formed a lifelong musical symbiosis that resulted in the creation of his most significant work,

21. Domenico Scarlatti: portrait (c1740) by Domingo Antonio de Velasco

a body of more than 500 single-movement 'sonatas' in binary form for unaccompanied keyboard. Maria Barbara married the Spanish Crown Prince Fernando and moved to Seville in 1729, and then to Madrid in 1733.

Scarlatti followed among her retainers and spent the last 28 years of his life in the relative obscurity of the Spanish court, performing whatever musical functions Maria Barbara assigned to him, with no record of complaint.

If Scarlatti was musically pre-eminent at the Spanish court from 1729 to 1737, his position must have changed on the arrival of Carlo Broschi, better known as Farinelli, one of the greatest of all castratos. In Madrid Farinelli's singing was confined to the private chambers of the kings, but he also supervised the productions of theatrical music. Neither the nature of Scarlatti's role at court nor how it related to Farinelli's after 1737 can be ascertained; there are no records of his participation, even as a continuo player, in the festivals that Farinelli directed, but in an official portrait of King Fernando, Maria Barbara and the royal household, painted by Jacopo Amiconi in 1752, Scarlatti and Farinelli are both prominently depicted at the forefront of the lofted gallery of musicians (see fig.20).

On 21 April 1738, at the Capuchin convent of S Antonio del Prado in Madrid, Scarlatti, under the sponsorship of King John V of Portugal, passed initiatory trials to become a Knight of the Order of Santiago. On 6 May 1739 Maria Catarina, his first wife, died; before 1742, he married Anastasia Maxarti Ximenes (orthography varies), the mother of his last four children. None of his nine children became a musician.

Scarlatti died in Madrid on 23 July 1757. The surviving scanty documentation means that little is known about him as a man. Various stories about his way of life, tastes, and character, especially the oft-repeated account of his passion for gambling, come from indirect and suspect sources. The well-known notion that he grew too fat in his later years to cross his hands at the keyboard has been scotched by the discovery in 1956 of a portrait of him painted by Domingo Antonio de Velasco about 1740 (fig.21); it depicts a newly dubbed knight in full regalia, constitutionally slender, with prominent cheekbones and forehead, with long thin arms and strong supple hands, well suited to the technical demands of his keyboard music.

CHAPTER TWO

Works

Until 1719, Domenico Scarlatti strove to establish a career as a composer in the world of *opera seria* over which his father Alessandro reigned. But his musical expressiveness was restricted by a style in which the composer merely provided a blueprint for the castratos or other performers; while others flourished, he languished. Even in the realm of sacred choral music, in which many aspects of his compositional technique ripened, the Neapolitan style's limitations of emotional range and motivic fantasy gave little scope to his latent individuality. An examination of the music of his Italian years shows that the level does not rise above that of professional competence.

After 1720, Scarlatti took advantage of his new freedom to alter his styles of life and composition. Free from the constraints of Neapolitan functional music, he could improvise and compose at the keyboard, exploring whatever path of abstract possibility his fingers could discover. Free from the domineering and critical person of his father, he could make his own mistakes and invest in his own ventures. Free from the unimaginative circles of Italian patronage, he could bask in the encouragement of Maria Barbara and her court. Titillated by the new sounds, sights and customs of Iberia, he could add new elements to his musical language. The resulting hundreds of movements in binary form for keyboard, each simply entitled 'sonata', that he wrote at some time during the last 35 years of his life, raised what Scarlatti himself called 'an ingenious jesting with art' into a uniquely wide-ranging and original corpus of music. These were no mere extensions of the stylized dances of the Baroque suite, but entirely fresh visions of the potentials of binary form; each sonata was an essay in the coordination and control of an unusual problem or problems such as arose from the employment of an eccentric gesture, a peculiar harmony or progression of chords, an irregular phrase or group of phrases, a strange type of motivic development, a tone-colour possible only on a Spanish harpsichord or a Florentine fortepiano, or some other unique problem. Above all, they explore new worlds of virtuoso technique, putting to new musical ends such devices as hand-crossing, rapid repetition of notes, arpeggio figurations rapidly traversing the length of the keyboard, and countless other difficult means of obtaining a devastating brilliance of effect.

The most characteristic of Scarlatti's harmonic mannerisms is the acciaccatura, which he used with greater frequency and variety than any other composer. Attempts to explain this practice in terms of polychords or other fanciful theoretical constructions are as unsuccessful as they are unnecessary. Gasparini and other 18th-century theorists defined the acciaccatura as a 'simultaneous mordent' (in other words, a lower auxiliary note struck together with its resolution). The difficulty experienced by the listener is that of accepting the dissonant note's immediate resolution back into its progenitor within the chord without requiring further resolution in subsequent chords. The most common acciaccatura

resembles the 5–4 dissonance in which the 4th above the bass must resolve downwards to a 3rd; but in all three of the situations cited in ex.1, as well as nearly every other of Scarlatti's acciaccaturas, this 4th has already resolved to the 5th above it and deserves no further part-writing consideration. Whether this use of the acciaccatura is to be linked with the techniques of the guitar music Scarlatti heard in Spain must be a matter for conjecture;

writers on his style have however commented on various instrumental imitations in his music, notably the rapid repeated notes or chords that recall the thrumming of the guitar and the fanfare-like passages that hint at the sound of trumpets or horns.

Auxiliary notes in Scarlatti sonatas, even when they resolve properly, manage to discover methods of effecting the process unknown elsewhere. In ex.2, the *c*♯″ and the later *b*♮′ resolve at the last possible instant before the left-hand chord change is articulated, to *d*♮″ and *c*♮′ respectively. The resolutions are artfully obscured by the intervening high pedal *g*‴s restruck throughout the bar. Scarlatti's literal and immediate reiteration of the

phrase is as if to convince the listener that the first playing was not in error.

The other primary source of exceptional harmonic usage in the Scarlatti sonata is what may be called the 'vamp': a section of indeterminate length, normally at the beginning of the second half of a binary movement, sounding like an improvised accompaniment waiting for the entry of an important musical event. It may vary in length from a few bars to a long group of phrases that can occupy two-thirds of the movement's second half. It opens with a figural pattern resembling that of an exploratory solo section in a fast movement of a Vivaldi concerto. But it is tonally much less predictable, teasing the listener, feinting in one direction and then another before reaching a goal different from the one expected. The harmonic rhythm is generally regular within the vamp, but may become extremely irregular towards the end of the longest examples. The part-writing moves clearly and logically, generally by step, but avoids obvious lines of continuation, mostly through the reinterpretation and redirection of leading notes in ways that are complex and difficult to follow. Ex.3 illustrates

some of the adventurous techniques of the vamp, combined with a characteristic nagging repetition of a short motif.

Ex.4 illustrates the originality of effect that Scarlatti could bring to the filigree surrounding a fairly straightforward sequence by the use of chromatic notes. The

prolongation of an A♭ chord from bar 23 to the downbeat of bar 26 establishes the nature of the section. The sequence progresses up a step to B♭ in bars 26–9 and to C in bars 29–31. Each step is provoked by the substitution of a chromatic note for a diatonic one at exactly that point in the scale where it could not be expected: the *a″* in bar 26 replaces the expected *a♭″*, and the *b″* in bar 29 replaces *b♭″*. The ascending whole-tone-scale fragments, although unusual, are less arresting than the bold stroke that produced them. With this sort of chromatic substitution established, Scarlatti could substitute *e''* for *e♭''* at the beginning of bar 31 to break the pattern of the sequence a bar earlier than expected.

Scarlatti's modulation depends largely on such bold strokes for its effects. Even when pivot chords effect a direct transfer from tonic to dominant or relative major, some attendant feature may be altered by one of these coups, producing some crooked transfer of register, chromatically changing part-crossing, common-note progression, modal alternation between parallel major and minor, false relation or the like. Each of Scarlatti's modulations is militantly individual and demands attention. He never wrote modulatory passages merely to shift from one chord prolongation to another, but tried to project a strength of purpose and a gestural significance in each one equivalent to that in the statement of a tonally stable theme or group of themes. The grand tour becomes an end in itself, with no wasted motion even when a seemingly circuitous route is chosen.

Scarlatti's binary form, outwardly complex and extremely variable, may be reduced to a useful outline. The first half begins, in the traditional manner, in the tonic, moving in major keys to the dominant, and in minor ones to the key of the dominant minor or (less often) the relative major; the second half continues the motion either directly or indirectly before circling back to the tonic. The early music in each half tends to be unstable in material and tonality, the later music just the opposite. The themes at the end of the first half are almost always transposed and repeated at the end of the second, but there is no recapitulation of the movement's opening in the tonic during the second half, and thus no sonata-allegro form (save in K159, and that seems to have been the result of an accident of motivic development). Unlike the stylized dance movements of the Baroque, each half of a Scarlatti sonata tends to be sectional, with many of its phrases coming to full cadences, many contrasts of material, and frequent shifts of rhythmic drive, which provide the sense of variety and freshness in each half that impresses and delights the listener.

The chief objection to this method is that, within each half, there may have to be so many stops and starts that momentum will be lost. Rutini, Alberti, Platti and other composers of this era often failed to solve that problem. The most characteristic way in which Scarlatti avoided this pitfall is his technique of phrase elision: for example, he may write an eight-bar phrase, complete up to its full cadence, and then repeat it, but at the close of the repetition the final bar or two may be eliminated in favour of the smooth early entrance of a new phrase, and the potential energy left over from the elided bars speeds the new material on its way. This procedure is even extended to the junction between the two halves of the binary form. In more than 100 sonatas, there are large curved lines above or below (or both) the final bar or bars of the first half (see ex.5), instructing the performer to omit those bars when playing the first half for the second time and proceed directly into the opening of the second half. This notation has long been understood by scholars, but it is excluded from the editions of the sonatas by Czerny, von Bülow, Farrenc, Tausig, Oesterle, Bartók, Buonamici, Georgii, Pauer, Longo, Granados, Godowsky, Sauer, Gerstenberg, Kirkpatrick and others, though not from the important edition by Kenneth Gilbert.

Ex.5 K535

Scarlatti often composed brief passages in imitation at the 5th or octave. Sometimes he began a piece in a manner indicating that fugal or some other orderly method of imitation is to serve as the structural basis, only to dismiss the idea; the grand Baroque fugal gesture had lost its potency and interest for him and became just one more of his contrasting textures. There are only six pieces that can reasonably be called fugues (K30, 41, 58, 93, 287 and 417), and each of these is in some way flighty, overcomposed or grotesque. K315 toys with the principles of fugue in an irrational, almost taunting manner; its opening motif reappears in a semi-fugal manner in bars 3, 5, 7, 9 (slightly altered), 11 and frequently thereafter.

CHAPTER THREE

Performance, sources, influence

Little information is available about ornamentation in 18th-century Spanish and Portuguese music. Most of the informed guesses about the performance of Scarlatti's ornaments have been extrapolated from Italian and German parallels: a reasonable expedient, although the evidence of the ornamental notation in Iberian pieces seems to indicate that the practice differs in several aspects from Baroque norms. Scarlatti's signs are restricted to small notes (many but not all of which seem to be best interpreted as appoggiaturas), the usual abbreviations for the trill, and the mysterious tremolo indications that have occasioned a good deal of concern and speculation (all one can say at present about this sign's possible meaning is that, whenever it appears, a mordent would seem most appropriate musically).

It has long been assumed that all Scarlatti's sonatas were composed for the harpsichord. A brief flurry of interest in the clavichord as the possible inspiration for some of the thinner-textured sonatas had to be put aside because of the lack of evidence for the existence of clavichords in Maria Barbara's courts. It is now known that at least three pieces (K287, K288 and K328) were meant for organ. Pianos, moreover, were owned and used in each of Maria Barbara's residences. Possibly hundreds of sonatas may have been intended for these delicate, single-escapement hammer-action instruments.

Most of the harpsichords for which the sonatas were written were made in Spain after the fashion of Italian builders; Maria Barbara's were largely one-manual, two-register, five-octave instruments with a clean, clear, delicate sound, very different from the Germanic or Flemish instruments favoured today. The fact that some sonatas have frequent hand-crossings while others do not may relate to the nature of the instrument for which particular pieces were written, as well as to the patrons for whom they were written.

The chronology of Scarlatti's sonatas, about which three numerical reckonings have been essayed, still remains uncertain. Before 1910 Alessandro Longo collected, grouped and numbered all the works then known; but his system of cataloguing was arbitrary. In the 1950s Ralph Kirkpatrick formulated a system that carefully followed the order of pieces in what he considered to be the best dated sources; but his calculations are flawed by the fact that no convincing relationship can be demonstrated between the dates of the copying of these sources and the dates of composition – all sources are copyists' manuscripts or printed editions, not directly traceable to the composer, and every autograph is lost. In 1967 Giorgio Pestelli attempted a listing based on stylistic criteria, which however hardly suffice for music so diverse in form, rich in material and intricate in tonality. All these lists of 'keyboard works' in fact include pieces for solo instruments with continuo.

A problem closely related to that of chronology is that of the grouping of movements into larger units. Most of the sonatas seem to be organized in pairs, according to key, at least in the principal sources. But a number of factors, notably the labelling of each

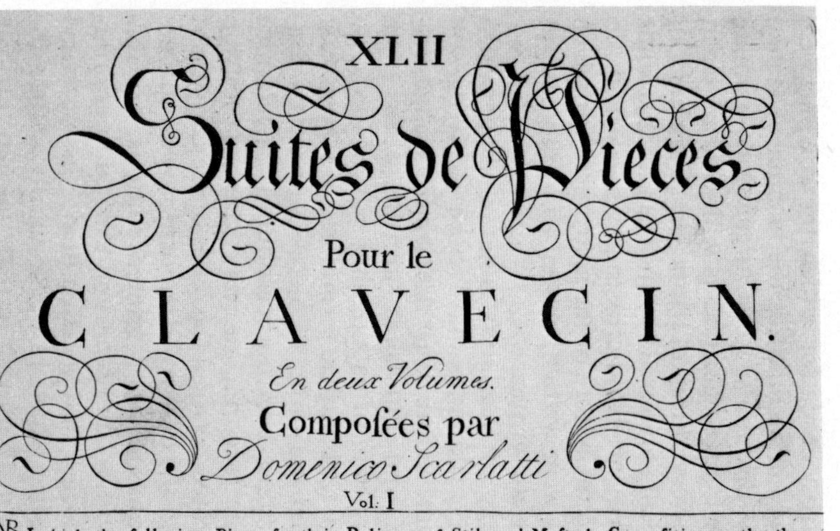

XLII

Suites de Pieces

Pour le

CLAVECIN.

En deux Volumes.

Composées par

Domenico Scarlatti

Vol: I

NB. I think the following Pieces for their Delicacy of Stile, and Masterly Composition, worthy the Attention of the Curious, Which I have Carefully revised & corrected from the Errors of the Press.

Thos: Roseingrave.

LONDON

Printed for, and sold by B: Cooke *at the* Golden Harp *in* New *street* Covt Garden; *Where may be had* Volume *the* 2d

this work contains 14 pieces more than any other Edition hitherto extant. 12 of which are by this Author, ye other 2 is over & above ye No. propos'd

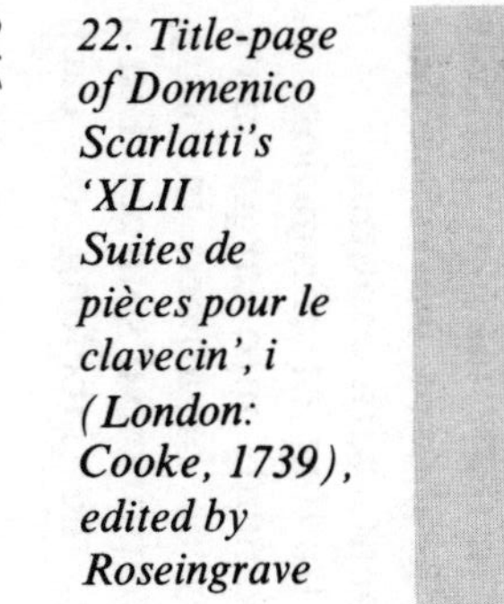

22. Title-page of Domenico Scarlatti's 'XLII Suites de pièces pour le clavecin', i (London: Cooke, 1739), edited by Roseingrave

movement as a separate sonata (unlike the practice of many contemporaries, notably Rutini and Alberti), the existence of a significant number of single movements among the pairs, and most of all the variant groupings among the best sources, suggest either that the pairs were an afterthought on the composer's part or the result of the intervention of the scribe or some other person. Kirkpatrick championed the paired movements; Pestelli rejected them. The pairing of movements in 18th-century Italian keyboard sonatas does not seem to conform to any pattern; nor is it usual for there to be any thematic or motivic connection between the pieces. There is thus no touchstone against which to measure the credibility of the pairs, some of which, particularly K347–8, 356–7, 443–4 and 526–7, seem to belong together for clear musical reasons. One may hope that further research will establish a definitive chronology and that the issue of the pairs will be resolved.

The primary sources comprise the following manuscripts: two sets, each of 15 volumes, both copied by the same Spanish scribe, now in the Arrigo Boito Conservatorio library in Parma (AG 31406–20) and the Biblioteca Marciana in Venice (9770–84); later Italian copies include the five thick volumes in the Santini collection, now at Münster (3964–8), and seven volumes, once the property of Brahms, now in the Gesellschaft der Musikfreunde library, Vienna (VII 28011 A–G); further manuscripts recently found in that library (Q 15112–20, Q 11432, Q 15126) may provide new information about the transmission and text of a number of the pieces. There are other, smaller manuscripts with significant textual readings or otherwise unknown sonatas (Paris, Bibliothèque de l'Arsenal, 6, 784,

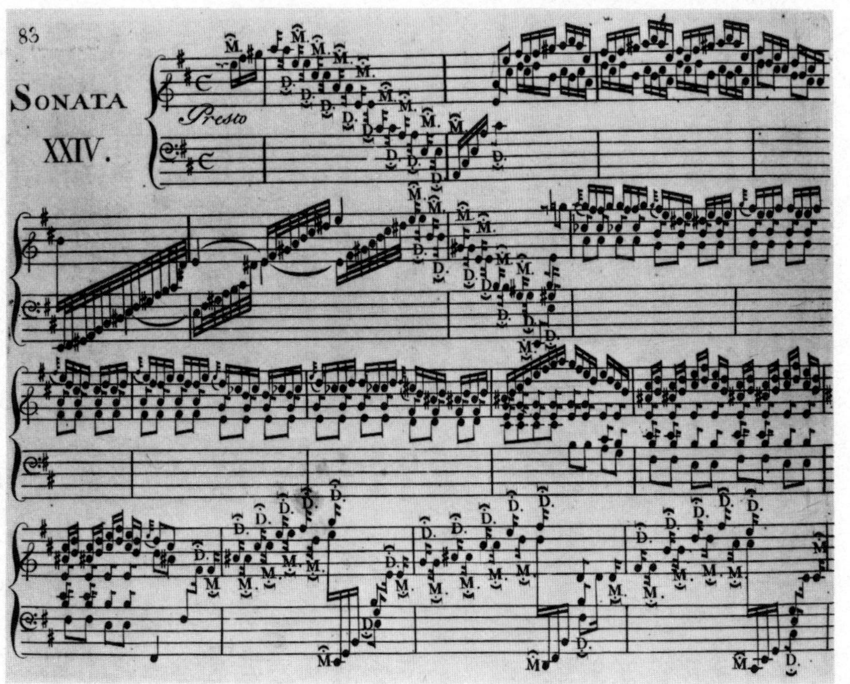

23. Opening of Sonata in A K24 *from Domenico Scarlatti's 'Essercizi per gravicembalo', engraved by Fortier (1738 or 1739)*

343; Cambridge, Fitzwilliam Museum, 32 F 12–13; London, British Library, Add.31553 and 14248; Bologna, Civico Museo Bibliografico Musicale, FF232 and KK96; Naples, Conservatorio di Musica, 18–3–11; Coimbra, Biblioteca Geral da Universidade, Mus.58; and Yale University, Music Library, Ma 31/Sca 7k/C 11).

Scarlatti's sonatas have had a chequered history in print, which bears heavily on the questions of their authenticity and of the textual accuracy with which they have been transmitted. The first of these publications, of 30 pieces singly called sonatas but collectively entitled *Essercizi per gravicembalo*, was issued in London in 1738 or early 1739 by Italian residents in England (possibly contacts of Farinelli), and was immediately pirated by Scarlatti's old acquaintance Thomas Roseingrave; that began a history of pirated or arranged editions which continued throughout the 18th century, particularly in Great Britain, where enthusiasm for the sonatas has never abated. Many notable 18th-century publishers in London, Paris and elsewhere issued collections, including some of arrangements (such as Avison's collection of concerti grossi after Scarlatti sonatas).

Scarlatti exerted considerable influence on the development of keyboard music, particularly in the Iberian peninsula, and also in England, where Burney regarded Joseph Kelway as 'leader of the Scarlatti sect' in London, and the keyboard music of several composers, notably Arne, shows traces of his style. Scarlatti's distinguished Portuguese colleague Carlos Seixas composed, among his many keyboard works, a few that resemble Scarlatti's, but mutual influence between them is still a matter for conjecture. The music of Antonio Soler, on the other hand, reveals strong influence; the two were probably in prolonged contact at the Escorial between 1752 and 1756. The tradition was extended through the next half-century, closing with the keyboard music of Félix Máximo López. An interesting figure among the Iberians influenced by Scarlatti is Sebastián Albero, an organist in the Spanish royal chapel about 1750; 30 of his sonatas in a Venice manuscript alongside Scarlatti's, copied in the same hand, include pieces aping many features of Scarlatti's form, rhetoric and tonal audacity, but never achieving the distinction of his model and thus showing the difficulty, if not impossibility, of isolating the factors contributing to the quality of music.

WORKS

(† – *doubtful*)

Numbers in right-hand margins denote references in the text.

OPERAS 328, 329, 335

(*lost unless otherwise stated*)

Ottavia ristituita al trono (melodramma, G. Convò), Naples, S Bartolomeo, ?Nov 1703, 31 arias and 2 duets, *I-Nc* 328

Giustino (dramma per musica, Convò, after N. Beregan), Naples, Palazzo Regio, 19 Dec 1703, 21 arias (incl. 7 or 8 by Legrenzi) and 3 duets, *Nc* 328

Irene (dramma per musica, adaptation of G. Frigimelica Roberti), Naples, S Bartolomeo, carn. 1704, 33 arias, *Nc* [rev. of orig. by C. F. Pollarolo] 328

Silvia (dramma pastorale, C. S. Capece), Rome, Palazzo Zuccari, 27 Jan 1710

Tolomeo e Alessandro, ovvero La corona disprezzata (dramma per musica, Capece), Rome, Palazzo Zuccari, 19 Jan 1711, MS score of Act 1 extant

Orlando, ovvero La gelosa pazzia (dramma, Capece, after Ariosto), Rome, Palazzo Zuccari, carn. 1711

Tetide in Sciro (dramma per musica, Capece), Rome, Palazzo Zuccari, 10 Jan 1712, full score, *I-Vsf*

Iphigenia in Aulide (dramma per musica, Capece, after Euripides), Rome, Palazzo Zuccari, 11 Jan 1713

Ifigenia in Tauri (dramma per musica, Capece, after Euripides), Rome, Palazzo Zuccari, ?15 Feb 1713, 2 (?4) arias, *D-Dlb*

Amor d'un ombra e gelosia d'un aura (dramma per musica, Capece), Rome, Palazzo Zuccari, 15 Jan 1714; rev. as Narciso (P. A. Rolli, after Capece), London, King's, 30 May 1720, with 2 arias and 2 duets added by T. Roseingrave, full score, *D-Hs*; short score arias pubd (London, 1720)

Ambleto (dramma per musica, Zeno and P. Pariati), Rome, Capranica, carn. 1715, 1 aria, *I-Bc*

La Dirindina (farsetta per musica, G. Gigli), intermezzo for Ambleto, unperf., full score, *Vlevi*

Intermedi pastorali, intermezzo in Ambleto, Rome, Capranica, carn. 1715

Berenice, regina d'Egitto, ovvero Le gare di amore e di politica (dramma per musica, A. Salvi), Rome, Capranica, carn. 1718, collab. N. Porpora, 5 (?7) arias, *D-MÜs*

ORATORIOS AND SERENATAS 329, 335

(*lost unless otherwise stated*)

La conversione di Clodoveo, re di Francia (oratorio, Capece), Rome, Palazzo Zuccari, ?Lent 1709

Applauso devoto al nome di Maria Santissima (serenata, Capece), Rome, Palazzo Zuccari, 1712

Applauso genetliaco (serenata), Rome, Portuguese Embassy, 1714

Contesa delle stagioni (serenata), S, S, A, T, chorus, 2 tpt, 2 hn, fl, str, Lisbon, Royal Palace, 6 Sept 1720, score of Part I, *I-Vnm*; ed. R. Fasano (Milan, 1965)

Cantata pastorale (serenata), Lisbon, Royal Palace, 27 Dec 1720

Serenata, Lisbon, 6 Sept 1722

Serenata, Lisbon, 27 Dec 1722

Festeggio armonico (serenata), Lisbon, Royal Palace, 11 Jan 1728

MASSES AND MOTETS 335

Missa, ?1712, ?lost

Missa quatuor vocum (g), SATB, *E-Mp*; ed. L. Bianchi (Rome, 1961)

†Dixit Dominus, lost; cited in A. Soler, *Llave de la modulación* (Madrid, 1762)

Iste confessor, S, SATB, bc, *I-Rvat*; pubd as suppl. to *Musica sacra*, iii (Milan, 1879)

†Lauda Jerusalem, lost; cited in A. Soler, *Llave de la modulación* (Madrid, 1762)

Laudate pueri, SATB, SATB, bc, *P-Lf*

Magnificat, SATB, *D-MÜs*

†Memento Domine David, SATB, *B*, *Dl*, *Mbs*, *MÜs*, *F-Pc*, *GB-Lbm*, *I-Bc*, *Mc*, *Nc* (probably by A. Scarlatti)

Miserere (e), SATB, SATB, *I-Rvat*

Miserere (g), SATB, SATB, *Rvat*, *P-Em*

Nisi quia Dominus, 4vv, ?lost

Salve regina (A), S, 2 vn, va, bc, *D-B*, *MÜs*, *I-Bc*, *Nc*; ed. R. Ewerhart (Cologne, 1960); ed. R. Leppard (London, 1979)

Salve regina (a), S, A, bc, *Bc*; ed. L. Hautus (Kassel, 1973)

Stabat mater, SSSSAATTBB, bc, *A-Wn*, *D-MÜs*, *I-Bc*, *Vc*; ed. A. Casella (Rome, 1941); ed. B. Somma (Rome, 1956); ed. in Accademia musicale, xxvii (1973); ed. J. Jürgens (Mainz, 1973)
Te Deum, SSAATTBB, org, *P-Lf* (score), *G* (parts)
Te gloriosus (for All Saints), SATB, bc, *Lf*

CANTATAS 329

Principal sources: *A-Wn*, *B-Bc*, *D-B*, *Dlb*, *Mbs*, *MÜs*, *SWl*, *F-Pc*, *Pn*, *GB-Lam*, *Lbm*, *Lcm*, *I-Bc*, *Bsp*, *Fc*, *Gi(l)*, *Nc*, *PAc*, *Pca*, *Rsc*, *US-Wc*

A chi nacque infelice, A, bc, ed. L. Bianchi (Milan, 1958); Ah, sei troppo infelice, S, bc, July 1705, ed. L. Bianchi (Milan, 1958); Al fin diviene amante, A, bc; Amenissimi prati, fiorite piagge, B, bc, ed. L. Hautus (Cologne, 1971); Bella rosa adorata, cara pompa di Flora, S, bc; †Belle pupille care, S, bc, 1697 (probably by Francesco Scarlatti); Cantata da recitarsi . . . la notte del Ss Natale, 24 Dec 1714 (text only, F. M. Gasparri); Cara qual hor lontano, S, bc; Care pupille belle, S, 2 vn, bc, July 1702; †Che pretendi, o tiranna, S, bc; Che si peni in amore, A, bc; Che vidi, o ciel, S, 2 vn, bc; Chi in catene ha il mio core, S, bc; Con qual cor mi chiedi pace, S, bc; Deh che fate o mie pupille, S, bc; Di Fille vendicarmi vorrei, S, bc; Dir vorrei, ah m'arrossisco, S, 2 vn, bc; Doppo lungo servire, A, 2 vn, bc, 2 July 1702; Dorme la rosa (B. Pamphili), S, bc; E pur per mia sventura, S, bc; E temerario ardire, S, bc; Fille già più non parlo, S, bc; Lontan da te mio bene, S, bc; †Mi tormenta il pensiero, S, bc, 10 March 1701; Ninfe belle e voi pastori, S, bc; No, non fuggire o Nice, S, bc; †Onde della mia Nera, A, bc; O qual meco Nice cangiata, S, 2 vn, bc
Pende la vita mia, S, bc; Piangete, occhi dolenti, S, 2 vn, bc; Pur nel sonno almen tal'ora (P. Metastasio), S, 2 vn, bc, ed. L. Bianchi (Rome, 1963); Qual pensier, quale ardire ti guida?, S, bc; Quando miro il vostro foco, A, bc; Quando penso a Daliso, S, bc; Rimirai la rosa, A, bc; Scritte con falso inganno, S, 2 vn, bc; Se dicessi ch'io t'amo, S, bc; Se fedele tu m'adori, S, 2 vn, bc; †Selve, caverne e monti, S, bc, ed. L. Hautus (Kassel, 1973); Se per un sol momento, S, S, bc; Se sai qual sia la pena, S, bc; Se ti dicesse un core, S, bc; †Sono un alma tormentata, S, bc, 1739; Sospendi o man per poco, S, bc; †T'amai, Clori, t'amai, S, bc; Tinte a note di sangue, S, 2 vn, bc; Ti ricorda o bella Irene, S, bc; Tirsi caro – Amata Fille, S, S, bc; †Tirsi, mentr'io dormiva, S, bc; Tu mi chiedi o mio ben, S, bc; V'adoro o luci belle, S, bc; †Vago il ciel non saria, S, bc; †Vuoi ch'io spiri tra i sospiri, 20 Sept 1699, S, bc (probably by A. Scarlatti)

INSTRUMENTAL ENSEMBLE

17 sinfonias, *F-Pn*: A, str, bc; G, fl, ob, str, bc; G, str, bc; D, ob, str, bc; a, 2 vn, bc; D, ob, 2 vn, bc; C, str, bc; B♭, ob, str, bc; d, ob, str, bc; G, ob, str, bc; C, ob, str, bc; G, ob, str, bc; G, ob, str, bc; G, fl, ob, str, bc; B♭, ob, str, bc; A, ob, str, bc; C, 2 ob, str, bc
†1 conc., F, hpd solo, 2 fl, 2 hn, 2 vn, va, bc, *D-B*, ? by G. Scarlatti

SONATAS FOR SOLO KEYBOARD 332, 335–43, 344–50

Catalogues in Longo (1906–8) [L], Kirkpatrick (1953) [K], Pestelli [P]
Editions: *Opere complete per clavicembalo di Domenico Scarlatti*, ed. A. Longo (Milan, 1906–8): i, L1–50; ii, L51–100; iii, L101–50; iv, L151–200; v, L201–50; vi, L251–300; vii, L301–50; viii, L351–400; ix, L401–50; x, L451–500; xi, S1–45 342, 345

D. Scarlatti: Sixty Sonatas, ed. R. Kirkpatrick (New York, 1953) [*]

D. Scarlatti: Complete Keyboard Works in Facsimile, ed. R. Kirkpatrick (New York, 1971–): i, K1–42; ii, K43–68, variants of K8, 31, 33, 37, 41; iii, K69–97, variants of K52, 53; iv, K98–123; v, K124–47; vi, K148–76; vii, K177–205; viii, K206–35; ix, K236–65; x, K266–95; xi, K296–325; xii, K326–57; xiii, K358–87; xiv, K388–417; xv, K418–53; xvi, K454–83; xvii, K484–513; xviii, K514–55 342, 345, 347

D. Scarlatti: Sonates, ed. K. Gilbert, Le pupitre (Paris, 1971–): xxxi, K1–52; xxxii, K53–103; xxxiii, K104–55; xxxiv, K156–205; xxxv, K206–55; xxxvi, K256–305; xxxvii, K306–57; xxxviii, K358–407; xxxix, K408–57; xl, K458–506; xli, K507–55 342

D. Scarlatti: Sonate per clavicembalo, ed. E. Fadini (Milan, 1978–)

Sources: *Essercizi per gravicembalo* (London, 1738 or 1739/*R*1967) [E] — *348*, 349

XLII Suites de pièces pour le clavecin, ed. T. Roseingrave (London, 1739) [R] — *346*, 349

Pièces pour le clavecin, 3 vols. (Paris, 1742–6, Boivin) [B]

Pièces pour le clavecin (Paris, before 1747, Boivin) [Bo]

Domenico Scarlatti: 26 Sonatas ineditas, ed. E. Granados (*c*1905) [G]

MS Sources:
D-MÜs 3964–8 [M] — 347
F-Pa 6, 784, 343 [PR] — 347
GB-Cfm Mus.32 F 13 [CF] — 349
GB-Lbm Add.31553, 14248 [LB] — 349
I-PAp AG 31406–20 [PA] — 347
I-Vnm 9770–84 [V] — 347
P-C Mus.58 [C] — 349
US-NH Ma 31/Sca 7k/C11 [NH] — 349

K	*P*	*L*	*Description*	*Primary source (variant)*	
1	57	366	d, C, Allegro	E1	
2	58	388	G, 3/8, Presto	E2	
3	59	378	a, ¢, Presto*	E3	
4	60	390	g, C, Allegro	E4	
5	61	367	d, 3/8, Allegro	E5	
6	62	479	F, 3/8, Allegro	E6	
7	63	379	a, 3/8, Presto*	E7	
8	64	488	g, 3/4, Allegro	E8 (R1)	
9	65	413	d, 6/8, Allegro	E9	
10	66	370	d, 3/8, Presto	E10	
11	67	352	c, C, —	E11	
12	68	489	g, C, Presto	E12	
13	69	486	G, 2/4, Presto	E13	
14	70	387	G, 12/8, Presto	E14	
15	71	374	e, 3/8, Allegro	E15	
16	72	397	B♭, ¢, Presto*	E16	
17	73	384	F, 3/8, Presto	E17	
18	74	416	d, C, Presto*	E18	
19	75	383	f, 2/4, Allegro	E19	
20	76	375	E, 2/4, Presto	E20	
21	77	363	D, 3/8, Allegro	E21	
22	78	360	c, 2/4, Allegro	E22	
23	79	411	D, C, Allegro	E23	
24	80	495	A, C, Presto	E24	
25	81	481	f♯, 2/4, Allegro	E25	
26	82	368	A, 3/8, Presto	E26	
27	83	449	b, 3/4, Allegro	E27	
28	84	373	E, 3/8, Presto*	E28	
29	85	461	D, C, Presto*	E29	
30	86	499	g, 6/8, Moderato	E30	343
31	19	231	g, 2/4, Allegro	R3	
32	14	423	d, 3/8, Aria	R6	
33	130	424	D, 3/8, Allegro	V xiv, 43 (R7)	
34	15	S7	d, 3/4, Larghetto	R9	
35	20	386	g, C, Allegro	R12	
36	91	245	a, 3/8, Allegro	V xiv, 25	
37	2	406	c, C, Allegro	V xiv, 41	
38	97	478	F, 3/8, Allegro	V xiv, 27	
39	53	391	A, C, Allegro	R28	
40	119	357	c, 3/4, Minuetto	R30	
41	37	—	d, C, Andante moderato	PA iii, 30 (R42)	343
42	120	S36	B♭, 3/4, Minuetto	R43	
43	133	40	g, 12/8, Allegrissimo	PA iii, 7	
44	116	432	F, 3/8, Allegro*	PA ii, 20	
45	230	265	D, 12/8, Allegro	V xiv, 3	
46	179	25	E, ¢, Allegro*	PA ii, 15	
47	115	46	B♭, C, Presto	PA iii, 11	
48	87	157	c, 3/8, Presto	PA ii, 24	
49	178	301	C, ¢, Presto	PA iii, 5	
50	144	440	f, 3/8, Allegro	PA iii, 22	

K	P	L	Description	Primary source (variant)	
51	151	20	E♭, C, Allegro	V xiv, 9	
52	41	267	d, C, Andante moderato*	V xiv, 10 (V xiv, 61)	
53	161	261	D, ¢, Presto	PA vi, 13	
54	147	241	a, 12/8, Allegro*	PA iii, 20	
55	117	335	G, 3/8, Presto	PA iii, 1	
56	50	356	c, 12/8, Allegro con spirito	PA ii, 25	
57	108	S38	B♭, 3/8, Allegro*	PA iii, 12	
58	39	158	c, C, Fuga	V xiv, 16	343
59	22	71	F, C, Allegro	V xiv, 17	
60	29	13	g, 3/4, —	V xiv, 19	
61	16	136	a, 2/4, —	V xiv, 20	
62	49	45	A, 3/8, Allegro	V xiv, 21	
63	32	84	G, 2/4, Capriccio: Allegro	V xiv, 23	
64	33	58	d, 2/4, Gavota: Allegro	V xiv, 24	
65	142	195	A, 3/8, Allegro	V xiv, 26	
66	134	496	B♭, C, Allegro	V xiv, 28	
67	125	32	f♯, C, Allegro	V xiv, 29	
68	7	114	E♭, 3/8, —	V xiv, 30	
69	42	382	f, 3/4, —	PA ii, 27	
70	21	50	B♭, C, —	V xiv, 34	
71	17	81	G, C, Allegro	V xiv, 35	
72	1	401	C, C, Allegro	V xiv, 36	
74	34	94	A, 2/4, Allegro	V xiv, 38	
75	35	53	G, 3/4, Allegro	V xiv, 39	
76	23	185	g, 3/8, Presto	V xiv, 40	
79	204	80	G, 3/8, Allegrissimo	V xiv, 45a	
80	28	—	G, 3/8, Minuet	V xiv, 45b	
82	25	30	F, 3/8, —	C2	
83	31	S31	A, ¢, —	V xiv, 48	
84	45	10	c, 3/4, —*	V xiv, 49	
85	24	166	F, C, —	C1	
86	122	403	C, C, Andante moderato	V xiv, 51	
87	43	33	b, 3/4, —	PA ii, 28	
92	44	362	d, 3/4, —	V xiv, 58	
93	38	336	g, C, Fuga	V xiv, 60	343

K	P	L	Description	Primary source (variant)	
94	27	—	F, 3/8, Minuet	C4	
96	210	465	D, 3/8, Allegrissimo*	PA iii, 29	
98	219	325	e, 3/8, Allegrissimo	PA iii, 19	
99	135	317	c, 3/4, Allegro	PA iii, 18	
100	232	355	C, 12/8, Allegro subbito	PA iii, 28	
101	156	494	A, 3/8, Allegro	PA iii, 26	
102	88	89	g, 3/8, Allegro	V xv, 4	
103	233	233	G, 12/8, Allegrissimo	V xv, 5	
104	109	442	G, 3/8, Allegro	PA iii, 2	
105	90	204	G, 3/8, —*	PA iii, 24	
106	197	437	F, ¢, Andante	PA iii, 15	340–41
107	98	474	F, 3/8, Allegro	PA iii, 16	
108	92	249	g, 3/8, Allegro	PA v, 12	
109	290	138	a, ¢, Andante adagio	PA iii, 3	
110	129	469	a, 3/8, Allegro	PA iii, 4	
111	99	130	g, 12/8, Allegro	PA iii, 17	
112	94	298	B♭, 3/8, Allegro	PA iii, 23	
113	160	345	A, ¢, Vivo	PA ii, 14	
114	141	344	A, 3/8, Con spirito è presto	PA iii, 27	
115	100	407	c, 3/4, Allegro*	PA iii, 13	
116	111	452	c, 3/8, Allegro*	PA iii, 14	
117	181	244	C, ¢, Allegro	V xv, 20	
118	266	122	D, ¢, Non presto	PA iii, 9	
119	217	415	D, 3/8, Allegro*	PA ii, 17	
120	146	215	d, 12/8, —*	PA ii, 16	
121	93	181	g, 3/8, Allegrissimo	PA iii, 8	
122	118	334	D, 3/8, Allegro	PA iii, 10	
123	180	111	E♭, ¢, Allegro	PA iii, 21	
124	110	232	G, 3/8, Allegro	PA ii, 3	
125	152	487	G, 3/8, Vivo	PA ii, 4	
126	128	402	c, 3/8, —	PA ii, 26	
127	198	186	A♭, ¢, Allegro	PA ii, 21	
128	199	296	b♭, ¢, Allegro	PA ii, 29	
129	148	460	c, 6/8, —	PA i, 29	
130	272	190	A♭, 3/8, Allegro	PA ii, 22	

131	154	300	b♭, 3/8, Allegro	PA ii, 30	
132	295	457	C, 3/4, Andante*	PA v, 5	338
133	218	282	C, 3/8, Allegro*	PA v, 6	
134	143	221	E, 2/4, Allegro	PA ii, 7	
135	234	224	E, 6/8, Allegro	PA ii, 8	
136	113	377	E, 3/8, Allegro	PA ii, 9	
137	231	315	D, 6/8, Allegro	PA ii, 6	
138	95	464	d, 3/8, —	PA ii, 5	
139	126	6	c, ¢, Presto	PA iii, 6	
140	127	107	D, c, —*	PA iii, 25	
141	271	422	d, 3/8, Allegro	LB 31553, 41	337
147	48	376	e, C, —	PR4	
148	291	64	a, 3/8, Andante	PA i, 1	
149	241	93	a, C, Allegro	PA i, 2	
150	205	117	F, 3/8, Allegro	PA i, 3	
151	238	330	F, 3/8, Andante Allegro	PA i, 4	
152	114	179	G, 3/8, Allegro	PA i, 5	
153	235	445	G, 12/8, Vivo	PA i, 6	
154	183	96	B♭, ¢, Allegro	PA i, 7	
155	208	197	B♭, 3/8, Allegro	PA i, 8	
156	248	101	C, C, Allegro	PA i, 9	
157	391	405	C, 3/8, Allegro	PA i, 10	
158	123	4	c, 3/8, Andante	PA i, 11	
159	418	104	C, 6/8, Allegro	PA i, 12	342
160	131	15	D, C, Allegro	PA i, 14	
161	216	417	D, 3/8, Allegro	PA i, 13	
162	162	21	E, 3/4, Andante	PA i, 15	
163	206	63	E, 3/8, —	PA i, 16	
164	274	59	D, 3/4, Andante moderato	PA i, 17	
165	292	52	C, 3/4, —	PA i, 18	
166	190	51	C, ¢, Allegro mà non molto	PA i, 19	
167	200	329	F, 3/4, Allegro	PA i, 21	
168	182	280	F, ¢, Vivo	PA i, 20	
169	247	331	G, C, Allegro con spirito	PA i, 22	
170	164	303	C, C, Andante moderato è cantabile	PA i, 23	
171	153	77	G, 3/8, Allegro	PA i, 24	
172	313	S40	B♭, 6/8, Allegro	PA i, 25	
173	51	447	b, 2/4, —	PA i, 26	
174	149	410	c, 6/8, Allegro	PA i, 27	
175	136	429	a, 2/4, Allegro*	PA i, 28	
176	163	163	d, ¢, Cantabile andante	PA i, 30	
177	184	364	D, ¢, Andante moderato	V ii, 1	
178	392	162	D, 3/8, Vivo	V ii, 2	
179	89	177	g, 3/8, Allegro	PA ii, 1	
180	192	272	G, ¢, Allegro vivo	PA ii, 2	
181	253	194	A, 2/4, Allegro	PA ii, 10	
182	207	139	A, 3/8, —	PA ii, 11	
183	150	473	f, 2/4, Allegro	PA ii, 12	
184	102	189	f, 3/8, Allegro	PA ii, 13	
185	121	173	f, ¢, Andante	PA ii, 18	
186	46	72	f, 3/8, Allegro	PA ii, 19	
187	145	285	f, 3/8, —	PA ii, 23	
188	213	239	a, 3/8, Allegro	PA iv, 5	
189	257	143	B♭, 3/4, Allegro	PA iv, 10	
190	256	250	B♭, 12/8, Vivo	PA iv, 11	
191	18	207	d, 3/4, Allegro	PA iv, 15	
192	322	216	E♭, ¢, Allegro	PA iv, 16	
193	254	142	E♭, 3/8, Allegro	PA iv, 17	339–40
194	479	28	F, 3/8, Andante	PA iv, 18	
195	185	S18	F, ¢, Vivo	PA iv, 19	
196	244	38	g, 2/4, Allegro	PA iv, 4	
197	124	147	b, C, Andante	PA iv, 9	
198	132	22	e, 3/4, Allegro	PA iv, 20	
199	276	253	C, 12/8 Andante moderato	PA vi, 29	
200	242	54	C, 2/4, Allegro	PA vi, 30	
201	252	129	G, 3/4, Vivo	PA iv, 8	
202	173	498	B♭, 3/8, Allegro	PA iv, 12	
203	96	380	e, 3/8, Vivo non molto	PA iv, 21	
204a	170	—	f, ¢, Allegro	PA iv, 22	
204b	255	—	f, 3/8, Allegro	PA iv, 23	
205	171	S23	F, ¢, Vivo	PA iv, 24	
206	307	257	E, ¢, Andante	PA v, 1	
207	140	371	E, 3/8, Allegro	PA v, 2	
208	315	238	A, C, Andante è cantabile*	PA iv, 1	337
209	209	428	A, 3/8, Allegro*	PA iv, 2	
210	293	123	G, 3/8, Andante	PA iv, 3	
211	277	133	A, ¢, —	PA iv, 6	

K	P	L	Description	Primary source (variant)
212	155	135	A, 3/8, Allegro molto	PA iv, 7
213	288	108	d, C, Andante	PA iv, 13
214	430	165	D, 12/8, Vivo	PA iv, 14
215	281	323	E, 3/4, —*	PA iv, 25
216	320	273	E, 3/4, Allegro*	PA iv, 26
217	287	42	a, 3/4, Andante	PA iv, 27
218	237	392	a, 6/8, Vivo	PA iv, 28
219	278	393	A, ¢, Andante	PA iv, 29
220	309	342	A, 3/8, Allegro	PA iv, 30
221	215	259	A, 3/8, Allegro	PA v, 3
222	236	309	A, 6/8, Vivo	PA v, 4
223	188	214	D, ¢, Allegro	PA v, 7
224	225	268	D, 3/8, Vivo	PA v, 8
225	202	351	C, 3/4, Allegro	PA v, 9
226	101	112	c, 3/8, Allegro	PA v, 10
227	52	347	b, 2/4, Allegro	PA v, 11
228	224	399	B♭, 3/8, Allegro	PA v, 13
229	139	199	B♭, 2/4, Allegro vivo	PA v, 14
230	47	354	c, ¢, Allegro	PA v, 15
231	393	409	C, 3/8, Allegro	PA v, 16
232	317	62	e, ¢, Andante	PA v, 17
233	497	467	e, 3/8, Allegro	PA v, 18
234	286	49	g, 3/4, Andante	PA v, 19
235	172	154	G, 3/8, Allegro	PA v, 20
236	201	161	D, C, Allegro	PA vi, 3
237	446	308	D, 3/8, Allegro	PA vi, 4
238	55	27	f, C, Andante*	PA v, 21
239	56	281	f, 3/4, Allegro*	PA v, 22
240	368	S29	G, ¢, Allegro	PA v, 23
241	431	180	G, 6/8, Allegro	PA v, 24
242	243	202	C, 2/4, Vivo	PA v, 25
243	394	353	C, 3/8, Allegro	PA v, 26
244	298	348	B, 3/8, Allegro	PA v, 27
245	299	450	B, 6/8, Allegro	PA v, 28
246	296	260	c♯, ¢, Allegro	PA v, 29
247	297	256	c♯, 3/8, Allegro	PA v, 30

K	P	L	Description	Primary source (variant)
248	187	S35	B♭, ¢, Allegro	PA vi, 1
249	424	39	B♭, 3/8, Allegro	PA vi, 2
250	461	174	C, 2/4, Allegro	PA vi, 5
251	314	305	C, 3/8, Allegro	PA vi, 6
252	203	159	E♭, 3/4, Allegro	PA vi, 7
253	239	320	E♭, 12/8, Allegro	PA vi, 8
254	186	219	c, ¢, Allegro	PA vi, 9
255	226	439	C, 3/8, Allegro	PA vi, 10
256	480	228	F, 3/4, Andante	PA vi, 11
257	138	169	F, 2/4, Allegro	PA vi, 12
258	494	178	D, 3/4, Andante	PA vi, 14
259	469	103	G, 3/4, Andante*	PA vi, 15
260	304	124	G, 3/4, Allegro*	PA vi, 16
261	300	148	B, 2/4, Allegro	PA vi, 17
262	301	446	B, 12/8, Vivo	PA vi, 18
263	283	321	e, ¢, Andante*	PA vi, 19
264	308	466	E, 3/8, Vivo*	PA vi, 20
265	168	S32	a, C, Allegro	PA vii, 16
266	251	48	B♭, C, Andante	PA vii, 4
267	363	434	B♭, 3/4, Allegro	PA vii, 5
268	369	41	A, ¢, Allegro	PA vi, 21
269	432	307	A, 6/8, Allegro	PA vi, 22
270	481	459	C, ¢, —	PA vi, 23
271	447	155	C, 3/8, Vivo	PA vi, 24
272	518	145	B♭, ¢, Allegro	PA vi, 25
273	174	398	B♭, 3/8, Vivo	PA vi, 26
274	491	297	F, ¢, Andante	PA vii, 1
275	330	328	F, 3/4, Allegro	PA vii, 2
276	433	S20	F, 3/8, Allegro	PA vii, 3
277	275	183	D, ¢, Cantabile andantino	PA vii, 6
278	434	S15	D, 6/8, Con velocita	PA vii, 7
279	306	468	A, ¢, Andante	PA vii, 8
280	395	237	A, 3/8, Allegro	PA vii, 9
281	289	56	D, 3/4, Andante	PA vii, 10
282	166	484	D, ¢, Allegro	PA vii, 11
283	482	318	G, ¢, Andante allegro	PA vii, 12

284	169	90	G, 3/8, Allegro	PA vii, 13	
285	321	91	A, ¢, Andante allegro	PA vii, 14	
286	410	394	A, 6/8, Allegro	PA vii, 15	
287	310	S9	D, C, Andante allegro	PA vii, 17	343, 344
288	311	57	D, 3/8, Allegro	PA vii, 18	344
289	249	78	G, 2/4, Allegro	PA vii, 19	
290	396	85	G, 3/8, Allegro	PA vii, 20	
291	282	61	e, ¢, Andante	PA vii, 21	
292	223	24	e, 3/8, Allegro	PA vii, 22	
293	157	S44	b, ¢, Allegro	PA vii, 23	
294	470	67	d, 3/4, Andante	PA vii, 24	
295	211	270	d, 3/8, Allegro	PA vii, 25	
296	305	198	F, 3/4, Andante	PA vii, 30	
297	448	S19	F, 3/8, Allegro	PA vii, 31	
298	194	S6	D, ¢, Allegro	PA vii, 26	
299	268	210	D, 3/8, Allegro	PA vii, 27	
300	312	92	A, 3/4, Andante	PA vii, 28	
301	361	493	A, C, Allegro	PA vii, 29	
302	279	7	c, 3/4, Andante	PA viii, 1	
303	212	9	c, 3/8, Allegro	PA viii, 2	
304	492	88	G, ¢, Andante cantabbile	PA viii, 3	
305	397	322	G, 6/8, Allegro	PA viii, 4	
306	456	16	E♭, ¢, Allegro	PA viii, 5	
307	449	115	E♭, 3/8, Allegro	PA viii, 6	
308	318	359	C, ¢, Cantabbile*	PA viii, 7	
309	333	454	C, ¢, Allegro*	PA viii, 8	
310	284	248	B♭, ¢, Andante	PA viii, 9	
311	227	144	B♭, 3/8, Allegro	PA viii, 10	
312	334	264	D, ¢, Allegro	PA viii, 11	
313	398	192	D, 3/8, Allegro	PA viii, 12	
314	505	441	G, ¢, Allegro	PA viii, 13	
315	54	235	g, 3/8, Allegro	PA viii, 14	343
316	193	299	F, ¢, Allegro	PA viii, 15	
317	258	66	F, 3/4, Allegrissimo	PA viii, 16	
318	302	31	F♯, ¢, Andante	PA viii, 17	
319	303	35	F♯, 6/8, Allegro	PA viii, 18	
320	335	341	A, ¢, Allegro	PA viii, 19	
321	450	258	A, 3/8, —	PA viii, 20	
322	360	483	A, ¢, Allegro	PA viii, 21	
323	411	95	A, 6/8, Allegro	PA viii, 22	
324	285	332	G, ¢, Andante	PA viii, 23	
325	451	37	G, 3/8, Con velocità	PA viii, 24	
326	336	201	C, ¢, Allegro	PA viii, 27	
327	399	152	C, 3/8, Allegro	PA viii, 28	
328	485	S27	G, 6/8, Andante comodo	PA viii, 25	344
329	337	S5	C, ¢, Allegro	PA viii, 26	
330	222	55	C, 3/8, Allegro	PA ix, 7	
331	471	18	B♭, 3/4, Andante	PA viii, 29	
332	519	141	B♭, ¢, Allegro	PA viii, 30	
333	338	269	D, ¢, Allegro	PA ix, 1	
334	412	100	B♭, 6/8, Allegro	PA ix, 2	
335	339	S10	D, ¢, Allegro	PA ix, 8	
336	262	337	D, 3/8, Allegro	PA ix, 9	
337	340	S26	G, ¢, Allegro	PA ix, 10	
338	400	87	G, 3/8, Allegro	PA ix, 11	
339	189	251	C, ¢, Allegro	PA ix, 12	
340	420	105	C, 6/8, Allegro	PA ix, 13	
341	103	140	a, 3/8, Allegro	PA ix, 14	
342	341	191	A, ¢, Allegro	PA ix, 15	
343	495	291	A, C, Allegro andante	PA ix, 16	
344	221	295	A, 3/8, Allegro	PA ix, 17	
345	342	306	D, ¢, Allegro	PA ix, 18	
346	250	60	D, 3/8, Allegro	PA ix, 19	
347	294	126	g, ¢, Moderato è cantabbile	PA ix, 20	347
348	462	127	G, 3/4, Prestissimo	PA ix, 21	347
349	452	170	F, 3/8, Allegro	PA ix, 22	
350	413	230	F, 6/8, Allegro	PA ix, 23	
351	165	S34	B♭, ¢, Andante	PA ix, 24	
352	343	S13	D, ¢, Allegro	PA ix, 3	
353	401	313	D, 3/8, Allegro	PA ix, 4	
354	486	68	F, 3/8, Andante	PA ix, 5	
355	344	S22	F, ¢, Allegro	PA ix, 6	
356	488	443	C, ¢, Con spirito andante	PA ix, 29	347
357	270	S45	C, 3/8, Allegro	PA ix, 30	347
358	457	412	D, 3/4, Allegro	PA x, 11	
359	425	448	D, 3/8, Allegrissimo	PA x, 12	
360	520	400	B♭, ¢, Allegro	PA ix, 25	

K	P	L	Description	Primary source (*variant*)
361	214	247	B♭, 3/8, —	PA ix, 26
362	159	156	c, ¢, Allegro	PA ix, 27
363	104	160	c, 3/8, Presto	PA ix, 28
364	345	436	f, ¢, Allegro	PA x, 1
365	112	480	f, 3/8, Allegro	PA x, 2
366	263	119	F, 2/4, Allegro*	PA x, 6
367	453	172	F, 3/8, Presto*	PA x, 7
368	506	S30	A, ¢, Allegro	PA x, 9
369	259	240	A, 3/8, Allegro	PA x, 10
370	346	316	E♭, ¢, Allegro	PA x, 13
371	264	17	E♭, 3/8, Allegro	PA x, 14
372	402	302	G, 6/8, Allegro	PA x, 15
373	158	98	g, ¢, Presto è fugato	PA x, 16
374	472	76	G, ¢, Andante	PA x, 17
375	414	389	G, 6/8, Allegro	PA x, 18
376	246	34	b, 3/4, Allegro	PA x, 19
377	245	263	b, 2/4, Allegrissimo	PA x, 20
378	347	276	F, ¢, Allegro	PA x, 21
379	107	73	F, 3/8, —	PA x, 22
380	483	23	E, 3/4, Andante commodo	PA x, 23
381	323	225	E, 3/8, Allegro	PA x, 24
382	508	S33	a, ¢, Allegro	PA x, 25
383	269	134	a, 3/8, Allegro	PA x, 26
384	487	2	C, ¢, Cantabbile andante	PA x, 27
385	220	284	C, 3/8, Allegro	PA x, 28
386	137	171	f, ¢, Presto	PA x, 29
387	415	175	f, 6/8, Veloce è fugato	PA x, 30
388	370	414	D, ¢, Presto	PA xi, 3
389	331	482	D, 3/4, Allegro	PA xi, 4
390	348	234	G, ¢, Allegro	PA xi, 1
391	364	79	G, 3/4, Minuet	PA xi, 2
392	371	246	B♭, ¢, Allegro	PA xi, 5
393	326	74	B♭, 3/4, Minuet	PA xi, 6
394	349	275	e, ¢, Allegro*	PA xi, 7
395	273	65	E, 3/8, Allegro*	PA xi, 8

K	P	L	Description	Primary source (*variant*)
396	435	110	d, ¢, Andante	PA xi, 9
397	325	208	D, 3/8, Minuet	PA xi, 10
398	493	218	C, 6/8, Andante	PA xi, 11
399	458	274	C, 3/8, Allegro	PA xi, 12
400	228	213	D, 3/8, Allegro	PA xi, 13
401	436	365	D, 6/8, Allegro	PA xi, 14
402	496	427	e, ¢, Andante*	PA xi, 15
403	437	470	E, 6/8, Allegro*	PA xi, 16
404	489	222	A, ¢, Andante	PA xi, 17
405	438	43	A, 6/8, Allegro	PA xi, 18
406	509	5	C, ¢, Allegro	PA xi, 19
407	521	S4	C, 3/8, Allegro	PA xi, 20
408	350	346	b, ¢, Andante	PA xi, 21
409	403	150	b, 3/8, Allegro	PA xi, 22
410	372	S43	B♭, ¢, Allegro	PA xi, 23
411	351	69	B♭, 3/4, Allegro	PA xi, 24
412	463	182	G, 2/4, Allegro	PA xi, 25
413	416	125	G, 6/8, Allegro	PA xi, 26
414	373	310	D, ¢, Allegro	PA x, 3
415	175	S11	D, 12/8, Pastoral; Allegro	PA x, 4
416	454	149	D, 3/8, Presto	PA x, 5
417	40	462	d, ¢, Allegro moderato	PA x, 8
418	510	26	F, ¢, Allegro	PA xi, 27
419	524	279	F, 3/8, Piu tosto presto che allegro	PA xi, 28
420	352	S2	C, ¢, Allegro*	PA xi, 29
421	459	252	C, 3/8, Allegro*	PA xi, 30
422	511	451	C, ¢, Allegro	PA xii, 12
423	455	102	C, 3/8, Presto	PA xii, 13
424	374	289	G, ¢, Allegro	PA xii, 14
425	426	333	G, 3/8, Allegro molto	PA xii, 15
426	500	128	g, 3/8, Andante*	PA xii, 16
427	464	286	G, C, Presto, quanto sia possibbile*	PA xii, 17
428	353	131	A, ¢, Allegro	PA xii, 18

429	439	132	A, 6/8, Allegro	PA xii, 19	
430	329	463	D, 3/8, Non presto mà a tempo di ballo	PA xii, 1	
431	365	83	G, 3/4, Allegro	PA xii, 2	
432	465	288	G, 3/4, Allegro	PA xii, 3	
433	440	453	G, 6/8, Vivo	PA xii, 4	
434	498	343	d, 3/4, Andante	PA xii, 5	
435	466	361	D, C, Allegro	PA xii, 6	
436	404	109	D, 3/8, Allegro	PA xii, 7	
437	499	278	F, 3/4, Andante commodo	PA xii, 8	
438	467	381	F, ¢, Allegro	PA xii, 9	
439	473	47	B♭, C, Moderato	PA xii, 10	
440	328	97	B♭, 3/4, Minuet	PA xii, 11	
441	375	S39	B♭, ¢, Allegro	PA xii, 20	
442	229	319	B♭, 3/8, Allegro	PA xii, 21	
443	376	418	D, ¢, Allegro	PA xii, 22	347
444	441	420	d, 6/8, Allegrissimo	PA xii, 23	347
445	468	385	F, C, Allegro, o presto	PA xii, 24	
446	177	433	F, 12/8, Pastorale; Allegrissimo	PA xii, 25	
447	191	294	f♯, ¢, Allegro	PA xii, 26	
448	261	485	f♯, 3/8, Allegro	PA xii, 27	
449	405	444	G, 3/8, Allegro	PA xii, 28	
450	422	338	g, C, Allegrissimo	PA xii, 29	
451	366	243	a, 3/4, Allegro	PA xii, 30	
452	195	—	A, ¢, Andante allegro	M ii, 51	
453	280	—	A, 3/4, Andante	M ii, 52	
454	423	184	G, 3/4, Andante spiritoso	PA xiii, 1	
455	354	209	G, ¢, Allegro	PA xiii, 2	
456	377	491	A, ¢, Allegro	PA xiii, 3	
457	442	292	A, 6/8, Allegro	PA xiii, 4	
458	260	212	D, 3/4, Allegro	PA xiii, 5	
459	167	S14	d, 3/8, Allegro	PA xiii, 6	
460	378	324	C, ¢, Allegro*	PA xiii, 7	
461	324	8	C, 3/8, Allegro*	PA xiii, 8	
462	474	438	f, 3/4, Andante	PA xiii, 9	
463	512	471	f, ¢, Molto allegro	PA xiii, 10	
464	460	151	C, ¢, Allegro	PA xiii, 11	
465	406	242	C, 3/8, Allegro	PA xiii, 12	
466	501	118	f, C, Andante moderato	PA xiii, 13	
467	513	476	f, 3/4, Allegrissimo	PA xiii, 14	
468	507	226	F, 3/4, Allegro	PA xiii, 15	
469	514	431	F, ¢, Allegro molto	PA xiii, 16	
470	379	304	G, ¢, Allegro*	PA xiii, 17	
471	327	82	G, 3/4, Minuet*	PA xiii, 18	
472	475	99	B♭, 3/4, Andante	PA xiii, 19	
473	355	229	B♭, ¢, Allegro molto	PA xiii, 20	
474	502	203	E♭, 3/4, Andante è cantabbile	PA xiii, 21	
475	319	220	E♭, ¢, Allegrissimo	PA xiii, 22	
476	427	340	g, 3/8, Allegro	PA xiii, 23	
477	419	290	G, 6/8, Allegrissimo	PA xiii, 24	
478	503	12	D, 3/4, Andante è cantabbile	PA xiii, 25	
479	380	S16	D, ¢, Allegrissimo	PA xiii, 26	
480	381	S8	D, ¢, Presto	PA xiii, 30	
481	504	187	f, ¢, Andante è cantabbile	PA xiii, 27	
482	356	435	F, ¢, Allegrissimo	PA xiii, 28	
483	407	472	F, 3/8, Presto	PA xiii, 29	
484	428	419	D, 3/8, Allegro	PA xiv, 1	
485	490	153	C, ¢, Andante è cantabile	PA xiv, 2	
486	515	455	C, ¢, Allegro	PA xiv, 3	
487	421	205	C, 3/8, Allegro	PA xiv, 4	
488	382	S37	B♭, ¢, Allegro	PA xiv, 5	
489	522	S41	B♭, 3/8, Allegro	PA xiv, 6	
490	476	206	D, ¢, Cantabile*	PA xiv, 7	337
491	484	164	D, 3/4, Allegro*	PA xiv, 8	
492	443	14	D, 6/8, Presto*	PA xiv, 9	
493	383	S24	G, ¢, Allegro*	PA xiv, 10	
494	444	287	G, 6/8, Allegro*	PA xiv, 11	
495	384	426	E, ¢, Allegro	PA xiv, 12	
496	332	372	E, 3/4, Allegro	PA xiv, 13	
497	357	146	b, ¢, Allegro	PA xiv, 14	
498	367	350	b, 3/4, Allegro	PA xiv, 15	
499	477	193	A, ¢, —	PA xiv, 16	
500	358	492	A, 3/4, Allegro	PA xiv, 17	

K	P	L	Description	Primary source (variant)	
501	385	137	C, ¢, Allegretto	PA xiv, 18	
502	408	3	C, 3/8, Allegro	PA xiv, 19	
503	196	196	B♭, ¢, Allegretto	PA xiv, 20	
504	265	29	B♭, 3/8, Allegro	PA xiv, 21	
505	386	326	F, ¢, Allegro non presto	PA xiv, 22	
506	409	70	F, 3/8, Allegro	PA xiv, 23	
507	478	113	E♭, 2/4, Andantino cantabile	PA xiv, 24	
508	516	19	E♭, 3/4, Allegro	PA xiv, 25	
509	387	311	D, ¢, Allegro	PA xiv, 26	
510	525	277	d, 3/4, Allegro molto	PA xiv, 27	
511	388	314	D, ¢, Allegro	PA xiv, 28	
512	359	339	D, 3/4, Allegro	PA xiv, 29	
513	176	S3	C, 12/8, Pastorale; Moderato*	PA xiv, 30	
514	389	1	C, ¢, Allegro	PA xv, 1	
515	417	255	C, 3/4, Allegro	PA xv, 2	
516	523	S12	d, 3/8, Allegretto*	PA xv, 3	
517	517	266	d, ¢, Prestissimo*	PA xv, 4	
518	390	116	F, ¢, Allegro*	PA xv, 5	
519	445	475	f, 3/8, Allegro assay*	PA xv, 6	
520	362	86	G, ¢, Allegretto	PA xv, 7	
521	429	408	G, 3/8, Allegro	PA xv, 8	
522	526	S25	G, ¢, Allegro	PA xv, 9	
523	527	490	G, 3/8, Allegro	PA xv, 10	
524	528	283	F, 3/4, Allegro	PA xv, 11	
525	529	188	F, 6/8, Allegro	PA xv, 12	
526	530	456	c, ¢, Allegro comodo	PA xv, 13	347
527	531	458	C, 3/4, Allegro assai	PA xv, 14	347
528	532	200	B♭, ¢, Allegro	PA xv, 15	
529	533	327	B♭, 3/8, Allegro	PA xv, 16	
530	534	44	E, 3/4, Allegro	PA xv, 17	
531	535	430	E, 6/8, Allegro	PA xv, 18	

K	P	L	Description	Primary source (variant)	
532	536	223	a, 3/8, Allegro	PA xv, 19	
533	537	395	A, ¢, Allegro assai	PA xv, 20	
534	538	11	D, ¢, Cantabbile	PA xv, 21	
535	539	262	D, 3/4, Allegro	PA xv, 22	342–3
536	540	236	A, ¢, Cantabbile	PA xv, 23	
537	541	293	A, 3/4, Prestissimo	PA xv, 24	
538	542	254	G, 3/8, Allegretto	PA xv, 25	
539	543	121	G, ¢, Allegro	PA xv, 26	
540	544	S17	F, ¢, Allegretto	PA xv, 27	
541	545	120	F, 6/8, Allegretto	PA xv, 28	
542	546	167	F, 3/4, Allegretto	PA xv, 29	
543	547	227	F, 6/8, Allegro	PA xv, 30	
544	548	497	B♭, 3/4, Cantabile*	PA xv, 31	
545	549	500	B♭, ¢, Prestissimo*	PA xv, 32	
546	550	312	g, 3/8, Cantabile	PA xv, 33	
547	551	S28	G, ¢, Allegro	PA xv, 34	
548	552	404	C, 3/8, Allegretto	PA xv, 35	
549	553	S1	C, ¢, Allegro	PA xv, 36	
550	554	S42	B♭, ¢, Allegretto	PA xv, 37	
551	555	396	B♭, 3/4, Allegro	PA xv, 38	
552	556	421	d, ¢, Allegretto	PA xv, 39	
553	557	425	d, 3/8, Allegro	PA xv, 40	
554	558	S21	F, ¢, Allegretto	PA xv, 41	
555	559	477	f, 6/8, Allegro	PA xv, 42	
SONATAS FOR SOLO INSTRUMENT AND CONTINUO					
73	30	217	c, 3/4, Allegro: C, 3/8, Minuetto	V xiv, 37	
77	10	168	d, 3/4, Moderato è cantabile; d, 3/8, Minuet	V xiv, 42	
78	26	75	F, 2/4, Gigha; F, 3/8, Minuet	V xiv, 44	

81	13	271	e, C, Grave; e, 2/4, Allegro; e, 3/4, Grave; e, 3/8, Allegro	V xiv, 46
88	8	36	g, C, Grave; g, 3/8, Andante moderato; g, 2/4, Allegro; g, 3/8, Minuet	V xiv, 53
89	12	211	d, C, Allegro; d, 3/4, Grave; d, 3/8, Allegro	V xiv, 54
90	9	106	d, C, Grave; d, 2/4, Allegro; d, 12/8, — ; d, 3/8, Allegro	V xiv, 55
91	11	176	G, C, Grave; G, 2/4, Allegro; G, 3/4, Grave; G, 3/8, Allegro	V xiv, 56

DOUBTFUL KEYBOARD SONATAS

(uncertain authenticity, or incomplete or poor texts in the primary sources)

95	—	358	C, 12/8, Vivace	Bo p.x, 16
97	5	—	g, 3/8, Allegro	B iii, 6
142	240	—	f♯, 12/8, Allegro	LB 31553, 42
143	267	—	C, 3/8, Allegro	LB 31553, 43
144	316	—	G, ¢, Cantabile	LB 31553, 44
145	105	369	D, 3/8, —	CF5
146	106	349	G, 3/8, —	CF7
—	—	—	C, 3/4, Presto	NH18
—	—	—	C, 9/8, Prestissimo	NH19
—	—	—	A, 3/8, —	G10
—	—	—	E, 3/8, —	G13
—	—	—	A, ¢, Allegro; A, 3/8, Spiritoso	LB 14248, f.15*v*

BIBLIOGRAPHY

BurneyH
A. Longo: *Domenico Scarlatti e la sua figura nella storia della musica* (Naples, 1913)
A. Cametti: 'Carlo Sigismondo Capeci (1652–1728), Alessandro e Domenico Scarlatti e la Regina di Polonia in Roma', *Musica d'oggi*, xiii (1931), 55
W. Gerstenberg: *Die Klavier-Kompositionen Domenico Scarlattis* (Regensburg, 1933/*R*1969)
L. Bauer: *Die Tätigkeit Domenico Scarlattis und der italienischen Meister in der ersten Hälfte des 18. Jahrhunderts in Spanien* (diss., U. of Munich, 1933)
S. Sitwell: *A Background for Domenico Scarlatti* (London, 1935)
C. Valabrega: *Il clavicembalista Domenico Scarlatti, il suo secolo, la sua opera* (Modena, 1937, rev. 2/1955)
S. A. Luciani: *Domenico Scarlatti* (Turin, 1939)
R. Newton: 'The English Cult of Domenico Scarlatti', *ML*, xx (1939), 138
Gli Scarlatti (Alessandro – Francesco – Pietro – Domenico – Giuseppe): note e documenti sulla vita e sulle opere, Chigiana, ii (1940)
S. A. Luciani: 'Postilla Scarlattiana', *RaM*, xliv (1940), 200
M. S. Kastner: *Contribución al estudio de la música española y portuguesa* (Lisbon, 1941)
S. A. Luciani: 'Un'opera inedita di Domenico Scarlatti', *RMI*, xlviii (1946), 433
C. Hopkinson: '18th-century Editions of the Keyboard Compositions of Domenico Scarlatti', *Transactions of the Edinburgh Bibliographical Society*, iii (1948), 49
R. B. Benton: 'Form in the Sonatas of Domenico Scarlatti', *MR*, xiii (1952), 264
R. Kirkpatrick: *Domenico Scarlatti* (Princeton, 1953, rev. 3/1968)
M. Bogianckino: *L'arte clavicembalista di Domenico Scarlatti* (Rome, 1956; Eng. trans., 1967)
A. Basso: *La formazione storica ed estetica della sonata di Domenico Scarlatti* (diss., U. of Turin, 1957)
A. Della Corte: 'Tetide in Sciro: l'opera di Domenico Scarlatti ritrovata', *RaM*, xxvii (1957), 281
H. Keller: *Domenico Scarlatti, ein Meister des Klaviers* (Leipzig, 1957)
R. Allorto: 'Clementi non ha plagiato Scarlatti', *Musica d'oggi*, new ser., ii (1959), 66
A. D. McCredie: 'Domenico Scarlatti and his Opera *Narcisso*', *AcM*, xxxiii (1961), 19
G. Pestelli: *Le sonate di Domenico Scarlatti: proposta di un ordinamento cronologico* (Turin, 1967)

Bibliography

P. Williams: 'The Harpsichord Acciaccatura: Theory and Practice in Harmony, 1650–1750', *MQ*, liv (1968), 503

J. L. Sheveloff: *The Keyboard Music of Domenico Scarlatti: a Reevaluation of the Present State of Knowledge in the Light of the Sources* (diss., Brandeis U., 1970)

L. Hautus: 'Zu dem Domenico Scarlatti zugeschriebenen *Capriccio fugato á dodici*', *Mf*, xxiv (1971), 294

——: 'Beitrag zur Datierung der Klavierwerke Domenico Scarlattis', *Mf*, xxv (1972), 59

G. Pannain: 'L'arte pianistica di Domenico Scarlatti', *Studi musicali*, i (1972), 133

S. Choi: *Newly Found 18th-century Manuscripts of Domenico Scarlatti's Sonatas and their Relationship to other 18th and Early 19th-century Sources* (diss., U. of Wisconsin, Madison, 1974)

R. Pagano: 'Le origini ed il primo statuto dell'Unione dei Musici intitolata a Santa Cecilia in Palermo', *RIM*, x (1975), 545

J. Clark: 'Domenico Scarlatti and Spanish Folk Music', *Early Music*, iv (1976), 19

R. Strohm: *Italienischen Opernarien des frühen Settecento (1720–1730)*, AnMc, no.16 (1976), 226

F. Degrada: 'Una sconosciuta esperienza teatrale di Domenico Scarlatti: *La Dirindina*', *Il palazzo incantato: studi sulla tradizione del melodramma dal Barocco al Romanticismo* (Fiesole, 1979), 67–97 [repr. from *Quadrivium*, xii (1971)]

A. Silbiger: 'Scarlatti Borrowings in Handel's Grand Concertos', *MT*, cxxv (1984), 93

Index

Index

Index